Strategic Emotional Involvement

Strategic Emotional Involvement

Lawrence E. Hedges, Ph.D.

With Original Contributions by

Anthony G. Brailow, Suzanne Buchanan, Charles Coverdale,
Carolyn Crawford, Jolyn Davidson, Jacquelyn Gillespie,
Ronald H. Hirz, Virginia Hunter, Sanford Shapiro,
Gayle Trenberth, and Sally Turner-Miller

JASON ARONSON INC.
Northvale, New Jersey
London

This book was set in 10 pt. Palatino by Alpha Graphics of Pittsfield, New Hampshire, and printed and bound by Book-mart Press of North Bergen, New Jersey.

Copyright © 1996 by Lawrence E. Hedges

10 9 8 7 6 5 4 3 2 1

All rights reserved. Printed in the United States of America. No part of this book may be used or reproduced in any manner whatsoever without written permission from Jason Aronson Inc. except in the case of brief quotations in reviews for inclusion in a magazine, newspaper, or broadcast.

Library of Congress Cataloging-in-Publication Data

Hedges, Lawrence E.
    Strategic emotional involvement / Lawrence E. Hedges; with original contributions by Anthony G. Brailow . . . [et al.].
       p.   cm.
    Includes bibliographical references and index.
    ISBN 1-56821-065-5
    1. Psychotherapist and patient. 2. Emotions—Therapeutic use.
3. Empathy. 4. Countertransference (Psychology) 5. Intimacy (Psychology) I. Brailow, Anthony G. II. Title.
    [DNLM: 1. Emotions. 2. Physician–Patient Relations.
3. Psychotherapy. BF 531 H453s 1994]
RC489.E45H43 1996
616.89'023—dc20
DNLM/DLC
for Library of Congress   94-11703

Manufactured in the United States of America. Jason Aronson Inc. offers books and cassettes. For information and catalog write to Jason Aronson Inc., 230 Livingston Street, Northvale, New Jersey 07647.

*To the many colleagues and clients
whose personal involvement over the years
has allowed these pages to come alive
with a deepened understanding
of the power of human emotional responsiveness*

CONTENTS

	Acknowledgments	ix
	Contributors	xi
	Introduction	xiii

PART I: UNDERSTANDING AND INTERPRETING THE EMOTIONAL RESPONSES OF THE THERAPIST

1	Emotional Responsiveness of the Therapist	3
2	Finding Ways to Be Together *Ronald H. Hirz*	7
3	Symbolic Enactments in Countertransference *Virginia Hunter*	25
4	The Relatedness Paradigm	39
5	Four Listening Perspectives	47

PART II: STRATEGIC EMOTIONAL INVOLVEMENT IN LISTENING TO PSYCHOTIC ISSUES

6	Emotional Involvement in Psychoses	57
7	Ensnared by Eros *Suzanne Buchanan*	79
8	Falling into a Pothole *Suzanne Buchanan*	91

PART III: STRATEGIC EMOTIONAL INVOLVEMENT IN LISTENING TO BORDERLINE ISSUES

9	Emotional Involvement in Symbiosis	103
10	*'Night, Mother* *Sally Turner-Miller*	127
11	The Snakebite *Carolyn Crawford*	141

12	Healing Abuse with Countertransference *Jolyn Davidson*	157
13	Replicating Incest *Gayle Trenberth*	183
14	Being As If Without Skin *Anthony G. Brailow*	197

PART IV: STRATEGIC EMOTIONAL INVOLVEMENT IN LISTENING TO NARCISSISTIC ISSUES

15	Emotional Involvement in Narcissism	207
16	Two Developmental Lines in Self Psychology: Selfobject Empathy and Interpretation *Charles Coverdale*	223
17	The Provocative Masochistic Patient: An Intersubjective Approach to Treatment *Sanford Shapiro*	231
18	A Countertransference Reaction to Budding Exhibitionism *Charles Coverdale*	243

PART V: STRATEGIC EMOTIONAL INVOLVEMENT IN LISTENING TO NEUROTIC ISSUES

| 19 | Emotional Involvement in Neurosis | 249 |
| 20 | The Sudden Violent Storm
Jacquelyn Gillespie | 277 |

PART VI: STRATEGIC EMOTIONAL INVOLVEMENT AND THE COUNTERTRANSFERENCE

21	Emotionality and Psychoanalysis	285
22	Emotionality and Human Relatedness	303
23	Working the Countertransference	311
	References	313
	Credits	323
	Index	325

ACKNOWLEDGMENTS

Clinical research necessarily requires many years and involves the contributions of many. This is the sixth volume to emerge from a study spanning two decades and involving over two hundred clinicians studying the therapeutic accomplishments of several thousand clients. We have worked together in teams and groups sharing our most interesting and difficult case work with each other, reading the psychoanalytic and object relations literature, bringing lecturers and consultants to our meetings, and studying published casework of master clinicians. The names of many of these contributing clinicians and researchers appear in *Listening Perspectives in Psychotherapy: Interpreting the Countertransference; Remembering, Repeating, and Working Through Childhood Trauma; Working the Organizing Experience;* and *In Search of the Lost Mother of Infancy.*

This is the casebook sequel to *Interpreting the Countertransference.* In that book I take the position that countertransference responsiveness is a vital working tool in the psychotherapeutic process. I issued the challenge for clinicians to come forth in an honest, forthright, and comprehensive way and to submit to the community of practitioners and to others interested in the inner workings of psychotherapy some of the difficult emotional entanglements that have resulted from working with early aspects of personality development. The eleven contributors to the present book responded to that challenge and the result is a remarkable set of reports of strategic emotional involvement unprecedented in the history of psychotherapy.

The ongoing support for this work has come from my daughter, Breta Lynne Hedges-Bonham, who has masterminded the computer and organized the manuscripts, and from my colleague and partner, Ray Michael Calabrese, who has effectively managed the entire project from the beginning. Jason Keyes has been instrumental in moving the last four manuscripts to press. Joan Carlson is responsible for the transcription of case conferences and numerous clinical vignettes.

The inspiration for documenting and publishing this research has come from Jason Aronson, who saw and understood my work from the beginning and who has encouraged me in the arduous task of getting the clinical data out of the consulting room, into an intensive group study process, and onto the printed page. Judy Cohen has shepherded endless pages of assorted mumblings and half-baked ideas of mine through a careful editing process that has brought life and illumination to the texts. This particular book owes its final organization and readability to the editorial expertise of Elaine Lindenblatt. Jason Aronson did the initial sculpting of the manuscript. David Kaplan followed up with careful and thoughtful copyediting that kept the text clear and incisive. Nancy J. D'Arrigo has worked with me to produce cover designs that embrace the work graphically.

To these wonderful people, to the numerous research participants—many of whom have been credited elsewhere—and to those who cannot be named who have laid bare their souls so that we might learn and grow, I give heartfelt thanks.

CONTRIBUTORS

Anthony G. Brailow, Ph.D., has twelve years of experience in the mental health field. He is currently a clinical psychologist with Children and Youth Services, Health Care Agency, Orange County, CA. He also conducts a private practice in clinical psychology and psychoanalytic psychotherapy.

Suzanne Buchanan, M.F.C.C., is in private practice in Lake Forest, CA, where her clinical focus is primitive human relatedness acquired in infancy and its expression in adult relationships.

Charles Coverdale, Ph.D., L.C.S.W., has been in practice since 1974 and is currently in Santa Monica, CA.

Carolyn Crawford, M.A., M.A., has been teaching emotionally disturbed and learning-disabled students for twenty-five years. During her career of educating difficult youths, she found considerable relief in the lessons of the psychoanalytical model. For the last nine years she has taught special education in a town of 350 on the slopes of the Sierra Nevada.

Jolyn Davidson, B.S.N., L.C.S.W., B.C.D., is currently in private practice as a licensed clinical social worker in Covina, CA, providing psychotherapy to children, adolescents, and adults. She is a graduate of the University of Washington School of Social Work. She served on the faculties of Biola University, La Mirada, CA, and Azusa Pacific University, Azusa, CA, at the latter as Associate Director of the Human Resource Leadership graduate program.

Jacquelyn Gillespie, Ph.D., recently retired from private practice as a clinical psychologist in Orange, CA. She continues to pursue her interest in object relations and has written on their manifestations in *The Projective Use of Mother-and-Child Drawings*.

Ronald H. Hirz, M.D., is an assistant clinical professor at the University of California, Irvine, Department of Psychiatry. He is in the private practice of psychotherapy in Tustin and Laguna Hills, CA, where he does long-term individual psychotherapy from a psychodynamic, intersubjective, and bioenergetically informed base, in addition to marital and family therapy.

Virginia Hunter, Ph.D., L.C.S.W., B.C.D., is an adult and child psychoanalyst who practices in Long Beach, CA, where she also sees couples, families, and groups, and supervises clinical work. A founding member of the Newport Psychoanalytic Institute, Dr. Hunter is especially interested in disorders of affect regulation, psychosomatic illness, and learning and creative difficulties. She is the author of *Psychoanalysts Talk*.

Sanford Shapiro, M.D., is a training and supervising analyst, San Diego Psychoanalytic Institute. He is Associate Clinical Professor of Psychiatry, University of California San Diego, School of Medicine, in La Jolla, CA. Dr. Shapiro is the author of *Talking with Patients: A Self Psychological View*.

Gayle Trenberth, Ph.D., has been a psychologist in private practice for the last eighteen years. She is a certified bioenergetics analyst, and has completed two years of study at the Newport Psychoanalytic Institute. She practices in Seal Beach, and is a founder of the Center for Integrative Psychotherapy in Redondo Beach, CA.

Sally Turner-Miller, Ph.D., is in private practice in Fullerton, CA, specializing in behavioral medicine, mind/body integration, hypnosis, and art therapy. She holds seven state credentials and has worked extensively with learning-disabled children. Dr. Miller is also a certified bioenergetics analyst, and has lectured for many years on parenting and communication.

INTRODUCTION

This book contains moving personal accounts written by therapists who have dared to extend themselves emotionally to the people with whom they work. The personal courage demonstrated by each contributing therapist has been supported over the years by numerous colleagues in individual psychotherapy consultation and case conference groups sponsored by the Listening Perspectives Study Center and the Newport Psychoanalytic Institute.

The chapters review the relevant scientific and philosophical issues that provide the backdrop for contemporary clinical work. Psychotherapy today is challenged as never before with the need to address the deepest issues of human personality formation. This vital work requires various forms of personal emotional responsiveness from the therapist that are aimed at providing a frame through which the most basic of human relatedness structures can be identified, understood, and transformed.

The current social-political-economic demand for quicker, more efficient psychotherapeutic approaches pales in the face of these profound tales of depth psychological contact and growth. Human understanding and transformation is simply not a quick and easy task, as the emotionally laden involvements of this book aptly illustrate.

But for therapists and social engineers focused on streamlining the delivery of mental health services, the kind of depth research presented in these pages is very illuminating. When we grasp what kinds of time and emotional involvement are required for significant personality transformation, then we can eliminate many such goals from the short-term applications currently required by medical, crisis intervention, and other limited marathon and self-help group approaches. That is, the task of separating out the kinds of transformational goals we can expect in long-term, in-depth individual psychotherapy from what is valuable and realistically achievable in time- or depth-limited psychotherapy is considerably clarified by this book. At present, the public is being sold an idealized psychotherapeutic bill of goods that simply cannot be delivered in abbreviated forms of therapeutic contact. Much can be accomplished in focused and limited forms of therapeutic contact. But significant time and emotional involvement are required to address in depth the human problems involved in childhood abuse and molestation, ritual abuse, abduction experiences, trauma due to violent intrusions, major eating disorders and addictions, and the insidious effects of more generalized borderline, narcissistic, and organizing (psychotic) personality structures.

Representatives of business, industry, and government cannot be expected to understand the distinctions between the need for efficient and limited applications of psychotherapeutic knowledge and the urgent need for the availability of the strong, longer-term approaches that are required for many people to lead fuller and more productive lives. It is the importance of the latter that stands out in bold relief in the vignettes presented here. And it is psychotherapists themselves who must inform all kinds of consumers of the distinctions between what can be accomplished in limited and focused work versus what kinds of human problems require more depth, and why making a depth resource available to many more individuals will be cost effective in the long run.

At present the social-political-economic approach to psychotherapy is penny-wise and dollar-foolish. As a society we pay heavily for not providing young parents with personalized experiences in understanding critical issues in the emotional development of their children, and for not making available to them knowledge and resources for enhancing their parenting skills. As a society we pay heavily for allowing people who have been damaged by childhood neglect and abuse to walk the streets, living on unemployment and emotional disability benefits, when we have the knowledge and skills to help them discover their creative and productive potentials that can make them more functional and productive. As a society we pay a heavy price for medical treatment as well as unemployment and disability benefits, for those who have not learned how to protect their emotional lives from intrusive stresses inherent in the modern workplace as well as home life. As a society we pay heavily in terms of public expenditures of welfare, medical care, and law enforcement when we fail to extend the psychological tools we have painstakingly developed for over a century into transformational work with socioeconomically depressed populations.

We are painfully aware that traditional values and social structures that in the past provided support and fostered growth have broken down and become ineffective. But we see all around us in a myriad of forms a hunger for self-knowledge, as the mushrooming of self-help literature and groups attests to, and a keen desire for full participation in the wider social community.

All people are capable of self-motivation and pride. Oppressed people want nothing more than to allow full reign to that motivation and pride through self-actualization experiences that can lead to personal fulfillment, social productivity, and an enhanced sense of well-being. But our changing society has not yet been willing to offer these people the psychological tools required to release them from continuing to live out strangulating, overlearned emotional relatedness patterns from their childhoods. By now it is evident that we do not learn to value ourselves or contribute to the well-being of those around us when we feel our importance is limited to the identification numbers we carry in our wallets. Value in human life is always to be found through personal involvement, which means emotional relatedness to others.

Exactly how people in contemporary society are to recover the lost sense of personal worth, the sense of pride in self-accomplishment, and the personal joy to be found in relatedness to others is, I believe, the most pressing question of our time. This book takes the position that whatever is important in human life connects to the ways individuals come to experience themselves in relation to others around them. The many affirmations that people are learning to make in limited-relatedness situations such as marathon experiences, ongoing self-help groups, and limited psychotherapies, are examples of these experiences. But the light that contemporary psychoanalytic understanding sheds on our problem makes clear that another approach is also required.

We now know that human beings overlearn a series of emotional relatedness patterns in the first five years of life. These overlearned relatedness patterns serve as enduring templates for perceiving, processing, and responding to our complex interpersonal environment. Until the individual later in life, working with more advanced mental capabilities, takes the opportunity to scrutinize his or her emotional responsiveness patterns through the mirroring possible in actual human relationships, his or her freedoms remain self-limited by personal forms of tunnel vision learned in the dominant emotional relationships of childhood.

This book clarifies how to identify and respond to the relatedness patterns that develop in human childhood and are retained in later life, as habitual modes of being. Strategic forms of emotional involvement on the part of a person in a listening/therapist role are discussed in detail. Then the listening perspective, which has evolved through psychoanalytic research for each of the four forms of strategic emotional involvement, is illustrated by highly emotionally-charged therapy reports recounted by courageous psychotherapists.

The reader is bound to find these intimate and personal accounts very moving, as each therapist relates a saga of how he or she came to understand and respond to the limiting emotional relatedness patterns of the person with whom he or she has worked. Until the principles of in-depth interpersonal involvement are better understood by many, we can expect the ills of modern society to continue. The bold therapist-adventurers whose work fills these pages propose exciting and futuristic ways of discovering themselves and the people around them through personal emotional involvement.

Lawrence E. Hedges
Modjeska Canyon, California
April, 1996

I

UNDERSTANDING AND INTERPRETING THE EMOTIONAL RESPONSES OF THE THERAPIST

1

Emotional Responsiveness of the Therapist

When we relate to one another we often forget that we do so primarily on the basis of our emotions. Darwin (1872) noted that twenty-six distinct facial expressions characterize primates. Infant researchers have found that shortly after birth mothers are able to identify this same number of emotions in their babies. Twelve-step program literature discusses the nature of these twenty-six basic human experiences. Emotional responsiveness can be seen to constitute the primary means of communication between infants and caregivers. A century of psychoanalytic research has demonstrated that personal patterns of interpersonal emotional responsiveness developed during infancy and early childhood remain fundamental to subsequent human interaction.

While people-watching in a crowd, we notice that we form various kinds of judgments. Our explicit judgments take the form of thoughts about a certain person. Our implicit judgments are present in silent emotional reactions we have toward that person. If we come to a favorable judgment based on our thoughts and emotions, we may find a way of striking up a conversation or introducing ourselves. But why out of a crowd did we select this particular person to relate to and not another? What special features of a person tend to attract or repel us? And what can we learn about ourselves based upon our emotional responsiveness to significant others? These questions take on special importance in light of the human tendency to be drawn toward people who relate in ways that cause us to repeat endlessly the emotional traumas from our past. Further, questions regarding the nature of our emotional involvements are of interest in light of the human tendency to do to others in relationships the very things that we have most hated having done to us in various ways throughout our lives.

When we form a relationship with another person, our emotional life becomes activated at once. If we have had prior occasion to think about the particular emotional responses elicited by this new relationship, then thoughts about our personal emotional patterns may arise as well. But more likely than not, when a stranger approaches to engage us we will not have explicitly thought about the complex emotions this new person will have the power to stir up in us. It will only be in the actual process of relating that we will come to know the other through mutually engaged emotional responsiveness. Moreover, it is through deep personal relating that we can come to discover many subtle and hidden aspects of ourselves.

This book portrays the emotional responsiveness of therapists (professional listeners) in relation to the people who approach them to speak about their lives. (I often use the terms *listener* and *speaker* to refer to roles customarily spoken of as *psychoanalyst, psychotherapist,* or *counsellor* and *analysand, patient,* or *client,* respectively.) Freud's (1912) seminal concept of transference refers to personal patterns of emotional responsiveness that the patient (speaker) brings to the analytic relationship. Freud (1915) uses the term *countertransference* to designate the personal patterns of emotional responsiveness that the listener (therapist) brings to the analytic relationship.

In-depth analytic experience requires that two people sustain a significant emotional relationship for a considerable period of time. But the vast literature on psychoanalysis and the psychodynamic psychotherapies focuses almost exclusively on the emotional life of only one participant—the experiencing speaker (the patient). In comparison, only a minuscule amount of attention has been given to the study of the emotional life of the other participant—the experiencing listener (the therapist). The reasons for this imbalance are many. Perhaps the most straightforward is simply the therapist's desire for privacy. Other reasons include the perennially uncertain position of the listener, who for very long periods of time necessarily skates on thin ice when trying to receive and understand with some degree of empathy and accuracy the relatedness experiences of the speaker. But perhaps the most imposing reason for the relative lack of study of the emotional life of the listener is the embarrassingly intense, subjectively compelling, and deeply personal emotional responsiveness that regularly punctuates the analytic relatedness situation.

Freud's intention was to formulate psychoanalysis along conceptual lines established by nineteenth century medical science. However, his texts regularly oscillate between an objective, deterministic approach and a humanistic, purposive approach. Throughout his lifetime Freud never relinquished his personal sense of identity as a philosopher. On occasion he even asked why psychoanalysis arose from the field of medicine rather than, say, religion, philosophy, the arts, or the humanities. But the facts of the history of psychoanalysis are that its powerful medical applications have inextricably colored, determined, and dominated the formation of its vocabulary and growing fabric of concerns. During the last two decades psychoanalysis has witnessed a radical shift in thought away from an emphasis on healing and toward an enterprise of consciousness expansion. The new conceptual paradigm of psychoanalysis that accents issues of interpersonal relatedness now calls for a systematic study of the emotional responsiveness of the therapist as well. Many ideas have begun to evolve to guide the therapist through some of the ambiguities and uncertainties that characterize contemporary psychoanalytic work.

Rudolf Ekstein, in his foreword to *Listening Perspectives in Psychotherapy* (Hedges 1983), envisioned a sequel entitled *Talking Perspectives in Psychotherapy*, which would survey speakers' ways of free associating in analysis. Ekstein writes, "It is my belief that each symptom, each emotional or mental illness, is in some way a Talking Perspective, a way of communicating, albeit a pathological way" (p. xiv). In a sense, this book is that sequel, because in the chapters that follow we hear speaking patients deeply engaging their listening therapists in complex and enigmatic webs spun on the basis of past patterns of emotional entanglement. The listener's critical tool for receiving this emotionally charged interactional material is the fabric of his or her own emotional life, replete with its idiosyncrasies that are also brought from the past. What sort of map can the listener and speaker use to sort out the intricate and interwoven meanings that are bound to emerge in the course of relating? The four *listening perspectives* that have served to organize my thinking and teaching for two decades provide ways of listening to the four distinct types of strategies of emotional involvement utilized by speakers in their relatedness experiences with listeners. In this text these four distinctly different forms of emotional relatedness will be studied in relation to how they may be empathically responded to with strategic emotional involvement on the part of the therapeutic listener in order to promote the psychoanalytic task.

The general approach that I pursue in this book is based upon two sets of assumptions. My starting point is always that of an experiencing listener empathically engaged with and relating to an experiencing speaker. The first set of assumptions is epistemological—basically that we can never know another human being completely or objectively. Using a series of philosophical considerations, I have argued for a radically revised philosophy of science more in keeping with the uncertainties of the quantum age than the positivist approach employed by Freud and classical psychoanalysis. Rather than deterministic objectivism, I have advocated approaches based on systematic subjectivism. This general metapsychological approach points toward a more specific metapsychology of listening perspectives based upon a second set of assumptions regarding the individual development of human relatedness potentials. Studies in clinical psychoanalysis, child development, and infant research point to four basic watersheds in the evolution of the human relatedness potential. The human environment over the millennia has come to respond differently to these four developmentally different forms of emotional relatedness. According to this view, the psychoanalytic task entails listening for what mode or modes of self and other relatedness are being spoken or lived at the moment or over time, and then seeking through empathy to establish interpersonal attunement through various forms of strategic emotional involvement. That is, in listening to interpersonal issues that are defined metaphorically as related to four watersheds of development of the human relatedness potential, the emotional life of the analytic speaker can be most effectively engaged or met through distinctly different strategic forms of emotional involvement.

This book discusses and illustrates contemporary approaches to understanding and interpreting the emotional responsiveness of the therapist, using first-hand accounts of therapist responsiveness. The moving and intense emotional encounters reported here are accounts written by colleagues who have participated with me in lengthy and in-depth studies of the complex cognitive, conative, and affective experiences that have been an integral part of our countertransference studies over the last decade.

Before proceeding to a discussion of the theoretical and technical considerations that provide the underpinning for the general listening perspectives approach, let us move straight to the heart of our subject matter by considering two clinicians' reports involving extremely difficult countertransference dilemmas. As the book proceeds the reader will be able to place these opening vignettes and the strategic emotional involvement required within an overall listening perspective context.

2

Finding Ways to Be Together

Ronald H. Hirz

Editor's Comments

From the first psychoanalytic case study (Anna O.) reported by Breuer and Freud (1893–1895), analysts have registered an awareness of the emotional responsiveness that this intense and intimate work generates. Freud's position (1915), which has become orthodoxy not only in psychoanalysis but in all derivative psychodynamic therapies, has basically considered emotional stirrings in the analyst as inevitable but potentially dangerous if not kept closely in check. This impediment theory of countertransference parallels Freud's general recommendation for psychoanalytic technique. The "opaque mirror" role of the analyst implies a position of neutrality and objectivity as well as a stance in which the analyst abstains from permitting his or her emotional reactions to enter directly into the analytic exchange.

By 1950 the analytic position was being interpreted by new generations of analysts to mean some sort of stoic forbearance or emotional distance. Heimann (1950) suggests that sterile forbearance was never Freud's intent but that all of the emotional responsiveness of the analyst must be employed in the understanding and interpreting activities of the analyst.

The analytic encounter you are about to read is disarmingly human and moving. It makes clear why traditional analytic technique has been unsuccessful at tapping the primary wellsprings of human spontaneity and creativity in people who experienced developmental difficulties in the earliest months of life. The analytic speaker has been willing to collaborate by providing her account of the first few years of therapy. We then hear how her analytic listener experienced the process. In a postscript I will discuss some issues that arise in trying to differentiate a corrective emotional experience from a psychoanalytic encounter on the earliest level of human organizational strivings.

SARAH'S STORY

I am Sarah, a middle-aged female professional with whom Ron has worked closely for the past three years, and with whom he is continuing to work at the present time. I am highly intelligent, well educated, and quite visible and successful within my professional field. I have worked with several psychotherapists in the past (primarily in long-term therapies), and I know myself to be very psychologically sophisticated in terms of my knowledge of process and content. My early history includes issues of emotional impoverishment, abandonment, and ongoing adolescent sexual abuse, resulting in difficulties in trusting and connecting. Despite many achievements, I have felt isolated, lonely, shameful, inadequate, depressed, and anxious for most of my life. My experiences throughout childhood taught me well to watch people carefully, believing in what I could see and physically feel, rather than believing in what was said. Words were not to be trusted, not congruent with what I was internally and often externally experiencing. I had also learned quite well how to hide reality from myself, constructing instead a fantasy family and a fantasy family life filled with warmth, loving, and caring, giving myself and others the appearance of a secure environment surrounded by love and warmth. I am now able to acknowledge and accept that this world existed only in my own needs and desires. I am beginning to grieve what I really did not have.

I first met Ron on the recommendation and with the encouragement of my physician, one person whose concern and caring I had come to trust fairly well. He told me about Ron, describing him as a kind and gentle person, professional and ethical. At the time I had some distinct issues that I needed to explore with someone outside my personal and professional communities. Although I asked Ron if he did long-term, in-depth psychotherapy, I also told him that I wanted to see him specifically to explore and resolve the pain and confusion of the ending of my last therapy. He asked me what I did with the anger I was carrying. I don't remember how I responded, but I was surprised that he could know that; I believed it was well hidden.

Little did he (or I) know then that we were opening Pandora's box, and that a lifetime of feelings would come tumbling out, threatening the two of us with drowning and exposing the two of us to having to deal with our own fears and our own feelings, without an already established road map or guide to lead us through the uncharted territory of feelings and experiences we had no way of knowing we would need to traverse before we would even begin to arrive at a stable and therapeutic working alliance. Although he was not aware of the extent of my emotional difficulties at the onset of our relationship, he soon realized that I was suffering with a major depression as well as with an anxiety disorder. He also learned (much to his consternation, I believe) shortly after our work commenced that I was frequently having suicidal thoughts and impulses, although I had never made an actual suicide attempt.

I now realize that, as the full extent of my current problems became clearer to him (and to me as well), he was feeling overwhelmed, inadequate, and guilty about being unequipped with what appeared to him to be the necessary personal and professional resources that were going to be needed, and very unsure that he could provide them. He has since acknowledged this, but at the time he did not; instead he spoke professionally and in a technically correct way. On what was to me a more believable level, I felt from him what seemed a reluctance to work with me, and a fear of me as well. I continued to become more and more depressed and anxious, having panic attacks, experiencing little relief even from the increasing doses of medication (Prozac, Wellbutrin, Desyrel, Xanax, Inderal and Stelazine) that he was prescribing. I now know that what he felt he was being asked to do he felt about as equipped for as circumnavigating the globe with a model of a flat earth. He felt that he was being asked to reorient his whole world, turning upside down and inside out all of the guidelines he had learned and followed so assiduously during the past years. As far as I was concerned, I felt ashamed and rejected because of the "size" of my feelings.

When I first entered treatment with him, I used to choose to sit on a couch near his chair. At one point, I remember trying to tell him, with words I could not really find, how frightened I was that he was going to hurt me badly. His response was that I might feel safer if I sat further away from him, on a chair on the other side of a low table. Somehow I knew that his suggestion of my moving away was at least in part determined by his desire to put me out of his space, to distance me to a place that felt safer for him. I could not express this in words, but I felt the same confusion, rejection, and depression that I had experienced as a child. Because I could not put this into words, Ron remained oblivious to my feelings about this (and perhaps to his own as well) for a long time.

I compliantly moved there, and remained there for a long time, each session feeling too far away to be safe and yet deterred by an invisible boundary that was as large and real to me as an "elephant in the living room." We did not discuss this, because I could not (and, because I felt I needed to protect myself from him, *would* not!) acknowledge either its invisible presence nor the degree of pain it was engendering. Instead I withdrew into myself more and more, sometimes spending long periods of each session locked in a "little room" somewhere inside me, a little room of my own in which I could be safer than I felt I was in the small consultation room that was later to become my "home." I now understand that the "little room" inside me was the place where I lived throughout my childhood and adolescence, and to some degree throughout my adult life as well.

Although he believed at the time that he could successfully hide what he was feeling and still function well with me using the techniques and patterns that were consistent with his earlier education and training, this turned out not to be the case. After about a year of our working together, with his often feeling overburdened and overwhelmed, and angry that he was feeling expected to work in ways that seemed so alien to him, he took what he has now described as a much-needed vacation. He needed to get a rest. Even though I was frequently withdrawn and afraid during our sessions, I was panicked at the idea of his leaving, and particularly upset and frightened at the idea that there would be no way to reach the only "lifeline" I felt I had. Although he later was to come to trust me, after the development of increased reciprocal openness and honesty between us, at the time of his vacation he was unwilling to provide me with a way to contact him, even through a colleague. He tried to convince me to see another therapist while he was away, to use the other therapist as a kind of interim object, and perhaps begin to develop a relationship with someone whom he said could be included in our work. I felt abandoned even by the suggestion, as well as feeling thrust away and discarded. I also believed at the time that he was then going to terminate working with me, abandoning me to the other clinician and thereby repeating one of the major traumas of my childhood. I did not know what to do, because I knew that I could not establish a strong or trusting-enough relationship with anyone else in such a brief time, and I felt that I wanted to die.

While he was gone, with the days stretching out in what seemed like an endless progression, I thought seriously about suicide many times. I also knew that although I did not want to continue working with him when he returned, I had no place else to go and no one else to whom to turn. A friend kept me company during that time, and encouraged me to return to therapy after Ron's vacation was concluded. I returned, only to continue to sit in that distant chair, and to withdraw to my own internal space.

I could not remember our sessions, nor could I remember his face or his voice. I had asked early in our work if I could tape our sessions; he had refused to permit it explaining that he did not want me to relive the experiences and the feelings of the session when I was alone. Although that made sense to me at the time, and even felt protective and caring, I still needed to capture his voice on tape, just as I needed to capture his picture on film. Eventually I felt safe enough to ask for both of these, and he was able to permit them. I listen to the tapes over and over while driving, about two hours a day. I get depressed and anxious more on weekends and only recently did Ron help me see that I did not play the tapes on the weekend because I was unable to create privacy from my husband in order to listen.

I asked Ron if he would touch my hand or my shoulder, or if I could touch him. His response was to turn to the literature to see if he could find validation for granting this request. When he finally touched my shoulder, it was with a touch so distant and stiff that the touch felt worse than his previous continued refusal. This served to more deeply confirm my idea that I was untouchable and undesirable, and that he wanted to keep as far away from me as possible, while still working with me, perhaps because of the hourly income I was providing for him. This culminated in a situation that was to bring our work to the brink of an abrupt ending, and to push me further toward suicide than I have ever gone. In a discussion that seemed to me to come from out of the blue, he told me that he had decided that if I became acutely suicidal I should call someone else or go to a hospital emergency room, and that if I needed to be hospitalized because of it, he would not see me there. To me this said clearly that he did not want to be there if and when he might be most desperately needed. Although he seemed to understand from my response that what had happened was damaging to whatever therapeutic alliance was struggling to exist, and clearly emotionally injurious to me, I could not listen to anything he said nor for a very long time could I hear his efforts to heal what had happened.

The weeks that followed were touch-and-go. I kept wanting to cancel all of my appointments, but knew I had nowhere else to go. I was afraid to stay and afraid to leave. I tried, very hesitantly and with great difficulty, to put into words what I was feeling. I was aware of the extent of the effort Ron was making, trying to stay with me, trying to hear unspoken words and to help me express inexpressible feelings. He also began, hesitantly, to be more open and truthful with me. I understand now how frightening and risk-taking exposing his own feelings must have felt to him. I could clearly differentiate between when he was being honest and self-exposing, and when he was hiding behind correct professional techniques and classical psychoanalytic guidelines. Each time he came out from behind his protective "front" I could hear him, and we could somehow begin to connect; each time he retreated, I withdrew into myself. We understand now that I desperately needed the experience of a whole person, someone who does not hide behind a blank screen, that I needed someone who presents congruity between his expressions and gestures, and his spoken word. This lack of congruity had done inestimable damage to me when I was growing up; I could not afford to repeat this in what was to be a healing situation. I needed, and needed badly, the acknowledgment of my reality, which meant his coming out of his traditional hiding place and meeting me straight on.

During that period of time I began to bring little things into the sessions with me. Some of them were "small child" things, such as a stuffed animal, some children's books that reminded me of some I had enjoyed as a child but that became lost to me as I grew older, as well as fruit and flowers that I had raised in my garden. Although I later learned that he was allergic to the flowers, he kept accepting them in an overly enthusiastic way that felt false to me. The fruit he flatly and abruptly refused to accept, nor did he seem to make any attempt to understand the unconscious message the fruit and the flowers were meant to communicate. Once again I felt hurt, rejected, barely tolerated, and judged to be a nuisance.

Much later, he told me of his allergic physical discomfort with the flowers, and referred briefly to his own early issues around food. Those words helped me to begin to make sense out of what had happened. Still later, he began to understand that my bringing the fruit did not require his eating it, appreciating it, enjoying it, keeping it, or taking it home for later consumption unless he wished to do so. Instead it was meant to communicate my feelings of awe and appreciation of the world of nature that surrounds us (and that held far more safety than did the world of people), and represented my perhaps immature and clumsy attempts to share those feelings with him and connect with him at the same time, even though I could not yet find the words with which to verbalize all of these feelings and needs.

As Ron came to understand this, he became more open and real about how he felt. In turn, I could respect his feelings without feeling patronized and falsely met, as I had felt previously. Although he is not encouraging me to bring small things (including food) to the office if I wish, this has become very difficult to do after the earlier rejections. At present, we (together) are trying to set this right; Ron is doing this with real patience, understanding, and honesty, and I am doing this by slowly risking despite my fears of his potential response.

We also realize now, as we did not know earlier, that many of the tangible items I brought to the office, my frequent inability to verbalize what I was feeling, my need to connect with him between sessions, and my fear of his potential abandonment were simultaneously replications of a very disturbed childhood, and at the same time a plea to Ron not only to allow me but even to help me relive and rework those earliest experiences over again.

Sometimes (recently, frequently, and more regularly) I can "go to a place" in early childhood where there are few words, but only an intense unfilled need for connection and contact. Now I can hold Ron's hand, and he can really hold mine in return. I can put my head against a pillow that rests in his lap or against his side. He will help me to maintain a deep silence that right now feels vital to me much of the time, instead of filling the silence with words. His words can create what to me feels like an emotional withdrawal. His thoughts may be about me, but I may not feel that they are attuned to my present emotional state, which his body can be and which I can detect and trust through any physical contact, even his hand. I can feel his protection and support, his caring and understanding in a way I could not do earlier in our work. I can finally be that little child I never could safely be, albeit for lonely short periods in the protection of his office and with his acceptance of the very strong need of mine to be soothed, protected, and accepted as I am. In exchange, I am becoming more able to verbalize as I had not been able to do, sharing my inner and outer experiences with Ron in a frightened but more freely and voluntarily expressed way. I still watch his response with guarded eyes, but I am experiencing him so much more of the time as demonstrating congruence between his words and his bodily expressions.

Over the past two years, since coming to the brink of therapeutic disaster, our mutual openness and honesty has slowly, often haltingly, grown and flourished. I do not always like what Ron says about how he is feeling, but I can deal with it far more easily than I could deal with the lack of congruence. We are able to make some much needed physical contact (touching of hands, a pat on the shoulder), which seems less needed now that it is available. Ron's touch no longer feels stiff and cold, but is often filled with warmth and caring.[1] I am coming to see him as a real person,

---

1. After this chapter was written and after extensive careful exploration of her experience of my touch, we constructed together a procedure whereby she could evoke memory of me and the safe emotional atmosphere that she experienced in my presence. The technique consisted of my pressing my hand into her shoulder so that she could clearly feel my fingertips and palm. Later, in my absence, she could re-evoke the feeling and sense of safety by pressing her own hand in a similar way on her shoulder, an act which has allowed her to tolerate the pain of my absence between visits.—R.H.

understanding on a level deeper than ever before how many feelings exist in a real relationship, and how those feelings can be handled with sensitivity and honesty so that they enhance rather than destroy the mutuality of the relationship. Collaborating on the writing of this chapter, with all of the open sharing and honesty that has been required of both of us, is an appropriate representational model of the therapeutic dialogue that Ron described recently as being a dialogue between two equal people, a dialogue that is enhancing of my dignity and worth, and helping to heal me.

RON'S STORY

Uncomfortable feelings that I experience with my patients, I have been taught, and I have fully accepted, are my responsibility to contain within myself, to find ways to understand, and to resolve them without the help or involvement of the patient. To involve the patient would be considered a burden to her and possibly damaging. In this particular therapy, my traditional training turned out to be all wrong; I had to learn to do just the opposite: it turned out that sharing the feelings that Sarah evoked in me, and eliciting her help in resolving them, is providing the "cure," while my first approach to contain it within myself led to therapeutic disasters, which fortunately have been survived and have healed slowly.

Sarah and I quickly formed a strong, positive therapeutic relationship that intensified when I acknowledged her profoundly disturbing suicidal feelings that previous therapists had failed to acknowledge to her. She quickly came to need me as a lifeline both during and in between sessions. She needed to touch me, which I had been trained was inappropriate and which I had a natural personal inclination to avoid except for brief handshakes, if initiated by the patient. She nonverbally asked for intense eye contact and later verbalized that need, but it was more than I could handle. I felt violated, intruded upon, smothered, exposed, and annihilated; I felt a loss of identity and privacy, and I felt I was being manipulated at different times. At first these experiences felt like malicious attacks, but later they would feel like honest appeals for understanding, help, and contact.

I was afraid to share these feelings with her for fear of making her worse. I felt that to be there for her and "take it" was the ethical thing to do.

She sensed and knew my discomfort all along, many times before I knew it, as my good-natured personality functioned with defenses against my awareness of discomfort. I later learned that my comfort was being able to be "in my head" and that my discomfort was in the giving in to the nonverbal relationship with Sarah in her overwhelming distress, without my intellectual defenses. I could not do both at the same time.

The first few times my discomfort emerged into my fully conscious awareness, I was too abrupt in moving to a new position where I felt safe. The abruptness, rather than the change itself, caused cataclysmic distress in Sarah, enormous psychic pain, panic, autistic withdrawal, intense suicidal preoccupation, and the inability to work or make significant contact during her therapy sessions. This caused me great distress out of sympathy for her, and when she was most angry I felt in fear of a malpractice suit.

During these episodes of disruption, Sarah would withdraw "into a box," and she felt a million miles away, abandoned, alone, and isolated. I learned that this occurred when she felt me to be emotionally withdrawing from her, usually before I knew I was withdrawing by speaking in "experience-distant" language or by inadvertent withdrawal of vocal affect or eye contact. I learned a lot from her about my own capacity to withdraw in these ways. In contrast I was not withdrawn in other ways from her. My internal private emotional concern, attachment, maternal preoccupation, intellectual curiosity, and moral commitment were not visible to her at the time. During these disruptions I would feel sad, helpless, and guilty. I would try various approaches to "get her back" including directly asking her to come back, and acknowledging how I thought I may have hurt her. What seemed to have the greatest impact, prior to our collaboration in developing "my emotional honesty," was my obvious sadness, which occurred several times when I read children's stories to her as a means of trying to make safe contact with her. Once I showed my sadness when she withdrew her hand from mine, sensing my hand's lifelessness, when I was trying to reestablish contact through our hands. I also repeatedly told her I wanted her to live. At times I was unable to respond with any thought, but simply telling her how sad I felt was helpful to her.

I was so flooded with feelings in her presence that I was unable to think. Her terror, anguish, and isolation from me were profoundly moving and I felt helpless to reach her with words. In fact, words just served to increase these symptoms. I had been trained "classically" not to touch the patient, not to gratify a patient with provisions such as food, and not to share my feelings. Attempts at clarifying or interpreting her negative transference were useless. She would remain in her withdrawn, suicidally preoccupied state.

I felt "over a barrel" because I felt at times she was a danger to herself (even though she promised she would not deliberately hurt herself) and I would have felt better if she were in the hospital. She would have had to go so far away to a hospital outside the community, where she could feel complete privacy, that I would not have been able to see her there. I believed that the loss of contact with me would have created a downward spiral, making her far worse instead of helping her to heal.

Sarah's need to make contact with me assumed overwhelming proportions. She would call and not be able to speak. I did not know what to say and I couldn't get her to get off the phone. I finally suggested that she page me, using a special code that we created, and I would page her back to let her know I had received her page. She felt greatly relieved because then she could "know that I could reach you if I had to." She described the pager as a "lifeline," and it acknowledged in a concrete way, the only way she in her "baby state" can understand, my inner awareness of her inner emotional state.

The pager caused one major problem, which we have overcome. When we sat far apart and my attention was momentarily withdrawn from her because my (vibrating) pager was activated, she would notice my withdrawal of attention and become deeply regressed because she did not see that I was just briefly attending to my pager and its message. She had personalized this momentary withdrawal of contact. Later, when we realized what had happened, we were able to make transference interpretations. She was able to acknowledge that "I realize that as a baby my mother must have acted mechanically and withdrawn attention from me without acknowledgment of me as a human being who would have feelings about my mother's withdrawal." More recently Sarah was able to detect my pager buzzing because she was sitting close to me. My turning my attention to the pager did not hurt her because she understood from her own direct experience why I was doing this.

When she stopped eating and lost sixty pounds in three months (she was overweight), I gave her hot milk every visit (three times a week) because she needed protein to prevent heart damage and I wanted to communicate that I wanted her to live. I felt manipulated into gratifying her but I wanted her to live, because she had a quasi-delusional belief that I did *not* want her to live. Transference interpretation of her mother's hostility did not help. I consulted several very warm and empathic psychoanalysts about this. Their concern seemed to be "to interpret the wish," as well as fearing that "the patient would have trouble giving up the gratification." Practically speaking, the technique was lifesaving even if it was not psychoanalytic, and it got through to her as words could not to any baby. And what about giving it up? In the fourth year we have begun to discuss it. She lamented that she had been weaned from a bottle to a cup on her first birthday. She believed it was much too soon. I suggested it was not the timing that was traumatic but the abruptness and most likely without her participation in the process.

Other aspects of creating contact and evocative memory for her have been to audiotape every session. She listens to the tapes several times between visits; there are times that she becomes depressed when she has been unable to listen to a tape for twenty-four hours. Listening to a tape usually improves her mood. She can now remember phrases I have said, like "take care of your health." She can now remember what my face looks like for about twenty-four hours. She has used a bottle of my cologne at times when she can't remember me.

She gets so soothed by the contact that she is disoriented and can't drive for as much as up to an hour after her session. So now I let her sleep in my back office for up to two hours, which is the calmest sleep she has ever known and from which she awakens profoundly refreshed. She says she feels "very young" in my office. I emphasize that I don't want her to feel this way outside my office when she must take care of herself.

Because of an impasse, we went together at my suggestion to see a consultant. During the visit Sarah started to rub the back of my hand with her thumb in an annoying way. I asked her if she knew that was annoying, and she acknowledged that she did, but added that she could not get herself to stop it until I asked her to do so. The consultant pointed out how I expected Sarah to take care of me, when in fact she was needing me to never expect that of her, just as a younger child might need. I can now add that we both agree that her failure to "acknowledge me as a person with feelings" replicates how her mother had treated her.

My newfound attunement to that need of hers to not have to be burdened by the expectation that she acknowledge me led to an opening up within me of more maternal caring and lessened the feelings of being provoked, tested, and narcissistically ignored. As a result I have been not so nonverbally hard on her and our relatedness became much softer both verbally and nonverbally. She was then able to be much more verbally communicative about many issues.

I started out not being sure whether it was all right to tell Sarah that I was concerned about her harming herself. I had been trained to not focus on that because it only gave the other person something to "blackmail" me with or it gave the other person a way to get my attention. It took some kind of a leap on my part to come to feel that I needed to tell her that I was concerned. Whatever I might be doing to give her attention or allow myself to be "blackmailed" was overridden by a basic human concern to be genuine with her. In addition, I felt that since I did care, why not share that with her? If I did not care, then saying that I cared would have been phony to say; however, since I did care, why hold that back? I was able to feel that I could risk telling her that and then learn from that whether it was helpful or not, rather than have a rule that I am absolutely supposed to avoid doing something because it might produce certain adverse results. I did learn from her how important and beneficial it was for me to have told her that I cared if she lived or died, and that I did not want her to hurt herself. It made her feel better and less self-destructive; it also made me feel better that I could share that feeling with her and not have to carry the burden of being quiet about it.

Sarah had explained that she had never known anyone in her childhood whose words could be believed. Therefore, I came to realize that it was necessary for her to understand what was going on within me in order to believe my words. At first I felt threatened because it seemed that I would have no area of privacy left for me. I later came to realize that I might as well acknowledge my inner feelings to her (and perhaps to myself as well).

She eventually convinced me that honesty with myself and her about my discomfort was the only salvation of the therapy. I then quickly learned how true this was. I would say, "I feel terrible about having these feelings about you, and I'm afraid of hurting you, but I am frightened of the intense and continuous eye contact that you try to establish with me. I know that you need it. You are not bad for wanting it. I wish I could give it to you, but for whatever reasons it causes me too much distress, I do not feel safe with it."

Interpretations have generally not had the impact in this particular therapy that merely acknowledging my countertransference has had. She has said, "I have never before had the chance to know another person so deeply and to validate my perceptions of that person by their own honest acknowledgments."

I feel that I could have claimed my own needs for security but it would have been at Sarah's expense. Even intensifying or prolonging her depressive symptoms, while I could feel individually relieved, felt terrible to me. I was unable to relieve my burden in this way because of what I only now recognize as an intense bond that I had formed along with Sarah's intense bond with me. I could have theoretically had her hospitalized to protect her life and protect my professional status but it would have broken our bond, which I felt was the only avenue to her regaining her emotional well-being.

Evidence of Sarah's improvement of her depression is indicated by much lower doses of medication (Wellbutrin, for example, was reduced from 450 mg/day to 150 mg/day); her increased ability to function professionally; and less regression in the sessions, resulting in greater capacity to confront verbally the painful issues from her past and in her current life. Negative transference was reduced and this appeared to have made for a more trusting therapeutic alliance. Our shared writing of this report has helped me to solidify my concepts regarding our work and has helped Sarah to work through her grief and rage regarding my difficulties in providing her with the therapy that was correct for her.

I have felt unable to write up the material without Sarah's involvement. I let her know that and asked her if she would help, and she was delighted. I feel that the process by which we created this written document together is similar to the processes of our therapeutic work. There are elements of symbiotic functioning in myself as well as in her. These include being exquisitely sensitive to her feelings of fear, anxiety, sadness, happiness, and joy. It could be called "co-dependent." I know that therapists are not supposed to be co-dependent. The fact is, I am generally not that way with my patients, and my being that way with this patient produced a large measure of loss of self-esteem and lack of self-confidence. I can view this now, among other things, as a countertransference reaction, one that is not a replication of a scenario of the patient or myself or based on my own so-called psychopathology, but rather is a replication of a normal developmental phase between an infant and a mother. The mother of an infant often experiences a loss of the sense of individual identity. Mothers who are uncomfortable with this loss, I believe, would be more susceptible to postpartum depression and are more likely to become emotionally distant from the baby and/or return to their work outside the home, leaving the baby in the care of someone else.

I have experienced those desires to withdraw but I have been drawn back repeatedly by my overriding concern for this woman. During the first year of therapy, she told me that she wished I could be her mother. She asked me why I cared about her and put up with her to the degree that I did. The only answer I could give her was that I was attached to her and that I had in some emotional way adopted her.

The enlistment of her participation in writing this story appears to be enormously gratifying to her as I expected it would. I continue to have some concern from the point of view of my classic psychoanalytic training, that this is "gratifying" the patient, specifically gratifying her narcissistic needs. From that perspective, I could acknowledge that view as a manipulation by the patient, or a mutual manipulation between the patient and myself. However, I can also see it another way, which I think is more fruitful, honest, and productive—I see it in terms of a primary narcissistic gratification, one that is absolutely essential to the healthy development of an infant.

To put the demands of this therapy into perspective, it must be stated that I could not have done it without the support of my wife, a colleague who understands the baby in adults, my psychoanalyst, and my supervisor. Their role was the allowance of the not-yet-understood needs of the patient and the simultaneous acknowledgment of my own personal needs. From Sarah's side, she could not have done it without her keen intelligence, great courage, psychological sophistication, and the support of her best friend and her personal physician.

I regret that I have not been able to present many significant details of her history and personal accomplishments due to the need for confidentiality. One profound benefit I have received from this work is a keen sense of my own subtle emotional withdrawal from people, of which I had not been aware. I can now understand much better my moment-to-moment realistic reactions to everyone with whom I make contact and my transference reactions as well. I learned this as Sarah reacted profoundly to my many episodes of subtle withdrawal.

My negative feelings regarding touching a patient had been reinforced by my traditional psychoanalytic teachers, my psychotherapy, and the literature. Kohut never acknowledged his use of physical contact, the two fingers his suicidal patient grasped, until his last public address days before his death.

The bioenergetics therapists, such as Robert Hilton writing in *Touching in Psychotherapy* (1990), have shown how useful and even essential touching is in psychotherapy if used in a respectful, nonintrusive way. I believe that my training in child psychiatry, infant research studies, experience with my own daughter as a baby, and contact with bioenergetics therapists have allowed me to integrate physical contact into psychoanalytically informed psychotherapy.

Winnicott spoke in Los Angeles around 1970 on dependence in childhood and in the psychoanalytic setting. Appearing almost as a parenthetic remark, he mentioned telling an analytic colleague about his desire to study the human environment as it relates to psychoanalysis. The response was that it would be considered an attack upon psychoanalysis as it did not involve intrapsychic phenomena. Winnicott shared with his American audience that he gave up pursuing this interest for thirty years! I don't think he really gave it up or we would not have his concept of the holding environment or his memorable expression "There is no such thing as a baby (without a mother to hold and contain the baby)." Margaret Little's account of her analysis by Winnicott describes sustained periods of physical contact that served as a concretely experienced holding environment (Little 1990).

Winnicott's first case presentation in the 1963 paper is much like Sarah, who felt easily annihilated. However, her regressed state prevented her from reality testing so that whatever she *felt* was experienced as being absolutely true. It took Kohut many years to give up his strict adherence to classical psychoanalysis and to give us what has become a foundation for understanding empathic attunement and intersubjectivity.

Theories and beliefs in science and therapy are subject to the same subjective, personal, unconscious forces that exist in everyday life. Theory in psychotherapy requires, therefore, having several theories and also the deep conviction that the therapist may have no theory with which to comprehend the patient, due to lack of existing knowledge, lack of training, or countertransference. Under these circumstances the therapist needs to appreciate that the more beliefs and theories can be suspended, the more the real patient may be discovered (Goldberg 1990).

Douglas Kirsner (1990) asks if it is possible for a psychoanalytic organization, which assumes a body of knowledge, to allow "mystics" (innovators, reformers, geniuses) to bloom within their ranks without producing disruption in the membership. I would say probably not. Organizational structure, like character structure, does not well tolerate the pain of transformation. Both will exert conservative forces to prevent change. I too resisted change from my more classical training, which had been ego syntonic. It met my needs for characterological defense. However, I was somehow caught up in an intense relationship with Sarah, and I decided to change because I did not want to lose her and I knew she was not capable of adapting to my needs. After four years she is now able to tolerate some disruptions and limit-setting, which is a sign of emotional maturation on her part.

Editor's Postscript

This in-progress account by the experiencing analytic speaker and the experiencing listener departs radically from the traditional psychoanalytic technique that Freud developed for the study of oedipal-level, triangular, neurotic issues. For many readers it begs the question of what exactly is meant by "psychoanalysis," and therefore, what psychic formations are to be considered analyzable? Freud based his notion of psychoanalysis on a nineteenth century model of chemistry—taking a complex compound and subjecting it to various conditions to break it down to reveal its essential components.

With neurotic issues, which Freud spent a lifetime studying, he formulated that complex oedipal issues could be broken down several ways. His topographical approach (1900) was formulated in order to break down the complex into unconscious, preconscious, and conscious elements—the first thought paradigm of psychoanalysis. By 1923 Freud had devised a second thought paradigm for breaking down psychic elements for study—the structural approach involving shifting balances and ratios of id, ego, and superego. Freud and classical analysts have strictly limited what is considered analyzable to psychic issues that demonstrate advanced oedipal (neurotic, triangular) structuring. It has not been until the gradual emergence of the third thought paradigm—relatedness—that preoedipal issues and structures have become available for analysis. This paradigm shift and the self and other relatedness listening perspectives will be discussed shortly.

In the foregoing account the reader will readily grasp that the issues brought up for study resemble early infantile strivings to connect, to feel safe in the presence of another, and to trust the reliable personality processes of the other even if they are not exactly what one desires or feels is needed at the moment. The account highlights the intense pain, sadness, and confusion that result when the other is not in a position to connect or when an achieved connection is lost.

But here a traditionalist will arise to say, "This is all very touching and is no doubt providing good support or a satisfactory 'corrective emotional experience,' but it is certainly not analysis." Based upon the accounts as provided I would have to agree that the analytic process is barely visible. But as a consultant on this work I am aware that a robust analytic process has indeed begun. But analysis of what? Certainly not an Oedipus complex or even a cohesive/fragmenting self structure. What is at stake at the organizing infantile level of human experience are the transferential structures that prohibit safe, smooth, and integrated interpersonal contacts or bonding experiences. Despite whatever other levels and forms of human competence the speaker brings to this dyadic exchange, she clearly knows that at root there is a deep disturbance or impediment in her ability to make full use of interpersonal intimacy. The focus of analytic study here is and will continue to be the "organizing transference," the fears and inhibitory structures that develop early in life to prevent full and efficient use of interpersonal resources for personal satisfaction and transformation.

The countertransference reported falls into several categories that will be discussed later under the heading of Organizing Countertransference. The therapist successfully avoids the first form of countertransference—the assumption that primitive mental states cannot be analyzed. His report clearly portrays the second form of countertransference—his fear of being the exclusive object of her intense infantile affects. At times we see his own organizing level of infantile experience—the third variety of organizing countertransference—surface when the patient withdraws, leaving him bereft, without sustaining connectedness after he has worked hard to find ways of reaching out and connecting with her. Not altogether evident in his report but clear to me from my consulting role has been the fourth form of countertransference—his instinctive withdrawal at times because of empathy with her processes. I find regularly that when speaker and listener begin to find some sort of reciprocal dance, with which they each are able to maintain comfort and sustained contact, the listener begins some sort of systematic and almost unconscious withdrawal. Sometimes a listener will become drowsy or inattentive or through more overt means begin to break the contact that has been painstakingly achieved by the work of both. While at times this is due to the activation of the listener's own organizing experience, many times it is the listener's empathy, his or her knowledge that sustained contact provokes the reliving of trauma by the speaker. The listener's almost automatic slowing down or interruption of the dance registers his or her awareness of the presence or threat of remembered trauma. I believe I have observed such empathic reactions in Ron on several occasions as he has intuitively de-intensified the relatedness connection to protect Sarah from overstimulation.

Where to from here? Both speaker and listener clearly believe they are embarking on some sort of "corrective emotional experience." That is, both accounts highlight the difficulty in achieving contact and the relief that ensues in one or both people when some form of mutually acceptable reliable contact or interaction can be achieved. But is the analytic goal with the organizing experience merely to learn to achieve reliable, satisfying, and usable interpersonal contact? It cannot be. If it were, the patient would not require an analyst but an empathic and attuned teacher—a person whose job it would be to teach her to achieve ways of feeling safe and comfortable relating to another person. Experience has shown that in adult life feeling safe in sustained contact simply cannot be taught. The psychoanalytic task is to begin analyzing the many ways in which a person has learned to avoid, to break off, to fear, to flee from human contact at all cost.

The analytic process focuses on analyzing the organizing (psychotic) transference structures that serve in various ways to prevent the establishment of relatedness, of relatedness patterns that have the potential of establishing a symbiotic dance. But breaks in connections, in interpersonally achieved thought links, in potentially transformative experiences cannot be studied except in the context of two people actually feeling affectively connected, being emotionally engaged with each other. Thus there are two phases to the analytic-interpretive process with organizing experience: first, two people finding ways to feel connected; and second, two people devoting themselves to noticing and suffering the transferential and countertransferential pains of what happens when the connection cannot, for whatever reasons, be sustained. As always, the focus of the analytic process (even in organizing or psychotic transference) is on breaking down previously established structures that serve as an impediment to further transformative experience. At the organizing level the analytic principle translates to a joint study of the affects, images, and concrete bodily sensations that both experience as a result of connecting and losing contact.

3

Symbolic Enactments in Countertransference

Virginia Hunter

Editor's Comments

Empathically engaging in symbiotic level ("borderline") issues and scenarios is generally thought to require more of the analyst in terms of self-extension and personal disclosure than empathic work with selfother ("narcissistic") and constant-other ("neurotic")–level issues. Therapists rightly experience concerns about engaging in various forms of more direct involvement and varied responsiveness than analytic technique has traditionally considered optimal. Having the "frame" as a backdrop to our work does serve as a constant reminder of a general direction that we know the best of relationships tend toward. However, to hold the traditionally developed frame as some sort of rigid morality or set of rules in an attempt to simplify the difficulties of analytic work is at best naive and at worst potentially destructive to the analytic process itself.

Empathic analysts who have been able to engage in deep symbiotic relatedness have regularly found that they have needed to extend themselves in various ways beyond the limits provided by the usual frame technique. Many analysts have refused to do so, considering such work as either "only supportive" or "unanalytic." Such epitaphs beg the question of what is meant by "psychoanalysis." Traditional technique was evolved for analyzing (understanding, taking apart) the triangular (oedipal, neurotic) relatedness issues experienced by people whose developmental opportunities have afforded them a good sense of self and other differentiation and constancy. Analysts have become aware that large numbers of people seeking therapy today have not achieved the requisite sense of independence and constancy for traditional analytic work. Furthermore, the analytic community has gradually begun to acknowledge that even with people who have achieved an advanced sense of constancy, the later selfobject and neurotic forms of relatedness always arise out of a person's previous relatedness experiences. Thus, in analytic work with all people, certain periods of experiencing symbiotic and organizing-level issues is not only expected but desirable for the sake of thoroughness. Strategic emotional involvement with symbiotic issues requires more than the customary restraint and abstinence, which constitute strategic emotional response for higher levels of personality development.

In the following case presentation the analyst has been able to formulate that many concrete enactments, which seem essential to the uninterrupted flow of analytic work with early relatedness issues, may be thought of as pretransitional object experiences. Drawing on the work of Winnicott, Segal, Giovacchini, and Searles, Hunter presents a series of interactions that, over time, enabled the patient in analysis to move from concrete levels of self and other experience to more abstract levels. This movement has been viewed by many analysts as the path to the development of the human capacity for the elaboration and use of complex symbols.

The analytic speaker described here, who is the in-depth subject of a recent book (Hunter 1994), has from the beginning some sense of what discrete symbols are; she understands that teddy bears can help in learning about complex experience. This capacity, which she brings to the question of concrete enactments and engagements, contrasts sharply with more primitive or organizing ways of experiencing objects. Tustin (1972, 1984) portrays more basic ways in which autistic children experience objects—as actual parts of their bodies or of the bodies of other people. The experience described here is also developmentally earlier than what Winnicott (1953) has called "transitional" experience, in which the Teddy stands for (symbolizes) the absent mother. Enactments in the therapeutic relationship and the function of these objects and enactments need to be formulated quite differently for organizing and symbiotic levels of self and other experience than for either constant self and other (neurotic) or selfother (narcissistic) experience.

In the following discussion the therapist acknowledges considerable countertransference involvement in the enactments and in her various concerns about them. But she is able to demonstrate that the symbolic enactments are in the service of empathic immersion in the very difficult symbiotic issue that the speaker brings to analysis.

INTRODUCTION

Patients who are psychotic or borderline, or who have "pockets" or areas where organizing, pregenital structures predominate, present technical issues and countertransference dilemmas that offer considerable challenge to both the patient and analyst. Issues that arise are related to symbiosis, fusion, holding, security, mirroring, attaching, trusting, object representation, the dangers of acting out, and the nature of the therapeutic alliance. Many emotional needs and traumas, along with developmental deficiencies, are evident and are likely to be complicated by concreteness in the patient's thoughts, needs, and object representations. Concreteness, of course, fluctuates according to the pervasiveness of the pregenital transference, along with the material that a patient is working on in a given session.

Ordinarily, patients reveal, in many ways, longings for concrete connections with the therapist, longings that for the patient may remain unconscious even as they are conveyed to the therapist. These longings may not be put into words, but in the countertransference they can be sensed by and resonate in the therapist. Such wishes or requests by the patient do not necessarily need to be verbally interpreted immediately. They may, in some instances, simply need to be sensed and accepted while they are being explored with extreme care and delicacy.

Under some conditions, patients' wishes may be represented in concrete enactments by the therapist and patient while, or even before, they are completely analyzed on the verbal level. What I am concerned with are those occasions when unconscious longings become crystallized in a patient's manipulation of a concrete object (or thing or phenomenon) in relation to the analyst, and the analyst's willing acceptance of the use of real objects in the therapeutic investigation of areas where words cannot yet go. Such objects I consider to be heirs of childhood transitional and pretransitional phenomena, directed now toward making a symbolic connection with the new object representation of the analyst or therapist.

When focus upon such objects occurs, it may need to be treated with considerable delicacy. Patients should not be humiliated or shamed by the therapist when exposing deeply hidden parts of themselves. The slightest hint that the therapist disapproves is likely to cause the patient's instant return from a therapeutic regression to a higher level of relatedness. Alternately, implicit judgments by the therapist may produce rage and withdrawal from the connection. In either case, these early pregenital wishes may remain hidden forever. While breaks in empathic attunement are inevitable in any analysis, the analyst can sometimes prevent such breaks from occurring at a time when maintenance of the therapeutic unity may be crucial to the patient's life or the survival of the analysis.

Let me illustrate my point through a few concrete examples. I believe that requests to borrow a magazine from the waiting room, a book from the office, a pen, or a paper clip; or the request by the patient to take the analyst's photograph, should all be responded to with positive interest. I first acknowledge such requests. Then we consider their possible positive and negative meanings. I never automatically refuse to consider requests. Depending upon my own countertransference resonance, I am often likely to accede to such requests if I feel they will deepen and facilitate the analysis. I will certainly do so when the requests for connection by use of a concretic symbol—which I call "symbolic enactments"—seem related to pregenital and preverbal material. The acceptance of concrete connections may facilitate and encourage entry, through regression, into areas of psychic development or repressed affects—or developmental arrest—that would otherwise remain inaccessible. We must be alert to such opportunities for allowing very important preverbal and verbal material to emerge from the unconscious. I have treated many patients who had already been "well analyzed" but who still had huge areas of painful affects locked in their mind and/or body. In them, their affects were rigidly separated from object relatedness.

Analysts such as Segal (1981) and Searles (1979b) have written about concrete thinking and structures in psychotics. Atwood and Stolorow (1984) have written about the significance in treatment "of enactment in concretizing and maintaining organizations of experience" (p. 91). I believe that there are pockets in most patients that concrete enactments may help to expose or reorganize. Winnicott (1953) states, "Transitional objects may be studied to help us understand the nature of the object; the infant's capacity to recognize the object as 'not me'; the place of the object outside, inside, at the border; the infant's capacity to create, think up, desire, originate and produce an object; and the initiation of an affectionate type of object relationship" (p. 230).

With patients who function on a higher level, responses involving thoughtful language and carefully phrased interpretations may be all that is necessary. I have been impressed, however, with how often even well-organized patients at some point wish to take something—even without permission—from the analyst's office or waiting room. These objects are held and cherished or even kept secret for a long time. But so long as they do remain secret and unshared, they are outside the analytic dialogue and may even have negative effects upon the treatment. After all, they were not offered by the analyst or shared by analyst and analysand. Patients are particularly resourceful at taking things from the waiting room, or creative in finding something they can "make do" as a transitional object, such as the bill, the envelope, or the analyst's signature on a canceled check. Transitional enactments are not always experienced positively. I remember a physician who expressed anger and hurt that I had been so "careless" as to put the stamp on his bill upside down!

The analyst must provide an empathetic environment in which the patient may expose and explore his/her secret desires, possessions, and thoughts. Acts of possession may remain secret and may derive from the patient's parenting, from psychoanalytic customs, and from the analyst's rigidity. Parents may have prohibited or attacked longings for attachment, or actual concrete symbols of or expressions of it. Analysts themselves have been burdened and inhibited by the "rules of abstinence." Such exchanges or needs must eventually be brought out into the open if they are to be analyzed. Often, during the termination phase, the patient reveals many meanings not verbalized earlier. Countertransference knowledge can be used in meaningful and deeply connecting ways when the exchange is brought into the dialogue.

I now turn to a case that represents, in a complex way, wishes for concrete symbolic objects and their use for therapeutic reasons. Interchange between analyst and patient of symbolic enactments through concrete objects will be discussed.

ROSLYN AND THE BEARS

Roslyn began treatment because of a pervasive feeling of depression, thoughts of suicide, and feelings of depersonalization. Even as she sought treatment, she was in the process of dropping out of a doctoral program where she had felt invisible and disconnected and became unable to continue. I saw her four or five times a week for many years; treatment itself was stressful for her and for long periods she could not tolerate the couch. She felt unbearably frightened, alone, or out of contact with me when reclining.

Here is the dynamic situation from several therapeutic frameworks. From a Kohutian perspective, Roslyn was unable to establish an idealizing transference because she felt she had to protect herself against me to avoid real annihilation (Hunter 1994). She could not make a safe attachment to her mother because her mother used her as a transitional object and made Roslyn a vehicle for her own attachment to reality (Giovacchini

1986). Her mother did not see Roslyn for herself. Due to Roslyn's uneasy, unsafe attachment to her mother, she was constantly losing and attacking the linkage between herself and others (Bion 1962). The image that she had of her mother was of a primitive internalized object that was aggressively saturated, so whenever she thought "mother," she thought "murder" (Volkan 1976). But the result, in accord with Bowlby's attachment theory, was that she found herself not profoundly, securely, and safely attached. She made her first attempt at this when she brought in the bear. But that comes later in the story! We analyzed these feelings and studied what helped her to feel safer. She often needed concrete, visible contact.

Her earliest memories, probably screen memories from around age 2, were of her mother and father fighting and blood everywhere. In later years, she did confirm that her mother had made a dramatic suicide attempt involving slashing her wrists in the bathroom. That was only one of many sources of her early memory of violence and her terror. No one ever discussed the terrifying happenings when she was a child. She remembers at an early age hiding in a clothes closet, hoping to avoid attacks. Indeed, her mother verbalized that she hated her and wanted her dead. There were constant physical and verbal attacks on the child. The verbal attacks were directed viciously and violently at any sense of self-worth or possible feeling of connection to a family member. Out of the blue, the mother would begin a tirade. "I wish you had never been born." "Your mouth does not look right; you are so ugly." "I could just kill you." "You ruined my life." "You made me ill." Such statements were experienced by Roslyn as meaning she was punished and cast into space because of her appalling, offensive, and disgusting lack of any redeeming reason to be cherished, comforted, protected, or even allowed to live. She felt in danger any time she was near her mother. Her father, who was passive, suffered from bleeding ulcers and nervous breakdowns. He encouraged the child to accept and tolerate her mother's "nervousness."

Despite her early traumas, and notwithstanding her frequent depressions and feelings of depersonalization, socially she was a charming, well-functioning, bright woman with a long and successful marriage and career. Her false self was accepted by all. This involved a presentation of herself as a "super-responsible" person. But the toll that this false self-representation had on her was also evident in her frequent migraine headaches. She seldom asserted herself, except professionally. She was accommodating and fearful of anyone's being angry at her. She was well oriented to time and place, but in the transference she was often terrified that we would kill each other. She felt that I would consider her a burden, be injured by her, and eventually wish to abandon, neglect, or kill her. It was dangerous to even think of trusting me. She felt that the only way I would be able to tolerate her was if she was undemanding, good, always adult, and showed no unpleasant desires or negative affects.

As Roslyn remembered her mother's attacks and described them, they had a frenzied quality in which the mother projected all of her negativity into the child. When washing the child's hair in the kitchen sink, the mother taunted the child with her ability and power to drown her if a whim made her so choose. In the transference, I was a "killer mother" and she was a "bad," vulnerable child who should either, herself, deaden all affects and desire, or else be killed by me. She expected little attunement or mirroring and certainly sought no "Mommy and me" enactments. To do so would be to seek a murderous possibility.

When she began treatment, I told her I had already booked an unusually long vacation for the following year and would be gone six weeks the next summer. When we began, the thought of the two extra weeks of vacation and separation seemed tolerable to her. At the outset, the high level of her social functioning, the facade of her false self, and my wish to treat her, deceived me as to the depth of her illness. My own countertransference wish to take this depressed patient into treatment made me see her transference needs as less intense than they would become.

Long before the time for my departure arrived, I was well aware of her absolute terror of separation. She fantasized breaking off a week earlier than necessary. She wanted to have a feeling of active control. She did not want to feel any of her feelings, and she also wished to keep her terribly regressed feelings a secret from me. Additionally, she wanted to have some feeling of active control by keeping everything inside herself. She could barely tolerate a dialogue with me; our relationship distressed her. As my departure time neared, she could make very little headway in sharing any feelings or thoughts whatsoever. I suggested, among other things, that the prospect of my leaving greatly diminished the little security and connection she felt in our relationship. It seemed that to be with me was almost as distressing as the prospect of being without me. When she did talk, suicide became an even more frequent topic, and themes of "dropping off the edge of the world" increased. She would not consider hospitalization, though my countertransference fears for her made me bring the subject up. Outside of our treatment room, she was quite capable of mobilizing her false self so that neither her husband nor the psychiatrist whom I had her consult earlier regarding medication would feel hospitalization was indicated. I worried that her inability to hold a mental representation of our connection and work would end her treatment or her life.

Then the issue I am choosing to call symbolic enactment came up. All at once she had an idea of what she wanted from me. Without warning, she brought me a small, white teddy bear about an inch long contained in a tiny, clear, plastic Ziploc jewelry bag, and she asked me to take it with me on my trip. Suddenly, she was animated. She herself was a world traveler and for the first time asked where I was going and shared her guesses. I answered her question because I believed that knowing would be more helpful than not knowing in the maintenance of our therapeutic alliance. I even gave her a copy of my itinerary through Poland, Russia, Mongolia, and on to Peking.

I encouraged her to talk about the bear and its meaning to her. At first she acted defensively, saying, "It's not important, forget it." She next depreciated me by saying, "Even if you said you would take it, you could always just leave it at home and I would never know." There was no recognition on her part of the possibility that for me to lie to her might entail a loss of personal integrity that I might find undesirable or intolerable. The closest she came to explaining what it meant was that it would magically keep me safe (from her rage?) and bring me back. Additionally, she felt I was identified with her to the extent that she felt I could not fail to come back, because I would be responsible enough to return her property to her. So the bear was many things: a concretized object representation, a magical object, a fetish, a good-luck charm. I would miraculously "come through" since I had the obligation of bringing the bear back to her. (That is, I was to be as "super-responsible" as she is.)

I interpreted that her wish to have me carry the bear with me might have an additional meaning: she might not trust that I would carry her in my heart and mind no matter where I went; she might think I would want to destroy our connection or vice versa. She acknowledged her fear that she was a burden I would be happy to leave behind and forget, but she tentatively acknowledged that if I did accept the bear it might be because I did feel some positive connection with her. I accepted the bear.

When a well-known analyst heard this story, he exclaimed: "What if it had been a brick?" But the point was, she had not offered me a brick. Clearly, she had given me something eminently portable. She did not want to burden me; she wanted to retain a concrete symbolic connection with me that I would find easy.

When I returned, she did not mention the bear for several sessions. I pondered this and was puzzled. Then she brought out material about her mother destroying whole picture albums and at other times cutting either the child or herself out of every available picture. Roslyn experienced these as clear messages that her mother wanted one or the other or both of them destroyed, along with any symbolic representations of the mother–child relation. I asked if these memories might help us understand her avoidance of any references to the bear. Tears ran down her face, and it was many minutes before she could nod, "Yes." I took the bear out of my purse and put it on the chest beside my chair. This simple gesture made her agitated and she seemed frightened. Out of my own wish to lessen whatever dread she was experiencing I said, "Miss Bear was a good traveling companion but is glad to be home." Roslyn's mood changed instantly, and her fears that any comment could have been meant as a criticism or an attack came pouring out.

This brings us to an important dynamic of this patient. Any direct reference to wanting or longing for a good mother or even the word *mother* in reference to our work remained, for years, extremely toxic and created an instant diminishment of feelings of safety in our relationship. So, if I had said anything in the transference regarding the bear, such as, "You must have longed to feel your mother was safe and wanted to keep you protected and with her and you must wish you could feel assured that I want to do what she never did," this would have produced an instant rejoinder: "You're not my mother! Don't use that word in relationship to us! I can't stand it! It's like putting me in a box with a snake!" This blockage made transference interpretations problematic and increased my countertransference frustrations and challenges.

The bear came up for the third time a year later, when Roslyn was going away on vacation. She informed me that she wanted to take it with her in order to assure her own safe trip and return. She likened it to a medallion of a Catholic saint. Thereafter, the bear made numerous trips with each of us.

Each of these was analyzed both before departures and following returns. We began to see that bear equaled "bearer of child," and I was to be the bearer of her childhood. Also, she was trying to "bare" her real feeling. A general deepening of our connection accompanied the analysis of the symbolic enactments. I made a second trip to China after several years of analysis with her, and was gone for a month. I brought her back a stuffed Panda bear about an inch and a quarter in size.

Why had I taken this new step? First, I had some countertransference guilt for leaving her for a long period again. Second, and more important, I wanted to give her confidence that there was reciprocity in our relationship and that I was willing to give back to her something like what she had initially given me. Third, I had a need in the countertransference to make a symbolic representation that I was neither snowy white, "all good," nor black, "all bad." Fourth, I wanted to try to create what I call a "stage for facilitation," upon which we could mutually examine her relation to her mother and work toward her acceptance of some possible trusting, nurturing relation with me.

Hanna Segal (1981), in writing about the importance of "symbolic equations," argues that "symbols [can] acquire new functions which change their character" (p. 55). By giving Roslyn the black and white "mother bear" to substitute for her internal image of the "mother snake," I felt I was trying to assist her in the process of modifying her symbol "mother" in order to allow her to imagine "mother" in other than a poisonous way. Segal continues: "The symbol is needed to lessen aggression from the original object and, in that way, to lessen the guilt and the fear of loss. The aim of the displacement is to save the object . . . " (p. 55). But Roslyn's displacement of "mother" to "snake" continued to destroy her experience of me as a "good enough" object; the substitution that I made from "mother = snake" to "mother = bear" (as "child = bear," and possibly to "therapist = bear = mother") was designed to assist her in the process of symbolic displacement. It was an interpretation at the level of symbols.

I gave a great deal of thought to how this gift might affect her, especially upon its initial presentation. I took special care to offer this "mother bear" without violating Roslyn's boundaries. After tentative discussion, I offered the new bear, a different species, to her in its own Ziploc bag, inside another Ziploc bag, with the original white bear who was in its own Ziploc bag. I did not want her to feel that her "own bear" was forced to be, even symbolically, mixed with my Panda bear without a boundary between them. The little Ziploc bags within a bag represented our continued isolation from each other along with the mutuality of our therapeutic relationship. She was greatly touched by my gesture, happy even, and took both bears home with her. Thereafter, she removed the bears from separate bags and kept them together in one bag.

Another stage of symbolic enactment occurred when Roslyn began playfully to design costumes for the bears, which related to the destination that either of us would have in our travels. We would have to figure out who had last had the bears. Were they in the chest beside my chair or in her bedside table? When I went off to Africa, the bears would be brought to me dressed in handmade safari costumes for the trip. When she went to England, the bears were cleverly dressed for England. When she traveled, she would bring the bears in to show me how they were dressed for her trip and for the bears to say goodbye to me. This was fun, creative, and playful for both of us. The new stage of childlike playfulness allowed many other important issues to emerge—verbally now—from the bear material. These bears became concretely related to issues of separation. They helped give her some security regarding separation and helped her come out of a period of depreciation and testing of me, which reflected her disappointment and terror with her mother during the developmental phase of basic trust. Originally the costumes of the bears had to be "perfect," or they would not be symbolically adequate. As time went on, however, they became symbolic "sketches." When she relaxed, she recalled how much she had resented her mother's constant handling and correcting of her to make her "look perfect."

The final stage, years later, of our use of the bears in our psychoanalytic dialogue was much more symbolic. On one occasion, at an advanced stage in treatment, following considerable reflection on my part and discussion with her, I offered her a crude watercolor that I had painted during my previous vacation, representing the two bears. Infrequently, during our work she brought in and used paints or colored pencils to try to depict her tightly contained or controlled feelings to symbolically represent her mother or her mother's teeth. That I had made this painting "proved" to her unconscious that I did think of her and her symbols while I am absent. This enabled her now to suggest that the bears did not need to go with me and she seemed comfortable in recognizing that we would remember each other during my absence and that our secure attachment would survive the separation. She framed a copy of this watercolor and gave it to me. She understood that I had mirrored her feeling of being exposed and vulnerable.

COUNTERTRANSFERENCE AND ITS USE IN TREATMENT: FINAL REFLECTIONS

Thus, the bears (1) started as symbolic object representations, which in their concreteness were definitely needed; (2) became objects of play in a game of "dress ups"; (3) provided new symbols for the mothering relation; (4) were allowed to become highly symbolic representations through the watercolor; and, finally, (5) could be represented by words and conscious thought. Similarly, at each stage we could analyze, first her terror of abandonment or attachment, which required her to possess a concrete object to hang onto; second, her wish to find a bridge in playfulness to a good-enough mother figure; and, third, her capacity to believe that I would remember her without the bears and that she would be able to hold on to me in her mind through mental representations.

Countertransferencewise, at the first stage I experienced a wish to ease her fears and to let her know that I wanted to return to our work. In the second stage, my countertransference centered around the pleasurable experience of mutuality and reciprocity in the game she created. In the third stage, I experienced countertransference pride that she was able to accept my symbolic representation and to trust me.

The work with this patient brought up many other countertransference questions. For example, inevitably I had to deal with feelings of guilt or shame that entered the countertransference. I was always asking myself: Should I be *acting* this or *saying* that? Is it inappropriate to offer the patient symbolic objects? Would doing so be "acting out" on my part? If so, would a recommendation for hospitalization or medication be less symbolic and therefore not constitute "acting out"? Will "acting out" facilitate or hinder the analysis, in contrast to talking out? Should I restrict myself to words and restrict the analysis to language? Would words necessarily communicate as fully as symbolic enactments do? Are words the only form of communication my colleagues would approve? Is what I am doing appropriate technically? Would I share this with a student or peers as a reasonable recommendation for treatment? Did it help the patient in ways she would not have been helped otherwise? The bottom line of how I would answer all these questions has to do with the basic consideration: How can the patient be helped? My aim is not only to analyze and understand but also to help the patient heal herself.

Another deeper, generalized area of countertransference consideration lay in my belief that through the bears she was allowing me access to preoedipal feelings that she could not put into words. I could help her put her feelings into symbolic enactments that enabled me to reflect back to her, "You must have needed to be safe and loved and cared for; and all those feelings were disappointed by your mother." Her symbolizations gave us deeper access to archaic thoughts and feelings. This takes us into an area of countertransference first described by Bollas (1987) as the "unthought known," and later elaborated by Hedges as "interpreting the countertransference" (1992). My patient was not and could not feel safe and be conscious, for many years, of her need to be loved, secure, and safely attached. She did convey these needs through her symbolizations. Long before she could be aware of her preoedipal traumas, I could understand them. I could be conscious of them and say them back to her, even as Roslyn remained unconscious of them because her hope, trust, faith, needs, and longings had been severely damaged during her very early life.

Without the symbolic enactments, I believe that language alone would not have been adequate for the patient to relinquish the false self and revitalize her real self. Of course, without the language, symbolic enactments would not have been good enough to cure her. In analysis of archaic preverbal issues, language, the analysis of enactments, and the willingness to give them can go hand in hand. The analyst must have the courage to plunge into the world of symbols and to participate in this world with the patient, to retain a capacity for wonder, and to tolerate mystery. Perhaps this is to say that the analyst must embrace his or her countertransference rather than to run away from it, and to use that mysterious world of the analyst's inner life as a bridge to the patient's self.

Editor's Postscript

Roslyn's bears played a significant role in enabling the analysis of certain symbiotic issues just as Hirz's concrete presence in the previous chapter made possible the beginning analysis of certain organizing issues. Hunter's sensitive care and responsiveness to these enactments constitutes strategic emotional involvement, which was shown to make the analysis of their meanings progressively possible. Hunter did not simply teach Roslyn about bears or how to do without them; rather, her strategic emotional involvement enabled an analysis of what the bears meant to Roslyn, and a breaking down of her concrete need for them.

The vignettes in Chapters 2 and 3 have been provided as opening illustrations of the kinds of countertransference issues with which clinicians grapple. Let us now turn to some of the philosophical, theoretical, and technical issues that form the backdrop for the wide range of countertransference responsiveness to be considered in detail in this book.

4

The Relatedness Paradigm

THE NEW PARADIGM OF PSYCHOANALYSIS

The major shift in thought taking place over the past several decades is a result of the collaboration of many people working together in consulting rooms to ascertain the most useful ways to approach the study of the human psyche. For reasons that will become clear as we consider the issues, the new paradigm is perhaps best designated "relatedness." The recurrent themes of this shift in thought can be briefly summarized.

The Shift from Healing to Consciousness Raising

More than merely relinquishing the medical model with its many metaphors of illness, pathology, symptoms, underlying causes, and cure, contemporary thinkers emphasize that the very words and concepts that characterize medically based thought affect us deeply. Just as the sexual revolution requires attention to nuance of speech and work on everyone's part in order to relinquish sexist language, our consciousness-raising goal in psychoanalysis requires that when speaking about human psyche and human behavior, we relinquish outmoded and inappropriate language borrowed from the medical model of illness. That analytic work continues to have numerous medical applications is not an argument for continuing to allow pathologizing and curing concepts to deviously undermine our more sophisticated efforts to elevate and expand consciousness. Part of this consciousness-raising effort involves dropping the social status designations such as "doctor," "therapist," and "patient" in favor of the more functional designations of "listener" or "receiver" and "speaker" or "narrator." "Analyst" might be retained if it were used to describe the relatedness function rather than the social role. Other language and thought shifts will arise in the course of this book that will serve to move us into a more refined consideration of the human psyche.

The Shift from Scientific Objectivity to Systematic Subjectivity

From time immemorial our language and general approach to gaining knowledge has been to define "things" that are "really out there" and then to study the relationships among those things. This general approach to knowledge has been canonized in Newton's view of the universe as a giant clockwork set in motion by the hand of God. The human (scientific) task is to discover the nature of God's handiwork. This classical approach to physics set the pace for the expansion of objective scientific study in the nineteenth century. But Einstein's theories and experiments have subsumed the findings of classical physics under the much broader principles of relativity. Subsequently, quantum mechanics and now chaos and turbulence studies are subsuming the findings of relativity under more encompassing ideas. But especially relevant for our studies in psyche is that twentieth-century science has completely abandoned the Newtonian assumptions and approaches upon which all existing clinical theories, stemming as they have from nineteenth century thought have been built.

Clinical studies are now left essentially without responsible epistemological foundations. Our observations painstakingly collected within a framework of objectivity and logical positivism must now be entirely reconceptualized within more encompassing frameworks that take into account the essentially arbitrary, subjective, relative, and participatory nature of all knowledge. Natterson (1991) goes so far as to say that in psychoanalysis, "The truth about the relevance of our subjectivity has been repressed. Therefore it has manifested itself in numerous displaced and disguised forms. It is now time to explore this vital area and recover the lost territory of therapist subjectivity as a powerful resource for well-being" (p. 193).

The Shift from Historical Truth to Narrative Truth

The greatest human truths have, since the beginning of time, been embedded in stories rich with image, symbol, archetype, and metaphor. Modern physicists never tire of bringing to mind ancient and world folklore as precedent for the new findings that are so shocking to contemporary observers, as though we are only now finding ways to document wisdom known to the ancients through their narrational renditions. Most aspects of human life can be viewed as essentially governed or influenced by the power of myth and metaphor. Clinical disciplines have traditionally adopted an objectivist language with a positivist search for the historical truths of individual humans. Contemporary psychoanalysts are making a compelling case for thinking of the analytic enterprise in terms of its mythic and narrational function in uncovering and expanding the truths of human consciousness.

The Shift from Classical and Relativity Theories to Quantum and Chaos Uncertainties

Heisenberg's mathematical matrices, which pointed toward experimentation that confirmed the existence of the fantastic and strange quantum world, no longer leave room for us to consider the makeup of the universe as certain or even finally and completely knowable to humans. His widely acclaimed uncertainty principle informs us, among other things, that we do not and cannot know what realities are doing when we are not observing them. All we can do is make probabilistic statements about how things are likely to appear when we do look (Heisenberg 1958).

Clinical language has not yet been modified to show a similar benefit from the new orientation toward subject matter required by quantum thinking, as have the other scientific disciplines. As analysts, are we not in a more humbled but advantageous position when we acknowledge that the definitive search for the psyche's features and laws is an ultimately uncertain endeavor? Can we not learn our lesson from the physicists and realize that ultimate certainty is, in principle, not possible, given the necessity of receiving sensory impressions from a universe that is infinitely weird and slippery to the touch, and the necessarily participatory quality of our observational stance?

From Mythical Beasts to Listening Perspectives

Projecting human issues, concerns, qualities, and forces onto external creatures and objects, as illustrated by a world full of mythical beasts, is a long-standing human thought habit. Fixing knowledge and thought in this way severely limits the vantage points that might conceivably be employed to attain various views and ideas about different features of our private lives. The listening perspective approach that I advocate offers a feasible and comprehensive way in which to organize the rich and diverse world of psychoanalytic concepts for the purpose of listening, in the broadest sense, to all dimensions of the analytic encounter. Rather than creating more mythical beasts by theorizing from a positivistic and objectivist standpoint, which can only serve to limit considerations, the listening perspective approach opts for the establishment of a series of arbitrarily but logically chosen vantage points from which to consider the subjective worlds that interplay in the analytic consulting room.

The basic psychoanalytic assumption about the human condition is that in the course of growing up, through exposure to various relationships, psyche and soma become progressively altered by a series of constricting transformations. The listening task is to discern from the actual facts of the analytic engagement, as Freud first did in the specimen case of psychoanalysis (Breuer and Freud 1893–1895), exactly how psyche can be observed to operate in this dyadic relationship here and now. Listening is not a passive or static activity but involves a variety of interactions that serve in the investigation of relatedness styles, modes, and patterns. As we are engaged for the purpose of investigating psyche's imprisonment, what kinds of responsiveness from the listener will serve to maximize this special opportunity for study and psychic expansion? The four listening perspectives have emerged from a century of psychoanalytic work, and their application to understanding interpersonal relatedness modes involves differential strategic emotional involvement on the part of speaker and listener.

The Shift from Frame Technique to Variable Responsiveness

Determining what constitutes optimal responsiveness on the part of a psychoanalyst has been one of the stickiest and most hotly debated topics over the years. Howard Bacal (1985) is generally credited with the term *optimal responsiveness*, which he substituted for Kohut's *optimally failing empathy*. Such considerations beg the question of what one takes our assumptions and purposes to be in psychoanalysis. Rudolf Ekstein (1984) goes so far as to say that we invent theories to justify what we intend to *do* in psychoanalysis! If so, then the listener has already decided beforehand what position and what value systems he or she endorses and what psychological effects he or she intends to promote! Freud himself chose to destroy rather than to publish a number of his papers on technique, presumably because he was unhappy with what he had been able to say regarding what kinds of responsiveness optimally encourage the psychoanalytic process.

Traditional technique has evolved as a *frame*work deliberately constructed to bring the targeted *neurotic* symptom into focus for study. So-called frame technique is based on a medical model that views "the illness" as an objectively definable entity. There is a history that must be brought to light and certain conditions have been considered favorable for that purpose. The patient is instructed to say all that comes to mind. The analyst is to provide private, nonintrusive, uninterrupted, emotionally neutral, constant, objective, nongratifying, nonseductive, and time-enclosed "evenly hovering attention."

The psychoanalytic situation has been written about widely (Langs 1982, Stone 1962). Until recently virtually all recommendations have centered around the traditional assumptions of this positivist, medically oriented paradigm designed for "curing" neurosis. After the inadequacies of this approach had become so glaring they could no longer be ignored, a series of "parameters" were proposed in the psychoanalytic literature as short-term measures to keep the treatment going until the need for the alteration of basic technique could be analyzed (Eissler 1953). It should be noted however, that a few farsighted analysts (Carl Jung, Sandor Ferenczi, Wilhelm Reich, and Franz Alexander, among them) intuitively grasped the severe limitations of application that Freud's classical technique necessarily introduced and, well ahead of their time, began experimenting with variations of technique designed to analyze so-called preoedipal or preneurotic personality constellations. Gradually, as the scope of psychoanalytic studies has expanded beyond the original paradigm for studying neurosis, an array of alternative techniques has been explored for treating the more deeply disturbed, or as we might now say, the developmentally earlier issues of the psyche.

In leaving behind medically styled diagnostic thinking and curative manipulations, the quest for objectively defined mythical beasts, and the belief in the attainability of historical truth, new criteria for optimal responsiveness begin to emerge. Traditional frame technique has indeed proven its virtues in listening to certain kinds of triangular, contingent relatedness forms labeled "neurotic." Heinz Kohut (1971, 1977a,b) has put forward another type of responsiveness, "self to selfobject resonance," for dealing with another set of relatedness situations ("narcissistic tensions," which will be discussed later). A number of other writers and practitioners have been experimenting with diverse kinds of responsiveness geared to maximize understanding of yet other types of preoedipal or preneurotic relatedness situations referred to as "borderline" and "organizing" or "psychotic" (Gedo 1979a,b, 1981, Giovacchini 1979a, Kernberg 1975, 1976, 1980a,b, Searles 1979a, Stolorow and Atwood 1979, Stolorow and Lachman 1980, Stolorow et al. 1987).

The assumptions guiding "variable responsiveness" as a technical procedure in a listening situation are based on our attempting to develop a series of listening perspectives for grasping different aspects of interpersonal relatedness. To consider relatedness styles other than those called "neurotic," different perspectives with different modes of responsiveness are required.

Parallel to the listening perspectives (to be discussed in the next chapter) for receiving information are a set of ideas about the kinds of engagements that might be anticipated and notions regarding what kinds of interpersonal responsiveness might serve the listener best in the task of understanding how the listener and speaker are experiencing the relationship at any moment in time. The listening perspectives and their companion notions concerning optimal responsiveness are conceived of as well-defined but somewhat arbitrary thought positions from which to grasp different kinds of human relatedness as they appear in analytic engagement. Each perspective is designed to listen to transferred relatedness arising from different eras in the speaker's developmental history. Each perspective implies a different kind of strategic emotional involvement for optimal psychoanalytic results.

Listening Perspectives with variable responsiveness techniques make no *a priori* assumptions about the true nature of the person in analysis or the unique story and interactions that will unfold. Nor do the listening perspectives make assumptions about the nature of limitations that a person might be experiencing, what these limitations may mean to the person, or what he or she may do to gain greater flexibility in living. Rather they are designed to help the listener maintain a consistent and coherent orientation within him- or herself. Listening perspectives function to establish a position of perennial uncertainty, of sophisticated unknowing, rather than making fixed (frame) assumptions that seek to establish a direction of certainty, of blind knowing, of predefined action.

A compass does not guide a ship but serves to orient the mind of the captain, who, depending on changing conditions and his varying intentions, will make decisions that take him to various destinations. Each member of a psychoanalytic couple has his or her private agenda for the enterprise. And each has broader, long-term goals. The listening perspective approach is designed to foster neither personal agendas nor any other personal goals per se, but rather to keep the couple oriented as to the ongoing nature of the personal emotional exchange that is in fact happening.

With the shift to the relatedness paradigm we have at last evolved a psychoanalytic approach to satisfy the demands of a quantum universe! With broadly defined listening perspectives we have a compass orienting us to a broad map of the world of human relatedness potentials. The listener and speaker set out on a journey together that evolves as a series of glimpses of interesting and curious happenings about which they come to weave an unfolding story of their adventures together and what they have made note of and called into question while they were together.

But like the compass, the listening perspectives did not simply float in out of the blue. Orientation can be accomplished in many ways. Before the compass, navigators either traveled treacherously close to shore, using visual means by day, or ventured out further when navigation by means of the stars was understood. On overcast days or nights navigation was dangerous. There are reasons for choosing to orient in certain ways and not in others. The various means for navigation were not developed completely arbitrarily or based merely on human whim. Orientation depended upon some familiar configurations, some "attractor"—the shoreline, the moving celestial bodies, or magnetic north. What strange attractors (Briggs and Peat 1984, Gleick 1987) might we discover in our orientation to elusive psyche? A century of study has led to the emergence of a set of ideas that have made possible preliminary definitions of the listening perspectives in terms fit for a quantum age. We are now ready to examine the historical considerations that have given rise to the listening perspectives of the relatedness paradigm before moving to an understanding of the listening perspectives themselves.

THE EMERGENCE OF "SELF AND OTHER REPRESENTATIONS"

Freud's first paradigm for thinking about psyche appeared at the turn of the century and highlighted the workings of the *dynamic unconscious*, wherein slips of the tongue, dream symbolism, and various hidden meanings in humor, sexuality, and other aspects of relatedness were studied for their determining unconscious power. By 1923, Freud changed emphasis in a paradigm shift that highlights the importance of considering personally constructed and evolving *internal structures* comprised of mental functions. Freud's *structural theory* was defined along the lines of shifting balances and ratios among instincts (the id), the forces of moderation (ego), and socially generated inhibitions (the superego).

The third paradigm, *relatedness*, traces its origins to Heinz Hartmann's (1950) conceptual distinction between Freud's concept of the *ego*, as agent or set of internalized and structuralized functions, and the *self* as an evolving and integrating subjective center of the personality. Edith Jacobson in "The Self and Object World" (1954), and in a 1964 follow-up book of the same title declared that in working with "more deeply disturbed" or "functionally depressed" people than psychoanalysts usually treated, she did not find Freud's concepts of id, ego, and superego helpful. Rather, she noted that the ways in which "more deeply disturbed" individuals *represent themselves in relation to significant others* provided more illumination for the analytic task. While Jacobson's landmark departure from Freudian structural theory has served to liberate psychoanalytic thinking for the elaboration of a new paradigm, it would now appear that both previous paradigms need to be fully elaborated *within* the new framework. That is, the conscious, preconscious, and unconscious aspects of id, ego, and superego need to be studied for their differential implications at each of the four major developmental watersheds of self and other relatedness.

These studies opened the way for a rich proliferation of ideas about how humans come to experience and represent themselves in relationship to important others in their lives. The extreme usefulness of conceptualizing human interactions in terms of the determining power of self and other representations has been repeatedly demonstrated in the psychoanalytic literature over the last three decades. Unfortunately, many thinkers have perpetuated the mythical-beast approach, thus maintaining a positivist slant in the study of mental representations, rather than leaving representations as a soft concept to describe the subjective organization of experience.

It takes a human infant very little time to realize that the key features of its environment to be studied and manipulated are human. Furthermore, infant researchers assure us that babies come into the world well equipped to begin vigorous work at once (Stern 1985). The central theoretical features of contemporary psychoanalysis—self and other representations as organizers of the psyche—is disarmingly simple to grasp. But for the analytic listener to learn how to discern each person's idiosyncratic forms of the self and other representation, to find sensible ways to think about these forms, and then to interpretively mirror these forms of experience to the speaker for analytic understanding comprise a formidable set of skills based upon numerous issues and complexities. It is in the development and application of these listening and responding skills that differential strategic emotional involvement is required.

5

Four Listening Perspectives

In 1983 I surveyed and organized the ideas and findings from a century of psychoanalytic research of self and other representations into four major categories designed to be utilized as perspectives for listening in relatedness situations (Hedges 1983). The liberating twist of the listening perspective approach is not to be found simply in the overall reorganization of familiar clinical concepts. Rather, a profound shift of mental organization on the part of the analytic listener is required. What follows is a brief summary of the four perspectives (Table 5–1), which are explicated more fully in Hedges 1983, 1992, 1994a,b,c.

LISTENING PERSPECTIVE I
THE PERSONALITY IN ORGANIZATION:
THE SEARCH FOR RELATEDNESS

This perspective for listening is based upon an appreciation of the many features of human intrauterine life and the neonate's rich experience potentials in the first few months after birth. During this period of human life an infant organizes sensorimotor and cognitive-affective channels toward the human environment. The earliest learning experiences of organizing mind/body channels for sustenance, comfort, safety, stimulation, and intelligibility provide a foundation for the development of subsequent patterns of relatedness.

Traditionally, persons functioning primarily or periodically in mental states rooted in early organizational experience have been referred to as psychotic, autistic, schizophrenic, manic-depressive, or paranoid-schizoid. But all humans have experienced this period of primary organization of psyche. All physically normal infants organize channels for reaching out and contacting the environment pre- and postnatally. Infants work to bring needed features of the environment to them by various means. All future somatic and psychic developments depend on how this process goes and

Table 5–1.
Listening Perspectives: Modes of Psychoanalytic Inquiry

I. **The personality in organization: the search for relatedness**
   Traditional diagnosis: Organizing personality/ psychosis
   Developmental metaphor: + or –4 months—focused attention vs. affective withdrawal
   Affects: Connecting or disconnecting, but often appearing inconsistent or chaotic to an observer
   Transference: Connection vs. rupture, discontinuity, and disjunction
   Resistance: To connections and consistent bonds
   Listening mode: Connecting, intercepting, linking
   Therapeutic modality: Focus on withdrawal/destruction of links—connecting as a result of mutual focus
   Countertransference: Fear of intensity of psychotic anxieties in both self and other

II. **Symbiosis and separation: mutually dependent relatedness**
   Traditional diagnosis: Borderline personality organization
   Developmental metaphor: 4–24 months—symbiosis and separation
   Affects: Split "all good" and "all bad"—ambitendent
   Transference: Replicated dyadic interactions
   Resistance: To assume responsibility for differentiating
   Listening mode: Interaction in replicated scenarios
   Therapeutic modality: Replication and differentiation—reverberation
   Countertransference: Reciprocal mother and infant positions—a "royal road to understanding merger relatedness"

III. **The emergent self: unilaterally dependent relatedness**
   Traditional diagnosis: Narcissistic personality organization
   Developmental metaphor: 24–36 months—rapprochement
   Affects: Dependent upon empathy of selfother
   Transference: Selfothers (grandiose, twin, idealized)
   Resistance: Shame and embarrassment over narcissism
   Listening mode: Engagement with ebb and flow of self experiences
   Therapeutic modality: Empathic attunement to self experiences—resonance
   Countertransference: Boredom, drowsiness, irritation—facilitating

IV. **Self and other constancy: independent relatedness**
   Traditional diagnosis: Neurotic personality organization
   Developmental metaphor: 36+ months—(Oedipal) triangulation
   Affects: Ambivalence; overstimulating affects repressed
   Transference: Constant, ambivalently held self and others
   Resistance: To the return of the repressed
   Listening mode: Evenly hovering attention/free association
   Therapeutic modality: Verbal—symbolic interpretation—reflection
   Countertransference: Overstimulating—an impediment

This table is revised from Hedges 1992.

how the body and psychic modes developed during this period serve to expand or to limit and constrict possibilities in ways specific to the infant and to the possibilities offered it by the immediately available facilitating environment.

Most psychoanalytic work sooner or later focuses on the primary relatedness modes that form the foundation of a person's basic somatic organization and emotional life. I call this the "organizing" period with its "organizing issues, aspects, or features" that remain embedded in body structure and in personality. This listening perspective is designed to orient the listener to the ways in which foundational organizing patterns (forms, modes, styles) can be discerned and responded to. The exact ways in which people search for and find satisfying relatedness and the ways in which people learn to accept defeat and to expect a loss or breaking of human contact are the focus of study in this listening mode. This perspective thus has applications not only for people formerly diagnosed with some sort of psychosis but also for the deepest layerings of learned experience of all people, which serves to determine an individual's fundamental orientation to the environment.

LISTENING PERSPECTIVE II
SYMBIOSIS AND SEPARATION:
MUTUALLY DEPENDENT RELATEDNESS

From the earliest beginnings of psyche, channels are organized on the basis of response from the mothering person's body and personality. We can see the "Mommy and me" dance that is forming in the mutual cuing behaviors being established by the third or fourth month of life. These psychological tendrils of mutual relatedness are metaphorically termed "symbiosis" by Margaret Mahler. These *internal states* that characterize the symbiosis of the infant are believed to evolve according to growing expectations of various likely interactions. In the symbiotic exchange that the infant overlearns, the response of each partner comes to depend upon the response of the other. Peaking by the twelfth to eighteenth month, the symbiotic mutuality, dyadic responsiveness, or forms of symbiotic exchange remain strong through the twenty-fourth to thirtieth month. (Infant researchers point out that human babies never engage in a true biological symbiosis with their mothers. But this criticism of Mahler's terminology misses completely her intent to define *internalized* psychic experience by use of a biological metaphor. I follow Mahler's intended use of the term *symbiosis* as a set of internalized interaction patterns that the infant develops in relation to early caregivers.) Basic character and body structure dates from early in this period as the constitutional and personality variables of the infant come into play with the environment, creating the first sense of psychological familiarity and stability.

The possible dimensions for construction of the merged dual-identity dance of the evolving symbiosis are defined and limited by the foundations of the available connect and disconnect modes that were laid down in the physical and psychical patternings established during the previous organizing period. The particular emotional and behavioral patterns established in this primary bonding relatedness are thought to follow us throughout our lives (as character structures) as we search for closeness, for intimacy, for security, for familiarity, for physical security, and for love. If some people's stylized search for security and love seems strange, perverse, addictive, or self-abusive, we can only assume that the adult search replicates in some deep emotional way the primary bonding pattern *as the infant and toddler experienced* symbiotic exchanges with his or her caregiving others. This listening perspective has been developed for use with what has come to be referred to broadly as "borderline personality organization" (Kernberg 1975), and is essentially a way of understanding various aspects of the preverbal interaction patterns that were established during the symbiotic and separating periods of human development.

All well-developed people evolved interactional patterns or scenarios related to basic emotional bonding or symbiotic experience. I define "scenario" as a *listening device* for highlighting the interactive nature of the early bonding experience as it manifests itself in the replicating transference based upon an analytic re-creation of relatedness forms, patterns, and modes of the symbiotic period (Hedges 1983). These patterns become transferentially replicated in some form when any two people attempt to engage each other emotionally. The (almost "knee-jerk") emotional dance that forms in any relationship can be studied in terms of an interaction, a drama, or set of scenarios that unfold based upon deeply entrenched ways each participant has established for experiencing and relating to another. This listening perspective seeks to bring under scrutiny the predominantly preverbal engagement patterns and body configurations that mean attachment, bonding, and love, regardless of what individualized forms those patterns may take. The notion of symbiosis should by no means be construed as searching for or finding harmony and bliss. Rather it is conceptualized as reflecting or representing the exact and idiosyncratic emotional relatedness patterns as recorded in the child's experience during the bonding period (roughly 4 to 24 months, peaking at 18 months).

LISTENING PERSPECTIVE III
THE EMERGENT SELF:
UNILATERALLY DEPENDENT RELATEDNESS

Mothers know altogether too well the point at which a child begins to develop his or her "own mind"—they call this period the "terrible twos." The bonding dance of union, merger, identity, and collusive engagement ends with "No!" Freud (1926a) establishes negation not only as the beginning of an individual's independent mental functioning but also as the beginning of language and culture. The child begins to refuse the (m)other's ways and to experiment with and insist upon his or her own ways. After the child establishes some right to autonomy we note the beginning development of what has been called by Kohut (1971) the "cohesive self." After establishing the right to a certain emotional separateness, the child reapproaches the mother on a new basis, this time for affirmation of whom he or she is coming to be. This process of attempting to consolidate the sense of self, which is prominent in Western cultures, may be observed from birth to death, Kohut tells us, but peaks in its emphasis in the third year of life, the subphase of separation-individuation that Mahler calls rapprochement. (Heinz Kohut in a discussion at the 1979 UCLA Self Psychology Conference was asked at which of Mahler's phases or subphases would he place the development of the cohesive self. He answered without hesitation, the rapprochement.)

The listening perspective for this process of ongoing consolidation of the self sense describes a "selfother tension,"[1] or the need to experience the reassuring, confirming, or inspiring other as a consolidating part of one's sense of self. Kohut uses the term *narcissistic* for the mirroring, twinship, and idealizing transferences that arise in analysis and are based on selfother tensions. The other is recognized as being a separate center of initiative but *used* as a cohesion building function of the self. Selfother tensions motivate the person to address or seek out some significant other in order to achieve a sense of wholeness and cohesion.[2] Kohut and the self psychologists have studied extensively how the self sense can be brought into focus in the analytic experience.

---

1. Kohut's term is *selfobject*, reflecting the traditional tendency in psychoanalysis to refer to significant others as love objects or objects of instinctual cathexis. "Selfother" reflects the more contemporary trend to think in terms of various self and other representations and experience.
2. During the late 1960s as Kohut was evolving his notions of the other being used to confirm the self, Winnicott (1969) was working on a similar concept—"the use of an object" as distinct from and arising later out of "object relating."

LISTENING PERSPECTIVE IV
SELF AND OTHER CONSTANCY:
INDEPENDENT RELATEDNESS

Freud first intuited that it was during the third through seventh years that the problems of independent psychic life were faced and worked through by children. Borrowing the mythic themes of Sophocles' *Oedipus Rex* and Shakespeare's *Hamlet*, Freud discovered in his own self-analysis (in 1897) the power of emotional triangulation. It is one thing to search for nurturance and intelligibility in the world (organizing period). It is yet another thing seek to establish dyadic reliability (symbiotic period). It is yet another experience to look to the other for consolidation of a sense of self (selfother period). But the most complicated aspects of human life develop when a full emotional awareness of third parties, of *contingent emotional relationships*, is integrated into psychic functioning. That is, the impact of the so-called oedipal triangulation experience relies upon the child's growing realization that each relationship exists within a broader set of contingencies determined by third parties. Symbolically and historically the third party is represented as Father or The Fathers. But in actual human experience, the third party appears along with language and cultural awareness—that which comes between Mommy and me—which intervenes in our private relationship and catapults our relatedness into the broader human community.

The third party elevates to the level of symbolic understanding, gives us an outside perspective (expressed in symbols) on every dyadic relationship we establish, and robs us of exclusive emotional ownership of the one whom we most wish to love. The researches a child conducts and the conclusions he or she draws about how triangles work in relationships form a strong emotional web that Freud first understood and referred to as the Oedipus complex. In this reading, what has been called castration anxiety can only refer to the anticipated loss of the personal power once experienced in dyadic relationship. It is the social order (the language system, "The Fathers") that intervenes to cut off this power.

The assumptions developed during this period are often conflictual and undergo repression. These patterns tend to govern subsequent relationships to such an extent that Freud labeled them "neurotic." The Freudian listening perspective operates on an entirely different plane (the cultural verbal/symbolic) than the three that precede it and can be thought of as leading toward independent relatedness. Loewald (1979) points out that Freud's notion of the power of unconscious psychic constellations *waning* throughout a lifetime contrasts sharply with his translator's term *"resolution of the Oedipus complex."*

SUMMARY

The listening perspective approach has emerged out of a myriad of considerations that have evolved over a century of psychoanalytic study. It is formulated in terms of a major paradigm shift that highlights (1) consciousness raising, (2) systematic subjectivity, (3) a search for narrational truth, (4) acknowledgment of the uncertainties of the participatory universe, (5) the systematic establishment of vantage points from which to listen, and (6) a variable responsiveness listening technique. The conceptual advance that the paradigm of self and object representations affords makes possible an approach to psychoanalytic inquiry based on differential listening to developmental issues and differential strategic emotional involvement. Countertransference responsiveness appropriate to each of the listening perspectives (see Table 5–1) will now be discussed in the next four parts of this book.

II

STRATEGIC EMOTIONAL INVOLVEMENT IN LISTENING TO PSYCHOTIC ISSUES

6

Emotional Involvement in Psychoses

Learning how to listen to issues involved in psychotic (organizing) states has been perhaps the most difficult challenge psychoanalysts have ever had to face. Over the course of time many psychoanalysts have tackled the problem of how to work with psychotic states (see Rickman 1957 and Rosenfeld 1987). The overwhelming conclusion has been that the verbal-symbolic free association technique developed by Freud for the treatment of neurosis can be, at best, a support to people suffering from psychosis. The minority opinion holds that psychotic states, like all psychic states, are transformable, given adequate motivation and appropriate environmental responsiveness. Notable is the work by many at Chestnut Lodge, the psychosis research project at Reiss-Davis Child Study Center, and the reports by Searles (1965, 1979a) and Giovacchini (1975a, 1979a, 1988). Little (1981) reports her transformative work with early developmental states and then recounts (Little 1990) her own analysis with Winnicott in which she herself experienced a regression of significant psychotic proportions.

STRATEGIC EMOTIONAL INVOLVEMENT IN THE SEARCH FOR RELATEDNESS[1]

To imagine what kinds of listener responsiveness might be expectable in organizing states we need but recall the kinds of reactions that parents have in the earliest months of their new baby's life. Yes, think of the happy Gerber baby and of the Holy Family, the joyous and beatific Madonna and Child. And yes, the thrills of new parenthood are many. But too often the horrible relatedness strain that parents and families of newborns experience

---

1. This section is reprinted with modifications from Hedges 1992.

is forgotten. Even in the best of circumstances, with a longed-for baby who is normal and healthy, marital and familial stress characterize the last months of pregnancy and the first few months of life. Feelings of abandonment, rejection, loss, disruption, jealousy, envy, and resentment—to mention only a few—characterize the general relatedness atmosphere before and after the new arrival. The couple's social and sexual relations are usually disrupted by the upheaval occasioned by the emotional preparation for new ties and new relationships that the baby's arrival creates. But as if the strain of all the shifting relatedness patterns is not enough, actually working out the ways and means of accommodating a highly dependent human being into daily schedules, family budget, sleep and feeding routines, and emotional awareness patterns takes just about every ounce of energy of everyone concerned. Sibling and oedipal rivalries (actual and transferential) are stirred up in everyone. Irritation and fatigue become the expectable rather than the exception. By the end of the baby's fourth month there are bags under both parents' eyes, severe feelings of deprivation and irritation reign supreme, marital and familial tensions are at an all-time high—in short, everyone is just about sick and tired of their lives being intruded upon by this "blessed event." Fortunately, not all is gloom and doom, for everyone is observing, nourishing, and in direct ways reaching out to find and know the new person in the family. Every day the baby does something new and endearing. Even the interruptions of sleep routine are bearable because everyone knows that the strained period will soon come to an end. The newly arrived creature will soon be showing signs of socialized and civilized behavior—like being able to stay on a reasonable feeding and sleeping schedule, like not crying interminably when no one and nothing can seem to provide reassurance. First we try one thing and if that doesn't work we try another. When one person becomes exhausted attending, another takes over. Parents begin to look lovingly into each other's eyes again, have an evening out, and use help in managing the daily tasks. "Look, he's becoming a regular person!" "See how she looks at me, watch her eyes move and her lovely smile." These responses from caregivers mark the beginning of the mutual cuing process, the internalization of a structure called symbiosis, the onset of a mutual dance in which two interact with one accord. In a family with more than one heavily invested caregiver, each dyadic exchange gradually assumes a characteristic life of its own.

But prior to the gradual establishment of mutual understandings and reciprocal behaviors between baby and caregivers, there is chaos, strain, confusion, bodily tension and stress, sleep disturbance, eating difficulties, and any number of psychological and physical disturbances. All of these and more can be expected in the countertransference responsiveness to organizing states. Searles (1979a) has been most courageous and influential in his writings that portray the disruptive, confusing, somatic, tension-filled, emotional responsiveness to his deeply disturbed patients. Likewise, Giovacchini (1979a,b) and Little (1981) write of the many disturbing experiences they have undergone while working with primitive transferences. Accounts of various kinds of therapist disturbances abound at centers that specialize in the treatment of psychoses (Ekstein and Motto 1966, Silver 1989). Hedges (1992) provides the first attempt to systematically define and organize countertransference responsiveness into different developmental levels and to specify a series of expectable countertransference responses in organizing states.

One important cue toward systematic study of organizing-level countertransference has been provided by Bion (1962, 1963), a British analyst, who for years studied the origins of the human thought process by studying psychotic states. Bion's overarching question revolved around the problem of how it is that one primate thinks and speaks while the others do not. Using a metaphor of container and contained, Bion noted how the human thought process begins. An infant is born into the world with a capacity for sensations (beta elements). On the basis of received sensations the baby gives out some cue regarding the state of the body/mind. The mothering person, drawing upon accumulated cultural wisdom regarding infantile needs, elects to do something that has the effect of altering the baby's bodily states and sensations. It is the (m)other who first thinks, thereby passing on some aspect of a complex cultural thought system that alters the sensation or tension states of the infant. After repeated instances of this containing of a state by the thoughts and actions of the mother, almost by classical conditioning the infant acquires the first elements of thought (alpha function). These elements might be some sense of anticipation based on mother's movements, some paired association of milk sensations with the smell of mother's breast, or some other pairing with the sound of her voice or the warmth of her touch. By means of the establishment of these rudimentary cycles from sensation-mother to thought-alteration-of-state-sensation, the whole complex web of human affectivity, movement, and thought evolves. Bion speaks of the "linking" of thought elements, initially accomplished through mother's body-thought system and later through complex interweaving of logical and symbolic thought. Extrapolating, it might be said that the formation of the symbiotic system of relating is comprised of a set of such baby–mother linking cycles that build and expand until the two come to move and live psychologically as though they were one. This at-one-ness might be considered as an attempt to re-create on a psychological plane the original sense of intrauterine union. It might be said that in various ways for the rest of our lives we seek state alterations that move toward replication of the interaction patterns by which we first managed to achieve this sense.

The aforementioned developmental sequences point toward a way to think about normal and expectable processes. Infant researchers are now discovering and defining many ways through which these early processes operate. But even in average expectable rearing situations, how often do baby's sensations go unresponded to, go unlinked to a greater thought system? When we observe organizing states in the analytic listening situation, even in the context of well-differentiated self and other constellations, we might surmise that in various areas the linking was inadequate or incomplete. In persons who tend to be considered psychotic in lifestyle, we might surmise massive failure of linkage, whereas in most babies many links were satisfactorily made and only certain areas have remained unresponded to. It is these areas that present themselves for analysis and often are referred to as a "psychotic core." I prefer to speak of "organizing" features or issues.

This way of thinking about links from bodily sensations to cultural thought systems (through mother's intelligent handling) that have the power to be transformative, points in the direction of a crucial problem area. Bollas (1979) speaks of this transformational process being accomplished by the baby's attachment to a transformational object. He further remarks that Freud's invention of the analytic situation unwittingly and forgivably represents an acting out of this early transformational setting. The implication is that even change at "higher" levels of integration requires the holding and containing of the early life processes to effect change.

Babies come into the world well equipped to search out and call for the kinds of help that they need in order to survive and thrive. Further, a certain special intelligence operates in maternal care that transforms sensation states into thought systems. Massive or partial failures of this transformational process are universal. When studying various organizing states analytically, we note that focus on the ways in which people orient for interpersonal contact and the ways in which they compulsively break off or prevent transformational contact from occurring yield crucial transference information. That is, transference memories become available for scrutiny in the analytic listening situation. These memories bear witness to the ways that the (m)other once was and was not available for transformational experience and, eventually, for symbiotic exchanges that have the power to bring somatic states into the realm of the psyche. Now, a few countertransference implications.

Considering early somatic states as idiosyncratic and ever changing according to principles that are at first unfamiliar to caregivers, we see that the key event in the organizing period is how the infant manages to reach out to others for transformational experiences. When these experiences have worked well to form connections to the other, patterns of symbiotic exchange form. When early sensations and yearnings are frustrated or go unresponded to in any of a variety of ways, the exact manner of the failure is recorded in body memory, and this early template for experience will be faithfully repeated as transference to the (failing) other. Winnicott (1949) makes this point in terms of early "persecutory experiences" that serve as patterns for the receipt of all later frustrations. The task of the analytic listener is first to discern these subtle patterns as they ebb and flow during the course of a clinical hour. That is, transference experience based on rupture and failure in regard to the earliest linking processes manifests itself in the fine details of a clinical hour as contact is invisibly sought and lost. Next, the listener must find ways of identifying and bringing under mutual scrutiny the moments in which and the means through which contact is transferentially broken. The listener, maintaining the sense of contact and continuity with the content of the interaction, will generally fail to discern when the speaker has silently and invisibly left, vanished, abandoned the emotional impact of the relatedness. The reason is simple enough. Most analytic listeners have themselves enjoyed favorable enough developmental experiences that they automatically assume contact or engagement if the person is talking, emoting, or otherwise apparently interacting. Close scrutiny of clinical sessions with people functioning at the organizing level at the time usually reveals, however, that the speaker is mimicking relatedness, thereby giving the listener the illusion (or delusion) that they are connected. It is my impression that most therapy that continues for protracted periods of time (ten, fifteen, or twenty years) has been conducted under these conditions. That is, the therapist was caught up in the content of the psychosis, rather than in pursuit of the process by diligent study of points of contact and transferential moments where that contact is broken. The content of the psychosis could be hallucinatory or delusional as in schizophrenia, or affect loaded as in the affect disorders. In following the material on people referred to as multiple personalities, as well as many of the eating disorders, perversions, addictions, and schizoid withdrawals, it appears that too often the analyst becomes caught up in the ebb and flow of the content, that is, the symptoms and conceptualizations of private life, so that the object relations process becomes completely lost from view and little reconstruction is possible. I call the break in contact the "appearance of 'the psychotic, overwhelming, or noxious mother,'" or the "breach" or "blockage" of the organizing channel to characterize the bringing to life in the transference moment the failure of the environment to meet some extension of the nascent self. It is only by scrutinizing many such interactions that the listener may begin to pick up on the moments of the break in contact.

The countertransference to organizing states will expectably be disorganized, chaotic, frustrating, anger provoking, fearful, dismaying, and generally filled with various emotions on the part of the analyst-listener that threaten to become disorienting and out of control. No wonder analysts have tended not to treat the organizing level, since their own personality is likely to be threatened with disruptive fragmentation! It seems that analysts empathically tuned in to the opening and closing of organizing channels of connection regularly and expectably become disrupted in their functioning. From observing the chaos generated in analytic listeners (my own included), when becoming aware of the abrupt and subtle ways in which people functioning in organizing states withdraw from or cut off connectedness, I believe that our own unmoderated, umet organizing states are activated. Restated, a listener subjected to idiosyncratically and/or misunderstood connections and disconnections from the engagement typically fails to notice what is happening, much in the same way that people occasionally find themselves automatically doctoring up a narration of their experiences so as to make a seamless fit to self-concepts, self-esteem, and the present narrational context. People catch themselves actually lying, subtly exaggerating, distorting, or otherwise altering facts in order to fit the perceived needs of the present context. So analytic listeners, in order to retain their sense of humanity and a sane orientation to the speaker, go to the greatest lengths to understand the content, thereby avoiding the deep-seated chaos and disorganization that would result if one were suddenly aware of being abandoned or rejected.

People who live most of their lives in organizing states learn to imitate or mimic human interaction patterns so as to "pass" in most everyday situations and thereby to delude the therapist into thinking them still connected. I refer to this self-structure based on imitation and mimicry the "mimical self." This structure contrasts sharply with Winnicott's notion of the "false self," which is a structure of later symbiotic life based upon relinquishing of a true, instinctively based self in favor of conforming to demands of the nurturing environment. Jerzy Kosinski's *Being There* (1970) depicts such a mimical self as Chance, a simpleton, becomes catapulted toward wealth and fame by being regarded by those around him as a wise man. In the movie version, Peter Sellers portrays the mimicry of the hapless fellow who only knows how "to watch." In one of the great sex scenes of all time, the millionaire's wife, played by Shirley MacLaine, is intent on seducing him. She asks how he likes it, not realizing that he hasn't the slightest notion about sexual interaction. He responds, "I like to watch," referring to television, since he doesn't understand human interactions and can only imitate. There follows a bizarre scene in which he proceeds to imitate stretching exercises he is watching on television, ending up standing on his head. All the while, she, in a black negligee, thinking she is exciting him, proceeds to masturbate to orgasm on the skin of a big black bear whose open jaws stare into the camera. *Being There* is a brilliant novel that not only captures the plight of the organizing state but the amazing extent to which people go not to notice psychotic disconnection. Only the black maid, who worked for the family that raised Chance, speaks the truth when she sees him being interviewed on network television as a celebrity, an authority on international economics. She turns to her family and declares, "This sho is a white man's wo'ld, that man ain't got nothing but bread puddin' 'tween his ears!"

People with organizing personalities often manage to develop good intelligence and skills and may be successful and highly placed in business, industry, politics, and the professions. But careful examination of their capacities for interpersonal relatedness places them at below the 4-month level, mimicking human life but knowing they are different, weird, strange, crazy, somehow not quite human.

While there is at present no known way to relate these disruptive countertransference reactions to the various contents and symptoms of organizing states, the responsiveness of the listener can point to the search for contact as well as the moments and means through which contact is regularly and compulsively thwarted. Transference has been the central tool of psychoanalysis from the beginning. In organizing states, the transference records the movement toward transformational experience and the breaks in contact that foreclose the transformational process. The literary work of Franz Kafka depicts beautifully and graphically the organizing struggle to reach out and make connections to a world that is unresponsive (Hedges 1983). By working together to learn to identify the times and styles of contact breaks, listener and speaker can analyze the transference to the psychotic or inadequately responsive mother that has been preventing the person from freely forming links that could move toward a fuller mutual cuing process of the symbiosis. It was Searles (1979a,b) who discovered that the reconstruction process in psychosis entails forming a symbiosis *de novo* with the actual person of the analyst. From here, self-identity and cohesion have an opportunity to develop for the first time. Some countertransference responses to organizing issues seem to represent the listener's retreat from the overpowering instinctual stimulation of the speaker. Other withdrawing or approaching countertransference responses seem to represent the listener's personal response to his or her failing or overwhelming mother of the organizing period. Yet other forms of countertransference to organizing issues represent listener empathy with the terrifying features of contact moments for the speaker. Here it is the listener, acting as proxy for the speaker, who withdraws from or breaks contact as an empathic response to the fear of the speaker.

Freud's formulations regarding transference identified a person's tendency to experience the current analytic relationship in terms of crucial relationships from the past. He was able to demonstrate successful analysis (understanding) of triangular structures formed during the oedipal period. Kohut demonstrated that a different technical notion was needed to analyze selfobject or selfother transferences from the phallic-narcissistic period of development. Many current approaches, including "interpreting the countertransference," are demonstrating the viability of analyzing the replicating transference to psychic formations of the symbiotic period. The organizing transference forms on the basis of early organizing channels being broken off.

FOUR TYPES OF COUNTERTRANSFERENCE TO THE ORGANIZING EXPERIENCE

Denial of Human Potential

The most common form of countertransference is viewing persons living pervasively organizing experiences as witches, evildoers, hopelessly psychotic, and in other ways not quite human. In this attitude is a denial of human potential and a denial of the possibility of being able to stimulate desire in such a way as to reawaken it and to analyze blocks to human relating. We hear, "I can't reach you, you are too sick. You are untreatable so we will lock you up or give you drugs to sedate or pacify you."

A Fear of Primitive Energy

When an analytic listener invites the organizing experience into a transference relationship, he or she is asking that the full impact of primitive aggressive and sexual energies be directed squarely at the person of the listener. Listeners fear the power of this experience because it can be quite disorienting and, if not carefully assessed and monitored, potentially dangerous. But fear of basic human affectivity is irrational and we now have at our disposal many rational ways of inviting and managing the organizing-level energies. The key technical consideration is not whether the person on the basis of *a priori* criteria is "treatable," but whether the listener has sufficient holding and supportive resource available to him or her on a practical basis to make the pursuit of treatment practical and safe for all concerned.

Encountering Our Own Organizing Experiences

When we as listeners invest ourselves emotionally in reaching out again and again to an analytic speaker only to be repeatedly abandoned or refused, it stimulates our own most primitive experiences of reaching out to our own caregivers during our organizing developmental period, hoping for a response and feeling traumatized when the desired response was not forthcoming. Our own "psychotic mother" transference reappears projected onto the analytic speaker as we attempt to provide systematic and sustained connection for people living organizing states. How each of us as individual practitioners develops staying power is the crucial question. Our own therapy is essential, as is consultation with colleagues during trying phases of this work. Attempting to work the organizing experience without adequate resource and backup support is like a single mother trying to manage a difficult or sick baby while holding down a job to support herself, caring for several other children, and trying to live some life of her own. We need support to do this kind of work.

Empathy Leading to Breaks in Contact

After the preliminary phases are well under way—that is, after the listener and speaker have established basic working rhythms that are comfortable and safe, and after the listener has been able to discern and bring up for discussion the specific ways in which the speaker engages in and searches for contact and then cuts off contact—we notice the speaker begins excitedly to see in outside contacts as well as in the analytic hour how the breaking of contact is being regularly accomplished. Speakers are often excited by the therapeutic process at this point because for the first time in their lives something is finally making sense about themselves. They begin a valiant struggle to maintain contact nearly everywhere they go, especially with the listener.

Then, we notice a tendency on the part of the listener to begin withdrawing into inattentiveness, preoccupation, or even drowsiness. This type of countertransference activity, which tends to occur only well into the treatment process, represents the listener's empathy for the terror that contact provides for the speaker. That is, the speaker for the first time in his or her life feels that he or she is hot on the trail of something that promises human satisfaction—sustained contact. But in the person's enthusiasm to achieve as much contact as possible as fast as possible, it is the listener who senses the speaker's internalized danger and in some way is deliberately (consciously or unconsciously) slowing things down a bit. This countertransference reaction can be shared with the speaker so that the two may gain a fuller appreciation of the joys and dangers of human contact.

COMMON CONCERNS IN THE LISTENING TASK

The remainder of this chapter discusses a series of issues and concerns that have caught the attention of analysts working with psychotic or organizing states.

Objective Hatred and Fear

In analyzing psychotic states Winnicott (1947) discovered that there are moments in which the analytic speaker seeks or expects hate from the analytic listener. Not to hate under these circumstances is not to be in touch with the private life of the speaker. In the passage below, Winnicott illustrates the importance of the listener being free to experience objective hate generated in the present from hate left over from the past and called out by the present event.

Winnicott reports that during the Second World War a 9-year-old boy was sent to an evacuation hostel because of truancy. He soon ran away—but not before Winnicott had interpreted one of his drawings as an attempt to run away so as to save the inside of his home and to preserve his mother from assault. Furthermore his running away was interpreted as his attempt to escape an internal world full of persecutors. Not surprisingly the boy turned up at a police station not far from Winnicott's home and the boy was taken in for three months by Winnicott and his wife—three months of hell, Winnicott reports. The first phase was dealt with by giving the boy complete freedom and a shilling whenever he went out. He had only to call and Winnicott would pick him up from whatever police station had taken charge of him. Soon the running away stopped and the boy began acting out the assault that he felt on the inside. In each crisis an interpretation was made no matter what hour of the day or night, creating a great trial for Winnicott and his wife.

> Did I hit him? The answer is no, I never hit. But I should have had to have done so if I had not known all about my hate and if I had not let him know about it too. At crises I would take him by bodily strength, without anger or blame, and put him outside the front door, whatever the weather or the time of day or night. There was a special bell he could ring, and he knew that if he rang it he would be readmitted and no word said about the past. He used this bell as soon as he had recovered from his maniacal attack.
> The important thing is that each time, just as I put him outside the door, I told him something; I said that what had happened had made me hate him. This was easy because it was so true . . . .
> Out of all the complexity of the problem of hate and its roots I want to rescue one thing, because I believe it has an importance for the analyst of psychotic patients. I suggest that the mother hates the baby before the baby hates the mother, and before the baby can know his mother hates him. [pp. 194–203]

In the analysis of a person living an organizing experience, many exchanges occur that elicit fear and hate in the listener. To be able to experience hatred and to report it requires a special empathic capacity of the analyst. However, knowing that the goal of an activity of the speaker is to stimulate hatred and to create a disconnection can sustain the listener in such a way that the disconnection can often be refused. Then the response to "Are you angry with me?" might be, "I easily could be and I did feel momentary flashes of anger. But I realize that somehow you are trying to show me something, so I'm less angry than I am puzzled and confused. I want to know what this is about, but right now I can find no way to think about it. Do you have any ideas?"

Winnicott's account suggests the inevitability of feeling angry or frightened by activities representing the organizing level of experience. It is critical for the analyst to be able to feel the primitive experience and to be able to report it. But it is equally critical to learn to process disruptive feelings in order to understand them as special communication rather than merely as provocations to be reacted to. The critical aspect of the communication will relate less to the content of the verbalization or exchange and more to the immediate and interpersonal context that is actually being lived out.

To be able to grasp the communication in terms of its disconnecting aim allows the possibility of securing the organizing transference for study.

Doing Exactly What We're Told

The following case report highlights the importance of the setting in the analysis of individuals who have had insufficient nurturance in the first months of life. On a Friday Winnicott (1964) has inadvertently failed to have an important feature of the room arranged just as the patient insists it must be and a disaster ensues. Finally the patient is able to ask what it is about her that makes people behave badly. Winnicott sees the opportunity to assure her it is not her on this occasion but a lapse in himself not related to her. He says she would rather believe she had caused it, and therefore that she had control over him. A flood of memories ensues regarding her father's character traits. Winnicott ends with, "The thing is, this is what I am like, and if you continue with me you will find I shall do similar things with unconscious motivation again because that is what I am like" (pp. 99–100).

Winnicott uses this occasion to be clear that with certain people, "It is always that if one provides certain conditions work can be done and if one does not provide these conditions work cannot be done and one might as well not try. The patient is not there to work with us except when we provide the conditions which are necessary" (p. 97). Winnicott clearly grasps the importance of providing the exact setting and kind of interaction called for by the speaker. He understands well the disasters that ensue if the listener fails to do exactly as he or she is told. But in the end he insists that he is a person with (sometimes unseemingly) unconscious motivations like every other person.

> It can easily be seen that one simply cannot afford to make these mistakes with patients who are more ill. By more ill I mean patients who have less healthy personality alongside their ill bit. The ill bit is just as ill in one as it is in another, and one cannot in any way lessen the adaptation to the patient's needs by knowing that the patient has a considerable amount of healthy personality. It is the ill bit that one is dealing with and it is as ill as possible.
>
> The astounding thing is that if one has a patient going through one of these phases one can adapt in a very detailed way to the patient's needs over a period of time; that is to say, in the hour that is set aside for this patient one can have a professional reliability which is very much unlike one's own unreliable personality. In time, however, one's own unreliability begins to seep through, and one of the dangers is that as soon as the patient begins to

get better in the sense of being able to allow one to lessen vigilance, one is liable to take a holiday, so to speak, and to rush forward with a show of one's own impulse. One cannot be blamed for being like this but it may lose a case that is going well. [pp. 96–102]

The addition we can now make to Winnicott's work is the importance of the listener tracking all untoward responses that the speaker has toward the listener and the analytic setting. Merely defending one's personality or one's practices misses entirely the context of the interaction and the disconnecting motivation. The message needs somehow to be, "I am what I am and I do what I do. By now you know me well enough to know that though I wish to be as responsive to your needs and requests as possible, my own needs and my own personality sometimes emerge. When this happens you fall into great distress. Can we look at what happens, at how you lose yourself, your mind and your body, in these moments, at how you lose me?" That is, the decisive analytic work is not done at moments when all goes well; rather, the appearance of the psychotic transference where it can be secured for analysis invariably occurs when some aspect of the analyst's response is failing or inadequate. Then the compulsion to disconnect arises, often in a very stormy way. True, one does one's best to avoid these abreactions. But also true is that it is only in these moments when transference analysis is possible.

Terror of Interpretive Control

Grinberg (1993) reports a spoiled interpretation resulting from counteridentification with a jazz musician. The interpretation stressed the positive transference implicit in a musical metaphor involving rhythm, melody, and harmony but missed the paranoid content involving envy and anxiety. The patient responds by speaking in a medical metaphor in which the doctor equipped with specialized apparatus gains a better knowledge of the patient than the patient himself has. The countertransference fantasy on the part of the analyst of a metronome to regulate, control, and direct the time in the client informed the analyst that the client was interested in learning about the timing and rhythm of the analyst so that he could control him. This paranoia had been stirred up by the beneficial effects that the analyst's words had on the client's diarrhea after a recent session. The terror of contact that has maintained this man in an organizing state is seen as related to the fear that interpretive contact can control him, that to open to the other is to be controlled by the other.

While I was listening to him I surprised myself with a parallel and simultaneous fantasy to have a metronome to regulate, control, and direct the time in him, that is to say, to have something which I already knew was lacking in him. I realized exactly at that moment all the play of his unconscious fantasy contained in his intense projective identification and also "how" I "counteridentified" myself projectively with a partial aspect of his, full of envy, and anxiety. One of the major effects of my "projective counteridentification" was the blind spot of the paranoid content of his attitude and my having stressed instead the positive aspect of the transference. The patient used it in a defensive way to pacify the persecutor, which I represented. But that was only his defense because of his anxiety and panic due to the power he thought I had. My words not only cured him of his diarrhea but also they gave him a physical stitch. I was in possession of a secret which he envied and feared because I could do what I wanted with him. He wanted to take this over so that he could limit its danger and also so that he could dominate me at the same time. For this he needed both to know me and to control me. It was for this that he "took" me into his own field, acoustics and music. He made me feel, projectively, what he had felt with me. My feeling of dislike corresponded to his feeling of anxiety. My admiration and envy reflected similar feelings which he had felt, and my need to use his terminology and concepts was the equivalent of his desire to take onto himself my special terminology and concepts. My fantasy of the metronome formed the response to his desire to use all kinds of medical apparatus so as to get to know me completely, that is to say, to control me. As a last resort, and as a transactional solution, he offered me his beat and timing in exchange for knowing mine. [pp. 182–183]

The Analyst's Values Under Attack

Giovacchini (1984) reports about a young college student who had managed to alienate a series of therapists. An audio recording of one of his analytic sessions was listened to by a number of Giovacchini's colleagues, all of whom found the young man irritating. In light of the man's obvious helplessness and vulnerability, it seemed strange that reactions were not more compassionate and tempered. Verbal "acting out" is discussed in terms of the person's exclusive occupation with reality and no corresponding ability to consider contributory internal factors. The student had seized upon the "science" of astrology through which he alienated his analyst, who took science seriously. Had his delusional needs been expressed more bizarrely, illogically, or flamboyantly the analyst probably would not have been threatened. A problem of delusional proportions had been obscured by a seemingly rational superstructure that seduced the therapist into arguing with the content rather than analyzing the intrapsychic motivations.

> This adolescent patient and many others like him, however, have a propensity to clothe their primary-process projections in secondary-process garments that represent areas the therapist *values*. Making astrology a science was the method this patient used. The therapist, who valued science, perceived how the patient distorted and made use of specious arguments. Since the therapist's value system and ego ideals included scientific integrity as a very important element, the patient's arguments, which were considered denigrations and falsifications of the scientific position, ran counter to his ego ideal, and he reacted. Undoubtedly, it would have been better for the therapist to continue focusing upon the delusional core, but this became especially difficult because the patient, by subtle means, upset the therapist's personal equilibrium. When the therapist became aware of what he was reacting to, the treatment lost its horrendous qualities. [pp. 328–332]

Knowing what one is reacting to indeed serves to reduce the disorganization of the therapist. But simply being more comfortable in the interaction is insufficient if the analyst has not been able to track the context of these subtle attempts to undermine the therapist's personal values. How exactly does this mode of disconnect operate? What aspect of organizing transference to the early environmental insufficiency is being represented in this interactive sequence? Are values per se the point? Perhaps the infant's needs in some way undermined the mother's values or vice versa. This might be a good clue and should be placed into the analytic dialogue as a possibility. But since content at the organizing level is rarely the central point of a communicative interaction, it seems more likely in the case cited that the speaker's emotionally irritating manner gives us a picture of disconnection caused by irritation or exasperation experienced by the mother or by the child, or by both.

At this level it is not safe to assume that the speaker is doing to the listener what was done to him, as we customarily assume with issues of symbiotic relatedness. This may be so, but a better hunch to consider is that the baby's irritability exasperated the mother to the point of disorganizing her psyche so she could not attend to the baby. But even this formulation may be too straightforward in that it uses representations of relatedness that tend to arise later than the organizing period. Analytic listening here would optimally attempt to track the search for relatedness to the point in the sessions that the irritation emerged either in the speaker or in the listener. What contact or potential contact has just occurred that must be blocked or destroyed by the irritation? What was the impending danger:

Loss of self into the other? Annihilation of the searching self by a finding self? A crippling sense of implosion or fragmentation that guards the threshold of connection? It is often as though, on a path to potential connection, an explosive emotional signpost is placed that says, "Never go there again." When potential connection approaches, the inner explosion threatens and the person searches for any means of flight. As if the speaker were to say, "By threatening his values, by throwing him off his equilibrium, I can prevent this connection that I know will be terrible because long ago I was traumatized by connection and I have learned not to risk interpersonal relating in those ways anymore."

Disconnecting Modes Compared to "Signal Anxiety"

The way of tracking the vicissitudes of organizing experience discussed in the preceding sections bears a resemblance to Freud's (1926b) thoughts on "signal anxiety." He hypothesized that when a person experiences some kind of uncontrollable trauma, he or she learns to experience an unconscious "signal anxiety." Formulating with neurosis in mind, Freud felt that signal anxiety served two purposes: (1) to warn the person of impending psychic danger, and (2) to maintain the previous trauma in a state of repression. But in experience at the organizing level the advanced capacity for dynamic repression has not developed. Instead, the traumatized area of the personality is thought to be known about but split off from the main personality, and thereby denied consistent conscious representation.

The danger signal at the organizing level is not merely an internalized sense of anxiety, but it manifests as an actual interpersonal enactment that serves to ward off connection, which is anticipated to be traumatic. That is, Freud's (1926b) formulation is that signal anxiety serves to ward off internalized (neurotic) danger situations. In contrast, at the organizing level the signal is an enactment, an actual breaking of interpersonal contact in an attempt to flee danger believed to be implicit in the world of relationships. What survives is a memory of actual trauma attributed to connecting. When people living organizing experiences begin to connect interpersonally, terrifying, confusing, and exhausting signal experiences begin to occur. Whenever one patient arrives telling me he's very tired, I respond immediately, "Oh, you've been relating again! How did it go this time?" In this manner I show a recognition of the experience he has come to tell me about—that relating is exhausting.

Experiencing Violence in the Countertransference

Searles (1979b) describes the frequent confusion between one's own impulses toward a speaker and those impulses that belong more rightly to the speaker. He relates this kind of confusion to a confusion we often feel in this work between inner and outer realities.

> [J]ust as it is to be assumed an inherent part of the work that the *patient* will develop a transference–borderline–psychosis or transference–psychosis, it is also to be assumed no less integrally that the *therapist* will develop—hopefully, to a limited, self-analytically explorable degree, appreciably sharable with the patient—an area of countertransference–borderline–psychosis or even countertransference psychosis. It should be unnecessary to emphasize that going crazy, whole hog, along with the patient will do no good and great harm. But I believe that we psychoanalytic therapists collectively will become, through the years, less readily scared and better able to take up this work and pursue it as a job to be done relatively successfully, as we become proportionately able, forthrightly and unashamedly, to take the measure of feelings we can *expect* ourselves to come to experience, naturally, in the course of working with these patients. [pp. 325–326]

Searles (1975) describes work he earlier supervised in which both he and the therapist felt a "threatened suspensefulness." The therapy ended when the patient ran away from the sanatorium and joined the Marines.

> Our last bit of information about him was a telephone call to the therapist from an official at an Army prison, stating that this man had stabbed a fellow Marine three times, that his victim was barely surviving, and that an investigation was under way to determine whether [the patient] was mentally competent to stand trial. The therapist and I agree that [the patient] had finally committed the violent act which we both had known he eventually would.... I want to emphasize the aspect of relief, of certainty, which this clearly afforded me and, I felt, the therapist also. It was as though the distinction between the patient's actualized murderousness and our own murderous fantasies and feeling was now clear beyond anyone's questioning it....
>
> Both the therapist and I, in relating to him, evidently had mobilized in ourselves such intensely conflicting feelings of love and murderous hatred that a regressive de-differentiation occurred in our respective ego-functioning, such that we attributed to the patient our own murderous hatred, and unconsciously hoped that he would give vicarious expression to our own violence, so as to restore the wall between him and us. More broadly put, such a patient evokes in one such intensely conflicting feelings that, at an uncon-

scious level, one's ego-functioning undergoes a pervasive de-differentiation: one loses the ability deeply to distinguish between one's self and the patient, and between the whole realms of fantasy and reality. Thus the patient's committing of a violent act serves not only to distinguish between one's own "fantasied" violence and his "real" violence but, more generally, serves to restore, in one, the distinction between the whole realms of fantasy and outer reality. [p. 288]

Loss of Body Integrity

Winnicott (1947) in the following vignette reports a general diminution in his overall work for several days until he has what he calls a "healing dream." In the dream he contrasts "castration anxiety" expectable as a countertransference reaction to his neurotic patients, with a more pervasive persecutory anxiety associated with body integrity.

Winnicott reports his dream in two parts. In the first part he was in a theater in the highest balcony (in England called the "gods") looking down on the people below in the stalls. He felt anxiety that he might lose a limb, similar to a feeling he had experienced on top of the Eiffel Tower that if he put his hand over the edge it would fall off on to the ground below. He labels this "ordinary castration anxiety" that he might develop in unconscious fantasy with his neurotic patients. In the second part of the dream he was aware that the people below in the stalls were watching a play and he was now related through them to what was going on on the stage. A new anxiety developed in which he had no right side of his body. This anxiety related to his psychotic patient who required that he have no relation to her body at all—she experienced herself as only a mind. What she needed was that he be only a mind speaking to a mind.

> At the culmination of my difficulties on the evening before the dream I had become irritated and had said that what she was needing of me was little better than hair-splitting. This had had a disastrous effect and it took many weeks for the analysis to recover from my lapse. The essential thing, however, was that I should understand my own anxiety and this was represented in the dream by the absence of the right side of my body when I tried to get into relation to the play that the people in the stalls were watching. This right side of my body was the side related to this particular patient and was therefore affected by her need to deny absolutely even an imaginative relationship of our bodies. This denial was producing in me this psychotic type of anxiety, much less tolerable than ordinary castration anxiety. Whatever other interpretation might be made in respect of this dream the result of my having dreamed it and remembered it was that I was able to take up this

analysis again and even to heal the harm done to it by my irritability which had its origin in a reactive anxiety or a quality that was appropriate to my contact with a patient with no body. [p. 198]

This patient's frantic insistence that Winnicott be with her to the extent of denying that they both have bodies is the kind of strange request that people living in an organizing state regularly make. If an analyst responds to these requests as merely provocative, manipulative, or demanding, then the possibility of watching the ebb and flow of connectedness that represents the organizing transference will be foreclosed. The content of the request might be understood in many ways but transformation will not occur until the transference implicit in the seduction toward contact (which inevitably must be broken) can be analyzed. Here the problem is so enigmatic and the patient is so entrenched in her pattern, that long periods of feeling victim to these aspects of her organizing transference are bound to occur before the analyst and patient succeed in studying the process together. Meanwhile, the intrusion into the analyst's psyche that the request represents must be borne and processed by the analyst.

This dream demonstrates the kinds of psychotic anxiety that are likely to be stirred up in the listening process. We see from his report that in session he had lost his stance of being receptive when he accused her of hair splitting. The temptation to confront aspects of the interaction that irritate the analyst arises regularly in this work. When one succumbs to the temptation, disaster always ensues. The alternative response when being berated, accused, neglected, and attacked by the speaker is to attempt to process what happened and why one is being stimulated to counterattack. But beyond the issue of whether the listener actually gives an irritable response or not, it is critical to develop the capacity for almost instantaneous recovery so that the process of disconnect can be studied while it is actually occurring. That is, it might be thought, in principle, that always avoiding these temptations to retaliation is a good thing. But it is simply not possible to avoid them. We will be used by the speaker for the purposes of accomplishing a break of contact, no matter how we behave. So while we try to be on our best behavior, it will only be a matter of time before even that will be attacked in one manner or another.

No matter how we conduct ourselves, the demands of the psychotic transference will become manifest and we will be found failing in one regard or another *so that* contact can be broken. If we reflect the attack and the implicit attempt to break contact, then that will be attacked, ad infinitum. So the critical variable in this kind of work is not the avoidance of the attack or even the avoidance of retaliation to the attack per se. The crucial variable is for the listener to be able to keep his or her observing ego functioning during the siege so what is happening can be studied.

On occasion, with a person I know well, I have lapsed into a silent position, making clear that I had no idea what to say, forcing the other (somewhat cruelly, I admit) to search for some understanding of what sort of situation we are in at that moment, and to begin to realize how nothing I could possibly say would foster connection. Paradoxically enough, as the person is able to search and to see the dilemma he or she is presenting, and to understand the untenable position I am in, contact is established or sustained for that time period.

The Pitfall of Addressing the False Self or the Mimical Self

Winnicott (1960) discusses his work with a successful woman who feels that her life has not started to exist. What she called her "Caretaker Self" he formulates as a false self based upon the infant's earliest relations to her environment. The extent to which the infant feels obliged to conform to maternal demand, she develops a self based not upon her own instinctual life but upon limitations of the environmental response. The false self stifles the true self that would otherwise manifest itself in spontaneous gesture so that motility and erotic life could freely develop in relation to important others. The implication of Winnicott's formulations are many. The false self may experience defeat in its attempt to defend the true self, resulting in despair and suicide. The false self may organize intelligence so that the mind becomes the location of the false self resulting in a radical split between intellectual activity and psychosomatic existence.

Winnicott (1960) speaks of the "good-enough mother" who is able to meet the omnipotent sense of her infant by implementation of the infant's expressions. The spontaneous gesture of the true self is thus met and responded to by the mother so that the ego gains strength. He holds that "The True Self does not become a living reality except as a result of the mother's repeated success in meeting the infant's spontaneous gesture or sensory hallucination" (p. 145). Winnicott links his formulations with Sechehaye's (1951) notion of "symbolic realization" but he corrects her notion. Rather than the symbol being made real, "it is the infant's *gesture or hallucination* that is made real, and the capacity of the infant *to use a symbol* is the result" (p. 145).

People who live most of their lives in organizing states learn to imitate or mimic human interaction patterns so as to "pass" in most everyday situations and thereby to delude the listener into thinking them still connected.

I refer to this self-structure based on imitation and mimicry the "mimical self." This structure contrasts sharply with Winnicott's notion of the "false self," which is a structure of later symbiotic life based upon relinquishing of a true instinctively based self in favor of conforming to the demands of the nurturing environment.

The analyst's countertransferential failure to see the false or mimical self formation can have deleterious consequences. The analyst can mistakenly believe that the person speaking is the real person when in fact the true self has no voice. Dialogue with the false, mimical, or intellectualizing self can continue indefinitely. Or, if when the false or mimical self begins to crumble, the analyst fails to respond to the sense of panic and dependency which emerges, an opportunity will be missed to analyze the regression to dependency experience. Analysts who are not prepared to follow false and mimical self structures until true regressed and dependent self states emerge ought to avoid taking on false self personalities, Winnicott believes.

Having looked at some countertransference difficulties frequently encountered in working with organizing issues, we turn to two more in-depth case studies in the following chapters.

7

Ensnared by Eros

Suzanne Buchanan

Editor's Comments

The ebb and flow of the connection/disconnection dimension is to the organizing experience, what verbal free association is to the neurotic experience. That is, the ability to free associate and the developing ability to sustain interpersonal connection are both unattainable goals that serve as perceivable backdrops against which glitches in the processes can be noted and studied. In the following account of a countertransference experience, a very attractive, seductive man succeeds in temporarily pulling the rug out from under his therapist by creating sexual arousal, first in himself and later in her. At one point he almost stops his therapy because he is failing to ensnare her in an emotional connection through the only means he feels he has at his disposal—Eros. Paradoxically, as the therapist permits herself to succumb to the arousal that for this patient spells connectedness, it gradually becomes clear how his lifelong passion of stimulating himself and women has backfired, repeatedly leaving him in a lost, lonely, and untransformed organizing state. His erotic stimulations function to destroy rather than create connections. Here we watch his erotic maneuvers nearly destroy once again his hope of someday feeling human. Freud (1905) has taught us not only that sexuality is ubiquitous but that it takes a myriad of forms. The analytic engagement reported here not only confirms Freud's correctness, but also points to forms and transformations of sexuality that Freud never dreamed of. Therapists tend to be unable or reluctant to discuss therapeutic involvements that include physiological arousal. Here you will watch a courageous and emotionally available therapist skillfully led into Eros's tender trap—and what a nightmare for her it is!—a trap that nonetheless appears therapeutically essential.

During twenty-five years of supervising and consulting on difficult cases, I have had frequent occasion to review therapeutic work in which the sexuality of the therapist has become somehow stimulated or engaged in response to the client's erotic transference or projective identifications. Recent national studies reveal that the overwhelming majority of therapists (87 percent) report experiencing sexual attraction to clients (Pope, Keith-Spiegel, and Tabachnick 1986). Further studies make clear that sexuality in therapists is poorly addressed in training programs (Pope, Sonne, and Holroyd 1993). The complexities of a newly licenced therapist trying to deal with powerful erotic/psychotic projections into the countertransference are amply illustrated in the study that follows.

ENSNARED BY EROS

I have real relatedness with Tom. We are bonded, have a language, jokes, topics of interest and, in general, a way we are when we are together. We eat and drink, laugh, cry, get angry or sad. We suffer together. We endure together. And we enjoy each other—and all this within the therapeutic hour. We are as real together as we know how to be. In addition to being real together there are times when we are able to observe the interaction that takes place between us as observers, commenting on the process, trying to understand what is going on. Oftentimes that understanding takes the form of trying to understand the past in the present. This activity is of much more importance to me than to Tom. Just being together is enough for Tom. We never know what can happen. As the relatedness evolves there is always that sense of being in uncharted waters.

Tom began therapy with a focus centered on stress reduction. When we first began he was in a state of complete exhaustion or collapse. His stress level was extreme and included bleeding ulcers. Our time together centered on his telling me about his anger and frustration with his job, his relationships, and life in general. He talked a lot about how his back and neck hurt. He was suffering from migraine headaches, long-term low back pain, sleeplessness at night, and extreme sleepiness during the day.

For me the work was not stimulating. He was a nice man who used words in a fun way and his sense of humor was enjoyable. I felt empathy for his suffering and said so. We began a course of relaxation exercises. Often during these times Tom would go into a deep sleep. I felt that he trusted me and this was a good indicator of his comfort with me. I was also comfortable with him.

At some point during the year it felt like we were stuck, like he and I were merely doing more of the same. He was making headway in stress management. He was much more relaxed, a lot less angry, and he was feeling considerably better. I found myself wondering, "Now what?" I did not sense that we had reached the end of our relating, by any means. Although his stress symptoms were lessened, I sensed that in time something more would come up.

Tom was a toucher. He found ways to stand just close enough to come into contact with me. He asked for a hug. He was able to pick up the fact that I was a toucher too and said so. I did not think too much about it at the time. Hugging seemed to me a ritualized way of greeting and parting, a lot like handshaking. I did not realize then the significance of touching or the possible danger or importance of it.

One day he came and told me he was going to stop coming to therapy. I was surprised. I felt we had a really good connection. I sensed that what we were doing and would do was important, yet he was terminating. I felt disappointed and confused. With seemingly nothing to lose I asked, "Tom, how do you feel about me?"

Heretofore the interaction had been nonstimulating. Surprisingly, this man who had not said too much to me of a personal nature began to tell me everything he liked about me from the top of my head to the tip of my toes and it was far from nonstimulating—in essence, he was the most seductive man I had ever met. I felt as if he had made love to me and yet I had all my clothes on. It was exciting. I thought to myself, "Wait a minute, should I be feeling this way? I am enjoying myself and him, and I feel confused." I had heard mention of something called sexual countertransference, but I had no personal notion of what that meant. Did I really want to mention this to my mentor/consultant? I had my doubts. Perhaps I could just go over the rules with Tom. This was probably some kind of brief passing experience. At this point I began to question the meaning of touching in this relationship.

Well, Tom decided to stay in therapy because he wanted to, because he was enjoying me, and he made it clear his interest was in me and not in therapy. Somehow that seemed okay. I knew that relatedness was the issue and that "therapy" was a word that did not mean anything to him. I told him that what we were doing was therapy and that not everyone did therapy the same way. My mentor, Dr. H., managed to give me some understanding of sexual transference and countertransference as potentially useful. I began to see that sexual feelings could be an expectable and acceptable part of therapy, under certain conditions. However, I experienced embarrassment, which I hated admitting. I sometimes felt guilty and uncomfortable about the strong sexual feelings and ideas about Tom that I found myself experiencing.

Tom just accepted how he felt and said that being with me was why he came and that he was not in agreement with my explanation about the potential role of feelings or their appropriate limits in therapy. We jokingly called it my "psycho-babble." I had very carefully explained to him that I understood how close he felt to me. And since he was a man with adult genitalia, of course that sense of closeness might register in his body as sexual attraction and arousal. I informed him that after an outside consultation I had found that this was not all that unusual. I assured him there was a lot we could both learn about him by studying such feelings. He laughed a little and said if I needed to think that way, that was okay. However, in his words, he was a "dirty old man who would like to jump your bones." When I asked Dr. H. how long Tom's response could go on this way, he said it could be some time.

Uncharted waters always have surprises. One day I was attempting to get into my office with a teapot full of water in one hand and the keys in the other when Tom showed up. When he was standing right behind me, I looked up at him. Suddenly he kissed me on the lips. I was horrified—not because he had kissed me but because my lips responded. *Now* what is going on? So far the uncharted waters have yielded up excitement, enjoyment, and now responding lips. Now I not only questioned touching in the present; I also talked with him about not misunderstanding or misreading the touching in the past. I was careful to explain that it would be unethical and unthinkable that I could ever become involved with him. I also told him to feel free to express his feelings and fantasies. He did so with real feeling.

Sessions continued and what I seemed to be seeing right before my eyes was a man falling in love with me. I found responsiveness within myself. I was learning to enjoy him more and more. One day he did verbalize that he loved me and he guessed he could never have me. I was feeling close to him and fond of him and sad. I said so.

It had become our custom to sit in two wing chairs that had an ottoman between them. And at the close of a session in the second year of therapy, Tom leapt from his chair. His knees landed on the ottoman between us and both his hands took hold of the ends of the arms of my wing chair. His face came very close to mine. He had pinned me in so I could not move. He had surprised me. Yet the movement was so like that of a very young boy that I found myself saying, after what seemed a long time, "Tom, I am not comfortable with this." He did not respond right away but in time he removed his hands and himself, remarking, "I have to make you more comfortable with me."

Tom is the first client I ever dreamt about. The theme was one of not being safe. To return to Dr. H., he told me that at the worst I might need to terminate the relationship if the transference became overly intrusive or threatened to become violent. The wing chair episode could be the beginning of something violent, so extreme caution with the transference was in order. I felt reassured by Dr. H.'s advice and his availabillty to me. I felt sad thinking about terminating what had become for me a very meaningful relationship.

I began the next session with Tom by recounting the wing chair experience. I spoke of how I felt about our last session, and of what I needed from him in the future: "We don't need me being afraid of you; if I'm afraid of you I won't be able to listen to you. What happened in our last meeting frightened me. I am not saying you're a 'bad boy.' But if I am worried about what you might do, I can't be tuned in to you. You must stay in your chair. You must not touch me or startle me. I want to work with you. I don't want to let you do anything that would make me have to end our relationship. I know you have intense feelings. There is a difference between intense feelings and actions. So from now on, stay in your chair. You must not touch me or startle me."

Tom's response was, "You don't need to be afraid. I need your approval. You remember I told you how frustrated I am, but I would rather have that frustration than not see you. We have such good nonverbal feeling."

What a relief. It would have broken my heart to have to end that there.

And so the uncharted waters continued. Things slowed down for awhile. The contact was mostly visual but it still seemed sexually stimulating to me. I was thinking about this man between sessions; I sometimes avoided his looking at me. He was clearly enjoying me in erotic ways. I wanted him to use me in the way he needed to, but what was all this sexual stimulation and what were those many thoughts about him between sessions? This felt confusing.

He said he kept thinking that one day I would give in and he would never tell, and that the rules are stupid; his only hope was that one day I would let down the final wall. He asked if this was going to be unrequited love.

I answered "yes." It felt tragic to me. I went to Dr. H. He said move away from the tragic sense and back to work. This was the first connection Tom had ever experienced that was near safe. We didn't know yet why he must experience it as so erotic.

I had a long period of time in which I felt frustrated, sexually aroused. I knew it was up to me to keep that wall up, to be there for Tom in the way that was best for him. This was hard. Sometimes I felt such intense longing for him that it was confusing. I felt embarrassed, silly, and guilty.

In an attempt to divert his attention while maintaining our relating, I introduced jigsaw puzzles. It turned out to be a very good idea, something we both enjoyed doing. I also thought it quite a good idea to sublimate some of those sexual feelings we each were having. I was feeling quite good about what I had done. But one day I was horrified to realize that I had cleverly introduced a way that to Tom virtually concretized the sexual act via puzzle pieces. So much for sublimation.

Well, we are still enjoying puzzling, as we have come to call it. Over time, the way we puzzle has grown to include more than just working in the same area of the puzzle; it includes my handing him pieces as I notice what he needs or might need. Now we have added another dimension of working parts of the puzzle each in our own little space, much like parallel play. Puzzling is still a warm, pleasant experience for both of us, a closeness without words.

One day during session he was looking into my eyes and I was looking back. I was feeling closer and closer to him. He was in his wing chair and I was in mine, and suddenly I felt myself merged with this man. It felt wonderful. I was struggling to say something and finally I asked him, "Tom, where are you?"

"Inside you."

It was time for session to end and I needed to hurry and get in my car and attend the weekly case conference group of which I am a member. My legs were weak, I was stumbling and lightheaded and feeling completely undone. Tom and I walked down the stairs to our respective cars. He remembered the no-touch rule. At the next session he commented on how hard it was, knowing he was not supposed to touch me and how much he wanted to help me. He knew how unorganized and out of charge of my own body I felt. Uncharted waters and more surprises. Back to Dr. H.

At our next meeting I told Tom I thought things were moving too fast. I hoped the roller coaster ride was not disturbing him too much. I recognized he was choosing to bare his soul to me and I was choosing to be open to it. I said, "Why would we want to stop that? We are finding out about parts of ourselves. Girlfriends and fucks are a dime a dozen but what we have is very, very special. Now we talk all we want about anything and it is rather nice that we have this law to keep us safe. Our being together sets off things in you and in me. It has sent me in a lot of different directions. As you know I am seeking consultation and I want you to know that I have support from other professionals also. I'll be okay. We have a very special relationship. Things happen in our relationship that don't happen other places. You know that mothers give birth to sons and have very special relationships. I am not saying that mothers never have sexual thoughts about their sons or sons about their mothers. But it is always fundamentally impossible for mothers and sons to have sex without it being destructive to both. Our relationship is special. To destroy this unbelievable thing we have developed would be very wrong. It's like incest. We have no choice but to keep going. This intensity of feeling could last a long time or it could come and go. We will do whatever we need to keep being together. I know you are suffering greatly. I too am suffering in my own way. Yet hope is increasing, our connection is good, and we are finding ways to process disconnections as they occur. Dr. H. says that when near-overwhelming feelings occur on either side, we need to consider how they disrupt our flow, our harmony together, and serve to throw us back into that lost and lonely place we know so well. I want to know myself and you want to know yourself and we are finding out about parts of ourselves." So on to more uncharted waters and more surprises.

The intrusive sexual transference continued. There were times when I think I managed things well, and there were other times when I visualized newspaper headlines telling some sordid story about me because I had let that wall give way inappropriately. I am thankful for Dr. H. and his continual belief that I can do this the right way, and for his suggestions and direction and all his understanding and empathy for both myself and my client.

At one point Dr. H. mentioned another therapist who might talk to me about having had a similar experience. We were able to meet and he had much empathy. What a relief to know that what was going on was happening not only to me.

Once before we left the parking lot Tom warned me to drive carefully. I asked him, "What would you do if something happened to me?" The look on his face was one of pure panic and told me all I needed to know. He had told me often of how much he liked "we." What we were doing together seemed very important to me and despite arousals I understood that what was happening was not adult sexuality. Tom had had a dream earlier in treatment of standing between two buildings with a woman. The buildings had no doors and no windows, no way in and no way out. The male–female togetherness was the only vestige of connection, the only possible bridge between two walled-off souls. This was the essence of his experience.

The sexual nature of the countertransference has currently been waning for me. Perhaps I am avoiding experiencing it. It was powerful, confusing, frustrating, and very disruptive at times to my functioning. Tom still mentions sexuality but the power of it is not so overwhelming to me any longer. That sense of "we-ness" is still there and growing even in new ways. Someday I hope Tom and I will understand and be able to verbalize about our voyage in a clear way. As of yet we are not there, and the waters are still largely uncharted.

Tom had another dream of being where several roads were under construction and yet there was no road that would take him to any destination as they were all unfinished. Roads connect people and places. I asked if it were okay that the roads were still being constructed. He said, "Yes, I think that is where we are." Life-giving connections are being built for Tom and that is enough for him. We are together doing the building. The threat of destructive sexuality has subsided as construction proceeds.

It feels like the right thing for both of us to be doing. I can't imagine it being possible to do this building together without uncharted waters or without surprises. There is a unique reality within our therapeutic hours together that just does not exist anywhere else for either one of us. It is a very special reality of attachment, closeness, comfort, play, struggle, and sometimes suffering. There is no real clear-cut blueprint for us. We have and are still creating a reality that is building structure and meaning into both of our existences to such an extent that neither one of us will ever be the same.

I am becoming more and more aware that if I stay present and am open he can find me. What he needs is to find me in his search for relatedness. Theory is a helpful guide and as a therapist I have great regard for theory. Human beings need other human beings who can be present not only with theory but with real aliveness, so that the search for relatedness results in useable human contact. That search can take many different forms. Sexual transference and countertransference is one of those forms. It was the way in which we initiated contact and began to study the breaks in contact, and eventually opened the way to other forms of human contact. We are all in search of human contact all our lives. When contact is empathic and timely it permits the transformation of our relatedness possibilities from concrete and disruptive forms into increasingly abstract, symbolic, coherent, and cooperative forms.

There are times of wonder when another person meets us in our search and out of the contact comes relatedness. Our forms and ways of searching for relating can be limited and they can expand. Our early experience with Mother limited each of our searches for relatedness in some way or another. We then look a long time for another human being who can meet us in our search for relatedness. I am grateful that I was open to Tom in his search for relatedness. I would not have wanted to miss any part of it!

I have come to believe that erotic or sexual energy was for each of us the channel open on an unconscious level that permitted us to connect and to have that connection displaced toward other kinds of connection. It was the way we had of connecting and developing relatedness. I think it has opened other ways of relating. The importance of this connection is that such an interaction was needed to establish relating and a very deep bond. Out of this bond came "we," and out of "we" will come "self" and "other" in some more differentiated way.

After I read this paper to Tom, he made it clear that his feelings for me were as strong as ever and that nothing had changed for him. He continues to express his feelings and wishes and his desire for me. He says that I know more about him than anyone and he enjoys being with me more than anyone. I recently told him that I thought when he was very young he gave up on being loved and that he then withdrew; he went inside himself and created an internal world of excitement. He said that could be true. I went on to say that I thought there were two Suzannes for him, the one in his created internal world who was perennially arousing and the one in the external world who shared our times together. He agreed. During our sessions he has experienced both the Suzanne in the room and the Suzanne in his internal world. We discussed how impossible it is at times to know the differences between the two experiences. Was it that he got overstimulated and then withdrew from contact, or that he was understimulated and withdrew into private stimulation?

Tom had a critical mother. He knows he is safe from criticism from me. Tom experienced some kind of early failure to be loved in a way that would permit him emotional growth. Tom has never been able to be involved with any woman in an integrated way involving sex and closeness. He does not know how to initiate contact this way. In his fantasies of sex with me he says, "You want it as much as I do." He tells me he would never do anything unless I wanted him to. These comments remind me of the primary infant bond in which the infant experiences Mother as passively merged with his own desire, a bond in which the infant is the one that needs to be loved and cared for.

My thinking at this point is that in some way Tom's primary love became overeroticized. Tom still desperately wants to be touched. This early primary longing and yearning to be touched is equated with love and is mixed with his biologically adult sexual desire. There is a confusion or fusion between his fantasy world of sexual fulfillment and the features he perceives in the external world.

In time, when enough psychic roads are built, we can expect that Tom will be able to connect with people in ways through which he can be integrated and find fulfillment in his external world rather than through his fantasized fulfillments that, in fact, are not fulfilling but excruciatingly painful, as his beginning complaints indicated. For now we can appreciate the constriction of his connections and the gradual expansion of symbiotic bonds in which psychic stimulation can empathically proceed between two people. His compulsive attempts to destroy the continuity of our connecting, our relatedness, with invasive hypersexuality have served throughout his life to insure that no transformation of his early internal world would occur. His pattern now slowly gives way to sustained and sustaining relatedness.

Editor's Postscript

Sexually sensitive interactions from psychotherapeutic work have seldom been reported in our literature, and certainly not in this uncertain and courageous manner. Training programs seldom, if ever, include courses designed to explore the sexuality of people training to be psychotherapists. Nor are issues of erotic transference and countertransference given an appropriate place in our training programs. As a profession, our neglect of studying sexual feelings in the therapeutic situation has no doubt contributed to the current state of affairs wherein the largest single cause of malpractice suits involves accusations of a sexual nature. The seemingly impenetrable wall of silence about sexual feelings in the therapist marks a taboo that is slowly being broken down by studies such as Pope's *Sexual Feelings in Psychotherapy* (1994) and V. Hilton's study "Sexuality in Psychotherapy" (in Hedges et al. in press). I have published an extended case study involving erotic transference and my countertransference response, illustrating some of the ways sexuality becomes activated in treating symbiotic-level issues (Hedges 1992, "A Countertransference Failure: The Case of Dora").

Traditionally trained therapists, with limited training in and understanding of the nature of primitive transference and expectable countertransference responsiveness to early developmental issues, no doubt experienced difficulty with the foregoing vignette. They might ask such questions as these: "Wasn't Suzanne being sexually provocative herself in the early stages? How clear was the therapist about her own boundaries? Did Suzanne get her own sexual and merger issues worked out in her own therapy? Didn't she actively participate in creating a mutually seductive situation?" I submit that this kind of Monday morning quarterbacking completely misses the point of what's happening in this sort of therapeutic relationship. People who get stuck on such questioning are not equipped to consider the vital nature of this kind of work. These questions do not help us consider therapeutic work that has a strong impact on early layerings of personality formation. People willing to sit on ethics committees and licensing boards to make judgments that significantly affect people's lives, without having obtained extensive advanced training in the kinds of transferences and countertransferences expectable when treating early developmental issues, are clearly operating unethically—making judgments beyond the limits of their expertise. (For an extended discussion of this issue see my chapters focusing on the inevitability of the dual relationship in psychotherapy in Hedges 1994a.)

I find that more often than not it is the less experienced therapists who dare reach out to clients in deeply personal and life-giving ways. In a certain sense it may be their naiveté and inexperience that allows them to be so courageous. And it is not surprising that in their eagerness and awkwardness they often get themselves into various kinds of pickles. More experienced therapists tend to be frightened by the obvious dangers such clients present, horrified by the relatedness they demand; these therapists thus remain largely content not to work transformationally with primitive personality issues. This is the first countertransference pitfall of dealing with organizing-level experience—not considering the client as a full and deserving human being.

For our purposes the crucial aspect of this vignette is that it allows us to think about the ways a sincere and well intentioned therapist who is receptive to deep personality issues may become emotionally involved and then derailed if not guided by theory and consultation. People dealing with organizing-level issues have a lifetime of experience in making sure that meaningful and potentially helpful human contact does not occur. Yet like Kafka's characters they continue to search in a myriad of ways for just the life-giving contact they compulsively foreclose once they get close enough to sense it. The very way in which they approach relatedness often insures that it will not occur. The internalized "psychotic mother" transference crops up and suddenly "something happens." What might have been usable contact is suddenly rendered useless. Such was the way with Tom's intense and intrusive sexuality—his lifelong way of making sure that he would never be able to connect to anyone. But Suzanne foiled him. She stood steady in the midst of her own psychic and somatic confusions, found consultative help, and slowly moved his seductive manipulations into a place where they could be seen for what they were, desperate attempts learned early in his life to foreclose useful but potentially terrifying contact. The dream of Tom and a woman (maleness and femaleness) standing between two closed-off buildings might be understood as not only a potential locus of linking but also a transference representation of how the gap between two is created and/or sustained.

The story of Tom and Suzanne continues from here with much working through to accomplish. Tom must find additional ways to ally himself with Suzanne in the therapeutic task of noticing how each potential contact is spoiled by the intrusion of overstimulation. He must come to understand how he perennially deprives himself of growth-producing experiences by trying to get her to be seductive with him and how he succeeds in alienating her through his seductions. Freud used the words "seduction" and "trauma" interchangeably to indicate that damaging human trauma is always the result of seductive stimulation that overwhelms the person's currently operative ego processes. Suzanne shows us how she allowed herself to become overwhelmed, traumatized to the point of threatening the ego processes required for maintaining a therapeutic stance. She then sought ego supports to help her perceive, integrate, and develop creative and usable responsiveness to Tom's lifelong self-destructive dilemmas. Did any of us imagine, when we decided to become therapists, that such demanding requirements might be made of us? I think not. But the choice later becomes clear: write people off as untreatable or roll up your sleeves and go to work! We can be grateful to Suzanne for being willing to submit this traumatizing and courageous piece of work for our consideration.

8

Falling into a Pothole

Suzanne Buchanan

Editor's Comments

The process of learning to make connections is a long, difficult, and often tedious one that requires a full measure of dedication on the part of a therapist. In organizing psychic states some of the earliest aspects of intra- and extrauterine life often seem manifest. We hear an ocean of images and thoughts that are unconnected or connected in strange, bizarre, and/or frightening ways. Organizing-level mental life reflects life's basic emotional concerns in the most concrete ways. Concrete responsiveness to these concerns is essential if transformative connections are to be made. Dreams and symbols can seldom be understood in customary ways.

In the following moving account of Michelle's therapy, we glimpse the transformative process slowly and painstakingly at work. Her dream about a horse falling in a pothole shows us the imagery employed by the speaker to describe her transformative journey and the potholes her horse keeps falling into as the two travel forward together. Tustin (1972, 1981) has written about the frequent preoccupation of autistic children with black holes. She decodes the fear of falling or getting sucked into a black hole as the terror of relatedness. According to the Tustin interpretation, the black hole represents the dangerous gap in the sensorium (the mouth?) where mother (the nipple?) once was—before the child psychologically withdrew into his or her private world. Tustin interprets in various ways to children that once their mother's body belonged to them and was under their control, but that something happened to take the control of that pleasure away—which has left them with a great longing for connection and for relatedness pleasure, a longing that is, nonetheless, terrifying because of their relatedness history. Whether such an interpretive angle might have been helpful in Michelle's developing relatedness to Suzanne is not clear from the information given. Were such an interpretive line to have an appeal to Michelle the flip side of connection—disconnection—could be analyzed in terms of the horse's fear of falling out of her safe private world into the potentially dangerous holes of relatedness repeatedly offered and nurtured by her therapist.

FALLING INTO A POTHOLE

She was terrified. Her posture was crouched, her head and eyes cast downward. She was like a scared, trapped, wounded animal. I thought if I listened I might hear her growl and hiss. Perhaps she might even attempt to bite me if I came too close. Yet she had come to see me of her own free will. How had she been so wounded? What was the trap constructed of that held her captive to so much emotional pain and terror? I felt and sensed an incredible amount of her emotional chaos and terror.

I began trying to glimpse her face—the color tone was muddy and her eyes were clouded. I felt helpless, useless, and generally powerless. One strong thing I have going for me is that I can hold on. But I had my doubts that I could get her to take anything from me. Her trap seemed so strong. Yet I had to try. This trap was crippling her and robbing her of life.

My goal was to stay present for any kind of contact I could get, even if it lasted for only a split second. Visual contact could be hard to get, so I'll keep on talking and wearing perfume and I will offer food and drink and move about from time to time. I want to be like Dolly Parton, that is, I don't want her to miss me! This is the kind of work that is like scraping down a mountain with your fingernails. There is gold in the mountain—the gold is the human spirit.

For this kind of therapy the therapist must not only want to do this kind of work but must also have sufficient support from a colleague or consultant. This kind of work is so demanding it is impossible to think of anyone doing it unless they get something back. It's just like when a mother has a baby. If the mother is unable or is not ready to receive the gift of this experience and pay the cost to receive this gift, then the experience will be aborted or fall short of its potential. Michelle had two therapists before she saw me. Neither therapist entered into the type of relationship necessary to provide a transformative experience.

So I began scraping at the mountain. The split second grew to a whole second, then to seconds, to minutes, and so on. As her narrative unfolded she began to reveal her captor to me. Her captor came in the form of sounds, images, and thoughts, very disconnected, except that her delusion of guilt connected these sounds and images and thoughts. She became guilty of doing horrible things; the worst was being a murderer.

This inner reality of Michelle's is more real than external reality when it lures and pulls her into the crazy world filled with terror, horror, and guilt. There is a part of her that torments and accuses her of being a killer. On top of that, she has to deal with the punishment of thinking that the authorities will come after her and take her away and imprison her, which would cause her to lose her family. In the beginning she was convinced she had done something awful and that she just could not remember it. She believed the images, sounds, and thoughts were proof of her guilt.

Progress has come slow and hard for Michelle, and has been a back-and-forth process. There have been phone calls between sessions. Some of these calls have come late at night on my home phone, which the answering machine picked up because I retire early. At times I have been so attuned to her that upon hearing her voice on the answering machine I answered her calls, because I could hear how agitated and terrified and out of control she was. This has been exhausting to her and to me.

Now at times our relationship is very draining to me and she has even asked if it is. I always try to be truthful with her. This work is emotionally demanding. Over time my hope has increased and feels solid. She needs a lot more of me than she can afford. Enough time with me is necessary for transformation to happen, otherwise we could do some kind of supportive therapy that would be inadequate at best. To settle for less would be a loss to her and her family. By now I have come to know other parts of her. There is much more than just the scared animal I first saw. There is a warm, sensitive, loving, creative young woman who is a mother to two darling little girls and wife to a salt-of-the-earth husband.

As the back-and-forth process continued it began turning into more of a touch-and-go process. If she is to get more of me, we must figure out what to do. Her resources are limited and so is my time. I care and am invested in her, and yet I can only work so many hours. I like doing this kind of work and I like working with her. I am committed to her and she is committed enough to her treatment to be working to support it. But can she work more? Not now, because she is decompensating and falling more and more into her trap, and the head voices and thoughts and visions of her tormentor are becoming more of a reality than her external reality. She is crying out to me more and more and I am feeling more and more helpless. In addition, there have been other stressors intruding into her life. Additional life stressors and too much stimulation exacerbate her tormentors by leaps and bounds.

At a certain point in treatment, even though she was trying, we were losing the battle to get her free from the trap. There is not enough external life support for the regression she is entering. Few people ever understand how hard we have to work to restore primitive parts of ourselves, just Dr. H. and a few colleagues. The world at large and her world in particular—her family, her friends, her work colleagues—have no idea. There is no self-help book that explains or gives credence to what we are doing. Her family seems to believe she can just get out of this trap by using her willpower. Not too many years ago cases like this were considered hopeless and untreatable by nearly everyone. The best thing to do was medicate the patient, lock her up, or give her limited supportive psychotherapy.

I thought if we could stop the intrusive quality of her daily life, lessen the stimulation, limit the demands on her, and get her into daily contact with me we would have a good chance. Several years earlier she had taken out a medical insurance policy that covered inpatient treatment. A resource at last. Now I need to find a hospital with a staff that is permissive and intuitive and that can be supportive of her issues and needs.

She agreed to hospitalization and this became a turning point in her therapy. What a relief! I don't know if I could have taken much more. She began to reconstitute quickly. In the hospital I saw a beautiful side of her emerge. Her eyes got brighter, her complexion became clearer, she had a great smile and sense of humor, and she made an impact on other patients by her loving, caring, and giving of herself. I had seen glimpses of her like this, but never with so much continuity. I long to see her so transformed that she does not have to have this back-and-forth process where one moment the internal chaotic torturous world is in gear and she feels trapped, crippled, and hopeless, and the next moment she can function in the external world with her internal world supportive of her and not in chaos.

Michelle works cutting hair to pay for three half-sessions a week with me. We need more but this is all she can afford or that she sees she can afford. A part of her transformation is in coming to understand that the time with me is an investment in her real and true self that she has to have. Part of what I feel to be a necessary therapeutic task for me is to convince her, and seduce her, if you will, into more time with me so that more transformation can occur.

And so Michelle's narrative continues to unfold and be transformed. At this point we are still in a back-and-forth process. I think she could regress again and need additional hospitalizations, and I have unshakable faith in her ability to transform and to rid herself of her tormentors that keep her captive as long as she cannot get enough of me. Dr. H. and my peers help and support me when the process is difficult for me.

Some clients are without obvious "smoking guns" in their history, such as child abuse, alcoholism, death of a parent, war, and so forth, and yet they still have tormentors and traps because something went wrong with the mother-child bond or disrupted the continuity of care in some way. Early disruption of continuity is a smoking gun. It's just that we tend not to recognize how venomous and destructive it is to human development. Our consciousness needs raising to appreciate that this is so.

Some days Michelle brings me things she has been creating. She is talented. "Why am I bringing these to you? It is just like I used to do with my Mom." We both laugh and I say, "Because you want to and need to."

"I wish you were my Mom. I think a lot about you. I want to make you things all the time. I wander around stores looking for things for you. Then I put them back. I can't afford all I want to get you or make for you."

Her creations and our talk about this process are one of the ways we connect and relate. It's a very positive way and we both enjoy it very much. It could yield more later in the process. But right now what is apparent is that it's a way that we have continuity without any stress and it's a pleasurable way to be together. Now she is thinking about me between sessions—she has me with her between sessions and one of the ways that is done is through her crafts and things she makes, some of which she gives me. It is a very creative way to have me with her and to have her with me.

Where we are today is that I am wanting to find ways to be more present in her mind and to have her take hold of me and not let go so she doesn't have to suffer all that torment and terror.

"Suzanne, I just feel crazy. What if I did kill someone? If I did I'll lose you, my kids, my husband. I see things, I hear things, things come into my mind and I can connect them. I must have done them if I can connect them. I feel things in my body down there or in my hand or foot. Why do I feel these things? I must have done it. It all fits together. There is a part of me that knows I could never do these things, but I connect them and if I connect them then I must have done them. I am so scared, Suzanne. I know you don't believe I did them. How can you be so sure? I can connect them, so I must have done them. I just don't know what I am going to do. I just do not know what I am going to do."

This is a small slice of the struggle that goes on for this courageous young woman between the external reality and the crazy chaotic internal reality. Her delusions of guilt are very real for her and are at war with her logical mind. These battles to get out of the trap that ensnares her can occupy large portions of her time and they disrupt her everyday life and cripple her in very significant ways. And yet she is creatively coping with a psychotic or organizing experience that is the result of some kind of early bonding failure or disruption that left her mind with large pockets of chaos over which she has very little control. Like Kafka in *The Trial*, Michelle searches for her guilt. She is guilty for being alive, for needing more than her mother could give her. When she connects to me the guilt lashes out at her again—connecting between her physical being and mine is what is forbidden.

Like all of us, Michelle was born with the capacity to be human and fueled by the search for relatedness, for to be human is to be related. She came into the world with needs for sustenance, comfort, safety, stimulation, and intelligibility. During the early part of her life something disrupted the organizing of her psyche through the normal channels of sensorimotor and cognitive-affective stimulation. The incompleteness of her psyche's organization shows up in her life today on a regular basis. And the attempt to establish organization through relatedness is regularly interrupted by guilt and punishment. It influences how she relates to herself and others and continues to direct and influence her destiny. The goal of our work together is to go beyond the limits of her early experience and to expand her ways of relating and being in the world. Right now her trap is that in some way her mother–child bond was not continuous or stable enough to establish reliable and safe connections, leaving her in periodic chaos. I assume as Michelle reached out for contact to Mother, Mother was not there due to her father's alcoholism or some fault in Mother, or some inability of Michelle's that prevented her from receiving what she needed. Her pervasive sense of guilt for murder may relate to her belief that it was her "badness" (her neediness) that made Mother disappear. All I can say at this point is that her search for human relatedness was not realized in a consistent-enough way to allow her a sense of safety, reliability, and sanity, and that this has resulted in her being trapped in an internal reality that is terrifying to her.

Michelle has made great strides toward establishing an internal psychic world that is not so terrifying. These strides are forged out of the bond and relatedness that we have developed together. Her self-development is now related to the bond that we have, out of which is coming a new psychic structure for her that will expand her capacity to relate. But when the sense of our own connection is overwhelming, she loses me; the torture and the terror emerge again. We have to take care to continue finding ways for her to get enough of me and to keep me with her. She has a few things I have given to her so she has me in her world in a concrete way, just as I have her in my world in a concrete way. Gradually Michelle is learning to have me with her in her mind. We are struggling together to come to understand how connections and/or the treatment of them cause the disruptions, and to create ways for her to take hold of me safely again. One night she phoned twice, and I did not get the messages until the next morning. The first call was about her terror with her chaotic world. The second call was about her thinking she had heard the phone ring, that I must be trying to call her—she was doing better now, she said. She had gone to the room where she works on her crafts and that had soothed her. She said she would call me the next day if she needed me.

Michelle brought in a little duck on a stick the other day. She came in walking it and giggling, "Push it, Suzanne, doesn't that feel fun?" So we are playing more. She is not so fretful and scared any more. At first I could not soothe or comfort her and this felt bad to me. Now I can soothe her and she is feeling more secure and is beginning to play and enjoy life and living. The symbiosis we have begun to develop has deeply affected me.

Dr. H.'s theories about how to connect and how to study disconnections have been like stepping stones through unknown areas guiding and directing our journey through the chaos of voices, tormenting thoughts, and delusional guilt. The search for relatedness has energized our direction from the early organizing level toward human milestones of development, into the beginnings of symbiosis. The milestone of individuation lies far ahead. This is an age-old road that all developing human beings must travel.

We all come into the world with endless ways we could be and soon adapt to those ways our mother will respond to; thus we each become limited even as we become connected in order to grow. On each journey I take with a client I too am offered a choice to expand my ways of being in the world. I often feel I can tell how much my clients are getting from me by how much I am getting in terms of my own personal expansion. There can be a danger to the therapist in these journeys—the danger is in either trying to expand beyond what one experiences as safe or passing up an opportunity to become expanded and thus transformed along with the client.

After reading this paper to Michelle, she remarked how happy she was when she first arrived and how sad she felt at the end of the session. Something had been lost as I read the paper—a piece of her chaotic internal world. She commented that at the last session what had meant the most to her was my saying that she would not have to lose me and she believed it. I interpreted that as one her fundamental issues, that she somehow early on lost Mom. I told her that now she was losing her chaotic Mom, that I was her psychic Mom for now, and that we were building a new psychic structure she could hold on to. There is always sadness when something familiar is lost. She also mentioned a dream about a horse that kept falling into a hole. I reminded her that her strongest bond had been with her horse and then I asked, "Is the horse okay after falling in the hole?"

"Yes."

"I'm that horse. I can fall in the hole with you and be okay and you can ride me out when you need to." She knew what I meant—she could hold on to my image. She still cannot recall my image all the time, but when she can the craziness stops.

Several weeks after hearing this paper she said, "Something has changed since you read me what you wrote about us. I don't know what exactly, but I'm better." Following her associations I think it is because she sensed through the paper that she lives in my mind and that I am committed to staying with her until she needs me no more.

Michelle still has times of falling into the psychotic pocket or, as we have come to say, "falling into the pothole in the road." She laughs when she can talk about riding me out of the hole and she is terrified when she fears she cannot. Now the frequency of falling into the potholes is less and the depth of them is smaller. Her psychic map for the journey of life is beginning to be more dependable for her.

Editor's Postscript

As in the previous chapter, Suzanne's style of working with organizing level issues or psychotic pockets will seem strange to readers not accustomed to working transformatively with this kind of regressive experience. To many her work toward soothing, containing, holding, calming, and connecting may seem merely supportive or like some form of simplistic reparenting. To many the work which involves many maternal impulses and feelings in the countertransference may appear to be simply an acting out of the therapist's own maternal nature.

In a seminar which was reported to me during my training, Anna Freud was quoted as responding to the question, "What distinguishes a psychoanalyst from other therapists?" Her response was, "A psychoanalyst uses the concept of the unconscious and the concepts of id, ego, and superego is his daily work." Following the expansion into the third paradigm of psychoanalysis we can now add, "The psychoanalytic therapist uses the concept of self and other representations is his or her daily work." The relatedness paradigm has made possible an extension of psychoanalytic work developmentally downward from oedipal neurotic structures into narcissistic, symbiotic/borderline, and psychotic/organizing level structures. The self and other representations involved at the organizing level are now known to involve a primitive transference structure that forecloses the development of more complex relatedness structures—either en masse or in encapsulated enclaves or pockets of dysfunction.

With Michelle we see that she has been able to develop an apparently ordinary life with a family and a successful work history. But when life's stresses overwhelm her she finds herself dropping into an organizing level pocket, to what many might call her psychotic core.

When Michelle first reports to Suzanne she presents a primitive, terrified, animal-like self and expects that her therapist will find a way to tame this animal and all of the inner monstrous thoughts. Slowly and thoughtfully we see Suzanne coaxing Michelle toward connection, much as E.T. was coaxed with Reese's Pieces. But simply encouraging and providing connections are not enough. Any well-intentioned helping person can provide coaxing and reinforcement. What is required is an analysis of the earliest level of self and other internal structuring that have served to prevent contact with others and a complete bonding experience for that person since infancy.

The treatment paradox is this: The person's mode of chronic disconnection contains the hidden psychotic or organizing transference. But disconnections cannot be consistently and fruitfully studied in the here-and-now by two until and unless there are some relatively safe, reliable, and rewarding ways of connecting that are available. So phase one of analyzing the organizing transference entails finding ways of being together that can be tolerated by both participating personalities. Thus the work is bound to appear strange or idiosyncratic to an outside viewer. A therapist accustomed to working with higher level issues may well wonder, "What exactly is going on here between these two?" But we often have the same question when we observe a new mother trying to connect with her baby. "What is she doing now? What's the purpose of that? Why is she doing it that particular way?" The answers, of course, become clear only upon close scrutiny of the personal and private natures of both mother and child. No mother–child combination gets along like any other. And so the work of establishing connections that have the possibility of leading toward a more complete bonding experience is always idiosyncratic and always appears peculiar to a casual observer—as it does here with Suzanne and Michelle. In finding ways to personally connect, the analytic couple is inextricably enmeshed in their most basic natures, their most basic quests to find rewarding human connections, and their most primitive means of avoiding, rupturing, and destroying connections once they are achieved.

Michelle's dream demonstrates her comprehension of what is going on in this analytic process. Her closest bond to date has been with her horse.

Now Suzanne stands in for the horse Michelle is riding. The horse keeps falling into potholes in the road they are traveling together. The internalized (m)other keeps threatening discontinuity—but the problem is perceived as external pitfalls that the couple encounters (such as sessions ending, answering machines being mechanical, or the therapist needing payment and weekend breaks). This is a strange metaphor indeed but it does capture what we perceive to be slowly happening as the two learn to ride things out together. The fear of falling into a black hole is an autistic expression for the fear of relatedness. Here two are threatened by holes previously made in the road but they are finding ways of staying together. Subsequent work will continue to focus on the nature of these potholes that now seem to be nonhuman and "out there." The organizing transference potholes, which threaten horse, rider, and relationship, can now begin to be analyzed by two as an internalized ("psychotic mother") structure developed in infancy that attempts to ensure that no personal or meaningful relationships will be permitted to exist.

III

STRATEGIC EMOTIONAL INVOLVEMENT IN LISTENING TO BORDERLINE ISSUES

9

Emotional Involvement in Symbiosis

THE SELF AND OTHER REPLICATION TRANSFERENCE[1]

Self and other configurations dating from the symbiotic period of human development, which expectably come into focus sooner or later, are secured for analysis through the replicating transference (Hedges 1983). Writers such as Winnicott, Ferenczi, and Balint hold that special provision needs to be made in the analytic relationship for these earlier relational issues to be seen and analyzed. Following Blanck and Blanck (1979), I speak of the transferences from this early period of development as more than mere transfer of instinctual feelings from oedipal parents (Hedges 1983). Symbiotic or early bonding experiences occurred at a time in the speaker's life when infant and caregiver engaged in a mutual cuing process in which two lived and experienced each other in many ways as one.

The replicating transference can be expected to be a reliving at an unconscious or preconscious emotional level of patterns, styles, and modes of relatedness once known in relation to the symbiotic other. In the original symbiosis, the mother is hooked by the power of the relatedness. In replication, the analyst must be equally hooked at *an emotional level* for the nature of the bond to begin to become apparent. Frequently in case conferences I hear a therapist making remarks such as: "I am going to present this case because somehow I find myself doing things I don't ordinarily do in my practice." "This person has a way of manipulating me that I find upsetting." "I feel like I'm being set up for something, that something isn't right, that I don't know what's going on with this person, that somehow I am being duped." Such expressions register the sense of interpersonal boundaries being tapped or stretched from the therapist's ordinarily expectable per-

---

1. This section is reprinted with modifications from Hedges 1992, pp. 160–175.

sonal and professional guidelines and limits. Studying how the listener experiences these boundary demands or violations begins to give clues to the preverbal emotional replication being lived out in the analytic interaction. Searles (1979a,b), Giovacchini (1979a,b), and Little (1981) provide numerous examples of this boundary stretching process and how they have been able to make it work in the service of analytic understanding. That is, in the countertransference responsiveness, emotional configurations come into play that are at once alien to the listener's personal preferred ways of experiencing relatedness situations, and at the same time often somehow deeply familiar within the listener's personality.

Another way of thinking about this is to say that the speaker has the project of attempting to communicate preverbal memories. In doing so he or she tends to ferret out and use various aspects of the analyst's personal responsiveness for the purpose of arranging an emotional replication of the way things once were. To the listener it often feels as though his or her Achilles' heel has been found, that the speaker has learned how to "push my buttons." In teaching I have often said that if I were to ask students to write three pages on their personal philosophy of life regarding how people are, how relationships should and should not be, and what they want and expect in interpersonal relatedness, we would no doubt be able to decipher many of the relatedness assumptions from their own symbiosis. That is, the earliest bond, the first love, and the foundational realities of our lives are derived from the assumptions we make about the environment and important people in it. This set of attitudes, beliefs, assumptions, and relatedness modes becomes so firmly entrenched that all intimate relationships for the remainder of our lives can be expected to touch upon how we experience the world and the realities of relatedness through symbiotic templates. The merged sense we have regarding how intimate relationships "should" be is so automatic and entrenched as to be readily confused with reality. A very definite set of expectations and relatedness difficulties arises and the speaker is adamant in insisting that such and such is the way things must go between us, or that such and such doesn't go here. Gradually the analytic listener feels closed in on all sides or backed into a corner until he or she can find a way to make an effective interpretive intervention; a way to "stand against the scenario" (Hedges 1983). The resistance is often so severe as to make relinquishing of the sought-for pattern almost an impossibility.

The first problem is for the listener to be able to place the difficulties in an interactive, symbiotic format so that exactly what the relatedness demand is comes into bold relief. Not only is this a cognitive task involving problem solving with new ideas, but the relatedness dimension itself necessarily has engaged the listener in many unconscious or automatic ways, so that the listener's own character defenses become activated and obscure the precise nature of the engagement. But even when observing a listener skilled enough to be able to see the relatedness dimension insisted on by the speaker, and even when the defensive structure of the listener can be more or less laid aside for the moment, making verbal interpretations of complex nonverbal experiences poses an entirely new set of problems. Therapists have been known to talk themselves blue in the face and what they were saying was well formulated but somehow it still didn't hit the mark. The speaker might even agree, even cognitively elaborate the therapist's ideas, or make behavioral changes in accordance with the interpretations, but still there is no connection to the deep, nonverbal emotional layers that the interactive dilemma springs from.

In my experience, verbal interpretations of preverbal symbiotic relatedness patterns are not effective until the issues are in active replication in the analytic relationship or a parallel relationship and unless the interpretation functions as some sort of active confrontation of the relatedness mode in the here and now present relating. "Confrontation" is used here cautiously, and does not mean that the person or behavior is being confronted, but rather, the forms, modes, or patterns of relating that arise from experiencing emotional relatedness templates from the past. As a device to aid in the interpretive process I have introduced the listening device of a scenario (Hedges 1983). Since the symbiosis consists of a set of stylized relatedness patterns and modes that cannot be spoken, if they are to become known they will manifest themselves in the non- or paraverbal exchanges between two people. As the exchange proceeds, a pattern of relating will emerge with regular expectations of how listener and speaker are to interact under varying conditions. The "Mommy and me are one" dimension becomes inadvertently or unwittingly lived out in the exchange, beginning with the dependency or care aspects implicit in the analytic situation. By looking for a recurring pattern or scenario that is regularly a part of the person's relatedness, the listener becomes aware that the "Mommy and me" interaction pattern gradually appears in each of its particulars as it is lived out in relatedness expectations.

Too rigid or too loose boundaries on the part of the listener may thwart the process. Unlike the study of neurosis, in which a series of rules or policies (the frame) are established to bring the neurotic longings sharply in focus, the study of symbiosis requires that the listener maintain whatever minimal limits and boundaries are needed to preserve personal and professional integrity, and then watch to see how the speaker chooses to structure the relatedness and attempts to play with, stretch, or violate what might otherwise be considered interpersonal boundaries. What can then be observed and opened to comment are the idiosyncratic ways in which the relationship becomes oriented and structured by the needs and demands of the speaker. That is, the replicating transference can be expected to be nonverbal and interactional in its impact, a silent development in the spontaneous relating of two human beings. A great deal of talk may occur as the listener attempts to inquire and offer ideas, but the crucial event of transformation will not occur as a result of verbal work, but rather of non- or paraverbal action or interaction.

Two major forms of the replication are to be watched for: the passive version and the active version. The passive replication, though often unnoticed for long periods, is the experience in the transference of the listener and the listening situation in some particular way like the preverbal interaction with an early caregiver. For example, the demand for a fee or for regular and timely appointments becomes experienced like some demand from a symbiotic parent for time and energy to be directed not as the infant/speaker would have it but as the parent/listener insists. An array of reactions might emerge: irritation, injury, rage, spite, excitement, rebellion, conformity, lust—each would represent the revival of some emotional relatedness mode from early childhood. Speaking these things is often welcome and well received but typically goes nowhere. In the replicated transference, in the passive or active forms, a certain emotional climate is set up by the speaker and the listener is expected to be in agreement or to conform to it. So long as the listener is living his or her part well, things go well. But when the listener fails to obey (inadvertently or through active confrontation of the scenario) the relatedness rules that have been laid down, a disturbance in the relationship ensues. This splitting of good and bad affective experiences keeps the listener on target in understanding the exact nature of the relatedness hopes and expectations.

Over time studies have led to consideration of active replication of a symbiotic dimension in which a role reversal is entailed. That is, the speaker is "doing unto the listener what was done unto him." A position of passive weakness or trauma is turned into active victory in the role reversal. The speaker acts instead of the parent, foisting onto the listener relatedness demands that the speaker once experienced being foisted upon him or her. Freud's (1915) formulation is that of turning passive trauma into active victory. Anna Freud's (1937) formulation is "identification with the aggressor." Her interpretation rests on the truism that no matter how good the parenting process, the parental ministration is frequently experienced by the infant as an aggressive intrusion into his or her space for instinctual expression. Klein (1946) formulates in terms of "projective identification," noting that early incorporated "bad objects" are made available for analysis by projection into the person of the analyst. Alice Balint (1943), in a brilliant tour de force, has detailed the process of primary identification and holds that we identify with what cannot be readily used and incorporated into the nurturing process. That is, it is the negative, the traumatic that poses a problem for the infant. In attempting to solve the problem of negative intrusions, the infant more or less builds a mental model of the parental emotional response that must be understood because it is intrusive. As the early model is built, it becomes a foundational and functional part of the early structure of the child's mind. In active replication transferences, these living modes based on primary identification emerge with clarity in the analytic interactions. These primary identifications, because of the global nature of infantile responsiveness, often manifest themselves in bodily constrictions, posturings, or gestures.

Symbiosis is considered a two-way street based on mutual mimicry and mutual exchange of affect tending to mirror each other. It is the disturbing aspects of this early mirror of mother that arise in and become identified with the replication transference so that the speaker acts in order to mother the listener in the same emotional ways in which he or she once felt mothered. Again, we tend to "do unto others what was done unto us." It is important here to remember that a scenario, thus constructed from observing the emotional exchange between speaker and listener, is not expected to be a re-creation of historical truth as it might have been viewed objectively at the time. Rather, the interactional patterns that become discerned, defined, and observed (shifting through analytic time) produce truths of an interactional-narrational sort. These reflect the internal experience of the infant as recorded in the body and the style of affect engagements with the other, rather than visual or cognitive memories of any real or discrete events. The pictures, affects, and words that emerge as a joint creation of the two participants serve to define real experiences of some sort and are often cast into a language of literal memory or of inferential reconstruction of past reality. It is certainly conceivable that early historical events may be recalled with accuracy, but it is also certain that we have no way of distinguishing the actual from the narrational based upon a reliving of the surviving affects.

Often a speaker will wonder if such and such an event that seems so true or is becoming so vivid in memory ever really happened. And if that memory is of a seduction, the speaker will frequently voice a sense of doubt about the badness of the supposed seducer and a sense of guilt for having in some way invited or enjoyed the seduction or abuse. It does little good to speculate about the veracity of the memory per se and certainly trusting the listener's gut level belief that it really did happen cannot be safe, since so much countertransference is being evoked at such times. The crucial aspect of the seduction hypothesis that Freud put forward early in his career is that each of us was actively invaded in many ways by caregivers. And, depending on the nature and extent of such seductive intrusions, narrative, cognitive, and visual memories can be expected to emerge in the course of analytic work. Freud's mistake was to get hooked on the question of whether the picture created in analysis was real or not. Others continue to do the same thing. There can be no doubt that seductions and abuses are widespread and that, whether or not a particular event can be depicted as happening on a particular date in history, a violation or series of seductive intrusions did occur, even if only in the overall atmosphere of caregiving that existed at the time. But of much greater importance than the actual veracity of a cetain seduction or abuse, and perhaps the reason so many get sidetracked on the question of its reality, is the question of how that seduction or abuse is being replicated in the here-and-now transference–countertransference engagement. Speaker and listener often get caught chasing red herrings about the past so that both cannot notice the abuse that is being experienced by the speaker at the hands of the listener in the here and now. Resistance and counterresistance obscure the replication as it is being actively lived out in the relationship. For this reason it is essential that therapists develop consultative resources for regularly reviewing their cases and searching for outside feedback on the state of the countertransference and the counterresistance to noticing how the symbiotic replications are developing. Replicating transferences are bound to develop with all people who have been fortunate enough to have experienced a symbiosis and who have developed the capacity for affective relatedness. The question in an analytic process is when and how it will reappear and what will the listener have done or failed to do to facilitate its emergence.

By now, most dynamically oriented therapists are fairly adept at noticing and verbalizing aspects of the passive replication. Therapists have learned to use parent–child metaphors to draw pictures, scenes, and adventures that may depict the ways in which the speaker is experiencing the listener as a parent. There are concepts, such as "good breast" and "bad breast," that give an image of the current experience to think about. Most therapists at this point in the history of psychotherapy are sensitive enough to the notion of transference to be able to endure rageful attacks and lustful seductions as a part of what people in analysis must communicate about their private lives. Much has been written on tactful and effective ways of handling such transferences when the speaker experiences the listener as parent or significant other. Still, we too often fail to speak what seems perfectly clear from the interaction as true, for fear the speaker will have an untoward reaction or reject the interpretation out of hand. Even if the idea is accepted and responded to, there is a sense that it did no good in terms of bringing relief to distress or a diminution of symptom-complaints.

But what is especially lacking are ideas, guidelines, and techniques on how to listen for and respond to the reversals, the active replication of the symbiotic issues. That is, when the "bad child" is being projected into us, when the aggressive parent imago seeks to attack or limit us, when we are the passive target for the victorious identificatory aggressions and seductions from the speaker's infantile history—how then do we receive and define the intrusions, the abuses, the identifications and projections that were once experienced? Moreover, how do we find words to begin capturing the experience we are having in the countertransference as a result of a successful replication of symbiotic patterns? Once again the parent–child metaphors will come to our rescue when trying to form pictures to depict what it feels like to be limited, abused, provoked, teased, tantalized, argued with, seduced, and so forth. But even if we have been more or less successful in fixing on crucial aspects of projected replication experiences and putting our experiences into words and pictures for ourselves, we face once again the problem of how to communicate our understandings so that the speaker can make use of them for transformational purposes. Whether the aspect of the countertransference life we are trying to bring to light is the passive or active replication, we repeatedly find that in trying to put preverbal affective experience that has a quality of relational reality into pictures, scenes, and words that might define that experience, our words essentially fall on deaf ears. Therapists often liken it to a mother speaking to an infant, explaining things that the infant has no way of grasping. The infant may listen intently, study mother's face and the sounds of her voice, and respond in a variety of ways, but the verbal understanding cannot be affectively received. For this reason, I believe therapists should attempt to verbalize their ideas whenever it seems sensible to do so, whether they seem to fall on deaf ears or not.

Kohut declares that a self develops because a mother addresses the child from the first day of life as though the child had a self. We need to keep in mind that many of our verbalizations are to keep ourselves oriented to the task at hand and may not yet be comprehensible to the speaker. Mother must find some other way of delivering whatever complex messages she intends to be fully received by children in the symbiotic period of development—through action or interaction of some sort. Mothers become geniuses at this nonverbal, interactive communication with their babies and it is this particular aspect of maternal care that may account for why this work is generally easier for women to learn to do. From early on little girls know that some day they are going to grow up and have a baby. They show intense interest in the mothering processes that often tend to pass completely by most little boys, whose developing masculine identifications are occupying their energies. By the time a woman trains to be a therapist she has likely participated in the emotional life of many babies, perhaps even her own, and is generally much better prepared to grasp the subtleties of nonverbal, active, and interactive communication than her male counterparts. We are hoping that enlightened parenting is serving to change some of this early sex role stereotyping, but as of today we remain profoundly affected by it.

The crucial twist that Bollas (1983) clarifies is that much of countertransference responsiveness can be considered a registration of the speaker's infantile past. Bollas holds that finding creative ways of speaking the countertransference is tantamount to putting words on preverbal experience that the speaker cannot at present verbalize. Speaking the countertransference represents interpreting the early mother–child idiom of being and relating. (For a series of typical or expectable scenarios that are encountered frequently by therapists in their efforts to grasp the nature of the symbiotic exchange, see Hedges 1983.) Resistance to the establishment of the replicating transference often is seen in the patient's fear of a real relationship with the analyst in the form of dependency, neglect, or some kind of seduction or abuse. The memory aspect here is not too difficult to see and interpret. A form of resistance to the neglectful, seductive, or abusive replication, which is often equaled by the strength of the counterresistance, is that of noticing how the replication is already happening between the two. But perhaps the most difficult resistance at this level is to seeing the destructive and masochistic aspects of the replication in such a way that the person feels impelled to relinquish the relatedness modes that form the core of his or her identity, the relatedness memories that have come to spell love, or mother, or safety, or familiarity.

The symbiotic relatedness modes are so foundational to the way we organize and orient our entire beings that a wholesale shift in lifestyle and interpersonal relatedness will be required. People are not only reluctant but terrified to give up ways of being that are basic to how they experience reality. The cry of resistance is always heard in one form or another, "I can't do it, you must do it for me!" It can take many forms: "I can't change without a completely safe relationship." "Unless I can be held and allowed complete internal integration of my true self I can't possibility develop." "Your style of working or personality simply will not allow me to do what

I must do. I need a therapist who . . ." The bottom line is "I can't (or won't) give it up." Symbiotic scenarios are like addictions; they fill in with something where complete satisfaction of the original yearnings is no longer possible. We can't return to the womb where all is safe or to the familiarity of a stable symbiotic dance. So the cry of "Mother, do it for me" in a thousand versions expresses our helplessness to have what we once knew was good and our refusal to develop ego strengths to cope with the world and to compromise our wishes with its demands. We only want to regress, to be allowed the safety and comfort that we know we once had and we still want to believe is possible. We do not want to hear the interpretation of active and passive scenarios because it would mean having to give up a way of relating dependently, safely, or familiarly with a maternal object who could be relied on for a set of responses—be they good or bad.

To relinquish long-held ways of relating is tantamount to giving up our mother, letting her die, being without our main ways of greeting the world. No wonder no one wants to individuate; it means a crumbling of ego function that was built on the old style of relating. And in the way of progress there is tremendous disruption, disorientation, and grief that our once-stable object relations are collapsing and we are fragmenting and losing our footing and our grip on what we once thought was real. I have observed the most painful and horrendous regressions in the service of therapeutic progress. More than once I have heard a person say, "Where is my old self? I used to be able to function even though I was screwed up," or "If I'd known how painful and disorganizing this process would be I don't know if I would have started." I have watched many therapeutic processes abort just on the brink of a major relinquishing of symbiotic relating—and all under some form of the guise "You must do it for me," or "I must feel good and you must provide those feelings for me." Sometimes speaker and listener find ways of rationalizing the failure and cheering each other up with a Hollywood sunset termination. Preferable is the greater honesty inherent when both end up feeling defeated that they have tried their best to make it safe for the fragmenting loss to occur, but as the psychotic aspects underneath are activated, the fears are too strong to continue.

In principle, I believe the relinquishing as well as a working through of the psychotic or organizing aspects is possible, but in practice we have to consider the personal resources available to the speaker at the time, the strength of the conditioning factors as originally laid down, and the analyst's preparedness to experience organizing regressions that a crumbling of symbiotic structures in the speaker is likely to stimulate. Freud's discussions of "negative therapeutic reactions" rest upon lifelong dependence, on overidealization, and on a penchant for moral masochism that the continued living out of the character scenario gratifies. And so the person on the threshold of cure abruptly aborts the therapeutic process, often disillusioned or enraged with the analyst (Freud 1923, 1924a, 1932).

The interpretive response to the insistence that "you must do it for me" is based on an understanding of how ego advances are accomplished in general but prototypically during the symbiosis when so many skills are being learned. Everyone learns for another. Children learn for mother and later for teachers, for love, and finally for the love involved in self-esteem. But mother's presence is required for venturing out at the symbiotic level. I believe likewise that in some way the real presence of the analyst in a supportive and reinforcing way is required at the point that a scenario is being relinquished. This is not the kind of support referred to in supportive psychotherapy, a giving up on the analyzability of something or someone. Nor is this support or active reinforcement focused at the level of behavior or getting better per se. The active and supportive intervention needs to be conceived like a "Mommy and me" project of learning to walk, to tie shoes, to draw, or to write.

The nascent ego in exploration and extension must be actively supported momentarily by an auxiliary ego until success in the new skill is achieved. At first this sounds like supporting behavior change or as though it may be too great a departure from the analytic stance (to break down structure) in the direction of a constructive or educative stance (to build up structure). In fact nothing could be further from the intent or outcome. From the study of long-term intensive psychotherapy with learning-disabled children, we find that many basic ego functions involved in perception, balance, coordination, orientation, and the later reading and writing, computational, and comprehending skills built upon basic modes remain defective until the object relations problems associated with the failure for the skills to mature have been solved. I have repeatedly watched numerous special education techniques produce minimal effects for several years until the object relations aspects are worked out in psychotherapy. Then the skills take a sudden leap, and even major jumps in IQ and achievement scores can be expected.

All people resist vigorously giving up their earliest and most foundational love bond in whatever form its memory is retained. And when it begins to crumble, suicidal and death fears abound that are properly interpreted as "You are dying; the only self you have ever known is being killed off. You are afraid because there is nothing in your life experience to suggest that things will ever be any different."

What follows is a series of reports that raise critical countertransference issues and show how listeners have conceptualized them and have been able to respond interpretively.

DOING UNTO OTHERS WHAT WAS DONE UNTO US

Grinberg (1993) reports on an obsessive man with a violent father who manages to elicit verbal abuse from his listener, which clearly represents the listener's acting out a projective identification. The man has identified with the aggressor and is mercilessly ill-treating his analyst and destroying whatever interpretations the analyst could make. This depreciating stance leaves the analyst not only the depository of the man's suffering aspect but attempts (defensively) to counteract its essentially masochistic meaning by reversing the reaction and sadistically acting it out on the analyst. In this brief account we see the "two-way street" of symbiosis. That is, rapid oscillations of self and other representations occur as first one party is victim and then the roles rapidly reverse. Listeners have considerable experience standing in the role of parental representations. But only recently are we learning to stand in the role of the child and suffer the experiences the speaker once suffered.

> This situation repeated itself intensely in the following session. The patient commenced a new attack on the interpretations of the previous sessions using his now classical destructive techniques in order to nullify them. The analyst felt that his patient was getting to the end of what he had made into an "unbearable nightmare," as he described it. There was something more than dislike and frustration in his work. He felt the attitude of the patient to be one in which he mercilessly had decided to ill-treat or destroy, one by one, all the interpretations.
>
> If the analyst had given way to his own impulses, which were well controlled, he would have gotten up and kicked the patient. This fantasy was that which directed his subsequent interpretation expressed with decided annoyance showing in his voice, interrupting his patient brusquely and telling him: "Just a moment, you are behaving in a way which makes me want to kick you; just like your brother and the rest did. It's the way you seem to want the whole world to be against you."
>
> After this intervention, the analyst thought the patient would not return. However, this did not happen and the analyst was able to see a decided change in the patient's attitude or behavior.
>
> Evidently, the interpretation was disturbing to the analyst because of the enormous emotional content which the analyst demonstrated and this was especially reflected in the analyst's tone of voice, the way he said it, and the intention; an almost conscious wanting to convert the interpretation into the concrete substitute for the "kick." This was due, in a large part, as the interpretation indicates, to the fact that he was the passive receptor of the persecutory objects which the patient projected into him as a result of the strong repetitive compulsion to look for aggressions. At another level of the transference relationship, the patient identified himself with the aggressors, plac-

ing, through projective identification, his punished self into the analyst, in order to make him suffer what the patient himself had suffered. The purpose of the projection was that the analyst was not only the depository of this suffering aspect, but changed it, giving it the quality of a reaction to counteract its masochistic meaning. This the analyst also did through the intervention. [pp. 185–186]

FRUSTRATION: IS IT MINE OR YOURS?

Savage (1987) reports an episode in which his speaker, by complaining about ill-treatment from his dentist, managed to frustrate and irritate his analytic listener. Savage finally related the position he felt the patient had created for him to his own experiences of oral deprivation and rage which the speaker's complaining arouses. The toothache went away when Savage found a way of commenting that the speaker's refusal to get better and his complaining served to subject the analyst to severe oral frustration in the manner in which the speaker's mother had frustrated him. He concludes that by becoming aware of the nature of the problem he was experiencing, he could grasp the nature of the patient's problem. The speaker's chaotic aggressive paranoid stance now seemed better understood. Savage did not make the error of assuming the frustration was only his own, thereby risking overlooking how effectively and creatively the patient was showing him the position he had in relation to his mother.

> Clearly the frustration of my own oral needs reawakened old and not completely resolved problems of orality and led to my retaliating by frustrating him at the oral level, by withholding my understanding and interpretations. Until I understood myself, I was unable to understand him. By becoming aware of my own problem, I was able to become aware of his. [p. 121]

FALLING INTO PROJECTIVE IDENTIFICATIONS

Epstein (1993) reports on an intelligent young college woman who repeatedly denigrates her listener by calling her intellectually deficient, self-indulgent, unsatisfying, frustrating, and disappointing. The listener in supervision discovers that her internal relationship with her own parent and child paralleled the projections of the patient, making it tempting to either defend herself, counterattack, reject, or appease her speaker—thus perpetuating the organization of her own internal self and other world.

Supervision permitted the listener to draw out the speaker's projections until her ego was ready to take them back. She said nothing to challenge the speaker's perception of her as banal, mentally deficient, or self-indulgent. Nor did she make the common error of offering a verbal interpretation such as, "I think you must be so intolerant of your own deficiencies that you are putting them into me and attacking them" (p. 383). Such a verbal interpretation during a phase of overt negative transference is likely either to be rejected or to prematurely disqualify the speaker's need to project her badness.

Epstein postulates that the listener's persisting attention to and study of the effects of his or her interventions contributes to the strengthening of the speaker's ego boundaries and to his or her developing sense of being a separate and significant person. A person whose internal world is split into good and bad self-other bondings often finds the analyst's objective interest alien, puzzling, frustrating, and anxiety arousing since the person is not internally organized as a full and separate person. The countertransference to the projection of such splits may be anger or destructiveness and acted out in such a way as to appease, blame, or attack the listener. Working through depends on the listener's capacity for sustaining or regaining rational judgment and observation so that interventions are based upon a comprehension of the interpersonal meanings of the ongoing interpersonal matrix.

Analytic progress depends on (1) the listener's ability to draw out the speaker's destructiveness, (2) the listener's enabling the speaker's internal parent to be more tolerant by accepting the speaker's projected intolerance, and (3) working through the listener's resistance to the speaker's efforts to nullify his or her separate existence. In this process the speaker's ego boundaries become strengthened, and her ability to tolerate bad feelings without having to project them increases. "She becomes more accepting of the reality of the two-person situation. In brief, such transactions provide a kind of calisthenics for the ego" (p. 385).

> In conclusion: in the patient's internal self-and-object-world, the persecutory parent's treatment of the inadequate child-self does not go unanswered. The persecuted child seeks vengeance and retaliates by frustrating the parent, going on strike for protracted periods of time, becoming passive, helpless, too infirm to perform—thereby inducing further attacks from the frustrated parent. Such was the case, I believe, with the patient under discussion.
>
> When the patient projects his or her bad self into the therapist, she provides him with an opportunity to break an internal vicious cycle. In this case, the therapist's interactions with the patient, which were shaped and sustained by her understanding of the countertransference data, ultimately

subdued the hatred and suffering of the patient's internal parent and gained its acceptance of her deficient, needy child, contributing thereby to the gradual growth of ego organization and strength. [p. 385]

LOSS OF INTELLECTUAL POTENCY

Following Bion, Money-Kyrle (1956) describes a set of events in which he identified introjectively with the speaker and then suffered attacks for mental incompetence, which the speaker feared in himself. The listener describes a delay in recognizing what had happened until a useful interpretation could be made.

> A neurotic patient, in whom paranoid and schizoid mechanisms were prominent, arrived for a session in considerable anxiety because he had not been able to work in his office. He had also felt vague on the way as if he might get lost or run over; and he despised himself for being useless. Remembering a similar occasion, on which he had felt depersonalized over a weekend and dreamed that he had left his "radar" set in a shop and would be unable to get it before Monday, I thought he had, in fantasy, left parts of his "good self" in me. But I was not very sure of this, or of other interpretations I began to give. And he, for his part, soon began to reject them all with a mounting degree of anger; and, at the same time, abused me for not helping. By the end of the session he was no longer depersonalized, but very angry and contemptuous instead. It was I who felt useless and bemused.
>
> When I eventually recognized my state at the end as so similar to what he had described as his at the beginning, I could almost feel the relief of a re-projection. By then the session was over. But he was in the same mood at the beginning of the next one—still very angry and contemptuous. I then told him I thought he felt he had reduced me to the state of useless vagueness he himself had been in; and that he felt he had done this by having me "on the mat," asking questions and rejecting the answers, in the way his legal father did. His response was striking. For the first time in two days, he became quiet and thoughtful. He then said this explained why he had been so angry with me yesterday: he had felt that all my interpretations referred to my illness and not to his. [p. 363]

GIVING SPEECH TO WHAT THE SPEAKER CANNOT

Pontalis (1977) believes that the current tendency to designate all the subjective responses induced in the listener as "countertransference" leads to banal generalities. In contrast, he notes the use of strong emotionally laden words when listeners describe countertransference reactions to specific casework. Fantasies are then no longer expressed in words but are embodied and acted out in the two-person exchange. The dilemma resulting from the speaker's refusal (or inability) to symbolize leads the analytic listener to form theories as if to give speech to what the speaker cannot.

> In such situations the analyst does not lack conceptual tools, inherited above all from Kleinianism, such as projective identification, the projection of a part of the self into another, whose otherness can be negatively defined as a *non*-ego. But if seeing these mechanisms helps him understand, it leaves him altogether defenceless. He then feels obliged to carry out the internal work whose movements Andre Green has tried to reconstitute: a psychical elaboration which, on the one hand, enables him to free himself of the extreme tension felt within the "too-much" of the session, and on the other hand, it makes up for the absence or the refusal on the part of the patient to "symbolize," as if it were up to the analyst to fantasize and imagine in order progressively to build a psychoanalytical space, by inventing the "theory" of his patient from what the latter arouses in him. [p. 163]

I have spoken of this process of speaking the emotionally laden projective identification as "interpreting the countertransference" (Hedges 1992). Bollas (1987) speaks of giving words to "the unthought known."

SPLIT AFFECT COUNTERTRANSFERENCE

Volkan (1968) holds that in a "split transference" it is not enough for the analytic listener to merely observe that a good or bad self or other representation has appeared. Each representation has a complex history of its own and is accompanied by a strong affective component. The following vignette illustrates how when the dead brother is externalized the speaker feels numb and dead, but when the early mother is externalized he feels alive and safe. It is the intense affective aspects of countertransference that give the listener a certain sense of what the historical details may have meant to the speaker.

> During the past year I have been psychoanalytically treating a young woman who declares that she is in communication with many spirits from another world. These are both good and bad spirits, and the patient sometimes feels them within herself. On occasion I am invested with them. This patient's self concept is accordingly fragmented and aligned in two opposing camps; sometimes she is an omnipotent savior; at other times she feels that she is dead. She is now a woman, then a man, and so on. The genetic aspects of

her psychopathology refer to the circumstances of her having been adopted as a newborn baby into a household in which a young man had died. The family was unable to grieve for him, and when the young man's sister aborted in the fifth month of her pregnancy, the patient was adopted, given the feminine version of the young man's name, and viewed as his reincarnation. Thus she was perceived by important others in her early life as half dead, half alive; half male, half female. The incompatible aspects of her self concept could not be integrated (mended) with the other self concepts as a little girl. My appreciation in analysis of how it had been for her as a child in this family was connected with the externalizations she made onto me. I felt numb and dead when the "dead" unit was in me, and enlivened and saved by her when her early mother's object representation was in me. My affective countertransference responses began to make sense as I learned more about her history and the details of her life. [pp. 447–448]

INTERPRETING PROJECTIVE COUNTERIDENTIFICATIONS

Grinberg (1993) defines "projective counteridentification" as an experience that the analyst has in response to a projective identification. He gives an example of a man in a training analysis projecting onto his analyst frustrations with one of his own patients, "who makes one work and does not gratify."

In an example, a student in psychoanalytic training came to his own analytic session after having analyzed a "difficult" patient. During the session with his own patient, the student had had the feeling of "killing himself," owing to his very active interpretations without obtaining any satisfactory result. He was depressed by his feeling of failure, and after communicating his experience and mood to his training analyst, he remained silent. While listening to his analyst's interpretations, which momentarily did not modify his state of mind, the student had the impression that the same situation he had been complaining about was being repeated, although with inverted roles. He realized that now it was his analyst who was "killing himself" to obtain some reaction from him, while he was acting in the same way as his patient had done. When, with some surprise, he communicated his impression to his analyst, the latter showed him that his behavior during the session had "compelled" (his own words) him to identify himself with the patient. The interpretation was then completed in this sense: the student envied his analyst for having better and easier patients (the student himself). A very intense projective identification had thus taken place, by means of which the student unconsciously wanted his analyst to experience his own difficulties. The student resorted to splitting, projecting his hampered and dissatisfied professional part onto the analyst, remaining with that part of himself identified with his own patient, "who makes one work and does not gratify." The training analyst had, in turn, "succumbed" to his patient's projection, and felt unconsciously compelled to "counteridentify" himself with the introjected part.

When this occurs—and this process is much more frequent than is usually believed—the analysand may have the magical unconscious feeling of having accomplished his own fantasies, by "placing" his parts on the object. This also may arouse in him a manic feeling of triumph over his analyst. [pp. 186–187]

Grinberg likens his concept of projective counteridentification to work described by Segal (1956), in which pseudo-happy dancing and singing about the consulting room is designed to make her listener sad, just as Ophelia's in *Hamlet* is designed to make her audience sad. He cites another example from Bion (1955) in which silence and tension projected onto the listener represent a fear of being attacked. When Bion interprets the speaker's fear that he will murder his analyst, the silence continues as the speaker clenches his fists until his knuckles become white. The interpretation had the effect of moving the fear of murder back into the patient's body.

PARADOXICAL THOUGHTS AS USABLE COUNTERTRANSFERENCE

De M'uzan (1976) holds that by confining oneself to the classical notions of countertransference, the listener is not able to grasp the range of psychic activity taking place within the analysis because certain aspects are outside the orbit of personal concerns as well as professional positions. He cites an example of a mild sense of depersonalization that resulted from a shift in the listener's narcissistic cathexes. The shift may well relate to psychic activity in the speaker that has not yet been detected. He believes that such countertransference activity occurs prior to any understanding of it as well as prior to the speaker's having formulated fantasies related to it.

De M'uzan postulates the existence of a "paradoxical system" of thought arising between the unconscious and the preconscious, consisting of a constant stream of images and ideas that fleetingly appear in the analyst's consciousness. In two extended case examples he illustrates the sudden appearance of paradoxical thoughts that serve as powerful interpretive tools. He holds that a listener's reluctance to acknowledge the existence of paradoxical thought is based upon a narcissistic need to maintain control and stability over the sense of identity and that much is lost in this defensive effort.

Alongside the conscious and unconscious processes taking place within him, how can the analyst recognize the existence of another register of psychic activity of which he is not even the subject strictly speaking? He experiences, identifies, associates, understands, transmits—that is the weft of his technique; he accepts as a matter of course the famous communication from unconscious to unconscious, but he is naturally reluctant to give a place to something undefined and uncontrolled, something that is radically foreign to him.

Thus the reticence that the paradoxical system inspires would be explained mainly by the threat it poses to the stability of our sense of identity. Our narcissism being shaken, we may think ourselves attacked and will defend ourselves most vigorously, still preferring to blame the effect on some personal problem, even though it may cause a technical blunder. In this connection, it is not out of the question that a secondary function of the extremely strict classical technique may be to protect the analyst against such instability. On the other hand, the tendency to grow drowsy, by which the analyst sometimes effects a narcissistic withdrawal, would be another way of protecting oneself—so radical a method, it is true, that it risks exceeding its goal, for by inhibiting the analyst's functional abilities, somnolence paralyzes the free play of the paradoxical system, precisely where one must let oneself go. Fortunately, however, it is not that easy to escape its action: the enormous power exerted by the object's representation, which is all the more firmly entrenched in its host in that it has a hold on part of his narcissistic libido, prevents the analyst from ever really keeping at a distance. [pp. 445–446]

Now the "royal road of countertransference to the merger experience" will be demonstrated through reference to a series of compelling, if not breathtaking, in-depth case studies.

EROTIC TRANSFERENCE AND COUNTERTRANSFERENCE

The leading cause of malpractice suits against clinicians is sexual involvement with the client. Little has been written to alert the practicing clinician to the clinical issues that lead to erotic countertransference experiences. In the following vignette Gorkin (1987) relates his own sexualized response to a sexualized transference and how he came to understand and work it through. He cites several ideas of Searles. These ideas are helpful in understanding what has happened when sexual involvement has occurred.

> A patient of mine in her mid-20s, K., developed an erotized transference in the second year of her four-year-long treatment. Dressed in carefully

matched, skin-tight outfits, K. frequently professed a wish to seduce me. At times, it seemed as if she came to her sessions primarily to accomplish this aim. K. did not talk easily and was in fact quite schizoid, although in the course of her years with me she did tell her sad story, the most poignant and important detail of which involved the death of her tyranically protective mother when K. was 11 years old.

At first, K.'s openly expressed wishes to be held, kissed, fondled, and penetrated were simply offputting to me. Although I kept my negative reactions to myself, I eagerly wished she would renounce these demands or, better yet, look at them as part of our analytic passion play. But they persisted in elemental force. As time went on I found myself, in turn, having sexual fantasies about her, wishing to do to her more or less what she wanted. I communicated none of this to her. I silently observed my countertransference, and I noticed that these sexual fantasies took on for me a deep wish to rescue her. A part of my ego accepted her demand, her argument, that if only I would have sex with her she could get better, and unless I did, she would never get better. The other part of my ego, the analyzing part, knew full well that this was folly. But the part of my ego that was locked into this fusion fantasy with her had become hooked, and it was then that I noticed another fantasy taking shape. I wished to have sex with her not simply to rescue her, but to rescue *me*. It would cure *me*. It is difficult to put this raw experience into words, but it was something of the order that I would be made whole and totally vital if only—and only if—I had sex with K.

In evaluating this primitive transference–countertransference matrix, I came to understand that for K. the desire for sex with me was the clearest, and perhaps the only, way she could communicate her yearning for contact with me—as a vital, nurturant, and ultimately symbiotic mother. It was this early contact that had been disrupted when her mother left her to go off to work when she was an infant, and that was symbolically repeated in her mother's death. In arousing my sexual wishes toward her, she was arousing my omnipotent and grandiose wish to be the all-good, symbiotic mother to her. As for *my* desire to be rescued by her, I believe it was activated by her wish, also omnipotent and grandiose, to be curative toward me, much as she still wished to make her idealized mother alive again, and much as she earlier had wished to make her mother supply the symbiotic oneness that had been prematurely disrupted. In sum, our mutual sexual fantasies were fundamentally in the service of recreating a Garden of Eden, a symbiotic oneness. They were for me, and I believe for K. too, more desperate than enticing. They were hardly ever fun.

Searles [1979a] has described a wide variety of countertransferential phenomena that occur in the treatment of primitive mental disorders. Although not dwelling at any length on sexualized countertransference, he notes how in the therapist's regression the wish to be curative toward the patient can take on the primitive urge to do so sexually. He writes, "It has long been my impression that a major reason for therapists' becoming actually sexually involved with patients is that the therapist's own therapeutic striving, desublimated to the level on which it was at work early in his childhood, has impelled him into this form of involvement with the patient. He has succumbed to the illusion that a magically curative copulation will resolve the patient's illness which tenaciously has resisted all the more sophisticated psychotherapeutic techniques learned in adult-life training and practice" (p. 431).

I agree with this observation. But my experience with K. and others has made it clear to me that the therapist also sometimes regressively wishes to be the one who is magically cured. While not specifically pointing this out, Searles's conception of the patient's need to be therapist to his analyst is in keeping with this view. In short, the "magically curative copulation" is desired by both, and for the same reason: to cure and be cured. The cure here is also magically elaborated by both. It is a cure in the form of a renaissance, in which an all-good oneness is reestablished. Mutual hostility is denied.

The mere experience of this form of sexualized countertransference need not lead to sexual acting out. The therapist's awareness of these induced feelings can help him know the patient and formulate interpretations to her. In addition, by sinking but not drowning in the countertransference, part of the therapist's ego remains aware of the "magical" nature of the copulation. This awareness helps the therapist avoid not only actual sexual activity with the patient, but also the more subtle forms that sexual acting out generally takes. [pp. 113–115]

SADISTIC SEXUAL COUNTERTRANSFERENCE FANTASIES

In the following account Gorkin (1987) illustrates how not being fully attentive to an early dream fragment and his own sadistic fantasies left room for a number of evasions and subtle types of acting out before the speaker's incest history emerged.

I have occasionally found that it has taken me a long while with a patient before the sexualized countertransference becomes conscious. And unfortunately, by that time, I have already blundered into a number of evasions or subtle types of acting out.

I remember, for instance, a 22-year-old woman, B., whose presenting problem was simply one of occasional anxiety attacks. B. had been married for two years, happily she thought. Before then, there had been "only a meaningless affair or two, nothing very much." B.'s manner was quiet and sweet, so sweet that I managed to overlook the portentousness of her first dream. This dream, told with a sense of girlish embarrassment, involved a scene at the home where she was raised along with her two older brothers.

In the backyard of that home, the family wash was hanging out to dry. Her bra and panties were noticeable among the clothing on the line. This dream fragment produced no associations, and when I mentioned something about washing one's dirty linen in public, B. shrugged it off with an air of insouciance.

There were few other dreams in the months following this initial fragment, and B. seemed to find it difficult to talk of her life or anyone in it. Eventually she did begin to discuss her husband, her family, and her work. Yet she did this in the most cursory way, *unless* I began to probe for details. In fact, that became our pattern: B. would offer up a piece of information, then remain silent, and I would hunt for details. My clue that I had entered into something of a morass with her was that I began to feel, during these probings, a sense of being teased. I also felt I was forcing myself upon her, and, in a sense, I was.

I gave up this hyperinquisitiveness—though I was at the time not sure of its underlying meaning—only to find myself engaged in a new form of acting out with her. This was a year and a half into the treatment, and B. had begun to warm up to me. Her warming, however, took on the aspect of a flirtatious baiting, and I found myself joining in, needling her back. It was during one of our exchanges that I noticed the emergence of sadistic sexual fantasies toward her. I wished to take her clothes off, tear them off, and grab her all over. These fantasies were attended less by warm feelings than by a sense of using her. Sadistically, I imagined how much she would like it, even though she would tell me to stop. I did not tell B. any of this, but instead waited for a relaxed moment, at which time I drew her attention to the teasing pattern of our exchanges. It was soon after this observation that B. finally revealed her dark secret: she had been incestuously involved with her brother. From the age of 11 to 13, she had frequent sexual contact with this older brother, whose first name, as it happened, was the same as mine. They had never had intercourse, but B. had submitted, at first reluctantly, to his requests to fondle her. Later she had often teased him into it. She also began to reveal with great shame her numerous fantasies of having sex with me, all of which involved my forcing her to do something against her will and ended in her humiliation.

I feel certain that, had I been more immediately aware of my sexualized countertransference, I would not have acted provocatively with her. Still, having done so, I felt that an acknowledgement of my role was needed. Thus stated: "You and I have become involved in a mutual teasing, which I have obviously enjoyed, and I imagine you have, too. But in so doing, I think that I have repeated with you, without actually having sex with you, some of that sexually provocative play that took place between you and your brother." This acknowledgement was fully accepted by B. In the following weeks, not only did she reveal further aspects of her history, but as we gave up the mutual provocativeness, her depression and anger became overt. This lasted for a long period. The sexual fantasies on my side, and on hers, were relinquished. Eventually, with the working through of the depression, a nonsexualized sense of warmth developed and maintained itself, for the most part, until the end of the treatment. [pp. 122–124]

A listener working with this woman would be wise to consider that this sadomasochistic-teasing scenario may not have begun at age 11 with her brother but can also be listened to as a screen memory—as an aspect of her original symbiotic exchange. Entertaining this listening possibility may clarify a number of the other enigmatic exchanges that also press toward a sense of mutually experienced oneness through titillating teasing.

EROTIC COUNTERTRANSFERENCE AS A CLUE TO GENDER-IDENTIFICATION ISSUES

Gorkin's (1987) sexualized fantasy about a 10-year-old boy patient alerts him early in the analysis to issues which were to unfold more clearly later. His account shows how a fantasy, in this case a specifically sexual one, can contain unconscious understanding of issues the patient has to work through.

> I had been working for several months with a 10-year-old boy, M., whose presenting symptom as described by the mother was a slackening in school work shortly after her divorce from M.'s father. The mother had custody of all three children: an older brother, M., and a younger sister. M. shrugged off any sadness or anger about the divorce and seemed to enter into the therapeutic relationship easily and openly. He drew pictures, usually of pirates and Superman-like figures, and he had a rather typical enthusiasm for playing "war" with plastic soldiers. He also was an ardent Yankee baseball fan; in fact, with the possible exception of the TV announcers, I cannot imagine anyone knowing more of the statistics—he called them "stats"—on the players.
>
> I highlight M.'s boyish interests because in spite of them, I gradually found myself reacting to him in ways I might have reacted to an alluring girl: as cute, endearingly charming, and above all, seductively cuddlesome. At times I wanted to throw my arms about him, squeeze him tight, give him a kiss. I felt him to be a lovely young girl. In attempting to sort out for myself whence this reaction came, I began to pay closer attention to the subtleties of M.'s interaction with me. I then began to notice how his movements had a kind of furtive quality to them. He occasionally would walk and almost brush up against me, cat-like. Also, some of his gestures, while not effeminate, took on a seductive cast—for example, a lingering look and slow running of his hand through his hair as he hesitated near the door at the end of the session.

Alerted by my countertransference to M., I began in the course of my sessions with the mother to question her on more of the details of M.'s family relationships. It was then that she recalled that M. had always been very jealous of his younger sister, who, as it turns out, was the father's favorite. Moreover, she remembered that when M. was a small boy he had often wanted to dress up in her clothing, although he had given this up when he entered school. She thought at the time that there was something "vaguely homosexual" about this, but she no longer worried about him. M., after all, had become "a real boy, a terrific athlete and baseball player."

It would take me too far afield to describe in any detail the course of M.'s three years of therapy with me. Suffice it to say that his sexual identity was substantially confused, and much work had to be done in this area. I believe that this issue would have become clear to me eventually even had I not been aware of my initial countertransferential response, and especially my sexual fantasy, toward M. as a seductive young girl. But my fantasy did prove to be an early, poignant, and accurate gauge of M.'s inner conflict. What is more, I found my countertransferential response useful throughout the therapy, particularly in gauging the progression, and at times regression, in M.'s therapeutic development. Finally, and perhaps most crucially, my awareness of the countertransference was of considerable help in preventing me from subtly acting out M.'s wish (and mine). Without this awareness it is likely that I would have unwittingly encouraged the perpetuation of, or brought about the premature renunciation of, M.'s (and my) wish for him to be a lovely young girl. [pp. 105–107]

The next five chapters involve lengthy studies that make clear how important it is to consider countertransference "the royal road to merger experience."

10

'Night, Mother

Sally Turner-Miller

Editor's Comments

Listeners frequently do not have the opportunity to see and to enjoy the fruits of their work. Practical issues as well as significant transference-countertransference dimensions may crop up to cut short the therapeutic relationship, leaving the listener bewildered, "holding the bag." Yet as often happens, perhaps years later, the listener by chance encounters news that attests to the powerful and beneficial effect on the person's life that the emergence of transference into the full light of day has had. Therapists tend to feel more secure when the transference manifestations are clarified (and "resolved") in the "working through" phase. But this was not Freud's criterion for cure. He believed that the mere establishment of the "transference neurosis" within consciousness was sufficient to merit the term *cure*. (For elaboration of Freud's position see Hedges 1983, pp. 36–41.) We do not have sufficient experience with the "transference symbiosis" to be so confident about a favorable outcome from the mere conscious experiencing of transference as Freud was about "transference neurosis," but I have the impression that in many instances of what the listener may consider "premature termination," the speaker's way of life has undergone transformations of considerable proportions. Perhaps the reader will be willing to speculate about what effects the following therapeutic relationship had on this analytic speaker who tells her story in terms of a familiar film plot.

The following vignette spans only one year but is intense, vivid, dangerous, and deeply disturbing to the therapist. Freud teaches that it is often necessary for people to find some way of turning passive trauma into active victory. This seems to be the nature of this patient's use of therapy and her therapist.

INTRODUCTION

This case vignette is written from my process notes as they occurred and from the patient's unsolicited letters and artwork presented to me, as well as dreams and other material from our sessions.

Notes from First Session (September)

Dark trouble. This particular referral source wouldn't send me such a nightmare; wouldn't even know a person like this. Listen to my naive, snob Pollyanna. Maybe I'm having a rough day. Impressions are unusually strong, so I'll jot them down. Maggie is a middle-aged woman, groomed but untidy. She has a worn, thrift-store look in a hand-crocheted sweater made of hard acrylic yarn. She doesn't hang together. Her body lacks structure, like jelly. Her large eyes not only stared, but looked through me so hard I felt very uncomfortable. She clutched her purse and told me I was her last stop! She doesn't mean today, either. I feel like I am an innocent person in the middle of some kind of dangerous conspiracy. This sounds so far out. I don't like how I feel. Perhaps next time will be different. Maybe I shouldn't take her on. I already told her I would and gave her another appointment. I feel compelled. Why? I saw and felt the desperation—there's my soft place again, the fundamental therapist functioning that is part of my own personal identity.

October Notes

Those eyes always look frightened, yet aggressive; like a caged animal cornered and ready for more trauma. Maggie tells me she cannot sleep and feels very agitated. She feels ugly, that she doesn't belong on earth, that others are better; that she is a child of God, but only a figment of God's imagination. "I feel like I don't exist." She feels set apart, more intelligent, and superior, even though others are experienced as "better" than she. She related her early history: she was adopted at 4 months after being in two foster homes. Her adopted mother was a nurse. Her natural mother was getting a divorce and the man she was remarrying did not want another man's child. She has two older brothers, also adopted (seven and eight years older, six months apart in age); one is an artist who has been on the missing person's list for years. Maggie bonded with her father, who died when she was 10. "Some part of me died when he died. My mother didn't tell me he died until after the funeral. I knew he was in the hospital and she wouldn't take me to see him."

The mother remarried when Maggie was 13. Maggie weighed 120 at the time of her father's death. Within two years, she weighed 225. Mother's new husband had a son who had sex in the afternoon with different people in front of her and masturbated all the time while she was around. "Mother never questioned why I hated him. My mother is like a black apple. I feel pain and darkness—no hope. Why bother? I'm tired. Nothing works. I feel pressure to not fail at therapy because I'll hurt and disappoint you. Same pressure in school—overwhelms and paralyzes me. I have wasted every gift I was given—that's why I deserve bad things. I don't know how this could have happened unless there's something wrong with me. If you can feel a piece of music that is me—then you can know me better. [She gave me a tape of her favorite classical music, a combination of Beethoven, Vivaldi, Handel, and movie themes.] I attract bad experiences because of being in a negative state—what you put out does come back to you."

I, the therapist, work hard at connection. There is a spark every now and then; I see a flash in Maggie's eyes that acknowledges that I am there. I feel morbid when I'm with her—I crave rest and sun. The connection process is so delicate and covered with black rot. I feel I'm with someone who is not pending death, but already is dead and covered with an afterdeath, tricking us at times to believe she is alive when I know she is dead in there. She is her own dead fetus. I have to provide meaningful existence for both of us when she is with me. Not only that, I have to obliterate the darkness first. When Maggie leaves, I open my office door to the outside. I take deep breaths.

November Notes: Catharsis of a Therapist

I'm trying to provide meaningful relatedness, processed through me to her to gradually soften her dead inner environment. Maggie splits off her weak ego capacity to differentiate and integrate the alive and nonalive components of her life. She craves to establish some kind of sustained connection, symbiotic tie with me even though it seems somehow life threatening to her. She unconsciously knows her limited experience of symbiosis to be so destructive, she loses either way. She wants me to be more powerful so I can be a successful mother to her and pull her from withdrawal and autism.

I am becoming more and more in touch with the heaviness I feel at attempting to be nurturing. My feelings shift from tenderness to disgust.

She activates my scorn and belittlement to such a degree that I wonder about myself. She comes into my office so full of superiority that I know within minutes she'll reduce me to feeling like a fraud. She fills the room with a hostile oozing energy that is full of vile hatred. In return, I find myself thinking: I hate you! I hate you! I hate working with you! You infect my practice. Go away—disappear—don't kill yourself; just get out of my space.

It's time to broach the all important subject of how bad I feel when I'm with Maggie. She needs to be enlightened about how she affects me. The countertransference is so pervasive, I can hardly breathe. I know how hated she was. She needs to know I know, to feel that I have some sense of it. She needs to hear that I mourn her lost humanity and that I cringe at her deadening processes. I dread it won't go smoothly; nothing is smooth with her. There's potential for eruption always there; like a diabetic pus that won't heal. Gloom and doom. When she canceled an appointment I couldn't even feel good about that. There's no relief for me. There's always shit somewhere.

She can't always remember me in between sessions—I can't forget her! I have made her a tape of my voice and had her take a Polaroid photo of me to carry around. She has a pillow of mine. I don't know what else to do—give blood? Listen to my sarcasm.

December Notes

Maggie has seemed docile and more connected to me for longer periods. I knew the time was as right as it would ever be. I basically said in words I hoped she would understand: "I have some very important things to share with you today. These are feelings, thoughts, observations about myself when I'm with you that may help us understand your difficulties even more. When you're very small and bad things happen, there are no words to describe or share with anyone because it is a preverbal period of our lives. The traumas and scary times become locked in our psyches and bodies and all we can do is cope defensively. We've worked on some of your defenses already; such as projection and denial. We have more to go, but today it is important to explore the feelings I have when I'm with you and even after you've left. Since there is no way for you to tell me just how terrible you feel, there is a therapeutic dance that goes on between us for you to show me somehow, someway, what goes on deep inside of you and you have shown me over and over.

"As we get to know one another I essentially become, in psychic experience, you the infant and you become your parents. Thus I come to know by living out your inner life. I know this sounds strange; but I also know you are extremely bright and will grasp this material. What I am developing is a fix on your very early development. You unconsciously become your parents; in particular your mother and foster mothers, and you act toward me as they did toward you. In this manner I become you as the infant. This is one of my jobs—to feel these emotions and share them with you and also to attempt to know what is not originating from my own personality dynamics. What is important is for us to know and understand your story. The powerful unconscious minds of both of us are at work here. When we are together, something different happens. We find out who we are more and more.

"Often and from the beginning, I experience intense feelings that are not common to me. I feel scared and confused around you. I feel I am not enough for you—that there is some awesome rage and chaos that I can't get out of easily. I feel depleted, drained of my life. I feel evil. As you listen to me, I'd like you to explore how this all might be representing your experience that is being made real to me. When I try to connect with you, I feel destroyed in my efforts. We know this is not your intention; not you, consciously. You are showing me something important. I even had a dream about this.

"There was a darling little blonde girl living around my house. She was so provocative and charming. She looked disheveled, though. I kept wanting to tidy her up. She was covered with something that had been there a long time, crusty and green. I was afraid to do that and knew it would take a long time. Somehow in this house my own mother was there. I loved the staircase because it was curving and graceful with a wooden bannister. My mother had it cut down to a horrid-looking stumpy stairs that didn't connect both floors. It looked awful and was crudely unfinished. I was very upset. The workmen were there defending it. I think this dream was about us and how our connection gets broken (the staircase) and how useless and helpless I am to make a significant difference. I offer so little comfort that you seem to be able to consistently use."

Maggie seemed somewhat dazed by this session and said she'd have to digest and listen to her music. I was so worried that her response wouldn't be constructive. The session had been very powerful. She said she felt okay leaving and that if she were overloaded, she would let me know. I checked on her later by phone.

The next session Maggie brought in two watercolor paintings that she said were provoked by our last meeting. One was a pregnant woman painted black with a fetus of blue with a red center. The other was a design with a dark center. She said, "This is what it's like to be in the black hole.

It starts at the center and bleeds out, the black hole contains it, controls it, and won't let it live. Strong at the center, filters out and muddies anything that's good. I'm surrounded by this black hole. The world is buzzing around outside. I know you know something. I know you don't know what it's like to be there, but something's different about us. I feel calmer."

January Notes

"The environment seems colder. Right now I feel like if I came to see you every day it still wouldn't be enough to fill me up. That's part of the reason it's scary for me. When will it ever be enough? I feel like a bottomless pit. Therapy is like a Band-Aid when I really need surgery. I am wearing tense armor, ready to be attacked. I feel constantly under attack. I feel so bad in the morning. I have so many parts. They leave me when I need them. There's a part that could be really strong like at work. There's a part that could help me do it, but leaves me and doesn't come down and help me down to basics. One part is such a bitch, outer-directed and twisted. She sits on my shoulder waiting to jump my guard. I've stopped seeing the beauty. Beauty supported me before. My head is in the clouds. My sand dollar has started to decay. My mother will never love me. There's nothing I can do. Look at me, I'm so fat. I have the body of an old lady. My left leg shakes. The ghosts of the past are here. I hear a strong persecuting voice. When I get hungry, the voice says 'Don't eat.' When I do, I feel like throwing up. I've done something bad. This depression. I am naturally attracted to the turbulent dark side. It's very seductive. It's where I feel alive being drawn toward it; it becomes like the black hole drawing me even tighter and farther than before. It's getting out of control. Part of the wall between me and others is that I stop at that hole."

Maggie brought me her "bad stuff" in a brown paper bag. Bad stuff refers to her favorite movies: *The Killing Fields, Death of a Salesman, Crimes of the Heart, Holocaust, Escape from Salvador,* and *Desert Bloom*. She told me she left the important one at home.

February Notes

This month is a therapist's nightmare; my basic nightmare. Maggie's hearing battling voices. One says, "You're fat and ugly; a failure. You'll never be good; you're not good. You can never be good. I hate you!" The other voice says, "You must be perfect. You can't fail or she won't love you." Shutting up the voices is taking all of her energy. She called me and told me she wants to kill herself and believes she can. I convinced her to go immediately to her favorite doctor, a gynecologist who has seen her a number of times. He and I talk and he is very helpful in convincing her to seek a psychiatric evaluation immediately. (Notice how she relates to a man at this time.) She refused hospitalization and the psychiatrist says he cannot involuntarily commit her at this moment. He prescribed Prozac, 20 mg daily. The gynecologist gave her Xanax samples to calm her. She comes to therapy with her favorite video (the important one she had left at home before): 'Night, Mother. She leaves it in my office to protect her from immediate suicide ideation and potential action. She reassures me that if I keep this video, she'll be safe.

'NIGHT, MOTHER

'Night, Mother is a play by Marsha Norman that won the Pulitzer Prize for drama in 1983. The subjects are suicide, love, and the meaning of life spoken in existential fashion. This disturbing play probes deeply into a mother–daughter symbiosis that ends in a suicide dance of the deepest despair and loneliness.

Of course, like the moth being attracted to the flame, Maggie happened upon this play in movie form, which, along with the original script, became her transitional object of sorts. She has read and watched it hundreds of times. The interaction between daughter Jessie and her Mama has struck a deep place within Maggie. She tells me it speaks to her like nothing else. She inadvertently discovered a replication of her internal script in the 'Night, Mother dance of the two characters. She is addicted to the 'Night, Mother interactions. She, like Jessie, wishes to die and knows that her life as she lives it has to end. Maggie even looks like Jessie, which probably increases her identification. She is sharing her guts with me in the form of this narrative. She is morbidly invested in every word. She wants me to join in.

Quotations from 'Night, Mother that illustrate the bittersweet symbiotic interactions between Jessie and Mama:

Jessie: I'm going to kill myself, Mama.
Mama: Very funny. Very funny.
Jessie: I am.
Mama: You are not! Don't even say such a thing, Jessie.
Jessie: How would you know if I didn't say it? You want it to be a surprise. You're lying there in your bed or maybe you're just brushing your teeth and you hear this . . . noise down the hall?
Mama: Kill yourself?

Jessie: Shoot myself. In a couple of hours.
Mama: It must be time for your medication.
Jessie: Took it already.
Mama: What's the matter with you?
Jessie: Not a thing. Feel fine.
Mama: You feel fine. You're just going to kill yourself.
Jessie: Waited until I feel good enough, in fact.
Mama: Don't make jokes, Jessie. I'm too old for jokes.
Jessie: It's not a joke, Mama.
Mama: You're not going to kill yourself, Jessie. You're not even upset! (Jessie smiles or laughs quietly, and Mama tries a different approach.) People don't really kill themselves Jessie. No ma'am, doesn't make sense, unless you're retarded or deranged, and you're as normal as they come, Jessie, for the most part. We're all afraid to die.
Jessie: I'm not Mama. I'm cold all the time, anyway.
Mama: That's ridiculous.
Jessie: It's exactly what I want. It's dark and quiet.
Mama: So is the backyard, Jessie. Close your eyes. Stuff cotton in your ears. Take a nap! It's quiet in your room. I'll leave the T.V. off all night.
Jessie: So quiet I don't know it's quiet. So nobody can get me.
Mama: You don't know what dead is like. It might not be quiet at all. What if it's like an alarm clock and you can't wake up so you can't shut it off. Ever.
Jessie: Dead is everybody and everything I ever knew, gone. Dead is dead quiet.
Mama: It's a sin. You'll go to hell.
Jessie: Uh-huh.
Mama: You will!
Jessie: Jesus was a suicide, if you ask me.
Mama: You'll go to hell just for saying that, Jessie.
Jessie: Mama . . . I'm just not having a very good time and I don't have any reason to think it'll get anything but worse. I'm tired. I'm hurt. I'm sad. I feel used.
Mama: Tired of what?
Jessie: It all.
Mama: What does that mean?
Jessie: I can't say it any better.
Mama: There's nothing real sad going on right now. If it was after your divorce or something, that would make sense.
Jessie: I can't do anything about my life, to change it, make it better, make it work. But I can stop it. Shut it down, turn it off like the radio when

there's nothing on I want to listen to. It's all I really have that belongs to me and I'm going to say what happens to it. And it's going to stop. And I'm going to stop it. So, let's just have a good time.

Mama: Have a good time!

Jessie: We can't go on fussing all night. I mean, I could ask you things I always wanted to know and you could make me some hot chocolate. The old way.

Mama: Why did Cecil leave you?

Jessie: Cecil left me because he made me choose between him and smoking.

Mama: Jessie, I know he wasn't that dumb.

Jessie: Smoking is the only thing I know that's always just what you think it's going to be. Just like it was the last time, right there when you want it and real quiet.

. . .

Jessie: (Standing up) It's time for me to go, Mama.

Mama: (Starting for her) No, Jessie, you've got all night!

Jessie: (As Mama grabs her) No, Mama.

Mama: It's not even ten o'clock.

Jessie: (Very calm) Let me go, Mama.

Mama: I can't. You can't go. You can't do this. You didn't say it would be so soon, Jessie. I'm scared. I love you.

Jessie: (Takes her hand away) Let go of me, Mama. I've said everything I had to say.

Mama: (Standing still a minute) You said you wanted to do my nails.

Jessie: (Taking a small step backward) I can't. It's too late.

Mama: It's not too late!

Jessie: Don't try and stop me, Mama, you can't do it.

Mama: (Grabbing her again, this time hard) I can too! I'll stand in front of this hall and you can't get past me. (They struggle.) You'll have to knock me down to get away from me, Jessie. I'm not about to let you . . .

Jessie: (Almost a whisper) 'Night, Mother. (She vanishes into her bedroom and we hear the door lock just as Mama gets to it.)

Mama: (Screams) Jessie! (Pounding on the door.) Jessie, you let me in there. Don't you do this, Jessie. I'm not going to stop screaming until you open this door, Jessie. Jessie! Jessie! Stop this! I didn't know! I was here with you all the time. How could I know you were so alone? (And Mama stops for a moment, breathless and frantic, putting her ear to the door, and when she doesn't hear anything, she stands up straight again and screams once more.) Jessie! Please! (And we hear the shot, and it sounds like an answer, it sounds like NO. Mama collapses against the door, tears streaming down her face, but not screaming anymore. In shock now.) Jessie, Jessie, child . . . Forgive me. (Pause) I thought you were mine.

Maggie wants me to play *'Night, Mother* with her. She has wanted this from the start. Of course, she couldn't tell me this. Watching the movie and reading the script has enlightened me. I feel like I've been struck in the head by lightning bolts. She carries the video around in a paper bag. She leaves it in my office for safekeeping with a great deal of pomp and circumstance. She tells me that as long as I have *'Night, Mother* in my possession, she won't do anything. She promises to leave it with me for so many weeks, then asks for it in the next session. Keep this dangerous movie away from me, she begs and then sneers at me and insists on having it back that instant! It's as if she gives me something precious then takes it away with sadistic pleasure. In spite of the rich material we discuss at length, the obsession exhausts us both.

I've had it with this *'Night, Mother* spook show. I hate feeling responsible for keeping Maggie alive, as if I could. I know the agony of Mama. It's my turn to let her know how much I detest being in this position. The dialogue from that session went like this: "I really want to relate to you in a warm and caring way. As long as I've known you, and before, you've been on a suicide course. I can't be warm and caring when you turn me into a hospital or police person whose job is to keep you from killing yourself. I don't want that job! I didn't train or sign up for that job. Your most important way to relate to life is in *'Night, Mother* games. I cannot play it with you. I will not be your " 'Night, Mother." It's not right for me. You've got to stop this! When you endanger your life, you can't have me. The hospital is *'Night, Mother*. The hospital's job is to keep you from killing yourself. Jessie had the last word with Mama, the blast of a gun. I know you're looking for a way to have the last word with me. You can have the last word. I just want to be free to do the work that needs to be done. I really want to relate to you. We can connect in a real way; as two warm loving humans." I gave her a candle from my office to light whenever she wanted to know I was there. She put it in her brown paper bag.

Maggie said somehow our last session when "I blew up at her" helped her to get some things into a new perspective, that she could feel me better.

She watched *'Night, Mother* again. She told me she could always really identify with Jessie's logic about killing herself. But this time she saw a girl who had lived a lifetime of pain that she never expressed to anyone and how no one picked up on her pain, so they thought everything was fine. She also saw someone who was already dead basically; that killing herself was just the completion of the physical act of something that had long been dead. She told me she now knows I know all this. She saw someone who was always taking care of all the chores and taking care of her mother. Even as she was going to kill herself, she continued to be responsible. It was as if she wanted to leave this world with as little mess as possible and without causing anybody any trouble. Like she just wants to slip away without a ripple, like the divers do when they do a perfect dive, without a ripple; without being noticed. "If you turned your back," she said, "you would never see it." It's like she had lived her life; she hadn't been noticed—made no impact at all. She saw someone who had been so hurt all her life, yet had not given voice to that pain until that one evening when all or part of it came out.

Maggie told me that now she sees why she identifies with that movie so much. Before she was not in touch with her feelings, yet she knew something important about her. Now, she says, just thinking about it gives her this anxious feeling in the pit of her stomach like something really bad is going to happen only she doesn't know quite what it is. Her hands become sweaty and she feels really nervous. Now, she's going to read the script again to see if she can experience it from a different perspective. She says that she can intellectually kind of understand where the mother is coming from, but mostly feels totally cut off from her and her feelings of pain, excuses, and reasons.

She told me she had the thought hit that what if she decided she'd had enough of this life and decided to kill herself because it seems like too much hell. And she killed herself only to find out that she was already in hell and that killing herself just got her a ticket to the same place. It would be horrible to realize that she was in hell all along and she thought it was just a really bad life!

May Notes

Maggie brought in dreams. First one: "I'm holding a baby. Did I have it or was it given to me? I didn't breast-feed. That's how I knew I didn't have the baby. The baby should eat now. I am confused, so I asked someone which formula is the best to feed."

Second dream: "I'm in an old house with an old man. The house was going to tumble down. Leave this. Leave this. I'm trying to stuff in a suitcase Christmas ornaments—clear balls with fish in them—going up to the top to get air."

Third dream, which is recurring: "I'm saving fish that are almost dead. I'm having one minute left to save them."

She reports feeling more balanced. She even smiles at me now.

June Notes

I told Maggie I wish there was some consistent way to reach out to her and some way for her to connect with my reaching out. She said she almost trusts me; that she trusts my insides and some small consistent actions that aren't always there. She can't find the words to explain. Words don't do any good. She's afraid I'll start beating her. She says she can see the craziness of *'Night, Mother* now and that she used to feel a victim of it.

July Notes

Maggie wants me to help her construct affirmations. I gave her: "I am a child of the universe. I have a right to be here on earth. I am a loving person." She told me she leaves here feeling more empty than when she comes. "I get stuck in between me and her; so divided and vivid. 'Her' is culturally fancy; is judgmental, can't condescend; is perfect. 'Me' is nothing." She wants her *'Night, Mother* video back. Says she can manage the feelings now. Dream: "I am on a bridge of feeling and you're my fairy godmother and this place isn't real and you can't do it for me, but you can help me understand and realize things. Then a bobcat appeared and wanted to kill an animal. I felt strong in the dream."

August Notes

"In the last couple of months I feel full sometimes. If I had known what it was going to take to get me here, I would have killed myself. It wasn't worth it; even as good as I feel now, compared to before. Once a week, I have energy—rumor has it that I may make it." Dream: "A friend and a baby are on a porch. My grandmother looks dead, but twitches. My brother and mother were there and said, she's dead. Twitching is normal. Grandmother's not dead—she gets up and walks around."

September Notes

Suicidal thoughts are different now, not as threatening. Maggie has "logical tapes" that stop the thoughts. She has developed enough of a false self or an observing ego now to monitor the warring voices of inner child and demonic parents. She began two college classes and ended up dropping both. Dream: "I asked you what do you think of your daughter? You said, 'I couldn't do without her. She's so good.'"

She wants a clean break from therapy. She can't afford the money or the pain of connecting. So we've been in termination process for two months now. By now Maggie has a large bill with me. Because she has so desperately needed therapy and because I have feared for her life, I have been very kind about not receiving payments. She owes me $5,000. I have helped her file for insurance several times and nothing remunerative happens; the insurance company stalls and denies payment for various reasons. I feel almost too tired to go after this account. She has no money and I don't press her now either. I am usually competent at solving insurance dilemmas and staying on top of accounts. Once again, I am the infant via the countertransference that cannot wage a battle against the all-powerful and withholding parent insurance company.

Now comes the final chapter. Maggie filed for bankruptcy. I received a notice in the mail two months after our last session. Balance zero. Her whereabouts unknown. It's as if the therapy was her birthright—that she shouldn't have to pay to exist in my office or anyone else's office. She did have the last word. I could hear her say to me "'Night, you fool." What she owed me is really what was owed to her in nature a thousand times over: a real mother with goodness and love. Emotional bankruptcy was filed on her a long time ago. She played it out to the bitter end.

Perhaps writing this vignette helps me let go. I thank Maggie for the invaluable lessons and poignant experiences of my own inner world. Because the therapy was not able to reach some kind of natural completion, not to mention the unpaid bill, I realize it was inevitable for me to feel frustrated as well as useful and nurturing. I am far wiser in my understanding of what takes place on a primitive level. For this I am grateful. From the position Maggie left me in I can now say, knowing what it means to her, "Good night, Mother." But at least it is I who am symbolically left for dead and she, as survivor, is on her own to find her way in the world. Wherever Maggie is, I wish her well.

11

The Snakebite

Carolyn Crawford

Editor's Comments

All helping professionals sooner or later find themselves in the grips of a countertransference response that represents their client's inner dilemmas. Most of the time this potentially helpful information goes unnoticed, is deliberately ignored, or is worked with too late to be of help. At the time of this episode, Carolyn Crawford was in training as a therapist while working as a high school teacher in a private school offering special educational and therapeutic opportunities to children with learning difficulties. In the following vignette Albert, her student, elicits intense sadism and helplessness from her as the two replicate a "terrible twos" oppositional scenario. She experiences first hand the terror of being damaged, the fear of drowning, and the venom of parents who hated Albert for being somehow (neurologically or mentally) disabled.

THE SNAKEBITE

Albert had been in my class for three years and he seemed, to me, to have made no appreciable change at all. Other teachers talked to him in the halls and complimented me on how much he had improved. It was true that Albert *was* able to do certain things better. His early conversational style had been reciting entire comedy albums by heart while staring at the ground immediately to my left—always to the left, never to the right. He had learned to look me in the eye while engaged in halting and laborious conversation. I supposed that making eye contact could be called an improvement, but it was rather like being skewered by two huge brown-irised spotlights.

In spite of the fact that my colleagues were impressed with Albert's newly developed social skills, I was not. The social realm continued to be very confusing to him. He could not understand subtleties of meaning and body language, but instead took things literally and imitated social behaviors in a rigid, concrete way. He was still the same lanky, near-vegetable who was assigned to me three years ago, showing no affect and no interest in maintaining his appearance. His short, thin, ungainly body, his lank, blonde hair, and his pale, expressionless face were all passive appeals for mothering that battered away at my subconscious. Any efforts I made that hinted at growing up and assuming responsibility for himself were met with mute obstinancy. He was on his way to institutionalization and there was nothing I could do to deflect his plodding, self-punishing course.

Others at the school with more experience and background felt that Albert was neurologically handicapped and thus was overachieving. He exhibited great skill with left-hemisphere tasks, such as reading, spelling, and memorization. However, when it came to right-hemisphere tasks—social intuition, reasoning, and the abstractions of the physical world (folding a shirt, catching a ball, or handling money)—Albert didn't have a clue. This disparity did indicate a possible neurological problem but Albert expressed anger by refusing to produce. This made it very difficult for me to tell when he could manage a right-hemisphere task but was refusing so he could engage me in battle, and when he was being asked to do something that was simply beyond his ability. He was my greatest burden. To leave him in peace was to watch him in slow death. To pressure him was to evoke stolid refusals and force me to behave sternly toward him.

As his graduation into a world he was totally unprepared for drew closer, I had a dream about him. Albert and I were hiking with a group of gray, somber strangers through a bushy countryside. Gradually, the landscape evolved into a marshy area. The strangers and I were following Albert along the banks of a brown sluggish river. I was feeling irked by his clumsy gait as he moved along the path. It was growing dark when we arrived at a channel crossing. A bridge of sorts, old pilings with planks laid precariously across from one to another, served as a way across the molasses-like water. I knew Albert had little chance of making the crossing, but I did not warn him. I watched as he stepped out upon the planks, teetering with each wooden step. The strangers silently moved forward and gathered around me. Together we watched Albert's progress. Amazingly, inch by inch he bumbled along successfully, but just as he almost reached the opposite shore, he stepped onto the last plank and toppled from sight into the river.

The strangers and I rushed forward across the bridge and leaped to the opposite bank to help him, but it was too dark and the river was too muddy. We could not see him at all. I rushed inland to some small cabins. I found one that was lit up. I banged on the door and a tired, drab housewife opened the door. I asked her for a telephone. She said they had no phone but she reached in the pocket of her flour-sack dress and offered me a dime. I asked for a flashlight. She handed me an oil lamp with no fuel. I ran back in the darkness to the riverbank.

I realized that next to the plank bridge there were steps that led down to a wooden landing. I bolted down the steps and found picnic tables laden with dozens of cardboard boxes full of flashlights and batteries moldering in the damp. I desperately searched through the boxes trying to find one that would work. I saw a flash of light below me. One of the strangers had succeeded in getting a flashlight to work and they were down a flight of stairs looking for Albert at the river's edge. I rushed down to them, becoming dimly aware that I was barefoot.

Then I saw him. He was lodged under some roots. The only parts of his body that were not under the water were his nose and his cow-like bulging eyes, staring hugely at me. I looked to see if he was injured. The water suddenly became quite clear around his legs. I could see that he had broken one leg. The bone had torn through the flesh. He was wedged. He could not be pulled out. Then I saw that the water and the landing stairs were snake-ridden. I could see a large green water moccasin curled up, resting, on Albert's other leg. There was no way Albert could be moved without being bitten. There was no way I could help him without being bitten. In fact, just standing there watching him was dangerous. I knew there was a water moccasin very close to my bare toes.

I ran back up the stairs to find the strangers. They were sitting very calmly around the picnic table, waiting for Albert to die. Albert, they said, was quite happy to die. Then he could go to God and he would finally be happy. I hated them and their Christian resignation but I knew Albert would be thinking those very thoughts. I kept seeing those passive brown eyes, waiting either for death by drowning or by snakebite. Why didn't he resist? Why didn't he thrash and struggle? Why did those huge brown disks glare at me with a silent request?

Then Flash, my Labrador retriever, came gamboling up, muddy and wet with the exhilaration of a romp in the bushes, in those snake-ridden bushes. I knew that he had been bitten. I could see the swollen bite on his belly. I could not let this innocent animal die, too. I had to make a choice between my loving pet and Albert. I knew it would not be Albert. How could I make such a choice? I couldn't tolerate the dilemma. I tore myself out of my dream. I awoke sitting upright, my nightgown clammy with sweat. I climbed out of bed and rushed to the living room to find my dog, sleeping peacefully on the couch. I was flooded with relief that at least *he* was healthy and safe.

My dream seemed to capture my countertransference with Albert. He was caught, trapped and dying. He wanted me to save him but there were insurmountable problems in my way, requiring more energy than I could bear to expend. I could not find any tool that would help to salvage him. He waited for me, an infant in a young man's body, to do what a good mother should do—but quite often these overgrown infants are abandoned by their mothers when they achieve sexual maturity. Like Albert's own mother, who suddenly discovered a need for a career when her son emerged confused from puberty, I too would rather run from him than face the possibility of snakebite. Albert, trapped in his swampy agony, was a terrible threat to me because *all* of the effort would have to come from me. So voracious was his need that he seemed able to deplete me completely, turning me into a dried-up husk of myself.

He continued to sit and wait for me to save him. He has waited for three years, hunkered, depressed and vulture-like, down at the far end of the classroom, patiently memorizing a new list of college-level spelling words, quietly listening and furtively glancing in my direction.

On my way to school the next day, I decided to try a new approach with him. I would forget about raising his test scores and try problem-solving activities instead. Using my best rendition of behavior modification, I would begin in an area of strength—reading and writing—and he would be rewarded with a treat of his choice when he had completed ten tasks.

Albert was an ardent Giants fan. He could quote the stats for the last ten years on any member of the team. I asked him if he would like to write a fan letter to one of his favorite players. He loved the idea and surprised me with his initiative in locating an address and writing his letter. One morning I checked the letter and asked him to make a final copy in ink. I estimated that he ought to have the letter ready in fifteen minutes. I asked him to look at the clock and tell me when he should have the letter finished. He said he didn't know what time it would be in fifteen minutes. I thought, he's stalling. He's not telling me the time because he wants to block this for some reason. Maybe he thinks he's done enough work for the day, or he wants more time to rewrite, or he doesn't think he should have to rewrite it in ink. Possibly I've overlooked whether or not he can tell time. I began to explore to determine whether this was another case of refusing to produce or something he really didn't understand.

I asked him to tell me the time. He did. I asked him how many minutes were between each number. Five minutes, he said. I asked him if he could multiply 5 times 3. He could. He knew that it took the second hand one minute to go around the clock face. He had been doing addition and subtraction of time problems for at least a year.

I was fairly sure that Albert could tell me what time it would be in 15 minutes but was feigning ignorance to oppose me. He had put me in this position many times before. Familiar frustration rose in me once again for this boy standing abjectly in front of me, eyes cast down at the ground immediately to my left. Inwardly, I fumed. I knew he could tell me the time! I was almost sure of it. Why was he doing this to me again!

I took a deep breath and patiently told him to go and stand in front of the clock and figure out what the time would be in fifteen minutes. I said that I knew he could give me the answer but was choosing not to. He obediently took his place in front of the clock at 9:20 A.M. He stayed there, silently shifting positions, until 4:00 P.M. Periodically, the other students would let him know they thought he was behaving like an idiot. He never complained, nor did he want his lunch. He seemed satisfied with his assignment. Naturally, I was the one who had to inquire about his bodily needs. He went to the bathroom, and came right back and took his place in front of the clock again. Once he attempted to pull a chair over and sit down, but I knew my cause was lost if I allowed him to get comfortable.

I would have rejoiced if he had rebelled. Throughout the day, I encouraged him to solve the problem and stop the ordeal but that only produced a momentary wooden imitation of Albert's notion of problem solving which soon subsided once again into stolid endurance. It was a battle of nerves, my conscience versus his iron core willfulness. Was I being cruel to a lad who was too handicapped to do what I was asking of him? Why didn't I just give in? I could have told him the time! What on earth was I doing! I missed my teaching aide, Drew. Of course this would happen when he was absent.

I began to wonder about myself. Who was I really? I had always thought of myself as a compassionate person, one who would not willingly mistreat others, yet look at what I was doing in front of a room full of witnesses! Albert had exposed me for what I really was, a humanitarian with feet of clay. I looked at him standing there, his back toward me. His wispy dishwater blonde hair was uncombed. His plaid shirt had slipped out the back of his oversized jeans. He shifted the weight of his skinny body from one leg to the other and searched for a place to put his hands while he waited patiently for me, his classroom mother, to come and produce for him. I felt only fury.

As each fifteen-minute interval dragged on toward the end of the school day, I began to suspect that he was waiting until the other students left so that he could have me all to himself—a sobering thought. Finally, after they had all cleared out, each one brimful with tidbits to tell their parents that evening, I began to question him again to be sure that he really did understand the basics of telling time. He did.

Doggedly I tried leading him to the answer. I asked him what time it was now and then I had him watch the clock, counting the second hand as it went around fifteen times. I asked him to subtract the time at the end of the counting sequence from the time at the beginning. All responses were correct.

"You're doing very well, Albert," I said encouragingly. "Can you think of a shortcut to determine what the time would be in fifteen minutes other than standing in front of the clock and counting the minutes?"

"No. There is no shortcut."

"What if I was going to meet a friend at a shopping center in fifteen minutes? How could I arrive on time, if I had to drive and watch the clock, too?"

Brushing aside the foolishness of my question, he declared, "There is no way you can get to the center on time. It is impossible, that is, unless you have something really special to do, like go out to dinner or have company over."

My sanity began to crumble. I was on the outer fringes of a new universe with a system of logic alien to my own. "I can't stand any more of this," I yelled, "I'm going to get a tape recorder. Nobody will believe this!"

Rushing to get a tape recorder, I hoped that if I could get this on tape, perhaps my supervisor could help me understand it all later. I slammed the classroom door shut, leaving my willing victim standing in front of the clock, and strode angrily across the patio through a descending winter dark to the main building. I was feeling imposed upon. There was no one around and the tape recorders were all locked up in a cupboard. I headed back to the classroom, thoroughly fed up, beaten, and ready to go home.

Furiously I entered the room, picked up my jacket and started to put it on. As I struggled with the sleeves, I grudgingly made one last attempt: "What time will it be in fifteen minutes?"

In a smug, satisfied voice, he said, "What's the matter, couldn't you find a tape recorder?"

I looked up in surprise. The bastard was looking me straight in the eyes and he had a smirk on his face! Never, in my three years of experience with him, had he ever used a tone of voice or displayed a face so full of the nuances of the moment. My rage momentarily canceled by shock, I tried again, "What time will it be in fifteen minutes?" It was then 4:17.

"4:32."

I couldn't believe it. It was a lucky guess. "What time will it be in fifteen minutes, if it's 4:30 now?"

"4:45."

The son of a bitch! He must have understood all along. He couldn't guess right twice in a row. "What time will it be in fifteen minutes if the time is twenty minutes to five?"

"4:55."

I felt like a fool. He had strung me along all day. It had been his show the entire time. I had been the victim, not him. He had waited until the very last minute, when he was about to lose me, to show that he was the one in charge. In a very tired voice, I asked, "How come you're doing it correctly now, Albert?"

"Well, I'll tell you but you really don't want to know. If you really want to know, I'll tell you, but you won't believe it." I was fed up with him and his ritualized conversations. I knew he wanted me to repeat the question—four or five times—before he would answer. Faced with my stony silence, he kept repeating himself over and over again.

"Well I'll tell you, if you really want to know, but you won't like the answer. But if you really do want to know, I'll tell you but it'll make you mad . . ." and finally, "Well, all right, I'll tell you. I prayed to the Lord God and he revealed the way to me."

I just stared at him. His eyes plummeted to the ground immediately to my left.

"Go home," I quietly told him. Even at the bitter end he had outmaneuvered me and wouldn't take responsibility for his production.

I went to school the next day with high hopes. My aide, Drew, a great source of comfort, would be back at work. I could hardly wait to tell him how Albert had finally revealed himself. Albert knew those answers and it would be hard for him to back down on them now, or so I thought.

I was too fearful of advancing into the nether reaches of twenty-minute time intervals so Drew and I started off with Albert in a pleasant supportive manner, asking him about fifteen-minute time periods. Sure enough he gave me the wrong answers. I took him to his desk and sat him down.

"Listen, Albert, you've been wanting one of those gold stars to go up on your chart, haven't you?"

"Yes, I would like that."

"And you'd really like to have one of the rewards that you've picked out, wouldn't you?"

"Yes."

"Here, Albert, take one of these stars out of the box and hold it in your hand. Now, I'm going to ask you three problems and if you can answer all three correctly, you get to put the star up."

Drew made noises about how wonderful this all was.

I asked him the first question. Wrong answer. Drew and I both gave him a pep talk and tried again. Three right answers—bam, bam, bam—right in a row. Gold star shining on his chart. Then he shut down.

I tried another gold star. I tried reasoning with him. In desperation, I asked him to pray to the Lord. Drew and I looked discreetly away while he did so. The Lord gave him the wrong answer.

"Well, sometimes I shut my mind to him and he can't get in."

"I'm confused, Albert. Do you want to get the right answers or the wrong ones?"

"Well, I want to get the right ones."

"Why?"

"So you'll go away and leave me alone."

In spite of the reasonableness of his answer, I confronted him. "Why did you say that, Albert? Did you want to hurt my feelings?" Inwardly I was saying my own little prayer that, yes, Albert would tell me he was angry.

"No, I didn't say that to hurt your feelings."

"I don't believe you, Albert. I would think that you'd feel pretty mad at me. Look what I did to you yesterday."

With a whoosh like someone had released the loose end of a full balloon, he blurted out, "Well, yes, I am mad at you for yesterday and I wanted you to know it!" He looked straight at me with a surprisingly eager gleam in his eyes. Again, for once his speech and gestures were normal, not memorized imitations. Internally, I gasped.

"Is that why you are giving me the wrong answers—because you're mad at me?"

"No, that's not why."

"How does it feel when you get the right answers, Albert?"

"It feels scary."

"How does it feel when you get the wrong answers?"

"It feels scary and kind of depressing."

"You mean because you've done the wrong thing again and you might get into trouble?"

"Yes."

"So, the thing that you feel most comfortable with is just keeping out of people's way, hoping they won't notice you."

"Yes, that's the way I like things to be."

"Well, you know, Albert, you've got to start giving the right answers. You've been hiding all your life and things aren't getting any better. Let's see if you can give me some right ones now. Take out another gold star and we'll try again." He gave me the wrong answers. I probably deserved it but I was furious. Was there no way to get this kid to produce on a regular basis?

"Albert, what happens when you give me the wrong answers? What do I do?"

"You get mad."

"Well I'm getting mad now. Is that what you want?" Evidently my having good feelings toward him and heart-to-heart talks had little value to him. Behavior modification wasn't working either; gold stars and rewards weren't enough of a payoff. It seemed that he was interested only in continuing the battle and the only way to get movement was through confrontation and threats. I felt a great kinship with his mother. I bet it took years to toilet-train him. No wonder she needed a career. I was beginning to think of finding another way of earning a living myself. I accepted my scripted part as villain and rose up to play my role.

"All right, I'd like you to go over there and stand in front of that clock all day again."

"No, I won't do it. I refuse."

Promising signs of rebellion, I thought. Still, my goal was a greater expression of anger or consistent production, not the old pattern of winning through obstinate refusal. "If you don't go and stand in front of that clock, I will have to do something really awful to you this time." I had no idea of what this new horror was to be.

"What is it? What would you do? What is it?" He kept repeating the question over and over again, his anxiety rising. I felt a small satisfaction in becoming the aggressor instead of the victim. Still I felt sure that, given Albert's great capacity for humiliation, I would have to do something truly terrible to him in order to make him produce. Again, I felt a wave of compassion for his mother. I could not bear the thought of spending another long day of playing the sadist in order to get him to perform.

Drew and I moved away from Albert and considered the problem together. We concluded that based upon yesterday's behavior, he might have prayed to the Lord and seen the light out of fear of being recorded. We decided that a worse threat to Albert might be videotaping him.

Happily, our idea enraged Albert. Drew and I were impressed with the vehemence of his response.

"There is no way! No way! You can't make me do it! I won't! I refuse!"

Drew calmly told him to come along with him to the video room. Albert kept up his stream of refusals while he helped Drew set up the equipment; a litany of determined oppositionality echoed through the hallways while his body compliantly helped to create his own humiliation.

After everything was set up, Drew craftily asked Albert if he would like to take a fifteen-minute break. Albert said yes. Drew asked when they should meet again. Albert gave the wrong answer. Fifteen minutes later, Albert was videotaped. He answered all the questions correctly.

Drew gave him another gold star and suggested that he might be able to go back and do it for me now. They came back to class. I gave him another gold star to hold and questioned him. He gave a wrong answer. Drew, exasperated, asked Albert to give me a wrong answer, not a right one. Albert did as he was asked.

"Good. Now that we've got that out of the way, give Carolyn the right answers!"

He gave me three right answers. I gave him a gold star and a pat on the back and told him that he had made me feel really good about him and wasn't that much nicer than having me mad at him. "Look at your chart, Albert. You've gotten yourself three gold stars today. Think how much closer you are to winning that reward!"

Drew said, "You can almost taste the pizza melting in your mouth, can't you, Albert?"

He gave us a happy grin.

When Albert earned his ten gold stars he was asked to choose his reward. As we expected, he chose going out for pizza. Drew and I asked him which of us should take him out for his treat. I held my breath. He mutely stabbed his long, bony finger at me, his personal torturer.

Oh God! Why me? I had been counting on his hating me. Those brown spotlights swiveled up to my face to see what I would say. I dredged up a smile from somewhere and told him how wonderful it was that he had picked me. Sigh.

I steeled myself for this encounter. Before we left for the pizza parlor I swore to Drew that since this was to be Albert's special treat I would not once correct him on his table manners. Albert tried very hard not to drop his slice upside-down on the red-checkered tablecloth, but hot pizza can be very slippery. For once those huge brown eyes were a haven for me as I consciously focused on them to avoid the rolling, heaving masticated pastry and cheese below, and the runnels of greasy sauce that wove their way down his chin to spatter upon his clean white shirt.

I put my eyes on his and kept them there, discovering that they had a new gear—automatic pilot. I engaged my ears and put my attention into them. Eventually, as I began to adjust to these imbalances, and data actually began to filter within, I forgot my distress at his table manners and found myself surprised at what a gentle kid he was, of his innocence and vulnerability. My expectations as a teacher had forced me into a role where

I had to make him produce. Now I discovered I had a different relationship with him. No longer did I view him as a stubborn half-wit whom I would much rather just avoid. Instead, I found myself feeling a rush of affection and pity for him.

He told me that in the first grade he overheard his teacher telling his parents he was mentally retarded. His parents were always convinced that his only future lay in a sheltered workshop. He had been certain of his mother's devotion but since she started a new career, he felt abandoned. He was ignorant of the most basic skills. I'd attempted to teach him a little cooking, cleaning, and laundry skills but these tasks were incomprehensible to him and took much more time than I could give him. Consider the tactile skill required to differentiate between hot and dry versus hot and wet clothes fresh from the dryer. Consider also the abstract geometry of folding a shirt.

On several occasions Albert has stated that I really didn't like him and would like to get rid of him. I asked him if he was afraid his folks felt the same way. His brown eyes pooled up and he said, "Yes I think they do want to get rid of me."

I confronted his oppositionality toward growing up by telling him that he put me in a bind. "You want me to explain everything to you and help you too much. When I do things for you that you really could do yourself, I'm helping you to stay helpless, to stay a little child. On the other hand, if I treat you more like an adult, you just disappear into the woodwork and never accomplish anything. Do you have any ideas about what I should do?"

"No."

"Well which would you prefer? Should I check your appearance every day, make sure you turn in your homework, remind you to do your classwork, and show you exactly how to do everything? Or should I treat you more like an adult? That means if you don't understand something, you will speak up, not hide and hope I don't notice. I'll treat you whichever way you want. I'll take care of you like a little boy, or I'll treat you more like an adult." He chose adulthood, possibly to avoid my wrath. We walked back to school with a new sense of camaraderie.

Albert did show much more improvement in those last few months before graduation. He spoke up more and voiced anger toward Drew and myself when he felt justified. Every time I noticed him hiding again, I asked him to look at how he was behaving and to choose again. I always appeared quite willing to take really good care of him if he wanted me to. He always chose growth.

Unfortunately, it happened much too late. Albert graduated and moved obediently into a sheltered workshop. I never saw him again.

COUNTERTRANSFERENCE COMMENTARY

As Albert and I approached termination, my guilt over not having done enough for him, my collusion in allowing him to hide and not grow up, forced me into conflict with him. Albert also knew that he had very little time left before he would lose what I could offer him. And so, we had to battle.

Had I been more aware at the time of my countertransference roles with Albert, perhaps I might have avoided such an intense battle, but I doubt it. I believe it was essential that I fought with him and lost, that I experienced the trauma of discovering cruelty in myself and finding myself helpless and in his control. It was only after I had experienced such an emotional roller coaster ride that I could finally see Albert as a real person and one for whom I felt affection. Ultimately, I believe that Albert was able to move forward only when we had achieved a relatedness that was mutual affection. Our conflict forced me to move past the role of a neglecting and hostile mother, past my own infantile place of hiding from him, into a more healthy, mothering relationship with him. It also forced him into forward movement and participation in his own growth.

Teachers, especially special education teachers, have to confront countertransference issues daily. We may face groups of very disturbed students for over six hours a day, and furthermore, we are expected to make them produce. Regardless of the fact that production, separation, and growing up are frequently at the very heart of these students' conflicts, teachers receive essentially no training in these psychological issues, other than group-management techniques. I was fortunate to be teaching in a clinical situation with plenty of support and supervision. Understanding countertransference was a tremendously liberating experience for me. It allowed me to move forward from feeling trapped by alien emotions to engagement with, and analysis of, these feelings. With understanding, even if it was only an approximation of reality, I could objectively grasp enough perspective to return to the conflict. I learned that the process, the struggle, is more important than the product. Albert and my supervisors taught me a great lesson. I wish more teachers could be as fortunate. When we don't understand the countertransference, abuse is only recycled.

Editor's Postscript

Helping persons in many different fields encounter daily in their work the same deep emotional projections and scenarios that we so painstakingly study over many months and years in psychotherapy and psychoanalysis.

But knowledge has yet to reach most of these workers as to how emotional reactions are projected into them, causing them to lose their usual professional stance and to collude with the longstanding devious relatedness patterns brought to the situation by the other person. Workers have not yet been taught how skillfully people come to use quirks in the helping person's personality in order to hook into their emotional responsiveness. Regularly bombarded with all manner of intense emotional responses, workers have not yet been shown how to use their own emotional reactions as tools for understanding the people who seek help from them.

In my experience consulting at schools, social agencies, church counseling centers, and community outreach organizations, as well as in courts with mediators, adoption workers, and judges, I have found willing learners. Hearing a case presentation and drawing out the complex and puzzling emotions necessarily stimulated in the worker by the projective identifications of the client allow the possibility of then showing the worker (and his or her peers and supervisors as well) the nature of the personal problem which is projected and registered in countertransference responsiveness. I find everywhere scores of well-intentioned, sensitive human beings striving to do the best work possible but feeling overwhelmed by strange and enigmatic affects that they are only too eager to talk about with a consultant, even in front of a group of peers who they know are similarly struggling against the emotional overload they feel.

Recently, in addressing a group of Superior Court judges and mediators involved in child custody decisions regarding the subject of projective identifications encountered in their work, I spoke of "reciprocal scripting." Most everyone these days understands the notion of scripting—that we each have an emotional life script that we manage to live out again and again in different situations. But the fresh twist is to learn that our life script also contains exactly what the other person is to say or do in response to us. That is, not only is each of us locked into endlessly repeating patterns of personal relating, but we are equally locked into finding, creating, or stimulating circumstances in which how the other person is supposed to relate or respond is also unwittingly scripted by us. With vignettes from therapy and extrapolations into parents fighting for custody of their children, I was able to demonstrate quickly what sitting ducks mediators and judges are to being snared into these reciprocal scripts by parents (and sometimes by attorneys), into knee-jerk responses and judgments which may have nothing to do with the task at hand of acting in the best interests of the child (Hedges 1994d).

In this chapter Crawford shows how the pressure of upcoming graduation and the spectre of an unnecessary placement in a sheltered workshop catapulted teacher and student into an intense battle that proved illuminating for both. Unfortunately, the encounter and the accompanying processing came too late to affect the child's next placement. But the relationship and the concluding episodes undoubtedly left an indelible mark on Albert's personality.

Therapists learning to work with children and adolescents often express discouragement to me: "I have only one hour a week with this child and then he goes back into that terrible situation—what I have to offer him is like a drop being swallowed up in an ocean. What impact can I possibly have?" I have a firm answer. We each learn patterns of relatedness skills as young children. Later we tend to find or create emotional situations where the fundamental templates of our inner lives can be played out. All it takes is one significant exception to that style—one violation or intrusion into the habitually lived mode—to permanently break the power of the original template. One relationship that stands as a significant exception to the rule is all it takes for a child to know that there is another way, that people can be different, that there are other options in the world though he or she may not yet be ready to try them out. One exception to his or her internal pattern of relatedness expectations sets a process going that cannot be stopped. I have been doing and supervising child therapy for so many years now that a wealth of corroborating evidence has come back to me of the incredibly powerful effects of a child finding a person whose attitude is strikingly different from what is expected, an approach to the child that is consistently caring and inquisitive. The therapist may only have one hour a week and maybe only a year or two to relate. But a therapist quietly enters the internal life of the child to disturb the existing equilibrium. The therapist shows unexpected acceptance, fondness, and curiosity. The interest is about who the child is, about why such and such must be true for him or her, about how feelings come into play not only in the world outside but here in this room during our special time together. No one has ever approached the child in such a persistent and inquiring manner—"Who are you Albert, I really want to know? Show me. Get me upset. Be obstinate. Humiliate yourself. Make me be cruel to you. Show me how you can do me in. Do whatever you have to to let me have a real experience of you. I may become confused, irritated, or exasperated in the process, but that won't matter. What matters is that we work on understanding one another."

Crawford's therapeutic stance had been operating quietly for three years leading up to this time of truth for both of them. Albert will never be the same. He will never again be able refuse, to deliberately give wrong answers, to humiliate himself, to provoke another without going through some additional process of knowing, of wondering, of questioning. He will not forget who first took a good hard look at him and deeply questioned his being, his learned inadequacy. He will not forget who first taught him how to empathically question himself. We will not know the effects of this questioning process on Albert's future, but we can he sure that Albert will no longer be simply naive to himself.

12

Healing Abuse with Countertransference

Jolyn Davidson

The creaky door jolted abruptly shut behind me as I entered the small wood and wire-meshed pigeon cage. I heard the padlock snap, ensuring my status as prisoner. My throat constricted and anxiety tightened my chest as I became acutely aware that I was standing in a 7- × 3-foot cage, lined with cooing, flapping, excreting birds. I tried to control the sinking knot by detaching, but really I was intensely alert.

Ronnie stood outside the cage and began his torture: "You have to stay there. I'm leaving you. I hope the birds shit on you." He walked away, around the corner of the nearby shed where I could not see him. Thoughts raced through my mind as I tried to contain my anxiety. I glanced around to see what part of the cage I could dismantle if he really did not come back to let me out. I started picking at the mesh but stopped myself. I told myself it would be important not to damage any part of the cage. As I tried to understand what was being re-created in the situation, I gave myself instructions, "Tune into your feelings, his feelings, and what is happening between us." But, in fact, I found myself trying not to think too much at all! I was trying to minimize the feelings that were flooding me.

After twenty minutes of silence, he again began to taunt me from a distance with hostile expressions, "How do you like it in there? You like being a helpless, tortured victim?" Then, he approached the cage to a point where I could see him. He poked at me through the wire holes with a stick and continued the harassment. I responded to his comments with my own, such as, "I don't like it in here. I feel trapped. I feel my trust was violated when I was tricked into the cage. I felt scared that you wouldn't come back." After further invectives, he shifted; "That's what it's like living here. I hate it. I want to get out. Everyone shits on me, and it's not my fault. I was deserted." I responded the best I could with empathy to what he said. He continued the verbal attacks. Then, he hesitantly unlocked the door. I stepped down saying, "I think I know a lot more now about how you feel. It is a terrifying and horrible feeling." He put his arms around me, his head on my shoulder, and sobbed, "I didn't know how else to tell you what I am really feeling."

Ronnie's schizophrenic father was physically abusive to both Ronnie and his older brother. His father would punish Ronnie with controlling, manipulative methods. In fact, he would torture Ronnie mentally, as well as physically. One example of a "minor" punishment was that the father would throw out all the tissues in a tissue box and make Ronnie refold and replace each one, then repeat the process several times. Ronnie's father died when Ronnie was about 7 years old.

Ronnie's mother struggled with a terminal illness from the time he was 6 years old, just before the time of his father's death, until her own death when Ronnie was 10 years old. Reports about the mother indicate she had some type of personality disorder. The mother tended to align with Ronnie's older brother and to identify Ronnie with his father. She was highly critical and demanding of Ronnie. Ronnie was required to provide for much of his mother's nursing care during her illness. Upon her death, Ronnie was placed in a group foster home, since no relatives would take him.

Once a week, I would do visitations to the foster home to have therapy sessions with some of the children who lived there. I utilized one of the rooms of the house for a therapy room or spent the therapy time with them on the grounds of the farm where they lived. I met Ronnie on one of my visits to the foster home. He had been at the home for four months. No problems with his behavior had been reported at that point.

One day, following Ronnie's first visit back home where his mother and father had lived, he began showing signs of extreme anxiety. He looked up at me with his big brown eyes and asked, "Can I see you for counseling? I'm hearing my mother, who is dead, tell me not to stop eating peanut brittle. She says that the food at this home is bad, because it isn't like her tastes. I'm scared that the voice will make me keep eating. I keep talking so I won't have to hear the voice." That began our eight-year journey into realms of each of us that has changed us both immensely.

I am writing to illustrate how I applied, learned, reapplied, and relearned, through a continual and evolving cycle, the principles of countertransference in a therapeutic exchange. The therapeutic relationship I am choosing to write about has had a profound impact on my personal life as well as on my clinical skill development. In addition, this case illustrates how countertransference can be used as a healing agent in therapy, rather than, as seen traditionally, as a nontherapeutic process.

Bollas (1983) describes working the countertransference. In the first phase of therapy, the therapist becomes aware of the personal idiom of the client, which is being projected into the analyst and/or externalized onto the atmosphere and interaction of the therapeutic situation.

Hedges (1983) differentiates two key variations of the processes of this phase: (1) "passive replication," in which the client assumes the child role in the same forms as he or she did with the parents; and (2) "active replication," in which the client externalizes the child's emotional role onto the therapist, which expresses the experience of, or identification with, the aggressive parenting process.

In phase two of therapy, according to the description given by Bollas, the therapist is able to confront the client with his or her personal style of interacting. Also, the therapist is able to confront the client with the meaning of the countertransference information that has emerged.

Working with Ronnie demonstrated these phases graphically. The following is a chronologically summarized description of the therapy with Ronnie, which spanned eight years. I have included notes regarding the symbiotic themes that emerged and how I used my own counterstransference experiences with him as a way to approach intervention aimed at healing the wounds he experienced from parental abuse.

Year 1: Eleven Years Old

The first period of individual therapy lasted eight months. Ronnie began to engage me, and I tried to engage him, using involvement in his activities. During sessions, we would play the organ together and make up songs about his feelings. We would talk while he worked on a garden to grow flowers for the owner of the foster home. He would work on his stamp collection and try to talk me into collecting and buying stamps for him. He resisted leaving sessions and once brought me a flower he had picked on his walk home from school. These interactions reenacted the passive replication process, in that he was trying to engage me like he had done with his mother and father. His attempts with his parents had not worked well, due to their lack of emotional availability. I found myself becoming very fond of him as we began forming a connection. His spontaneous expressions of engagement were sporadic, however, as much of the time he approached and then pulled back from the emotional connection with me.

In this initial stage of therapy, several key symbiotic themes that would thread their way through the therapy had already become apparent. The main themes of Ronnie's therapy were (1) being destroyed and wanting to destroy others, (2) damage, (3) receiving inadequate and insufficient supplies from others, and (4) death/loss/abandonment.

The themes of being destroyed and wanting to destroy others became more pronounced as treatment progressed. Ronnie became increasingly demanding and intrusive in therapy and with others in his environment. In his stories, he began expressing rage about being abused by his father. For example, once when we were making up songs on the organ, he began singing, "We are on the Starship Enterprise. Our mission is to kill an alien man. He is being punished in Hell forever for mistreating a little girl. In fact, I am going to torture him."

He then began acting out this transference rage about his father with his foster parents. He had occasional episodes of hitting at them. He would complain loudly that they were being abusive in the way they treated him. I had to work with the foster parents on ways to respond to him so that his aggression could be contained. From the standpoint of Ronnie's therapy I would rather not have intervened, but this was part of my role at the foster home.

Also, as treatment progressed, through active replication, Ronnie began directing the abuse he had experienced from his father onto me by angrily calling me names at times. Interpretations at this point would have been premature and useless. We were just beginning to create a picture of his symbiotic themes. My main goal, at this point, was to connect with him, to become a part of the symbiotic structure he experienced, and to help him feel heard. Instead of interpretation, I responded with comments such as, "You are mad. What are you mad about? What's happening?" I wanted him to learn to identify his affect, speak about the issues, and see the connection of the affect with the precipitants so that we could negotiate solutions that would help him develop. My interactions with him at this point also included affirming his strengths, validating his feelings, and understanding his persecutory feelings. We dealt with pragmatic issues related to his daily living. I tried to engage him in talking about his frustrations of the week.

It is significant to note that these aggressive and complaining behaviors alternated with the engaging, charming attempts to reach out and connect with the therapist and others. That is, the passive replication process, in which Ronnie tried to engage adults as an endearing child, alternated with the active replication process, in which he was identified with and reenacted the aggressiveness of his parents.

Another key symbiotic theme that became apparent as the initial treatment progressed revolved around the issue of damage. Questions he continually raised verbally and in action were: "Who damaged me? Who do I damage? How was I damaged? What do I do with the damage?" In my interactions with Ronnie, I attempted to be aware of this theme and how he struggled with the issue of damage in the transference relationship with me and with everyone in his environment. Also, to utilize the benefits of the countertransference aspect of treatment, I continually had to ask myself questions as well: "How does he damage me? How does he experience me damaging him?" What became apparent was that, for him, involvement meant injury. His internal experience was that "when I am beaten, I experience a love bond."

Due to the foster home's limited resources, when Ronnie's acute anxiety and acting out behaviors subsided, the foster parents stopped individual treatment. They decided to start him in a peer-group therapy experience with me to assist him in development of his social skills and to improve his ability to relate to peers. Both Ronnie and I were not pleased about that. I was frustrated that individual treatment had to stop and that he had to be in group, which I felt was premature for him. Being in the group setting would change the nature of how I would need to interact with him, which would alter the nature of the therapeutic relationship. He was angry about not being able to continue individual treatment but wanted to stay connected with me. We talked about how group would be difficult for him, since he felt very threatened by peers. We looked at how we would try to manage the transition together, given the foster parents' decision.

For the next twelve-week period in group, Ronnie alternated between efforts to control group members and the therapist, and episodes in which he would withdraw from the group in order to feel safe. He attempted to align and identify with the therapist by taking a therapist role at times. He had marked difficulty sharing the time and attention of the therapist with others. At times, he was cooperative and attempted to please others.

When threatened, Ronnie became verbally aggressive and defensive. On one occasion, he became enraged, tore a book apart, and threw it across the room at a peer. I found myself limit-setting with him yet trying to scramble to respond to his feelings and to help him contain himself. In my countertransference, I felt off balance at the rapidity of his mood shifts, which is how he felt with his schizophrenic father and, probably, borderline mother. In the active replication, he was the out of control, aggressive parent. My role as the child was to contain and calm down the parent so I could feel safe and stable.

In addition, Ronnie's attempts to control and gain attention would result in peers verbally attacking him. This, also, was a form of the passive replication in that he was in the abused child role. In my countertransference response, I found myself wanting to be very protective of him. He had re-created in the abuse situation the opportunity for me to respond protectively, which his mother had not done when his father had been abusive to him.

Interlude

By the end of group, Ronnie's foster parents reported he was more cooperative and was relating better with peers. They stopped treatment at this point. There was a fifteen-month break in treatment, during which I interacted briefly with Ronnie during my visits to the home in order to keep some kind of connection with him.

Year 2: Thirteen Years Old

Ronnie started therapy again, at his own request, to get relief from his pain, aloneness, sadness, and anger with how his foster parents were handling him. He was markedly depressed. His request was supported by the foster parents due to their frustration with his increasing acting-out behaviors: argumentativeness, low frustration tolerance, demand for immediate gratification, verbal abusiveness of foster parents, physical aggressiveness, defensiveness, and resistance to any limit-setting. Again, the aggressive and angry behaviors continued to alternate with expressions of guilt, apologies, and attempts to gain nurturance from the foster parents. I came to understand this as a further part of the active replication process. His parents would be abusive, then try to reengage him so that he would meet their emotional needs.

During this phase of treatment, I began experiencing a tug of war within Ronnie. He was struggling more obviously with wanting to be close, alternating with a fear of being hurt and unsafe. He punished and detached from me with direct verbal rage and silence. I began to experience that no matter what I tried to do, whether it was empathy, interpetation, or reflection, it was always inadequate and a point he could use to become abusive with me. This became one of the major themes of work with Ronnie.

At this point in therapy, his foster parents *required* he be in long-term treatment. This requirement increased his rage, because he was no longer in control of the decision. Up to this point, he had been the one to approach me to request treatment. I attempted to give him as much control as possible in the sessions, but this did not ease his sense of being violated. He began verbally attacking me and therapy. His complaint was that he *had* to come and that therapy was damaging him. In addition, at times, he talked directly about being angry with God and everyone else that he had to be in a foster home and not with his relatives. Through projective identification, he often succeeded in turning me into the bad/aggressive parent. At the same time, he would be in the active replication stance of attacking me for not behaving how he wanted.

During this period, another aspect of the inadequacy/insufficiency theme of our work had emerged: I don't have enough and you must give it to me. From the aggressive assaults, Ronnie would switch back to a more passive replication stance of engaging me in his creations. I became aware that these "gifts" of himself, that is, creating/talking, were paired with "if I give to others, they must be willing to give back to me for being willing to give." Or, stated as a symbiotic scenario, "I give to you and no matter what you give back, it is not enough, and I am enraged." Gradually, I became aware that what I was to "give back" to him was "to fix him up," that is, "make the pain go away." We talked about the pain and about his justifiable anger at being damaged.

I began to experience more and more demands and desperate attempts to control me, which was how Ronnie experienced his parents. He demanded that I let him read his file, make things better for him, and do *exactly* what he wanted. Frequently, I felt helpless with his demands, especially when any attempts I made to respond to him were rejected. "Therapy is a waste of time. It doesn't help." Again, I felt that it was premature to speak my countertransference feelings of helplessness. Instead, I empathized with his feelings of despair and hopelessness. Also, I presented to him this idea: "*You* are in charge and control of whether therapy helps you, but I want to be with you and support you as you are trying to work on the pain."

As we continued to work on the issues about the damage Ronnie had experienced, the death theme became a major focus of treatment as he grappled with his parents' deaths. We used many death analogies to explore the idea that trying to deny or to bury the pain and rage would not make the feelings go away. He began to experience episodes of self-rage and guilt. He blamed himself for his mother's death. He frequently sobbed in sessions. My responses were aimed at being empathetic and trying to maintain the connection with him. He felt caught in the pain and despair of having no one to love him.

At this stage, Ronnie experienced me more directly as part of the world that "screwed things up for him." As an active replication of the parent process, he began expressing his rage about this to me, not just verbally but physically as well. He began throwing small things at me. He tried to turn a large oak table over on me. I felt afraid of the rage being directed at me. Frequently, he would hurl accusations at me that I caused him pain. He demanded special attention and pressed the limits of the therapy structure, for example, asking to go fishing at the nearby pond. He saw himself as an empty shell that could not be filled. I had to take active steps to stop the physical acting out, by structuring the environment to have someone else nearby and to verbally set limits on the aggression, in order to provide for its containment.

At this point, I did not utilize my countertransference feelings related to the anger in an interpretive or confrontive way to any great extent, as he was not able to tolerate those interventions yet. Instead, I tried to perceive and identify his needs and dilemmas. I focused on providing verbal and nonverbal empathic identification of his feelings and needs, on containment of the rage, and on negotiating solutions to his dilemmas wherever possible. I did use my own feelings of helplessness and frustration as a way to speak with him about his own experiences with his parents.

As time progressed, however, we began to move into what Bollas identified as phase two of therapy, in which I more actively began confronting Ronnie with his personal style of interacting and the countertransference information. Ronnie presented me with several stories during this period, as he was working very hard on his issues. At times, I would have difficulty understanding the meaning of the stories. I would reflect what he was saying incorrectly. When this occurred, rage would fill his face. He would get agitated and say, "You don't understand. You're not stupid. Figure it out."

At this point, I began to speak the countertransference feelings. I responded, "It's very hard for me to be trying my hardest to understand and still I miss what you're trying to tell me. I'm frustrated because I want to give you what you're asking for and yet sometimes I'm not able to. I'm scared because I know how mad that makes you. I wonder if that's how you've felt at times, trying to understand what people [at this point, speaking of his parents directly was a taboo] around you are wanting, and not feeling able to give them what they want. Even when you're trying very hard, you still get in trouble."

After this, Ronnie became quiet for a few minutes, then said, "For the first time last night, I realized my foster father reminds me of my dad. He's mean to me. They look alike. He puts me on unfair restrictions. I got the idea while looking at a picture of Dad. Dad got rid of me by dying. He got rid of himself by dying, because he had a death wish. I tried to do what he wanted, but it was never right."

Another session graphically portrayed how Ronnie felt. When he came into the session, he checked to see if I had done the assignment he had given me the week before. I was to inquire about getting permission to take him for a ride in my car. No matter what explanation I gave for not being able to take him out in my car, he rejected it. I responded empathetically to how frustrated and hurt he must feel that I wasn't able to give him what he wanted.

Then, he proceeded to give many analogies of how scars work. "I have scars all over. They never go away, and they hurt more if they're bumped or hit. Seeing you is the same as hitting open wounds. It's like there is a dragon in a cave. It is melting an ant down with its flame so that the ant is surrounded by molten gold. It's still alive, but it can't breathe, so it ends up dying. Before it does, the ant tries, and others try to set him free, but it's impossible to change anything. It's like a diamond that has been etched, but the etching can't be removed, even with a thousand years of rubbing. I've tried."

Again, I am turned into a persecutory figure in the passive replication. Also, I am experienced as someone he feels is trying to help him. At this point, it feels like I am both the mother and father. I tried to interpret what I was hearing, "It's like you are this small person in a very dangerous place. It feels like I and others are attacking and trying to destroy you. You are still alive but having a hard time surviving. You have some sense that others, and you yourself, are trying to protect and help you, but it seems impossible that anything can be changed so that you can live and be safe." He relaxed and nodded affirmatively. I mentioned, "Maybe there is a more helpful way to deal with the etching than to try to rub it off, to make it not exist."

After this session, he began demanding, "If you cared, why don't you see me for free? Why do you see me?" Also, he began dealing more directly with the issues regarding the death of his mother, his missing her, and his being angry because she left. Understanding and speaking his dilemma facilitated his exploring more directly the pain and vulnerability he felt about his mother's abandonment by death.

One session a few months later, after he returned from Christmas break with his relatives, he began complaining bitterly about everything at the foster home. When I asked him how Christmas had gone, he said "I had a bad time," but would not elaborate. I brought up a sarcastic comment I had been told he made to the foster parents that week and asked what he had been feeling. He laughed and made a sarcastic comment about me. Again, he was engaged in active replication.

At that point, I decided to bring up my countertransference feelings directly. I said, "Now I know what it feels like to be Ronnie." He demanded, "How does it feel?" I responded, "Not good when I get picked on." He laughed, but did not criticize me the rest of the session. Later in the session, he talked about his relatives criticizing him when he had been on vacation. As he left therapy, he said, "Bye, Mom." In this, he was clearly expressing the wish for the mother he never had. We knew the experience we were having was the emotional bond of a mother and son.

After this, for a time, he became less demanding and intrusive in general. However, on a few occasions, he began pushing me in "play" maneuvers and subtly threatening me. For example, he brought a wooden spoon into session and kept hitting his leg with it while glowering at me. He began demanding, again, that I let him out of therapy. Again, the active replication was occurring. Still, he alternated the threatening stance with the desire for connectedness. He stated his ambivalence, "Sometimes I think you are the most fun person in the world, but most of the time, I hate you."

Year 3: Fourteen Years Old

Ronnie began being able to utilize me to learn and practice new ways to ask for what he wanted from the foster parents during this period. He became less bossy in therapy and apologized after he would make a sarcastic comment about therapy. It was at this point I made a six-week teaching trip to China. I felt that in order to assist him with object constancy development and to prevent him from being overwhelmed with another abandonment experience, I needed to keep in contact with him during this time.

We spent a great deal of time, during the two sessions before I left, going over my trip itinerary with a map and discussing the trip. He asked, "Are you worried about being bombed and coming back with a toe tag?" He was fearful of my not coming back, which would replicate his mother's death. I told him, "I'm planning to come back to you in one piece." We set up a plan to have me send him cards and call. He resisted leaving the therapy room that day. "Do I have to go?" he asked, and he put his arm around me briefly as he was leaving.

The final session before I left, he brought in two duck feathers, stating, "Birds of a feather flock together." He gave me one and kept one for himself. I said, "I will have this one with me so I won't be apart from you in my thoughts."

When I returned from the trip, Ronnie came up to me in the living room and gave me a hug. Smiling and joking, he pronounced that he hadn't missed me. However, the foster parents reported he had talked about me the whole six weeks and had been obviously pleased by my cards and call. He then demanded, "How long do I still have to be in therapy?" I felt tired and, being faced so soon with the pressure of this intense, ongoing battle, I responded in a joking way, "I'm *never* going to let you stop!" He grinned and trotted happily away!

After this, Ronnie became kinder to the animals at the farm. He began talking about his feelings more directly with much less acting out. Generally, he was less angry unless set off by a particular incident. His social involvement increased with a variety of activities. He began teasing me, "Good morning, witch," when he entered the therapy room. I would say something like, "Oh my gosh, I left my broomstick at home today," or "I care about you, too," and he would laugh or sputter, depending on his mood. He talked about the way his family members knew they were close and connected was to "rag" on each other. He was unable to speak his positive transference feelings directly. So, our interactions became liberally sprinkled with him "ragging" on me and me responding in a joking and accepting way with some light teasing back.

Ronnie continued working directly on his feelings about the abuse, the abandonment, and his struggle to survive. For example, one day he took me down to the fishing pond. He caught a small fish and threw it on the ground about six feet from the water. It flopped around frantically. I felt caught with frustration that abuse was occurring, and in a dilemma about how to respond. I protested about him treating the fish in a cruel way and my desire that he not leave it to die. I wanted to throw it back in the lake myself but wanted to learn what he was trying to communicate to me, so I waited. He said, "It's survival of the fittest. If it wants to live, it'll get itself back in the water." I told him, "I think it might need some help along with the will to live, since it isn't in its own element and doesn't have the ability to totally protect itself." He agreed to move it closer to the water, so that, eventually, it was able to flop itself back into the pond and swim away. He then said, "I feel sad when I think of my mother, but that's normal. Dad beat and did crazy things to my mother, my brother, and me. I don't know why my mom protected me more than my brother."

In this experience, Ronnie had created a situation in which I assumed the role of his mother, he the father, and the fish himself. I had to be the protesting mother saving him from the abusing father. In addition, I think he wanted to see how I would handle his feelings of struggling to survive and feeling that it was totally up to him to survive. I think the negotiation to move the fish closer to, but not into, the water was a way we kept the thought that he had to work and to will to heal the damage he had experienced. Also, that it was all right, and maybe even necessary, to let someone help and support him in the healing process. The final freedom was up to him. This became an ongoing theme of therapy. It can be surmised that his inability, due to actual historical circumstances, to successfully negotiate such triangular relationships resulted in his remaining emotionally stuck in dyadic relationships that were abusive but nevertheless familiar and more tolerable.

During the weeks that followed, Ronnie showed signs of internal shifting in several areas. He became increasingly more comfortable talking about his mother's death. He received an award for being the most improved at the home. One incident occurred in which he reported helping a younger peer with his attitude and behavior toward adults. He said to the peer, "I've just come through that this year. I want to help you." At this point, he was becoming able to introject positive aspects of the therapist. He reported to me that "he reminds me of me." He sang joking songs about people at his home that were of a "ragging" nature. I enjoyed them. If he sang one about me, I joined in and playfully added lyrics to make me sound "bad," also. He and I enjoyed this thoroughly.

That year, a boy at school Ronnie knew fairly well committed suicide. When he did not bring this up in therapy, I asked him about his feelings about the situation. He became angry that I brought it up and told me the incident didn't affect him at all and had nothing to do with his parents' deaths. He was avoiding the painful feelings during this time of less intense pain.

During that period, Ronnie had to miss one session and left a note for me. The note read, "Dear #1. Sorry I can't see you today. I have a tennis game. (If I knew of a basketball team that met every Wednesday (therapy day), I'd join it!!) HA HA Signed, Your Insane Patient." This was an example of his expression of connectedness.

Several weeks after this, Ronnie began directing nonjoking derogatory comments at me again. I continued the process of confronting him more directly with his personal style and with the meaning of the countertransference information. I pointed out, "I've noticed that when you've been dumped on during the week, you do that to me to let me know how you feel." He became very quiet and made a brief comment about not having a good weekend at his relative's house.

As I was leaving one night, Ronnie stopped me and demanded I see him that very moment. He was very angry about a conflict he had with the foster father and was feeling unwanted after a weekend with his relatives. He talked about this directly rather than taking an active replication mode of communicating. The rage began to subside, and he said, "It's hard to feel good and positive when things get painful." He was beginning to speak of the dilemma of splitting. We talked of the need to learn to hold the positive and negative together so that the negative would not destroy the positive.

Two days later, I received an emergency call from Ronnie. He had had an altercation with his foster father that became physical. They were pushing and shoving each other. Ronnie was threatening suicide if the foster father did not remove the unfair restrictions he had placed on Ronnie. I let him talk for a long time and responded as empathetically as possible. I pressed him, as well, to promise he wouldn't hurt himself before our next session. He promised, "99.9 percent." He was in tears when I asked for 100 percent. He said, "I won't tell you 100 percent that I won't die, because that's what my mom did. I won't do to you what she did to me." He promised he would call if he felt worse. We worked on managing his anger at the foster father. I was serving as a container for his rage.

At the next session, Ronnie put his head on my shoulder when he walked in the door and said, "See, I told you your chances were good that I wouldn't kill myself." We worked on his opportunity to make choices and take control over areas he was able to, such as his responses to situations. We talked of the incidences of the foster father's unfairness and how the erratic parenting reminded him of his father. He pushed the transference discussion away, as it was too much for him to deal with at the time.

Ronnie began focusing more directly on how mean and withholding others were to him. He was able to acknowledge that his own angry, mean, and punishing behaviors were a way to let others know how he felt. Also, he acknowledged he would use aggression to push people away because he was afraid they would die. He reported plucking the feathers from his pigeons. Also, he had poked the eye out of one of his birds when he hadn't liked how it was behaving. He said, "Poking the eye out was a mistake. I just wanted to hurt him. I feel guilty about that." This was the first time he did not defend his aggression and acknowledged it was wrong.

In addition to hurting the birds, Ronnie expressed feeling relief and pleasure when he punished himself by doing such things as breaking his stereo. A few times he joked, "I could hurt myself with my knife if I wanted." I asked the foster parents to monitor his knife use. We worked together on him learning ways to handle his frustration and anger with others in ways that were not destructive to others or to himself. We explored the idea that the main ways he had learned to handle his feelings were ways he had learned from his parents. Again, we discussed how he communicated his own experience by treating others the way he had been treated. We identified the problems with communicating feelings in indirect ways. We talked of his fears that people he became attached to might die and how he still blamed himself for his mother's death.

During one session we had at the pigeon cage, Ronnie demonstrated how he had taught the pigeons to "kiss" him by holding one's beak up to his lips. He said, "They are my family. No one ever better try to take them away!" He then told me about a goat that had died that week at the farm. He had made a grave for it, to "show respect." He said, "It wasn't his fault he died." He wanted affirmation from me that it was acceptable to make a grave for the goat. I felt at this point that he wanted my engagement and affirmation that it was all right to "bury the dead," psychologically connecting that event with letting go of his mother and the anger he felt at her and himself for her dying.

Ronnie began to talk of his need to learn to control his manipulations and to let go of his demands that people be perfect. He began buying more pigeons to add to his "family." He was very conscientious in taking care of them and spent hours fixing the cage and cleaning and feeding them. During sessions, he frequently had me participate in the caretaking process.

He continued to express the frustration he felt when others did not give him what he wanted. We had agreed earlier that if we were to go out of the therapy room during a session, we could only talk to each other and not with others, because therapy was our time together. For several sessions, he tested this limit by speaking to others and trying to engage them in conversation as we walked by them. When I protested, he said, "I call others Bitch if they don't give me what I want and Half Bitch if they do." There was some teasing and telling me not to get jealous of him talking with others during "our time." Again, he had re-created a scenario for me to experience his own frustration, and we were able to talk about this directly. Later, he said, "God is being good to me. It's not His fault my parents died."

Year 4: Fifteen Years Old

One evening, I received an emergency call from Ronnie. He was having suicidal thoughts and wanted to punish others. He would not discuss what had occurred to set off these feelings. He had no plans to hurt himself but used the call as a way to contain his feelings and to get himself back under control. Later, I found out he had had an episode of trying to punish a peer who had been intrusive and abusive to him by putting a pillow over the peer's face. He had been able to back off from the peer by himself. We spent time interpreting this episode and set up arrangements with the foster parents to provide closer supervision.

After this, Ronnie began making comments such as, "I wish you were my friend. You're okay as a friend, but not as my shrink." He wanted therapy to go faster, and we talked about the possibility of sessions twice a week. Unfortunately, the foster parents were not able to make that provision.

One session, while we were down at the pigeon cages, Ronnie showed me a ground squirrel that he had killed, because it had killed one of his baby pigeons. He reported, "I kicked it to death, then chopped its head off to make sure he was dead. And don't you make any shrink comments about it!" I protested that he would not let me be myself. Then, he began killing ants vigorously with bug spray "because they hurt the pigeons and take their food."

This occurred around Mother's Day, and I inquired how he was doing with his feelings about it. He became enraged that I brought it up, but cried on my shoulder. He said, "I'm afraid if I let go of the image of my mother that I will be damaged even more. So, I bury my feelings so I won't lose the pain. I'm afraid counseling will make me lose her." He would not discuss these fears.

The next session, Ronnie manipulated the situation to get me into a meeting with the owner of the foster home. I was aware of this but knew he was again creating a setting in which I was to experience certain things. He would not discuss it with me. At this meeting he lodged multiple complaints about me to her and asked her to punish me for bringing up the pain about his mother. I said, "You felt invaded and hurt last week even though my intent was to be caring. I really blew it. You felt very threatened and angry last week, and you want me to feel threatened and hurt today." He responded, "Yes, you're right!" He had experienced me as the hurtful father and felt he could look to the owner of the foster home as the "good mother" to protect him. His purpose was to "kill me." He believed he had the power to "kill" me, that is, to stop the therapy, but was pleased that he did not.

In the following session, I talked of feeling concerned that he thought I wanted him to forget his mother. I told him, "I want to help you remember her in all the ways you want to. You can't, if you try not to think of her. You can't get over her death, but you can remember her without so much pain." He was able to explore these issues.

A few weeks later, at the pigeon cage, Ronnie showed me a squirrel he had caught "trying to hurt my pigeons." He demanded, "You pick a burial site for him while I kill him." He was very insistent. I said, "I feel very uncomfortable participating in this." He said, "You lived on a farm. You know it's okay to keep your animals safe by killing predators." I responded, "Yes, I know that has to be done sometimes, but I don't feel comfortable with this. It feels like something more is happening. You're trying to tell me something important. I feel torn—to stay so I can understand what you want me to know and not to stay because I don't want to participate in the killing. I think this has to do with your parents, but I know you've forbidden me to bring them up right now." He continued to be insistent. By this time, our time was up, and I let him know I had to leave.

It was the following week that the incident occurred in which Ronnie locked me in the pigeon cage. He was graphically trying to help me understand what he had been trying to tell me the week before! He was trying to engage me in feeling his trauma and in taking action to protect and vindicate him from the internalized abuse he felt.

After this, several sessions occurred around a police investigation of an older man Ronnie had spent time with as a father figure before he came to the foster home. The man was being investigated for child molestation, and Ronnie was interviewed by the police. He was angry and protective of the man. He denied the man had hurt him in any way. Still, he was not allowed to have any contact with the man.

One day, during the weeks that surrounded the investigation, Ronnie entered the therapy room angrily. He shoved me several times and pinned me against the wall. When the foster father knocked on the door, Ronnie would not allow me to answer. The foster father entered the room with a key. Ronnie backed off but kept yelling and trying to intimidate the foster father into letting him out of therapy. Ronnie threatened, "What would you do if I put Jolyn into the hospital?" The foster father told Ronnie that he would be hospitalized in a mental hospital if necessary. Ronnie stood in the hallway, kicking the doorpost the rest of the session. He talked of his pain in therapy because he has to deal with painful issues. Also, we talked again of his striking out following his being hurt by someone. We explored the connection of his anger to the child molestation investigation. I again served as a container for his rage.

The next several weeks, while Ronnie was physically agitated, I required that the foster father observe from a distance during the sessions. Ronnie tried to manipulate me into making the foster father leave the area. He talked of being upset that I didn't trust him. I told him, "I need to be able to trust myself to know how you are feeling, and that didn't happen last week." He seemed to accept this and did not press further. In fact, he later asked me to call him while he would be on vacation for the following three weeks. He was planning to be with his relatives and was feeling quite vulnerable. Again, he said, "I want you to be my friend, not my therapist."

Following this event, a month passed in which he talked of the only consistency in his life being therapy, getting yelled at by the foster parents, and feeding his pigeons. With the pigeons, he kept the cages very clean so he wouldn't "lose his birds through illness." This was a passive replication of his role with his mother. He talked of identifying with one bird: a whiner and fighter, who wanted to be hand-fed. He was feeding one that was damaged and had been rejected by its parents. He was trying to save it. At this point, he was taking a more nurturing stance and was able to internalize the therapist. Also, he began talking about his feelings toward me. He said, "I'm angry with you because you can't be with me every day." We talked about the frustration of this and of my role as his therapist. He would not discuss his fantasies about me as mother directly.

The next session, Ronnie tried to get me to let him work with some electrical power equipment at the home. This would have put us in a position to interact with other people and to be so noisy that we would not be able to hear each other talk. I reminded him of the limits about being out of the therapy room that we had previously agreed to follow. Just the two of us were to be together. I pointed out that perhaps his request was a way not to interact with me. He became angry that I was not cooperating, and said, "It's not fair that adults can set limits and kids can't." I agreed with him. Then he proceeded to "make" me sit on a box and to not let me talk for the first part of the session. I began to protest playfully: "I hate it when others make me do what I don't want to do. I think it's not fair to be punished just because I don't do what you want." He laughed and released me from my "restriction." This was a way to speak the countertransference feelings I had in order to reflect his own feelings of frustration that he could not control others.

Toward the end of this session, Ronnie asked, "What would you do if someone lied to you 95 percent of the time?" He refused to speak directly about who he was referring to. I spoke of having to choose what I would do. I gave some alternatives: "#1. To say 'to hell with you, I can't trust you' and then to reject the person all together; or #2. To acknowledge the person's limitations and take the positive experiences the person offers, when I am able to, and not demand that he or she be different." We used an analogy of one of his pigeons, which only had one wing: appreciate the bird for the enjoyment it brings, though it can't fly; or demand that it be perfect and fly; or kill it because it can't.

We focused on his right and responsibility to choose his responses, which was an important issue for him. I asked him if he wanted to punish me at times because I don't meet all of his needs. He acknowledged this slightly but also began talking about other specific people he was angry with who did not meet his needs who were the focus of his attention that week.

Year 5: Sixteen Years Old

Several months went by in which Ronnie was able to connect more positively and to share his thoughts and feelings with me and others at his home more directly. His grades were up to a 3.5 grade point average. He was getting positive feedback from all those who had contact with him. He was actively making plans for summer, possibly some travel. He was able to handle the limits of his home much better. He made comments about letting go of his attachment expectations of a person whom he had been trying to get to love him for years but who was not able to love.

In these months, we continued to focus on his ability to make choices and to be in charge of how he handles the situations he faces daily. He still would throw in comments that reflected feelings of ambivalence toward me, for example, "I'm going to tell others you are a pedophile. They're getting rid of pedophiles, you know." Then he laughed. In the midst of this, he teasingly told me I had "ninety-one sessions left to cure" him, meaning until he was 18 and could leave the foster home. He jokingly said, "I won't do anything to help myself until they pay me!" We, again, spoke of his opportunity to make choices about his life.

Several weeks later, Ronnie began to express more directly his fear that I would be forgotten by him after he graduated the following year and finished therapy. He called me a few names, and at the end of the session, he threw some toys around to "make a mess," aiming some of the small, not hurtful, items at me. He asked, "How long do you think it will take you to clean this up?" I responded, "I'm not sure if you are trying to get me mad, get me to set limits, or if this mess to clean up is a way for you to stay with me after you leave." He responded by going over to the couch and lying down. He said, "I'm going to go to sleep and stay." He did this for a few minutes. Later, as he left the session, I said, "Even when you leave, you are a part of me, and I am a part of you. But, it's hard to leave." He expressed wishes that he could live with me.

Ronnie directly talked about his outrage at being an orphan and about the injustices and inequality in the world during this phase of treatment. In a previous session, we had used the analogy of being in a card game and being dealt a bad hand. We had spoken of the choice we had to make of how to handle that, that is, to fold, stop playing the game and walk away, or to try to make choices about the cards to improve the chances of winning. During this session, he said, "Sometimes I don't want to be alive, but you don't want me to fold my hand. I need a family, but I can't have one now. I used to feel guilty for my mom dying and that I had to live here. But I'm intelligent and know now it's not my fault. I was angry at God for a long time, but it's not His fault either." He was moving into more acceptance. He also made a side comment, "I guess I better get used to you, because I am going to marry someone like you." We did not have time to pursue discussion of his marriage fantasy at that point.

Later, Ronnie again talked of wanting out of therapy, but his ambivalence about therapy, his living situation, and the loss of his mother through death continued to be apparent. He would sing songs to me to the tune of "This Land is Your Land." He sang, "This shrink is your shrink, this shrink is my shrink." One session, down at the pigeon cage, he talked of separating the young pigeons from the old ones because, "It will help them learn to be independent sooner if they are orphans."

He cried over the loss of his mother. "I'm afraid to be angry at my mother because it might destroy the good parts of her. But, I could only remember one good thing about my mother at first. She fixed me up after my dad abused me. But she didn't protect me from the abuse. She was beaten by my dad, also."

He continued to try to integrate his thoughts about his life. For the first time, he spoke at length, specifically, about his father. He said, "I've been analyzing myself and trying to put the pieces back together. I'm aware of how angry I am at my father for his abuse, like pouring motor oil over me and beating me with a switch. He was schizophrenic, switching from one personality to another—nice to mad. I was terrified of him. Sometimes I play like my dad by not letting myself experience the good parts of life. Sometimes I'm afraid I may become schizophrenic, especially when I hit things and throw the pigeons when I'm mad."

As this exploration continued, we talked about some of his anger at me and others as being tied in with his anger for not getting what he needed from his parents. We talked directly about ways to protect himself from victimization. We worked on ways to manage his anger when he feels others are victimizing him. We discussed his fear of becoming schizophrenic. Ronnie summarized his solution to the dilemma of his ambivalence when he gave an analogy of letting go of an old bicycle and getting a new one. He identified the good and bad parts about the process. He also said, "You can stay mad forever because the new isn't like the old, but that keeps you from having fun on the new."

Several months later, another segment of rage emerged over the issues of loss, pain, and death. At one point he said, "I want to let my mother be dead and still feel the pain. I want you to let me be dead to you. And you not to forget me, but keep me as in the past." He was wanting me to experience my loss of him and to work through the loss, so that he could resolve the loss of his mother through me.

During these months, we explored issues related to borderline characteristics: projection of the rage, detachment, fear of loss of control, and object splitting. He was continuing to project his fear, rage, pain, and abandonment from the past onto the relationship with me and others. We continued to look at the way he resisted therapy as the way the parents resisted connecting with him. It was important, at this point, that the anger and rage be allowed to continue to emerge, so we could continue to deal with the transference issues.

Following another weekend with his relatives, Ronnie allowed himself to continue his grieving. He was tearful and angry: "I can't change my life and bring my parents back or make them be non-abusers. No one wants me. No one will be there at my graduation. No one will be there to dance at my wedding." This rage episode also coincided with him being rejected from the sports team at school and being hurt emotionally by his coach. He allowed himself to grieve about that, also.

At one point in the struggle with the foster parents, when he was displacing his rage on me, he said, "Don't take it personally, Jolyn. I like you. I'd come to counseling anyway, but I have to fight it because *they* are telling me I have to come to therapy." I reassured him: "I understand that you need to fight against them so that you don't have to feel so powerless and out of control in your life."

Year 6: Seventeen Years Old

During the sixth year of treatment, another episode occurred in which Ronnie again entered the therapy room, enraged about having to come to counseling. He refused to talk about what had happened that really had made him angry. He demanded, "You have to choose another kid in the home to work with, because they abuse drugs, and I don't. I'm not crazy." I asked, "Why don't you use drugs?" He answered, "Because I have hope that I will have an okay life. I feel helpless and mad because I can't make others be what I want or give them what I want. I don't know why I haven't killed myself yet." I asked, "Why haven't you?" He responded, "Because I want something better for myself."

He continued to verbally rage, then suddenly threw game boxes at me, hitting my head and ribs before I could get up from the chair. He threw a table over so that it scraped the side of a cabinet. He yelled, "You can't tell anyone I did that, because if you do, I'll sue you." I reminded him of the limits about damaging. I worked with him to contain his rage. In the process of doing so, Ronnie pronounced, "I want to stay the way I am. It's my choice. All I have left is my will and my foster parents are taking that away from me, too. Just let me crawl into a corner and be safe." He sat down in a chair, curled up slightly, and cried for awhile. Then, he began hyperventilating until, gradually, he calmed himself down.

Ronnie silently refused to leave at the end of the session. I tried to offer that he could stay in a room down the hall until he felt able to leave, but he refused. He lay down on the couch and appeared to sleep. I sat with him in silence for forty-five minutes. At that point, I had to see another person. I told him that if he wanted me to, I would ask his foster parents if he could have the rest of the day off. He did not respond to that, but eventually he uncurled himself from his fetal position on the couch and left the room.

During the next few sessions, I again had one of the foster parents be nearby until I felt Ronnie was more stable. In one of those sessions, Ronnie was able to speak directly about finding out that his only other key relative was ill and might be dying. He was able to connect his feelings of vulnerability, helplessness, and rage about this with the previous week's rage-displacement episode in therapy. We talked of how hard it is to have things feel better but then to have other frightening things happen that we have no control over.

Also, Ronnie's fear of connection and loss were evidenced when he began insisting, "You have to fix me up. I'm not going to let you help me, though. It's your fault I'm upset. Therapy is like a glass ball with a cottage, water, and snow in it. It's like you shaking me up each week. I'm the snow that gets agitated." He continued the session with verbal aggression. He talked openly of how he used his violence as a way to get me to reject him. We explored how painful it was to experience all of these overwhelming feelings and to work them through in therapy.

Following this, Ronnie began the next session by verbally attacking and denigrating me. He expounded, "I made gallows for both of us to hang on, but I want to kick your chair out first." I spoke directly of my countertransference feelings at that point. I stated, "Sometimes your anger is frightening to me, Ronnie, as well as to you. I'm sorry I haven't told you that directly. Sometimes I have tried to handle my fear by detaching when I'm feeling unsafe to protect myself. I'm sorry I can't give you everything you need. I want to. I get sad and frustrated that I am unable to meet all of your needs. I know you struggle with these same feelings, also." He immediately calmed down and responded, "At least you're human too, now."

We discussed ways this was related to the active replication of experiences with his parents, his ambivalence, and human limitation. We talked about how he used the verbal attacks as a way to engage me. We proceeded to explore the need to discern the differences between caring and not caring, his demands that others care 100 percent or he decides they don't care, his refusal to communicate what would mean caring to him, and his detachment and difficulty trusting that anyone could be there for him. We used the analogy of him caring for his pigeons though he wasn't 100 percent a perfect caregiver. He said, "Why are you talking to me this way? You haven't talked to me this way for a long time." I acknowledged that I had not been able to give to him all that he needed due to my own struggles making it hard to be as available to him as I wanted.

Using my countertransference feelings along with interpretive exploration at this time seemed to contain and calm him. The sessions following this were less intense, with his making only occasional sarcastic comments about looking for ways to abuse me. He began talking about how much smarter than other kids he is and he looked to me for confirmation. This seemed to indicate some emerging narcissism, in which he was beginning to use me as a selfobject.

At one point, Ronnie said, "You're a fake. You can't say how life works, since you're not 80 years old. You don't know much more than me. You know more about some things than me. I know more about some things than you." We talked about the truth in these ideas. He was looking for ways to unify the splitting of the idealization and denigration.

In the fall of Ronnie's senior year, we discussed the relative value of different possible termination dates. We considered ending therapy in four months, when he turned 18. To do so would give him several months to see me around the home after termination until he left at graduation. Otherwise, if we continued sessions until he moved out of the home at graduation, it would be a more abrupt ending. He chose to set the ending of therapy at the earlier time.

A traumatic incident occurred several weeks following the setting of a termination date. One day, as we approached Ronnie's pigeon cage, he realized something was wrong. He ran up to the cage and yelled out that all his birds were dead. He was angry, but attempted to treat the situation pragmatically. I found tears running down my face. He said, "There's no point in getting upset. You just cry and get tired." He asked, "Why are you upset?" I responded, "Because they are a part of our lives. They are important to you and me. I'm sad and upset because you've lost more of your family." He seemed to ponder my response.

Then Ronnie proceeded to give me instructions to assist him in cleaning up the feathers, blood, and body parts. He was trying, agitatedly, to figure out how the birds had been killed, that is, by an animal or a person. At one point, he had me hold a gunny sack while he proceeded to drop body parts into it. He placed the beak of one pigeon between the fingers of both hands, moved it back and forth as if it were talking, and said, "Goodbye, Ronnie. Don't worry about us. We will be with your mother in heaven." I stood there choking on my feelings. I was still in shock, but he seemed to be staying detached. At one point, he instructed me to feed the few remaining birds. He declared, "Because, that's your job—to take care of the sick, hurting birds who are left without their family."

I sent a note of concern to Ronnie and called him during the following week to express my concern about his loss. At the next session he said, endearingly, "Hello, Shrink-i-poo. Are you still upset?" I mentioned that I still felt sad and angry. He wanted to know why I didn't just forget about it. I explained, "I need to let myself feel my feelings, so that the sadness will heal and leave the good memories, as well as the hard ones, of our times with your pigeons." He seemed pleased and was able to listen to what I said about resolving loss issues.

Ronnie expressed anger because the foster parents did not show more concern about the situation and because some people actually thought he might have killed the birds himself. He was pleased that I had sent him a card and was concerned. He said, "I wish I could make you feel better." This emerging concern for my feelings represents a reorganization into a new mode of relatedness. My emotional engagement in the loss was an important part of his process of working through his parents' deaths.

Year 7: Eighteen Years Old

Termination issues came more to the forefront during this time. He had only five months left before graduation and only two weeks of therapy. He talked about it being good that the birds were gone, because he wouldn't have a way to care for them after he left. He didn't want them left for others to care for, since they might not be cared for adequately. He was speaking of his own experience.

We walked back to the pigeon cage, talking about his leaving. I mentioned, "There have been a lot of changes since you've been here." He wanted to know, "Why did you say that?" I said, "I notice things like that when I or others are beginning to leave." He said, "I don't have anything to say about that, so you don't need to bring it up." I stated, "There are all sorts of ways to leave others." He responded, "Do you want me to stay in therapy longer so I can learn how to leave?" It was more of a statement than a question. By this time, we were back in the therapy room. He went over to the couch and curled up, stating, "I'm going to take a quick nap."

Two sessions later, we had our last session. He talked about everything but it being our last session. I sat silently at first, but tears began to trickle down my cheek. He asked, "What are you crying for?" I responded, "I'm sad because I won't see you any more in the same way. I will miss you." He began to show internalization of the therapist's role. He asked, "Will you be okay? If you need to talk to me you can have my phone number." He reminded me he would be all right. I said, "I know, but I'm still sad." Several times that day, he came by to check on me and seemed pleased that I was still grieving.

DISCUSSION: THE COUNTERTRANSFERENCE

With Ronnie, I had found myself in an emotional kaleidoscope: I wanted to protect him from some of the hurt, abuse, and lack of understanding from others—to be the "Good Mother." I wanted to escape from him when I felt threatened and intruded on by his aggressive, abusive behaviors. I felt compelled by him to reject him in a hostile, abusive way. I felt pressured by his insistence that I be the perfectly bonded, symbiotic mother. His frequent demands that I rescue him—fix things up for him—left me feeling helpless and frustrated. I found my own ego functioning pressed and at times regressed. At times, my own identity was pushed to fluctuate between being an "all-good" therapist when he was responding delightfully, and an "all-bad" therapist when his rage at me would become so intense that I felt overwhelmed and inadequate. All of these countertransference feelings were part of the replication process. The pain of the rage episodes left me dreading the times, which I knew would come, in which I would be placed in the "bad object" position again. I even had thoughts of quitting my profession as a therapist, so I would not have to be so emotionally overloaded!

Feeling these many things was painful, but I needed to experience them in order to be empathetically available to learn the unconscious aspects of Ronnie's life and then work them out with him. I needed to feel what he felt, so we could begin talking about his feelings and finding ways to move him out of his destructive symbiotic mode of relatedness.

In the process of therapy, Ronnie created the conditions for me to experience his aggressive, abusive, and inadequate father and mother through the active replication process. As I reflected, interpreted, and replicated with him how his anger was a way to communicate and connect with others but sabotaged his need for closeness, he began to be able to speak more directly about his needs and feelings. He began to find more effective ways to take care of those aspects of himself.

Ronnie still has a challenge ahead of him in navigating through the pain and patterns that still cause him problems at times. However, much progress toward individuation occurred during the course of therapy. He was able to resolve his grief about the death of his parents on a deeper level. His ego structures developed to the point where he was able to manage his affects more effectively. He was able to form more positive connections with others. Although, as Ronnie put it, his "scars" were still there, there was much healing that occurred around the pain and trauma.

Participating with Ronnie during these eight years of his life has provided me the opportunity to resolve some of my own experiences with loss to a greater degree. In experiencing and managing his affects, I too had to learn to know and to respond to my own in more profound ways. The intensity and duration of merging with him symbiotically and moving out of the symbiosis to promote individuation definitely replicated the "mothering" process. I am grateful that Ronnie has been a part of my life, and that he was able to show me about his life by replicating it emotionally in our interactions together.

Even at the end of treatment, in his aloofness over the death of the pigeons and his loss of me, he succeeded in showing me how it felt for him to have someone who he knew loved him leave. This is what Freud refers to as turning passive trauma into active victory, what Anna Freud called identification with the aggressor, and what Hedges calls active replication of the symbiotic scenario.

Though the content of our sessions often centered on what could be recalled—the abuse, the illnesses, and the deaths—throughout the process, I was aware we were jointly creating an interactive narration about what it is like to have a schizophrenic father and a mother who loves you but cannot stay affectively in tune. By the time we enacted our last leave-taking, we both understood the elusive features of his primary love bond. It was work that took the cooperation of two.

Editor's Postscript

We could not hope for a more beautiful or moving account to bring into focus the ways in which countertransference can be interpretively used to liberate a person from the bondage of a skewed character structure and a history of traumatic loss. We see the "terrible twos" quality of relating that regularly marks the relinquishment of the symbiotic bond and a few touches of narcissistic self-aggrandizement that move Ronnie on his path to more ordinary forms of relatedness. Jolyn even describes several instances of mother–father–child triangulation that had begun. This story makes clear the long time required for reparative work and the deep and intense emotional involvement from the therapist necessary to heal the wounds of being an emotional orphan.

ized harmony and love

13

Replicating Incest

Gayle Trenberth

Editor's Comments

Mahler (1968) has borrowed from biology the term *symbiosis* to describe the intrapsychic (internal) state in which self and other are experienced as a single unit reciprocally interacting with each other. Little (1981) has felt that this metaphor implies two bodies interacting and has proposed the even stronger term *basic unity* to indicate that the origins of human psychic life spring from a psychological sense of unity that the speaker experiences as one. Researchers in the field of infancy have criticized Mahler's term on the basis of laboratory observations of mothers and babies, which demonstrate that infants have a robust sense of self and independence from birth, albeit a rudimentary one. In common clinical parlance Mahler's term has come to be used to describe some sort of pathological dependency, which characterizes "low level," "primitive," or "borderline psychotic" states. Alternatively, clinicians seem to conceptualize a working or "good" symbiotic relationship as some sort of idealized, beatific harmony and love between mother and child, which the listener and speaker are striving to establish in their relationship since in infancy the client presumably experienced a faulty symbiosis.

These varying usages and criticisms of the term *symbiosis* fail to grasp Mahler's original explicit (psychoanalytic) intent to describe the subjective psychological (intrapsychic) state of an infant. These usages and criticisms spring from a social psychology (objective) point of view in which one is looking from the outside at two bodies interacting. This view, which may be easier to grasp than the intrapsychic view, misses Mahler's stated intent and weakens the use of the term for psychoanalytic purposes.

I follow Mahler's original intent and use *symbiosis* not to describe a state between two people or a state of blissful at-oneness. Rather, I have considered the age period of roughly 4 to 24 months to be a time when the growing child becomes inculcated with his or her basic sense of human reality. The child is organizing experiences and memory around some rudimentary sense of me-ness and other-ness that are not altogether distinct. We know that primary communication is established by means of interpersonal interaction and emotional exchange. Memories of this symbiotic period can be expected to be recorded in somatic structure and interpersonal emotional responsiveness patterns. I speak of *scenarios* as stylized modes of interaction that can be observed to occur regularly between the experiencing listener and the experiencing speaker in the analytic situation. (See Hedges [1983, pp. 165–196] for an extended discussion of scenarios and an explication of a series of typical scenarios encountered in borderline personality organization.) As a listening device a scenario is defined as an observable representation of a pattern of self- and other-relatedness established early in life and continuing to be lived out with others in and out of the analytic setting. I have spoken of *replicating transference* to identify those characterological scenarios that are played out emotionally or relived interpersonally in the course of analysis (Hedges 1983, 1992). The ways in which the speaker engages the listener tend toward an actual replication of a stylized emotional interaction thought to stem from the symbiotic or characterological level of human development.

In the following vignette you will see the extent to which therapists are often called upon to step out of their accustomed role and to be present while a person explores his or her personal interaction patterns deeply buried in what Bollas (1987) has called the "unthought known." The therapist's strategic emotional involvement here is seen to facilitate the emergence of replicated transference scenarios so that they can be lived, spoken, and analyzed.

REPLICATING INCEST

In thinking about using case material to examine the utilization of the countertransference in the therapy of symbiotic states, I realized this account needed to be very personal. It needed to be the personal story of two people being together, with all levels of our conscious and unconscious minds/bodies resonating together in order to *know* together what needed to be known. So this account is the personal story of Gayle and Benna during the time of our therapy when the symbiotic link or scenario was in full replication between us. Benna, a young, single working woman whom I saw several times weekly for a number of years, agreed to allow her journals of the therapy to be used in presenting our story.

Writing this piece has been difficult. Over the course of six weeks I found myself putting off the reading of notes and journals, thinking about declining the offer to write about this time with Benna. Finally I realized I dreaded reimmersing myself in that period of time when I felt violated and violating, helpless and powerful, loved and raped, raping and loving. The emotional world between Benna and myself was chaotic during this time, and very difficult for either one of us to endure.

Benna began seeing me in the spring of 1982. At that time I was a licensed psychologist in training to become a bioenergetics analyst, and using many body-oriented techniques. My background had been existential/humanistic, with some psychodynamic influence. When Benna began to see me, I was using a therapeutic framework that engaged the patient emotionally and physically.

Benna began the first session stating that she wanted to explore issues around incest with her brothers and her relationships with men. A 29-year-old woman who had never dated and never had sex outside of the incest, she had crushes on men who were either health providers or authority figures. She was positive that the incest was prohibiting her from having actual relationships with men. Benna had five years of college and was within a few units of graduating, but showed no interest in returning to school. She was articulate and seemed very intelligent. Her boss, for whom she worked as a secretary, had encouraged her to seek therapy due to her manic behavior on the job.

She had undergone extensive therapy in the past, and had been hospitalized two times for suicide attempts in her early 20s. She had taken antidepressants in the past and found them ineffective. As she talked in that initial session, she had an anticipation and eagerness that caught my interest; I did not sense any mania or depression. I felt an excitement about working with her, which at the time I attributed to her psychological savvy and her willingness to be in therapy. Benna's journal comments about the first two sessions were: "Initial visit—liked her" and "Scary, but really wonderful."

Within a month, I was trying various body-oriented techniques. Bioenergetics, founded by Alexander Lowen, is the study of the human personality in terms of the energetic processes of the body. Lowen hypothesized that character structure was not only in the psychology of an individual but also structured in the body. The body's available energy, and how that energy becomes constricted or expanded in the musculature, is a mirror of the psychological defenses the individual created to handle the early childhood environment. I saw Benna's character structure as masochistic, using Lowen's typologies. As described in *Bioenergetics* (Lowen 1975), the masochistic character shows a submissive attitude in his or her outward behavior, and is inwardly hostile, spiteful, and negative with feelings of superiority. According to this view the masochist's body is fully charged energetically, but the charge is held. The musculature is holding aggression and self-assertion back from expression.

The constrictions in Benna's musculature and the incest material she had presented had me convinced that we needed to work on her expressing her anger. I would suggest various exercises to free the muscular holding in her back and arms, and she would do them in a mechanical, disassociated way. I remember the way she would hit a couch with a tennis racket, holding her breath, not making a sound, jaw locked, toes curled on the carpet, clearly doing it for me. There was no cathartic expression. I felt some frustration, but thought that she must be very frightened and that we could work on the muscular holding until her resistance was reduced.

By the third month, Benna was writing in her journal such entries as "Hold me!" and "So much rage, but no words—I need you!" I did not know about these feelings as Benna felt she needed to keep them secret. She was beginning to call between sessions, and to ask for extra sessions on occasion. She began to talk about her fears of "regressing," of becoming a little girl in our work. She began alternating between needing me and wanting to be "little" with me, and hating herself and me for those feelings. She would push me away, then reach out to me. Her insistence and need were so great that by the autumn of that first year I was holding Benna (in bioenergetic fashion), or she would lay her head on a blanket in my lap. Then I would get calls between sessions that she was quitting therapy. She was now coming twice a week, with extra sessions here and there. I was fairly calm during this time, staying warm but clinical.

Looking back I see this first year and the next one as the time when Benna and I came together—first as two "objects," two people wanting to trust, two subjective worlds. We slowly became human to one another, and then began the replication of the symbiotic dance. The overall theme of this time was around needing me: Was it okay? Could I tolerate her need? Could she tolerate her need? And underneath that theme was another: Can she get me to love her, and when I do love her, can she feel it? Benna seemed to feel that my loving her, if she could really feel it, would be the resolution of her childhood loss.

Benna's loss was severe. She had a seemingly narcissistic/borderline mother, who would react with anger and violence to any moves Benna made toward emotional separation. Her mother had the attitude that the girls in the family, Benna and a younger sister, were there to "service" the men in the family, the father and four brothers. For Benna, servicing the "boys" became sexual when she was 5 years old. The incest had a sadistic quality to it. The father, in particular, was violent in his sexual use of Benna. Benna longed for a relationship in which she felt loved, safe, and contained, yet she feared that connection tremendously. She felt that being loved would drive her crazy. Love as experienced in Benna's family *was* crazy. Her father was violent, and her mother would cling to the child one moment and then react with rage the next. The rhythm of the "Mommy and me" dyad was chaotic. Love was always chaos. Love offered today could only have that same chaotic rhythm, or so Benna feared.

Two years into the therapy, Benna was calling me twice a day during the week (or more), and once a day on the weekends. She was still seeing me twice a week and often needed more contact. There was a definite sense of her intense need for this level of contact. Sometimes that contact would be in the form of waiting for me between sessions, to have a word with me or to get a hug. Sometimes she would sit in the waiting room for hours watching me come in and out of the office. She would watch me from her car in the parking lot of the office. She often seemed frightened or desperate during these contacts. Although I did not know it at the time, she had found out where I lived and where my parents lived. She made it her business to know quite a bit about how I spent my time, whom I saw for my personal therapy, and who my friends were. As these things came to light I was amazed at her detective work. I was also beginning to feel watched and invaded.

Invasion became a way of our relating together. I felt that I invaded Benna in the sessions frequently. I invaded her with my words, with my questions, with my bioenergetic exercises. She spent much of the time in sessions silent and unwilling to talk, as I poked and prodded. She would begin sentences and not finish them, leaving me hanging, until I poked and prodded again. She would look at me and say, "You know what it is, why do I have to say it?" or "Can't you guess at what I'm thinking?" I would become annoyed, frustrated, or bored with the silences. I felt like the violator, trying to force something out of her or even to force myself into her world. In between sessions I would receive 10-, 15-, and 20-minute messages of her talking, and crying—and, yes, whining. It wasn't that she was in danger or without social supports. Rather, a style, a mode of being with and without Mother, was being lived out, represented in this manner. My life came to feel constantly interrupted by these calls. I began to approach my answering machine with dread. And yet she seemed in such emotional pain that I didn't feel I could set limits on the calling, at least not at this time. Those recorded calls were also often my only source of information from Benna, since the sessions were basically silent.

Looking back, I realize that the whiny, dreadful chaos of the "Mommy and me" dyad had been re-created between us. I was filled with dread, frustration, and confusion; I felt overwhelmed, angry, at a loss, and afraid, all of which needed to be held back because of the intensity of Benna's pain. I began to feel my own musculature holding in, holding back, all of my emotional life being subtly stifled. This must have been Benna's experience as a child.

In session, when there was communication, the content of the therapy was around the incest memories. Benna would begin to report having disturbing experiences outside the sessions (seeing images of people, feeling bugs crawling on her). These symptoms became our red flag that a memory was trying to surface. She would demand that something be done to give her relief. She did not want medication from me; she wanted protection. I would have her lie down, relax, imagine the scene, and her body would abreact as she reviewed her incest memories. She would leave the session distraught, wanting to die, hating herself, hating me. In allowing her to remember and abreact I felt I was "doing it" to her, as if I were raping her. Then with the flood of phone calls and notes about how terrible she felt, I would feel helpless and invaded—as if we both were victims. There were a few times when she felt suicidal and took pills, and twice she mutilated herself slightly. Then I felt raped. I did love her, and to have her harm herself was torturous for me. Finally, I was very angry and confronted her by saying that if she continued to hurt herself in these ways, I couldn't be with her, it hurt me too much. To my surprise, she felt relieved, loved, and was willing to abide by some "rules" we laid down around hurting herself. It seemed that the intensity of my reaction gave her a sense of contact, connection, and containment.

In the fall of 1984, I entered the training program at the Newport Psychoanalytic Institute to further my understanding in object relations. My work at the institute began to provide me with a theoretical frame with which to understand my experiences with Benna. I began to see her presentation of the incest memories not merely, or even significantly, as the recovery of memory, but more importantly as Benna's way of relating to me. Later I realized that reliving those memories through our interaction and the resulting torrent of feeling was her vehicle to re-create the symbiosis with me in a way we both could come to experience and understand.

In October of 1984, Benna wrote in her journal: "At this moment I am having a difficult time because I feel like I want *all* of her attention, *all* of the time. I want her now; not for any specific reason, but because I want it." At the time she wrote this, she was reexperiencing a particularly violent body memory, and for the first time came to believe that her father had had sex with her. She was devastated by the belief/knowledge. There followed a torrent of suicidal feeling, many phone calls, notes, and waiting-room contacts. At one point she asked if I thought she'd made up this memory about her father. I asked her what her motivation would be to make it up. "To get more attention? You already have a lot of my attention." Benna was stunned. She did not experience the extent to which I was available to her. And I was stunned—how could I do more?

In January 1985, without my knowledge, Benna found out that I had sold my home and was moving. She came to our session angry and withdrawn and demanded, "What do you want to do?" I commented that she looked angry, and she said, "I don't want to talk, I'm tired of this." I asked if there was a way to be with me without feeling forced to do something she didn't want to do. Her response was, "I don't want anything from you, I'm tired of wanting, I'm tired of being so transparent." By this time I felt very puzzled, and I looked at her questioningly. She looked at me and said, "Why don't you just tell me?" And then, "Are you going to move away?" She began to cry. She said, "I feel like I'm losing my comfort, knowing where you are." I explained that I was relocating nearby. She was relieved but still distressed that she had lost a reliable fix on me.

Benna wrote the following in her journal:

January 20, 1985

> I just want to get a chance to put some of this down, to help me to sort it out a bit, so that I can get some perspective on what I am doing, how I am acting out, lashing out, and probably hurting myself more than I am hurting Gayle.
>
> What is, exactly, the issue? Well, that question in itself is impossible. Nothing about what we have been doing the last three years is exact. Nothing is just what it is, everything is enmeshed and tangled and intertwined. Nothing just exists by itself. What most probably prompted my reactions, the event that I am most reacting to, is the selling of Gayle's house, which means she will be moving. That's where the facts, the exactness, ends. This is where stupid feelings take over. The fact is that I probably will find out where she lives even if she doesn't tell me. I know that I am good at finding those kinds of things out. So, let's talk about the feelings then. I feel horrible. Too vague, too general, Gayle would say. Okay, I am feeling that I am losing her. I am having to face that I don't have her, I am not as big a part of her life as I want to be, and that hurts, and she knows how deeply that hurts, but she isn't willing to do anything to change that. In other words, she is

not going to love me more just to make me feel better, which leads directly to the other issue, it probably wouldn't matter anyway, how intensely she loved me, it will never make up for the terror, pain, betrayal, shame and other shit of my life.

So, what am I doing . . . I am trying to get a reaction from her, and she won't react. I want to hurt her like I am hurting, and the only way I know how to do that is to hurt myself, and I am not willing to do that at this point in time. I also know that my withdrawing, for whatever reasons, makes it difficult for her. At this time it feels like I am pulling back for a few different reasons. (1) To protect myself—I perceive her moving as potential for a great loss, face it, it will be a loss, as she said, a bigger chunk of her life will no longer be so readily available to me, something I used to use to comfort myself is no longer there. (2) I am angry with her and I will show her, I won't talk—no, I plan to talk while in her office, but I will not call anymore, I will cut her out of my life as much as possible. It won't be hard, it will become as easy as it is to be away from Pat and Rhea. It hurt a lot initially, but now I know it's not such a big deal. People come and people go. (3) I am pulling back in response to the feeling that I am getting very close to something that feels like it could shatter my entire world. I *know* I have had that feeling before, I know that the memory when I felt like my dad wanted me to die made me feel like my world was going to end, and it didn't, so I know that no matter what the memory may be it probably won't be so bad . . . but there is always the tiniest seed of doubt.

Benna's solution to my move was to call later that evening and cancel her session scheduled for the following Thursday. I called back to say, "I want to see you even if you don't want to see me." She said she had been trying to shut down, that she felt so dependent on me. Not knowing where I was going to move had scared her. I told her that I wanted to explore her feelings more, but that if she really wanted to know where I was moving by the time I moved, I would tell her. She sighed, and said, "I was afraid you'd let me go."

Under the threat of separation generated by my moving, another cycle of pain/chaos/dread began. It reestablished our "connection."

The next Thursday, Benna had a horrific memory during our session about the incest with her brothers. She called during the next three days, sometimes angry, sometimes in pain. By Sunday morning, Benna called saying she wanted to die. She said the memory made her feel discarded and empty, and she couldn't find any reason to live. After we talked awhile, she said she wanted to commit to not hurting herself until tomorrow but that felt too long, so I suggested I call her back that evening.

I found myself restless all day with a sense of dread, trying to decide if she should be hospitalized, feeling responsible for her life. When I called her back, she said she still felt very suicidal, so we discussed hospitalization. She said her previous experiences in the hospital had frightened her, and she did not want to be hospitalized again. She agreed to call a friend over to spend the night with her, and called me back thirty minutes later to tell me the friend had arrived.

In the next session Benna continued with her memory, which involved her brother threatening to kill her with a knife. Benna said, "Why didn't he do it, why didn't he finish it?" I said, "I don't think it was about killing you, Benna, I think he wanted to feel he had an impact on someone . . . he could feel real by scaring you." She said, "We aren't very different then." I saw this as my chance to interpret: "You never felt real to your parents, and when you threaten to hurt yourself, it is to feel real to me. If you're real to me, you'll exist. Perhaps this is how your mother felt real . . . by scaring you." Benna began to look "removed" at my interpretation, and left the session seemingly disconnected. However, in the next session she was very open to the contact between us, putting her head in my lap, scanning my face like an infant, eyes open and connected. She said, "If I died I wouldn't know stuff, would I, like your touching my head?" She seemed peaceful and content.

In February, Benna and I went through yet another cycle of crisis, chaos, dread, need, confrontation, and finally connection. At one point, she left this message:

> Hi, it's Benna. I'm sorry to be so stupid. It occurs to me all the whining, and all the burning myself, and all the attention in the world isn't going to make a difference. I can be as stupid and horrible as humanly possible, and it's not going to help. The problem is that it feels like nothing's going to help. I can't see how I'm ever going to be a real person. I don't know why people care. Anyone loving me doesn't make sense to me, and I'm so tired. It's hard to keep hanging on to something I can't believe most of the time. Goodbye.

Feeling alarmed, I called her back and she reassured me she was not going to hurt herself but wanted me to know how hard it was just to exist, how "unreal" she felt. The metacommunication was that I was not providing a response that made her feel real, real in relation to me.

By this time in the work, such conversations made me feel tossed on a storm of violent feelings and experiences. When I thought of Benna, which I did all the time because of the constant turmoil, I felt frightened; I had a sense of dread, not knowing where I stood, while also feeling responsible for her life or death. At times I felt angry, and wanted to scream "Stop it!" I felt battered and out of control of the therapy.

When I sought consultation, my supervisor suggested that simply remembering the incest was not the issue. Benna was trying to create a bond with me. The only bond she knew as love, as Mother, was rape. The supervisor also suggested that much of her behavior was coming out of a need to "track" me, the way an infant tracks the mother with his/her eyes. He suggested that I set telephone appointment times at my convenience and call her every day for five minutes just to connect, to touch base. I was appalled at the idea. It felt like I would be drawn further into chaos, and the sense of being responsible would become enormous.

He pointed out that I was having daily contact anyway. The erratic contact was clearly a burden for both of us, and some regularity and limitation might help me to feel more in charge of the contact, safer in my role.

In early March I proposed the idea to Benna in the following way:

> I've been thinking about the tracking you've been doing—wanting to know where I am—and was trying to think of a way to meet that need. I was thinking about scheduling a daily five minute phone call where we could chat or talk or just connect. In these five minutes we can talk about anything—music you're listening to, what's on your mind, what you're doing, what I'm doing. It doesn't have to be serious. It's just for us to have the connection. I'm saying this because I don't want you to think you have to come up with some struggle to tell me about. If it's there, we'll talk about it, if not, we'll talk about whatever.

Her response was euphoric. She wrote in her journal:

> I had called Gayle on Tuesday and asked if I could see her on that day. I was feeling very despondent and couldn't even talk, I just wanted her to hold me. She said that she was not able to see me on Tuesday, but would see me at noon on Wednesday. I wasn't sure that I wanted to see her on Wednesday, but she insisted. Sure enough, on Wednesday I was still feeling like I wanted to be not in this world. When I got to Gayle's office, I couldn't talk, I could barely keep my eyes open. It was scary at one time because I was lying down, and I kept feeling like I was becoming part of the couch. Gayle made me run my fingers over the cushions and feel how different that felt than my skin, but I kept feeling like I was disappearing into the couch, so I sat up and leaned on Gayle instead. I kept feeling like I wasn't feeling anything, so I asked Gayle to talk. She said, good, because she had something she wanted to talk about. She said that she had been doing some thinking and felt that I really needed more contact, and I certainly couldn't afford to see her more often, so she had decided that we would talk on the

phone every day. I could only talk for 5 minutes, and I could talk about whatever I wanted. I didn't have to be upset or talk about "heavy" stuff, mostly it is a chance for each of us to find out where the other is, what kind of day they had, what they have planned for the day ahead. She will call me, even on Saturday and Sunday!!! I kept saying: "Are You Sure?!" I felt that there was no way I could get any more unless I got it myself and kept it hidden, and now here is this woman giving me more of herself, showing me that I can be close to her, I don't have to do it in secret. I am awestruck. . . .

We are dealing with something different now. Suddenly I am catapulted into infancy. I don't know how I got there. Suddenly everything is different. The explanations I used to rely on no longer hold true. Sensations are different, and nothing makes sense. I don't know anything about this phase so I am totally at Gayle's mercy. How did this happen . . . ?

The euphoria wore off quickly, and Benna began to experience profound distress. I was offering her a different form of (symbiotic) connection with me, no longer based on rape/terror/chaos. The "Mommy and me" connection that Benna knew and understood might die. If we could experience a different way of interacting, it meant the loss of the way in which Benna organized her sense of self, and her sense of the "other." Her old scenario had been successfully confronted but now Benna was terrified. She wrote in her journal:

March 16, 1985

I haven't been writing as much as I would really like to, there is an awful lot to record, all kinds of new things, words, thoughts, feelings pop out when I am with Gayle that I hadn't the faintest idea roamed inside me at all. Most of it has been given impetus by this new twist in my relationship with Gayle, a twist that I have craved, yet at the same time it scares the shit out of me. I have spent the last two or three sessions explaining to her how dangerous it is and how she is deliberately throwing caution to the wind, so to speak, and leading me to my death. She maintains that we are ready to face whatever it is that we need to face, she acknowledges that indeed, it is dangerous, but that I am able to go to that place now. She says that she is confident that she is ready to go there, and that she watches me look at her and track her and sees some trust and peace in my eyes from time to time and feels that I am also able to do what must be done. I explain everything a million times. I tell her that there are three basic things about my existence: (1) That there is nothing pure in me. . . . I absolutely don't have any idea what is real and what isn't real. I am not just sad, most likely my sadness is contrived in order to manipulate whatever situation I happen to be in at any given time.

NOTHING JUST IS. (2) To love me is a very dangerous prospect. I will make you crazy. You will do awful things to me because you loved me and it made you crazy. (3) If you love me it is dangerous because I will die. It is the point of origin for me. I love you, you love me, I want, you give to me, I want more, you give more, I want even more, it is too much, you turn away and leave because I am too much, I die because when you leave you take away everything that keeps me alive. Those are the three things that are central to knowing what I am about.

On Thursday I begged Gayle to stop calling me. I sobbed and pleaded to stop before it was too late. She won't, I don't think she has any concept of how exceedingly terrified I am.

After Benna experienced that neither one of us was destroyed by the nightly contact, both of us began to enjoy the connection. Sometimes we talked about serious things, sometimes just chatted, sometimes we listened to each other breathe for five minutes. Sanity returned to the therapy. Benna and I kept confronting the theme that rape is love, but now Benna *talked* about the longing to do something to herself or generate an internal or external crisis to feel close to me, rather than actually doing it. We kept exploring different ways for her to let me in, accept and feel the relationship. Her activity of recovering memories took a back seat for the next three years while she worked on an integration of self and her relationship to me. Later, when we returned to the memories, she could experience her grief and anger without the emotional disintegration that was her clarion call to mother love.

After a year and a half of calling every day, both Benna and I recognized that she no longer needed (or even wanted) the routine calls. We had established a new form of relating and now she was beginning to separate and come into her own being. Tentatively, experimentally, we changed the "rules." I realized how the daily contact had enabled an intimacy and knowing of each other that was profound, and that I would miss the daily connection and feel my own loss at "not knowing" about Benna in a daily way. It was a bittersweet feeling—separation, loss, and excitement at the next phase of our work.

The story of Benna and Gayle continued through many twists and turns. However, the experiences, the engagement, and the learning that occurred during the time recounted here remained powerful for both of us. Benna has progressed dramatically in her work, and is now employed as a vice president in a large company. She is dating occasionally, enjoying relationships more, and exhibiting no acting out of her earlier concerns.

Editor's Postscript

The portion of therapy reported by Trenberth here is full of trials for the therapist as well as for the client. Chaos, threat, and dread in the countertransference signaled the replication of the symbiotic transference, complete with its intrusion, incest, and rape themes. Timely and empathic speaking of the countertransference served to interpret the structure of relatedness this woman has lived with all of her life. As with all preverbal psychic structures, interpretation entails more than mere verbalization of the relational dynamic. The preverbal scenario from the realm of the unthought known has to be somehow lived out by two in order to be known and then to be interpretively confronted by the listener. The interpretive work is not complete until the speaker has grasped the nature of the mode of interaction that he or she has retained and found some way of relinquishing in the here and now in relation to the listener. This giving up a lifelong (survival) relatedness mode always feels like a form of death or suicide to the speaker and is usually represented and interpretable as such.

An interesting feature of Trenberth's account is the appearance of "recovered memories" just at the point that the mutilating, raping transference was becoming established. For the therapist to have gotten sidetracked from studying the therapeutic relationship into the progressive elaboration of memories would have been to collude with the resistance to reexperiencing in the here and now the transferentially horrifying chaos and intensity of threat with the therapist. When the therapist assures Benna that she isn't moving anywhere and insists on having brief contact every day to ensure the continuity of the relationship, there is simultaneous relief and terror of what the new contact may mean to be experienced. Predictably, the production of recovered memories drops off as the daily relationship and its fears can be experienced and processed reliably by the two. I have written extensively on the phenomena of recovered memories in psychotherapy, concluding that, apart from abuse that can be fairly readily recalled, the painstaking elaboration and expansion of memories is a different process (Hedges 1994a). A century of psychoanalytic research into memories recovered in therapy points toward infantile strain trauma leaving scars that cannot be remembered in ordinary ways through pictures and stories. But the person knows something dreadful happened to him or her long ago that cannot be readily recalled. In therapy one enters an altered state in which one's best dream-like unconscious imaginative creativity goes to work to generate pictorial and narrational metaphors of what the intrusion, deprivation, neglect, or strain trauma in infancy was like. The need for such imaginative constructions in order to express deep experience diminishes when the speaker and listener in therapy are able to move the locus of experience from the inner stage of dream time into the actual drama of the ongoing therapeutic relationship, where it can be known with even greater clarity by two through mutual transference and countertransference experiencing. This brief account of a particularly difficult portion of a lengthy working through therapeutic process stands in stark contrast to the simplified recovery approach of "remember, be validated, and seek redress" that is currently in vogue and is leaving so many therapists seriously at risk for malpractice charges.

14

Being As If Without Skin

Anthony G. Brailow

Editor's Comments

Professional listeners frequently have had the uncanny experience of feeling that their mind is somehow being read by the speaker. While each instance of perceived mind-reading needs careful study, it would appear that it is the least developed speakers or the least developed parts of their personalities that connect in deep, intuitive ways with the emotional life of the listener. The quality and content of the emotional response in the listener often gives important leads toward understanding the experience of the speaker.

In the following set of events we see that the listener's otherwise private life comes under scrutiny by the speaker—not because she realistically wants to torment him, but because skinlessness is a part of her psychic experience, which she has no words for. She must show him herself by how she relates to him—by doing to him what was done to her, by showing him how it feels to be "as if without skin."

All manner of variations in interpersonal boundaries manifest themselves in the analytic situation. If the listener merely views attempted intrusions into his or her private sphere as provocations, as a nuisance, or as symptoms against which to establish firm limits and boundaries, then an important feature of the analysis may be overlooked. To ignore countertransference stirrings that arise in relation to pressure on the listener's sense of boundary is to look deliberately away from the material being presented.

Strategic emotional involvement in instances of boundary pressures entails coming to feel the nature of the intrusions and then interpreting by speaking in an empathic manner the nature of the feelings being stirred up. This process does not represent a personal disclosure on the part of the listener, but rather constitutes the interpretive work with the symbiotic scenario. How to proceed with this kind of work is illustrated in the following report.

BEING AS IF WITHOUT SKIN[1]

I awoke with my mind preoccupied with how I was going to get through the day of seeing patients without burdening them with my own distress. The night before I had told my wife I wanted a separation. I wanted to conceal my pain so as not to interfere or block what my patients needed to work with. I had a session scheduled with my own therapist early in the day, which would help. In particular my thoughts went to the last session of the day I would have with Sally. She could "read me," that is, my moods, thoughts, and feelings so well—often before I was conscious of them myself. I searched for some way to prevent that from occurring. Of course being the professional I am, I told myself that my concern was for her so as not to intrude on or to interrupt Sally's free associations—to maintain the "blank screen" at all costs.

However, I now realize it was also to protect me. I didn't want to be invaded, to have my private emotions and thoughts "known" before I wanted to share them.

I had my own therapy session. I did my catharting and, feeling some relief, I steeled myself for the day of sessions with patients that awaited me. I did quite well most of the day, setting aside my own preoccupations and staying connected to my patients. But then Sally arrived. We entered my office and as we were exchanging greetings and sitting down, Sally exclaimed: "Oh my God! Something awful is happening to you." Assuming my best empathic stance, I responded, "I appreciate your concern and awareness. I am going through some personal changes that are quite disruptive and painful, but I will be able to handle them satisfactorily and be just fine." She was clearly hurt by what she experienced as my rebuff saying, "Oh, excuse me, I am going where I am not wanted."

At that moment I realized the foolhardiness of my efforts at "protecting her" and the deception I was trying to foist on us both, which she could clearly see. It was inevitable that Sally was going to know of my distress, verbalize it, and want me to respond not necessarily with the facts but to the reality that she could plainly see. The only way she could respond was to "know." Because for her we were one. We existed together in the room

---

1. Other casework with Sally is discussed at length in Hedges 1992, pp. 309–352.

as if there were nothing separating us—no barriers, no interpersonal distance, not even skin. This has been her persistent experience of me. What was so damaging about what she experienced as the deception and the rebuff was not that I would or would not tell her what the facts were with me, but that it wasn't her I was protecting but myself, from the continual invasion of myself I had to experience in order to relate to her. My emotional experience with her had been for some time now that of sitting in the consulting room two hours a week as if there were no skin protecting me, containing me. Her panic was not that I wasn't sharing, per se, but that I was masking my true feelings in a cloak of what she had come to call "acting the professional." Further, she would often fear that I would be so consumed with my own issues that I would not be able to listen to her—that she would feel "there isn't room for me."

By acknowledging the deception and confronting the dilemma before us openly with Sally, contact was reestablished and therapy could proceed including addressing her concerns about my personal life intruding and not allowing room for Sally's and my work together.

I want now to further elaborate on my wish to protect myself from the sense of intrusion and invasion I often experienced in our work together and the way in which my cloaking it as "acting professional," was a replication of the way in which her mother and the new baby, Sally, related. To do this it is necessary to provide some background information. Sally is a married woman in her early forties whom I have been seeing for five years twice weekly. Her presenting symptoms related to a long-term depression that had reemerged relative to marital conflict, struggles with her children, and a general sense of complete dissatisfaction with her life and herself. She was born with a facial disfigurement covering most of one side of her face. She wore extensive heavy special makeup to hide the disfigurement. She further revealed a history of repeated abuse in the form of inappropriate and loose limits around sexual behavior by her parents and being fondled by her grandfather over a period of several years.

Sally had become quite adept at hiding her birthmark, which at the outset of therapy was not immediately apparent to me. Over time she began to discuss a secret she wanted to share with me but was terrified of disclosing. Eventually the secret became the birthmark which she would describe as a deformity. She would describe herself as not being normal—as an "alien not belonging to this world." In session after session she would use words to describe herself like, "abnormal," "defective," "deformed." I found myself feeling increasingly uncomfortable and angry with a sense of sorrow and hurt that she could only see a small part of who she was. As she would describe and discuss herself with great conviction and belief in these terms, I began, just as firmly, to confront these perceptions and attempted to point out how we all have handicaps of one sort or another. At times, I would become quite distressed at what felt to me to be such a distorted, painful, and negative self-concept. I desperately wanted to help this patient free herself from the pain of feeling as if she were deformed, when in my mind she really wasn't.

Frustrated at my inability to help this woman find a more "real" self concept, I sought consultation in a countertransference study group I belonged to. As I presented the case in group I found myself stumbling anxiously over the words *deformed* and *deformity* and getting angry as I described her intransigence in maintaining her negative self concept. I had to ask what was my anxiety over these words? What did my anger and frustration conceal? It became clear to me that just as desperately and firmly as Sally was trying to describe for me the reality of her world, I was trying to deny and conceal it. Not to do so would require acknowledging the pain and discomfort one has at confronting a person with some physical or other abnormality. Neither the wish to stare nor the impulse to turn away are acceptable if we are to respond directly and humanly. The group began speculating about what it must have been like for her mother, the first person who saw Sally after she was born with a visible defect. A working hypothesis arose from group discussion that my anxiety and denial where a replication of what her mother may have experienced when first engaging with Sally.

The next session with Sally I shared with her my new understanding by acknowledging that her reality is that she is deformed and abnormal. I still remember the hesitation and fluttering heart I felt as I uttered those words. Her secret was not that she had a birthmark or birth defect per se. Her secret was that she knew she was deformed and abnormal but that she was not permitted to say it. She always had to act as though she weren't, and as though people didn't notice or were not turned away by it—even though she knew they were. After sitting together and acknowledging Sally's world and all the feelings about it, the forbidden secret could begin to unfold, the trauma could begin to heal, and the possibility of a new life, a new way of being even if still hidden from awareness, could begin.

The dilemma with which I began this chapter was resolved in one sense by the open admission of the deception and my willingness to understand that to maintain connectedness with this woman required that I allow myself to be vulnerable to what to me felt like invasions of privacy, intrusions into my very being. Her only way of experiencing—of feeling real—was knowing her therapist and feeling that she existed within *his* existence because her real existence was not acknowledged in her childhood. By acknowledging her realistic place in my life, contact was reestablished with Sally and our work together continued.

It became critical for me to understand that the position required of me in order to maintain emotional contact with her is precisely the position Sally had to take as an infant vis-à-vis her mother. The price she paid for feeling in contact with her mother was to remain skinless, constantly vulnerable to violation, intrusion, and abuse. The truth of her own identity could not be acknowledged; her reality had to be as a part of mother's reality. The necessary replication of this relatedness scenario replete with intrusions and abuse from both parties within the therapy allowed Sally to first replicate and teach her way of relating to the therapist, and then for her, in alliance with the therapist, to take a stand against the abuse and intrusions.[2]

In the safe haven of the alliance Sally was able to gradually express her rage and hate at the abuse she exposed herself to in order to feel connected, to begin saying "no more," and to begin developing limits, boundaries, and ultimately a skin. In the course of our work there were many times when Sally experienced me as being preoccupied or unable to be completely available to her due to feelings or events in my life outside the clinical hour. The breach or damage she experienced was not so much that there was a realistic preoccupation or intrusion, but that rather than share them openly, I would try to conceal them (prevent the invasion), thereby rupturing the replicated merger bond between us. I would relate to her as if we were separate with "skin" between us, when in her world there was none and she needed me to relate to her skinlessness in order for her to feel safe and connected.

The gradual development of a psychic "skin" heralded a major developmental shift for Sally. She no longer was restricted to experiencing the therapist and herself as "one" without boundaries or skin separating us, but began to experience us as separate individuals, each with our own intactness defined by "skin." It is at this point that we find ourselves at the time of this writing. Recently, after an eight-week leave for a hysterectomy, Sally returned to announce that she wanted to terminate therapy (as if she were saying of our relationship and possibly about having a baby, "If I can't relate skinlessly, if have to acknowledge separateness, I don't want to relate at all").

In the process of discussing the possibility of termination, a new form of the skin versus skinless relatedness metaphor began to emerge. As Sally

---

2. The nature of the replication as it emerged in this case is discussed in detail in Chapters 12 and 13 of Hedges 1992.

has begun to be able to experience herself and myself as separate individuals, I have acquired in her mind a private life that I have the power not to share with her if I choose not to. She says, "Your private life comes first, I am not important any more." But now the challenge has shifted to, "Can we still feel connected and continue to maintain the intimacy required for the therapy to continue if we are separate people who sometimes choose not to share all parts of their private lives?"

By recognizing that Sally now has a nascent capacity to relate to me as a separate individual, it is necessary to take a stand against the old way of relating as if "skinless." The opportunity now exists to begin to relate in a new way that protects and respects the intactness of the individual rather than providing abuse or invasions. In the initial explorations of my separateness stance, Sally has expressed it as my becoming "stronger," namely, that my willingness to be vulnerable and share aspects of my personal life with her in the past was "showing my weakness." Not doing so now is seen as relating from strength. Allowing invasions was the way all the old abusive objects were related to and, "I will never allow that to happen again."

Sally's expressed wish to terminate represents her growing awareness of our psychological separateness as well as her complete lack of knowledge of how two separate people can enjoy each other and sustain a relationship. She cannot relate in the old way of merging with me by way of being skinless. My "private life" prevents that. Feeling that she will be unable to achieve the intimacy and safety to move forward in the therapy relationship, she only can imagine terminating the relationship. Whether we can find ways to take up the challenge presented, to continue to explore all the intricacies and meanings of boundaryless and bounded relating, or whether Sally must in fact experience her separateness by terminating and taking with her all the growth she has accomplished and the internalized intimate relationship we established, remains to be seen.

Throughout our relationship when the metaphor of relating "skinless" has arisen I have consistently verbalized the dilemma of trying to reconcile my traditional analytic training of maintaining the "blank screen" with my growing understanding and respect for what was required from both of us to maintain the relatedness bond that allowed therapy to proceed. The question for us to consider would be posed as, "Is this useful to you? Does it help facilitate your work and expand your understanding of your world?" This is, of course, part of the issue and a very appropriate question to struggle with continually, but it begs part of the question. When I first became aware of my own reactions and feelings of intrusion, invasion, and discomfort, I lacked the courage to express these reactions and feelings directly to Sally. I did not use them to further understand and reflect back what her experience of her mother and the world must have been like. In retrospect, my reluctance to speak my discomfort and thereby to interpret her childhood sense of being invaded appears to have slowed down our work considerably. What is clear, retrospectively, is that until skinlessness could be replicated in the transference/countertransference dimension, we could not move from skinless relating to relating from within our own skins.

Editor's Postscript

Followup work showed that Sally's hysterectomy and relinquishing the possibility of having a baby were indeed related to her feeling that she had to give up her infantile skinless orientation in relation to her therapist so that the business of relating and growing could continue.

Brailow's remarks underline the impression I have had for some time that therapists are much too reluctant to begin interpretive work directly utilizing countertransference responses. When we are speaking countertransference feelings in the spirit of offering a piece of projected information back to the speaker, we necessarily do so cautiously and tentatively. We are aware that countertransference responsiveness is always filtered through our personalities, through the entire history of our own personal relationships, so that we can only have "ballpark" impressions. That is, the impressions arising from the emotional responses of the therapist are bound to be less than correct because of how they were achieved. They must always be thrown back to the speaker as loose hunches submitted for accurate refinement. But because our impressions are necessarily inexact is no cause to unduly withhold them. In traditional analysis of neurosis, restraint in this regard was and is well advised because the contents of the repressed unconscious are specific and need no suggestions from us in order to emerge accurately—only help in the analysis of the resistance to their emergence. But the unthought known has never been put into words, images, thoughts, and stories; only projected emotionally into various relationships with various results. We can speak the result of the projection—how it is affecting us—and open up possibilities of representation for the speaker. Therapists who need to be correct in their interpretations had better stick to analyzing pure neurotics. The rest of us go nip and tuck, jointly creating a narrative which fits well for the moment, which is subject to revision at any time, which opens possibilities for further elaboration, and which in time allows for the expansion of psychic structure by bringing old and limiting structures to light as they operate in the here-and-now therapeutic relationship.

The case studies in this part of the book have been selected to illustrate the intimate and enmeshed strategic emotional involvement which is necessarily involved in analyzing replicating transferences originating during the symbiotic period of psychic development. Having begun with cases illustrating strategic emotional involvement with organizing/psychotic features of personality and having now considered borderline/symbiotic features, we are ready to move up the developmental ladder to the third year of life to consider strategic emotional involvement with narcissistic/selfother features of personality.

IV

STRATEGIC EMOTIONAL INVOLVEMENT IN LISTENING TO NARCISSISTIC ISSUES

15

Emotional Involvement in Narcissism

The psychological approaches which have been spawned by the work of Heinz Kohut (1971) are imbued with a special richness of emotional involvement. In his seminal monograph he considers typical countertransferences to the three varieties of narcissistic or selfobject constellations he defines: the idealizing, the mirror, and the twinship transferences.

STRATEGIC EMOTIONAL INVOLVEMENT TO IDEALIZING, MIRROR, AND TWINSHIP TRANSFERENCES[1]

Kohut (1971) indicates that, as might be expected, the analyst's major responses to idealizing transferences are rooted in his or her own narcissism, especially in areas of unresolved narcissism. He discussed the case of Miss L., who began an intense idealizing transference to her analyst at the outset of treatment. One of her early dreams contained the figure of an inspired and idealized priest, relating to her Roman Catholic background. Though not in direct response to her dream, the analyst did subsequently indicate that he was not a Roman Catholic. He did so in a move motivated by her supposed need to have a minimum understanding of the realities of their situation since her grasp on reality was in his opinion somewhat tenuous. Kohut discerned the beginning of a stalemate in the analysis dating from this remark. He interpreted her dream as an initial tentative transference step toward reinstating an attitude of idealizing religious devotion from adolescence, an attitude that seems to have had its origin in early childhood. Later material from the analysis indicated that these early idealizations had been an attempt to escape from the threat of bizarre tensions

---

1. This section is reprinted with modifications from Hedges 1992, pp. 192–196.

and fantasies caused by traumatic stimulations and frustrations from her parents. The analyst's remark that he was not Catholic, not like the priest of her dreams, and therefore not an idealized good and healthy version of herself, was received as a rebuff leading to a stalemate.

> The analytically unwarranted rejection of the patient's idealizing attitudes is usually motivated by a defensive fending off of painful narcissistic tensions (experienced as embarrassment, self-consciousness, and shame, and leading even to hypochondriacal preoccupations) which are generated in the analyst when the repressed fantasies of his grandiose self become stimulated by the patient's idealization. [p. 262]

The analyst's uneasiness at being idealized is especially likely to occur if the idealization is early in the analysis and rapid. Discomfort with such idealization is to some extent universal and proverbial: "Praise to the face is a disgrace!" Even analysts usually comfortable with their own narcissism may be tempted to fend off the patient's admiration. The rejection of the idealization may be blunt, or subtle, or premature, or may express itself in no more than a slight overobjectivity or coolness in manner, or in a tendency to be jocular and to disparage the idealization in a humorous and kindly way. Kohut maintains, "during those phases of the analysis of narcissistic character disturbance when an idealizing transference begins to germinate, there is only one correct analytic attitude: to accept the admiration" (p. 264). An automatic emphasis on the analyst's realistic qualities in contrast to a patient's idealization is no more justified than an analyst's protestation at the first hint of an oedipal striving that he is not his patient's parent.

In later phases of analysis, the idealizing transference begins to be worked through. Whereas in the early phases of idealization the analyst may feel oppressed by the stimulation of his narcissistic fantasies, in the working through phase he may resent being belittled by the very person who had earlier idealized him. Exaggerated fault-finding and belittling can also occur as defenses against the establishment of idealizing transferences. But the attacks that occur during the working-through period may be especially oppressive as the angry disappointment that follows disillusionment and that precedes the waves of withdrawal of idealizing libido from the analyst often fasten onto some aspect or another of the analyst's actual emotional, intellectual, physical, or social shortcomings. According to Kohut:

> The analyst thus becomes aware of these alternations between admiration and contempt and will be capable of viewing with optimal objectivity the

attacks which are directed against him, because he can comprehend them within the context of the analysand's needs during the analytic process. He will grasp the dynamic interplay between the patient's attacks on him, the loosening of the idealizing cathexes, and the gradual strengthening of certain internalized narcissistic structures (e.g., of the patient's ideals). [p. 269]

The rewards of watching such a growth process support the analyst when the process proves to be especially stressful.

According to Kohut, the analyst's responses to the mirror transferences are determined by the level of professional experience in handling narcissistic issues, the state of his or her narcissism, and the current state of mind. In the narrow mirror transference the analyst is "the well-determined target of the patient's demands that he reflect, echo, approve, and admire his exhibitionism and greatness" (p. 270). However, in the alter-ego or twinship transference, the grandiose self experiences the representation of the analyst as a part of itself, thus blotting out the person of the analyst so completely that he is deprived even of that minimum narcissistic sense that is afforded in the reflective function of the mirror transference. The analyst's optimal responses to the unfolding of the mirror transference are (1) interpretations of resistances against the revelation of his grandiosity, and (2) demonstrations that not only did grandiosity and exhibitionism once play a phase-appropriate role, but that they must now be allowed access to consciousness. It may be difficult for the analyst to tolerate a situation in which he or she is reduced to the seemingly passive role of mirroring infantile narcissism in order to unconsciously interfere with the establishment or maintenance of the mirror transference. When the listener attempts to respond to the twinship transference, the most common danger is boredom, a lack of emotional involvement with the person, and precarious maintenance of attention (with or without drowsiness), including secondary reactions such as irritation, overt anger, exhortations, forced interpretation of resistances and other rationalized forms of acting out the tensions and impatience arising from minimal narcissistic stimulation.

> True alertness and concentration during prolonged periods of observation can be maintained only when the observer's psyche is engaged in depth. Manifestations of object-directed strivings always tend to evoke emotional response in those toward whom they are directed. Thus, even while the analyst is still at sea about the specific meaning of his patient's communications, the observation of (object-instinctual) transference manifestations is not usually boring to him. The situation is, of course, different in the case of the analyst's defensive boredom. Although in these instances the analyst understands the transference meaning of the patient's communications only

too well, he does not want to understand it. He may, for example, be unconsciously stimulated by libidinal transference appeals and therefore defend himself, by an attitude of disinterest, against the patient's attempt to seduce him. In all these instances we are dealing not with genuine boredom but with the rejection of an emotional involvement (including preconscious attention) which is currently present below the surface layer of the analyst's personality. [Kohut 1971, pp. 274–275]

With idealizing transferences, the analyst's attention may become engaged more easily than with mirror and twinship transferences, in which the grandiose self merges with representations of the analyst. This can become tantamount to total enslavement, making it difficult to be attentive for long periods of time. Many such difficulties are amenable to amelioration through supervision, in which the consultant is able to demonstrate the very important function that the analyst is performing. Thus, countertransferences to mirroring, twinning, and idealizing transferences may act as facilitations to understanding the nature of the transference and in providing optimal responsiveness. Other difficulties of a more chronic nature may require more analysis of the analyst's narcissistic vulnerabilities. Deep fears of merger that need personal attention may account for tensions of some analysts.

STRATEGIC EMOTIONAL INVOLVEMENT AND THE INTERSUBJECTIVE FIELD

One group of clinicians and therapists, notably Stolorow, Atwood, Brandchaft, and colleagues (1994), is developing extensively its ideas on the "intersubjective field." Elaborating Kohut's general model of self to selfobject resonance, these clinicians have been studying the conjunctions and disjunctions of subjective worlds. This way of thinking offers a fresh angle on the problem of the emotional involvement of the listener. The starting point for their work is that both participants in the analytic dialogue arrive with subjective worlds that each have a long history. As the relationship evolves the focus comes to be on places where subjectivity collides. Analytic work revolves around both participants exploring their subjective reaction to points of disjunction. The refreshing aspect of this approach is that deep structures of subjectivity are assumed to be operating within both listener and speaker as they relate to one another. Thus careful scrutiny of the emotional involvement of the listener is a matter of routine.

We will next consider empathy in some detail, then turn to a vignette by Wolf highlighting the vicissitudes of countertransference from a self psychology point of view. With Coverdale we will consider developmental lines of empathy and interpretation and watch how he manages to remain empathically immersed in two episodes involving strategic emotional involvement. A case study by Shapiro follows, illustrating the utilization of both the Kohutian approach as well as the intersubjective perspective.

ON EMPATHY[2]

Kohut (1959) formulated that the data of psychoanalysis have always been personal introspections and that the mode of observation in psychoanalysis is vicarious introspection, which he termed *empathy*. Introspection and empathy form the limits beyond which psychoanalysis as a discipline cannot go.

Kohut bitterly complained to the last days of his life that people misused his notion of empathy to mean something like syrupy sweet kindness or sympathy and that people were attempting to exalt empathy as something inherently good. He delighted in giving the example of the sirens that the Nazis put on their dive bombers to strike terror into the hearts of their victims as an instance of perfect empathy being used for destructive purposes. Empathy is to be understood solely as a mode of observation. Only late in life was Kohut reluctantly pushed into conceding that empathic observation in psychoanalysis does, in fact, have a certain beneficial effect beyond its usefulness as a research tool. Since the development of concepts concerning self-cohesion stood in the center of Kohut's investigations, he stated the benefits he saw in terms of the consolidating and firming effects on the self of admiring, confirming, and inspiring responses from empathic selfothers.

I wish now to broaden the purview of empathy. It seems useful to consider psychoanalytic narrations and interactions as a successively expanding compilation of forms for expressing experience. Experience itself is comprised of yet another set of forms for providing versions of activities. Consciousness must be classed as a network of forms for communicating, sharing, or comparing experiences of activity.

In the present context, empathy is taken as one person's private and personal ways of sensing, imagining, and thinking about how another person organizes and narrates his or her understanding of personal actions and activities, in a world partially or largely thought to be his or her construction. Much of the activity of empathy is likely to be unconscious,

---

2. This section is reprinted with modifications from Hedges 1992, pp. 137–147.

especially at the beginning of the analytic relationship. Gradually, however, the analyst constructs various versions of what he or she considers to be the person's narrational contexts.

A limitation of Kohut's work on empathy is that self is only one of a number of important interwoven strands involved in individual human development. His insightful work on self-to-selfother resonance is one, albeit an important one, of perhaps many potentially definable forms in human life and activity. My own work has sought to separate out four clearly definable categories of human experience and activity. I have elaborated four corresponding listening perspectives as modes of psychoanalytic inquiry, or as guidelines for considering different modes of relatedness. Each of these distinctly different modes of relatedness is associated with different forms of empathic response. The modes of empathy can be summarized now within a context of form realities.

FOUR EMPATHIC MODES

1. *Organizing forms and activities* are perhaps best met with what may be called interception or interceptive contact. The most basic forms of orienting, organizing, and ordering of affective and sensorimotor response seem facilitated by their being contacted while in active exploratory or manipulative extension. An infant's, child's, or adult's tentative extensions into the environment may result in a variety of consequences. Those that put him or her into safe and reliable contact with the human environment are those that are met with various forms of reliable, warm, human responsiveness. Orienting, organizing, and ordering extensions not warmly or safely met in a timely fashion result in psychological enclaves of autosensuousness (Tustin 1984) leading to forms of entanglement with dangerous, threatening, seductive, nonhuman, mechanical, or erratic environmental figures or features. Many culturally defined forms exist to encourage patient waiting until an infant is in a position of extension in which he/she may benefit from human contact (interception of movement). The psychoanalytic tradition has evolved a variety of patience-inducing concepts that represent analogous forms for providing availability and responsiveness for the organizing aspects of personality. In persons or areas of a person where there has been an early traumatic history we will be concerned primarily with the way contact, once established, is broken off. The exact mode or style of destroying life giving (form providing) contact represents a transference from earliest experiences in which contact was either not maintained satisfactorily or was traumatically disrupted. Systematic study of

stimulation associated with feelings of attraction, rivalry, jealousy, and injury permits the assimilation of social codes on a different plane than previously possible—the so-called crystallization of the superego. Full emotional capacity to consider others as separate centers of initiative with separate interests and motivations introduces the realistic possibility of personal injury (e.g., so-called castration) and gives rise to various forms of distrust. That others' personal and narcissistic investments constitute a danger is a reality to be reckoned with, Kohut says. Not to notice in oneself or in others unacceptable forms of attraction, aggression, jealousy, or injury is the dominant way of dealing with these intense forms of stimulation in the oedipal mode. Freud formulated this policy as one of not noticing, as unconscious defensive activity, which he categorized as various forms of repression. In order to master the intensity of the Oedipus complex, a person must learn to sublimate or at least not to notice stimulation that would disrupt the continuity of the sense of self.

Historically, empathic contact with repressed oedipal activities through carefully timed and tactfully delivered verbal-symbolic interpretations has been the central thrust of the psychoanalytic enterprise. Freud's insistent advocation of a strictly verbal-symbolic, interpretive approach and his gradual limiting of the population of the analyzable to neurotics has led to much dissension. At present, Freud's obstinate consistency can be seen as limiting to analytic work with preoedipal issues, but as clarifying with regard to the value of abstinence and verbal interpretation for understanding and analyzing personal (neurotic) activities constellated and integrated in the abstract symbolic mode of Oedipus, who blinded himself, symbolizing his wish not to see (be overstimulated by) relating others.

Kohut (1982) has argued convincingly that optimally empathic oedipal figures are successful to a large degree in limiting overstimulation during this period, thus preventing the formation of excessive defensive activity and neurotic constellations. It can be added to Kohut's observation that empathic responsiveness to self-cohesion modes from important others prevents excessive fragmentation during self-consolidation. Furthermore, appropriate empathic responsiveness forestalls extensive good-bad splitting in the symbiosis and separating modes as well as needless searching and floundering in organizing modes. Kohut (1982) has maintained that the traditional psychoanalytic emphases on lust and destruction have overshadowed the positive trends of stimulating love and assertiveness that are possible with positively resonating parental selfothers. In addition, emphasis on self fragmentation, good-bad splitting, and chaotic or bizarre behaviors have also tended to overshadow the positive aspects of developmentally determined modes and activities when more appropriate forms of empathic responsiveness are available from the parents and/or the analytic listener.

EMPATHIC MODES AS FORMS "FROM ABOVE"

The gradual refinement of developmental theory and technique has made possible the extension of the concept of empathy to at least three preoedipal modes that do not include verbal-symbolic interpretive activity as a consistent response. Interception of organizing activity, replication of symbiotic and separating interactions, and repetition of selfother resonance all represent major modes of listening to and empathizing with various preoedipal aspects or features of personality. These empathic modes have evolved to supplement the traditional empathic mode of verbal-symbolic interpretation. In order to avoid confusion, a mode is conceptualized adverbially as a way of seeking contact with another. However, a mode usually stems from preestablished forms or patterns and/or rapidly becomes a form of address to the other.

In many instances, what passes for empathic response differs little from sympathy and by itself has no useful effect in psychoanalysis. Everyone has seen or heard of instances in which an analyst has continued for a protracted period of time in genuine sympathetic immersion with a person who has realized only limited personal gains as a result. The effect is at best benign or helpful in promoting an ameliorated life adjustment. One might liken such a situation to transitivism or sympathetic parallel play in young children who, though they may enjoy one another and may react intensely to each other's play, are quite unable to elevate their level of mutual relatedness without intervention of the kind that recognizes or implies higher (more comprehensive or flexible) relatedness options. Children can be told to be considerate and they can indeed be taught not to create a ruckus with one another, but differentiated capacities for self-confirmation and mutual consideration come from somewhere else. Where? Clearly from something that can be described as a learning, modeling, or identification effect. That is, empathy if it is to be transformationally effective, must come "from above." And what can this mean?

Returning to our main topic to shed light on the problem of empathy, we can only consider others fully when we know what it means to be considered. We can only know how to confirm another struggling self when we know what it means to feel confirmed. We can only tolerate separating opposition when we understand how crucial it is that our opposition be received tolerably. We can only permit ourselves to be drawn into a symbiotic replication when we know how important it feels to have someone fully involved in our subjective world. We can only know how to wait for and to discern extensions that can be momentarily met if our own extensions have been adequately met. Different modes of empathy are necessarily derived from identificatory experiences of others listening to us or being with us in increasingly broader, more flexible, or more comprehensive ways, or as it were, "from above," in a hierarchy of complexity in human responsiveness.

A Kohutian truism, which is confirmable in the more differentiated self and otherness states, relates to the consequences of empathic failure. Kohut predicts increased tension, fragmentation, and loss of self-esteem following an empathic failure. This prediction indeed appears to hold true when it is the self that needs confirming. However, in symbiotic and organizing activities, the results of empathic failure may be manifold and are generally not well described by merely referring to them as increases in tension, fragmentations of the self, or losses in self-esteem. For example, one person may experience a relief at a certain type of symbiotic failure in empathy because, as with the original symbiotic partner, failure means that the experienced battering or abuse (connection) comes momentarily to an end. Conversely, for someone else, certain kinds of intrusion or abuse might signal interpersonal contact and a consequent relief from a terrible period of isolation and loneliness. By the same token, either an empathic connection or failure to connect to organizing features might, depending upon the original caregiving situation, either permit or prevent a withdrawal into hallucinatory experience, a flight into manic elation, or an escalation of depression or paranoid rage. A placid interval may mean to a mother that the baby is content, while it may represent to the infant a state of depletion resulting in disappointment or failure to attain his or her subjective aims.

Contrary to Kohut's general assertions regarding empathic resonance at the level of self-cohesion striving, it is not possible in the short run to predict with certainty the consequences of empathic contact or empathic failure in pre-cohesive self states. Paradoxes and surprises abound in preoedipal activities in which a person's strivings may resemble a young child's attempting to master the nuances of a complex environment with certain limitations in knowledge or communication skills. Misunderstandings between child and caregiver are common occurrences rather than exceptions. However, a persistent baby and a devoted caregiver in time do develop a mutual cuing system (the symbiosis), which is a fairly reliable communication system. How many instances have we all encountered of well intentioned empathic response that failed to meet the mark in terms of tension release?

Empathy, if it is to be accurate and comprehensive, and if it is to promote greater flexibility, must come "from above," that is, be derived from more encompassing, more abstract, or more flexible forms of understanding. The empathizer must be able to convey a sense of understanding of and tolerance for the personal concerns and positions being expressed, sought, or presented for interaction or interception. That a baby will be happier and healthier with a clean diaper is no consolation to the angry, kicking, screaming child who has been interrupted in absorbing pursuits. Mother's understanding and tolerance of the rage and its causes will make it possible for her to survive the infant's attacks without retaliation until soon the two are laughing and cooing together to the smell of fresh talcum and the sense of a clean diaper, a nice baby and a happy mother. The expectable provocations of "the terrible twos," and "adolescent rebellion" are common examples of personal activities that try a parent's (or therapist's) patience. In these cases empathy can only mean a willingness to engage in a fray so that the opposing self can experience an independent consolidation. There are also various seductions that must be accepted and lived through in some suitable manner. Whether the seduction is to some form of organizing contact, merger, self-confirmation, or incestuous activity, empathizing means receiving the wishes and impulses openly and being prepared to be available, supportive, and responsive when inevitable limits and disappointments arise.

Formulating empathic observation as consisting of a variety of forms of self and other relating potentials expands Kohut's fundamental notion of empathy as vicarious introspection centering around the cohesion and fragmentation of the sense of self. Some of the complexities of this expanded definition of empathy with different developmental concerns have just been considered. But one particularly interesting problem in analytic empathy arises when considering the organizing level of self and other relatedness experience. As has already been stated, at this level the main transference formation that persistently appears is a break, a breach, a foreclosure of an interpersonal connection. That is—whether the person lives pervasively in organizing experiences or only lives out limited pockets of organizing experience—when the possibility of an interpersonal connection presents itself the internalized transferential mode of disconnection appears in short order. Primordial connections with an other that were traumatic (over- or understimulating) have left their mark in a knee-jerk tendency to avoid all emotionally similar situations in the future. And what is emotionally similar in the perceptual field of an infant may be fairly encompassing.

The avoidance of connectedness thus conditioned in infancy has serious implications for the formation of symbiotic mutual cuing connections since whole areas of a person's creativity and spontaneity may be cut off from the influence of ongoing developmental processes. Analytic listeners are accustomed to thinking that empathy means connecting with the person's immediate experience and in so doing tend to follow the content and process of engagement as the analytic speaker offers it. But people who have significant areas of undeveloped organizing experience have become masters at moving quickly from a point of potential contact to content that appears to continue the connection but that in fact stops or prevents the possibility of a genuine give-and-take or I-thou reciprocal relationship from proceeding. Empathy here entails walking a tightrope between following and allowing the disconnection and alternatively somehow intervening at the moment of disconnection in order to hold the person emotionally present while the terror of connecting can be brought forward in the transference and can be experienced with the listener. The technical problem is that to empathize with the immediate subjective concern or content misses the invisible transference structure that seeks to avoid empathic connection because in the primordial past connection was traumatic.

VYING FOR APPROVAL: A MINI-FRAGMENTATION

Countertransference in analytic work aimed at studying the cohesion and fragmentation of self states often takes the form of the analytic listener not comprehending the kind of selfother (selfobject) resonance required by the speaker at a particular moment in time. Wolf (1993) illustrates just such a failure of empathy due to his being preoccupied with separation issues at the time and the resulting sequelae.

> The analysand was a 38-year-old physician in the third year of his analysis. The patient had come into treatment because of recurrent episodes of severe depression. The first depressive episode had been precipitated when the patient and his wife had been summoned to a school conference with his son's teacher. The teacher had complained that the youngster presented a behavioral problem to the school. Significant in this analysand's past history was the loss of his mother because of illness during the patient's infancy. Following this loss, there had occurred several years of institutionalization. As a matter of fact, his childhood was almost empty of sustaining psychological relationships except for the idealized institutional authorities and for a kindly and admired grandfather with whom he had sufficient contact to establish a meaningful relationship. In the structure of this patient's

self, then, there remained a central defect associated with insufficient confirming-mirroring responses from the caregiving self-objects of his early institutional years. However, he had learned to elicit a modicum of confirming responses from the institutional authorities by being a good boy, an eagerly compliant and helpful child. He thus was able to build a precariously established compensatory structure (Kohut 1977a), which was strengthened by the relationship with the grandfather and that covered the defective part of his self, allowing him to function in life with a measure of healthy zest, joy, and creativity until the sudden breakdown into depression. Before that breakdown the patient had arranged to maintain and strengthen the compensatory structure of his self by maintaining institutional affiliation (e.g., medical school, hospital, professional societies) whereby being a good student or active member he could continue to receive the sustaining responses from the self-objects now represented by the institutional authorities.

When his son—with whom the patient in normal parental manner was identified because he experienced him as part of his self—then suddenly was the object of severe criticism by the school authorities, and the patient was helpless in doing anything to effect the usual gratifying compliance with the idealized yet dreaded authorities, his depression came to the fore.

During the analysis we worked to ameliorate somewhat the core defect by analyzing the depressive episodes precipitated by weekends and other disruptions in the continuity of the relationship to the analyst as mirroring-confirming self-object. While there was some reduction in sensitivity to separation, the main work of the analysis and its main effectiveness was in the area of analyzing and thereby reconstructing and strengthening the damaged compensatory structures. The patient derived additional strength from an elucidation of the protective function of the compensatory structure vis-à-vis the depressive core.

I will now illustrate the subtly intertwined roles of transference and countertransference in the working-through process. The patient had a close friend who was taken seriously ill and though the patient initially attempted to prescribe for his friend, he recognized, with interpretive help from me, that his excessive involvement was motivated more by his need to be the good boy who takes care rather than by considerations of his friend's welfare. One day, soon thereafter, the patient told me that he had prevailed upon his friend to accept the care of another physician who then had promptly hospitalized his friend. For various reasons my attention at the time had been drawn to the aspect of separation from his friend and to the institutionalization of his friend in a hospital. My comments, therefore, were directed toward clarifying my patient's reactions to the separation, an issue that had always been a sensitive one. He listened politely and I did not notice any particular affective reaction. Next day, however, he complained of waking up with a great deal of anxiety and now he was feeling depressed. Moreover, this always well-dressed man that day was wearing a clashing color combination that struck me as unusually disharmonious. His voice was testy and I recognized that the patient was in a state of what we had come to call a "mini-fragmentation."

Asking myself where I had failed, perhaps the previous day, to properly understand and respond to the patient, I could not come to any answer until my patient remarked that I had not said anything about how well he had coped with delivering his friend to the hospital. Then I recognized what had happened. The patient, after my previous interpretations about his motivation for taking care of his friend, had decided that I would be pleased if he withdrew from taking care of the friend. I had become for the patient like the institutional authority of his childhood and when he told me, apparently proudly, that he had been a good boy and let another physician help his friend, he expected a confirming acknowledgment. Such an acknowledgment would have meant to him acceptance by the self-object as worthy to share in the idealized self-object's power and righteousness. At the same time and at a deeper level he was also exhibiting himself proudly as the perfect good boy for which he demanded confirming responses from a mirroring self-object. Having recognized the dynamics of the transference disruption, I could interpret it to the patient, who almost immediately calmed down. His mini-fragmentation subsided. [pp. 456–459]

Empathy is not enough if it only means sympathy or if it is limited to the understanding of certain forms of relatedness. Comprehensive psychoanalytic empathy is based on an assimilation of a variety of developmentally determined modes and forms. Indeed, the role of the empathizer is a form. The role inherited by the analytic position is endowed with several thousand years of form-filled tradition in addition to the specific rituals and requirements that twentieth century professional life has added. Empathy is not enough until it includes an understanding of the full human repertoire of developmental patterns, modes, codes, and forms. The analytic position is a specially contrived form with a variety of modes for understanding established patterns of personal activity. Sustaining the analytic position inadvertently fosters the systematic expansion of personal realities through an enhanced process of personal reverberation with the form-filled human milieu via the living presence of the analytic listener.

STRATEGIC EMOTIONAL INVOLVEMENT TO UNILATERALLY DEPENDENT RELATEDNESS

Strategic emotional response to narcissistic features of personality entails empathically tuning into the speaker's needs to be affirmed through mirroring, to be confirmed through twinning, and to be inspired through idealization of the listener. The speaker needs to use the listener to perform these self enhancing functions much as one might use a hand to perform various self functions—thus the reason for the term "selfother" or "selfobject": the listener psychologically uses the other as a part of self.

Boredom, drowsiness, and/or irritation are among the expectable countertransference responses to being used as a part of someone else's psyche. That is, one's own narcissism is not being adequately responded to. Kohut suggests that these responses may serve as red flags to mark areas where the speaker's narcissism is active and needs analytic attention. Hence the emotional involvement can be facilitating to the analysis.

What follows are two wonderful vignettes by Charles Coverdale that illustrate some of the ways in which countertransference to selfother transferences may evolve.

16

Two Developmental Lines in Self Psychology:
Selfobject Empathy and Interpretation

Charles Coverdale

Editor's Comments

In Kohut's last speech, at a self psychology conference held at the University of California at Berkeley, October 5, 1981, he called for an elaboration of the developmental lines of empathy and interpretation. Following Kohut, Coverdale (1983) formulates and illustrates those lines.[1]

While what I present here relates to highly controversial issues, my purpose is neither to settle controversy nor add to it; rather, to put forth the importance of individual experience. I am thankful to Dr. Kohut for his inspiration and for providing a theoretical framework that brought cohesion to this work. The major issue, so vigorously contested, has to do with the role of empathy. Is it a tool for analytic observation and nothing more, or does this human capacity provide elements of a cure? The second issue, somewhat incidental to the first, concerns the gratification versus interpretation debate. Do we love our patients into health or analyze them toward cure?

---

1. This section is reprinted with modifications from Coverdale 1983, pp. 93–99.

The vignette to be considered presents arguments for each side of these two much-disputed issues. It also demonstrates how not only are we selfobjects for our patients but they too serve as selfobjects for us.

The controversy not only exists between self psychologists and other analytically oriented practitioners, but also within self psychology. Indeed, the writings of Kohut take one side at one time and stand in contradiction at another. On the one hand he notes that the therapeutic aim is not indulgence but mastery based on insight, achieved in a setting of tolerable abstinence. One need not provide love and kindness, because understanding and interpretation are sufficient. On the contrary, we are advised that an attitude of cautious reserve and overly muted responsiveness will have deleterious consequences; that if the emerging grandiosity and idealization are not dealt with properly, the result will not lead to cohesion of the self but rather to disintegration. We are warned not to interfere with the patient's needs for phase-appropriate mirroring and idealizing (Kohut 1977a).

Shortly before his death in October 1981, Kohut, speaking at the University of California at Berkeley, stated that empathy is a method of observation that does not cure. In the same talk he later said that analysis cures by giving explanation through interpretation, based on empathic understanding.

Empathy creates the selfobject matrix and selfobjects provide reassuring functions. At times we are to interpret the patient's subjective experience of us as selfobjects. At other times we are to function simply as selfobjects—new editions. Reconciling these divergent views requires a developmental perspective, which will now be illustrated with the aid of the following case.

The patient is a single woman in her late twenties. Due to financial considerations she was seen once weekly for 16 months and subsequently twice weekly. Presenting complaints were that relationships became inevitably ruinous, and that although she was accomplished in her field, she felt compelled to hide her accomplishments, in spite of strong wishes to be known. In the worst of times she felt she was dying and was obsessed with mirrors that were cracked, shattered, or warped (which may give a hint as to the type of transference that developed).

Of the 28 months that she had been in therapy, I will present aspects of the last 12. During this time she sometimes used the analytic couch and sometimes sat in a chair facing me.

Before a holiday 16 months into therapy, she spontaneously hugged me at the session's end to thank me for helping her prepare for a visit with her family in another state. Returning from her visit, she was very quiet and often silent for almost two months. During this time my hand drifted toward her head on several occasions, as she lay on the couch facing away. I offered numerous interpretations about her need to be touched, held, or to have physical contact, based on my unusual countertransference reaction, and each time without effect. This was a time of real impasse.

Then, one session I watched my hand drift over, almost involuntarily, and come to rest on her head. The impasse ended immediately with a flood of tears and associations. She recalled feeling that her mother did not touch her, did not want her, did not like being pregnant or giving birth. She remembered that when she was a toddler her mother had teased about not being her mother. She also reported that two months previously, when she had hugged me, her perception was that I had stood with my arms at my side. In fact, I had reciprocated in kind.

Pressing her hand to the back of mine as it rested on her head she asked, "Are you comfortable touching me?" I explained that I had been reluctant but that I now understood how my reluctance had worsened her situation.

Where the numerous attempts at verbal interpretation had failed, the physical interpretation based in archaic empathy had succeeded. However, one can imagine a negative effect in similar situations. If, to give only one example, a therapist were to reach out to a patient based in his/her own archaic feelings of helplessness, the patient would sense only the therapist's ineffectual helplessness.

I had been reluctant to touch this patient. I had learned all the good reasons not to touch patients. This well-advised tradition, which began with Freud in his work with neurotics, remains of value with most patients. Further, with this attractive woman I had to question my own unconscious motivation thoroughly.

In this instance an interpretation in concrete and physical terms seemed called for and, like any good interpretation, worked. Empathic contact here served as a tool for observation, a way to gather data. The empathy also proved curative. That is, my archaic, empathic response effected a change. From a developmental perspective, one can imagine the ludicrous scene of a mother responding to her desperate infant by commenting from across the room, "I can see how much you need to be held."

A very active period in this patient's analysis followed. Her needs to be loved and touched became understood as did her reactions to a mother who was unable to respond to such clear but silent, empathically communicated messages. The "vague" states of mind, which had reportedly troubled her all her life, subsided. I spent one memorable session with her, both of us in silence and quite content. Sitting behind her, I noticed, much to my surprise, that my arms were in position as if I were holding a sleeping child.

Twenty months into treatment as she began to feel more touchable, the issue became one of being seen, looked at, mirrored. She wanted to be seen, but not exposed. When she felt unobserved, she withdrew, felt ghost-like and unsure of her existence. Increasing "sexiness" was accompanied by feelings of embarrassment and shame—in keeping with her early experiences of thwarted exhibitionism, and also contributed to by what she accurately perceived as my discomfort. A session from the twenty-second month of treatment, presented directly from process notes, will illustrate.

> Dressed in a very sexy manner she comes in quite happy only to become quickly self-conscious. She says she doesn't know what to say. I put forth the possibility of her wanting a different response from me than what she is getting. She said she felt good about me all week but now was having difficulty with continuity. I noted she was dressed in a way that's really "out there" (a term she used meaning showing herself, putting herself forward, wanting recognition) particularly considering that she had just come from work. She says she's decided to just be "out there" regardless of the response from co-workers but with me she feels self-conscious, noting that she is blushing. I suggest that perhaps she wants to be more "out there" with me. "No." After a time, I say perhaps this is her way of telling us what happened in the past when she put herself forward. "No." She withdraws into silence and after ten minutes appears to withdraw still further. In touch with my discomfort over the mild attraction stimulated within me, I ask if she feels I'm different than usual. "No." After another period of time I ask if she sees me as a little more reserved, inhibited than usual. "Yes." No longer withdrawn, she says she does not want to review what's gone wrong in her past but to focus on my reserved quality. I tell her I feel a little inhibited in appreciating her body today. She says she can understand my role and really appreciates it, telling me about a friend at work who had an experience with a therapist who was not so clear about his role. But, she emphasizes, she wants me to appreciate her body and like looking at her. I comment that the issue has changed from being touched to being seen. She applies this to all areas of her life and tells me, "It doesn't seem like contact is an important issue today, rather it's being admired and feeling good about myself that's important."

As time passed a firmer sense of who she was and an increased capacity to feel more lovable developed. The next phase of therapy had to do with loving, in the sense of what she had to give or offer. This perceptive patient was aware that my needs to be useful interfered with her needs to experience the value of what *she* had to offer. She was also aware of how my professional limitations interfered with her expressing her love for me.

Nevertheless, she told me that she loved me, and while my overt response sat well with me, I felt too caring toward her. Thus, in response I said, "This seems like an important feeling to feel," yet internally the situation seemed erotically tinged.

I soon realized I was still wanting to respond to this patient in archaic and, therefore, concrete ways because I had been in touch with her concrete ways of receiving. She wanted my appreciation and I wished to provide it in a way which I knew she could receive. My interpretive abilities had been formerly undermined because interpretation represents a higher level of empathy than she was ready for. But while the patient required archaic empathy previously, she now needed understanding on a higher level. My continued caring at an archaic level would now be prone to misinterpretation by a patient who could have seen my feelings for her as romantic. My sense of concern about this hour could now be understood: archaic empathic response was no longer appropriate.

The next session she was angry with me. I commented that recently our relationship seemed to be an impediment to her growth. She confirmed with a flood of associations about how her father's basic message was "to stay, and have everything she wanted; or to go, and die." The question became, could she be "out there" without jeopardizing her relationship with me? A higher form of verbal interpretation was now appropriate. I gave her messages such as, "No one ever backed you up as you moved away."

Twenty-four months into treatment she told me, "Being known by you has grounded parts of my personality." At 25 months she spent a week with her mother—after ten years of little contact. She noted that in her mother's presence she felt unsubstantial. She realized her perceptions had always been sharp, yet had gone without Mother's support and validation. She recognized her mother's gross inability to relate to her, and characterized Mother as "wearing a mask of supernormalcy which served as a cover for craziness." Yet she felt compassion for Mother, for "Mother was the way she was, because she couldn't be any other way."

A week's vacation with Mother brought on a month's regression during which she turned to me for selfobject functions that had been stimulated but unmet by Mother. She expressed increased needs for confirmation of her experience, as well as for archaic forms of mirroring. The form of my empathic contact with her regressed briefly also during this month. For example, more than usual, I enjoyed looking at her. "Do you enjoy looking at me?" she asked. "Yes," I replied.

My enjoyment of her was accompanied by a great sadness for her mother. I said, "What a shame for anyone to miss out on this experience." With that, the regression ended.

I was to experience more sadness with her for her parents as she described how moving forward and away had been accompanied at first by painful feelings between herself and her family, and then by their indifference. On many levels they were deprived of the valuable experience of enjoying her as she was.

What a rewarding, moving, and enjoyable experience it has been for me to provide her with mirroring in different forms in accordance with her different developmental phases. For a mother, father or therapist to be so preoccupied with themselves, their troubles, or the task of doing a good job that they miss this kind of experience seems most regrettable for them as well as for their children or patients.

In reviewing, she thanked me for helping her learn that she is touchable, lovable, and that her love and all she has to offer is worthwhile. In turn, I thanked her for all that I had learned and received. She responded, "It was that which made the experience possible."

Opponents of the psychology of the self complain that it is a lovey-dovey kind of therapy. In looking at this case one may ask, "Was this patient cured by love?" The answer may be, "No, but somewhat." Greenson (1967, 1978) maintains that the analyst's capacity to love is an essential tool of the job. This patient was aware of my love for her; I mirrored her like the daughter I never had and like the mother who might have enjoyed her but did not. I also grew by experiencing myself in the gleam of her eye. It's often a two-way mirror. Not only was I a good selfobject for her but she had become a special kind of selfobject for me.

Her life has changed from relationships that become inevitably ruinous to experiences with men and women that provide an enhancing, valuable, selfobject milieu. Perhaps more significant is a relationship with a particular man, which clearly demonstrates the beginnings of object love based on mutual consideration.

How was she helped? First, my understanding of her needs and feelings served to confirm her experience, and at times her existence. Second, interpretations in genetic, dynamic, and psycho-economic terms, based in empathic understanding, progressed from archaic forms to higher forms. She first had to experience herself through the gleam in my eye before she could feel her own pride, value, and goodness. Following this, we could share in enjoying her important achievements.

Earlier developmental phases require archaic forms of empathic contact. Later developmental phases require higher levels of empathy. Empathic contact through interpretive activity assumes a level of complex symbolic communication and becomes assimilated—to use Piaget's (1937, 1962) terms—into an already existing schema.

The selfobject is, by Kohut's definition, a developmental agent. Initially, selfobjects provide functions that the self cannot provide. Later, through transmuting internalizations, the individual is increasingly more able to provide functions for him/herself that previously required the participation of selfobjects. Different forms of empathic contact are appropriate for different developmental levels.

With the help of my patient, I have come to understand that empathy serves as a tool for analytic observation as well as sometimes providing certain elements essential to the curative process. With certain patients, or at particular times, empathy serves as a method of observation only and nothing more. But with other patients, or at other times, empathic contact actually contributes toward the cure.

Editor's Postscript

These clinical illustrations hardly do justice to the richness and complexity of concepts developed by Kohut and others under the rubric of the psychology of the self. All that can be done here is to point toward an important developmental phase and a specialized way of listening to persons whose personalities have become locked in an incessant search for a cohesive self through obtaining confirming responses from outside selfobjects. In contrasting the Freudian and Kohutian perspectives at the level of clinical *listening*, one can readily appreciate these listening frames have different applications. In listening to persons with a neurotic personality organization, the subjective experiences of drive, conflict, and defense will be foremost. In listening to persons with narcissistic personality organization, the experiences of self cohesion and fragmentation in relation to selfobjects will take center stage. Careful listening to the way each person experiences self and others can prevent massive empathy failures.

Traditionalists accustomed to listening for drive motivations, structural conflict, and defensive disguises express concern that the Kohut selfobject perspective focuses excessively on the manifest content while ignoring the latent causes and resistances. This argument loses its strength when one considers that, by definition, the narcissistic personality organization precedes in development the oedipal period in which the drives become crystallized (or constituted as such in conscious experience) so that (repressive) processes of defense become necessary. If the person arrested at the selfobject phase *experiences* no drives, structural conflict, or defenses as such, there is less need for manifest disguise and, therefore, less need for the analyst to be concerned about the manifest/latent distinction as a tool for listening. This point is made especially clear when Kohut (1984) talks about "self state" dreams. Stolorow and Atwood (1981) make a similar point about preoedipal dreams and there being less need for disguise since structural conflict is *not* an experience of central importance to these people. Yet more convincing here is Langs's (1982) argument that the *adaptive context* of the psychotherapy situation itself will be experienced and expressed in latent terms (i.e., encoded derivative communications). Adapting Langs's ideas to the present purposes of listening to the way a person experiences self and others, one might expect in preoedipal developmental arrests that whatever latent meanings are to be understood will relate *less* to internal conflict and more to the experience of the adaptive interpersonal context of therapy. Different people present different listening challenges to the therapist that are based upon their developmental level of self and other differentiation. Different experiences appear to require different ways of listening and the Kohut listening model is securely fixed on a certain phase of developmental experience.

17

The Provocative Masochistic Patient: An Intersubjective Approach to Treatment[1]

Sanford Shapiro

Provocative behavior and other expressions of negative feelings are normal during any psychoanalysis or intensive psychotherapy. Analysts who face such transferences should maintain a therapeutic stance of understanding and should interpret rather than become defensive or punitive. This task is not too difficult when anger at the analyst is direct and well focused. However, some patients, particularly masochistic ones, often express anger more subtly and provocatively, thus making it difficult for analysts to maintain a therapeutic equilibrium.

The early phase of analysis with such patients is generally rapid and satisfying. The patient works hard and develops good insights, leading to an amelioration of symptoms. Then, just when the patient's quality of life seems to be improving, changes take place. For example, patients who were scrupulously punctual start coming late or just cancel sessions, or they may delay payments or complain that no progress is being made. These patients may even complain that the analysis is making them worse. In some cases, patients may register more than one of these complaints.

Sometimes these patients will respond positively to interpretations that demonstrate the therapist's understanding of the patient's underlying fear

---

1. This chapter is reprinted from the *Bulletin of the Menninger Clinic*, 1989, vol. 53, pp. 319–330.

of negative feelings. Often, however, these patients get worse instead of better. These "negative therapeutic reactions" often seem related to conflicts over unconscious guilt feelings, yet interpretations in this vein may further frustrate both patient and analyst (Brandchaft 1983, Freud 1918, 1955). Some analysts may conclude that the patient is not analyzable or that treatment requires the introduction of parameters.

In this chapter, I will offer some guidelines for dealing with sadomasochistic transference phenomena. These guidelines are derived from classical psychoanalytic theory, with enhancements from the writings of Winnicott, Gill, Kohut, Brandchaft, and Stolorow. I will describe in detail some challenging analytic sequences to illustrate the development of these transferences, resistances to their emergence, and the interpretation of these resistances. I will also describe some of my own thoughts during these stormy periods.

THERAPEUTIC GUIDELINES

In an early paper on masochistic transferences, Brenner (1959) advised the analyst to avoid being "unconsciously tempted to participate with the patient in . . . sadomasochistic behavior: to become angry at the patient, to feel hopeless and defeated by him, or to demonstrate either affection or aversion in whatever way" (p. 223). "A model of behavior for the analyst to follow," Brenner suggested, "is that of an understanding adult . . . dealing reasonably with a sulky, stubborn, provocative child. If the adult is wise and not unduly involved emotionally with the child, he is not upset or disturbed by such a child's behavior but remains calmly observant and understanding whatever may be the child's attempts to seduce and provoke him into a sadomasochistic episode." Brenner added "that this is easier said than done but . . . it is not impossible, and . . . is essential to the optimal analytic treatment of the masochistic patient" (p. 224).

No adult can remain calm and understanding in the face of a healthy child's provocative behavior, such as in a normal 2-year-old or in a vigorous adolescent. Likewise, no matter how understanding analysts are, at some point they will become angry at such patients or feel hopeless and defeated by them.

The model of behavior that I recommend is one of survival. The analyst who can survive these assaults without either feeling destroyed or making interpretations that leave the patient feeling destroyed can use these countertransference reactions as opportunities to enhance understanding and to further the analytic process. The analyst's perception of the patient's behavior as a manifestation of underlying psychopathology rather than as an attempt to use the analyst in a healing process creates a disruption that hampers the analytic process. Interpretations that the patient is resisting, is angry at the analyst, or envies and wishes to devalue the analyst often lead the patient to feel criticized and defective. The patient's self-esteem becomes further impaired and the treatment alliance breaks down.

I define the treatment alliance as a manifestation of a basic selfobject tie in which the patient feels understood. A disruption in this tie can lead to a breakdown in the treatment alliance and, if not resolved, to an impasse in the analysis (Brandchaft and Stolorow 1984). Many sensitive therapists intuitively grasp this truth but are unable to translate this intuition into principles of technique that can be applied by their students.

Learning to understand the concept of selfobject transferences (dimensions of transference in which the patient perceives the analyst as providing a function) has greatly expanded my ability to work with patients who become intensely provocative during an analysis (Kohut 1971). I use the term *provocative* to refer to those actions or attitudes by the patient that cast me in roles foreign to my own self-perception. For instance, I do not see myself as a molester or a sadist. I originally viewed such experiences as an attack on me, as evidence of a patient's aggressive strivings. An interpretation based on this understanding often led my patients to feel hurt and guilty, which in turn led to a disruption in the treatment alliance. The alliance would be reestablished when I could understand that the patient was engaging me in reliving an early traumatic experience in an attempt to complete an essential developmental task that previously had been blocked.

Masochistic patients often describe one parent as cruel or demeaning and the other as withdrawn or indifferent. The child's developing sense of self requires some human contact to maintain a sense of realness or aliveness. If the price for this human contact is suffering, pain, and humiliation, the child has no choice—the alternative is isolation or psychic death. The patient whose case I will discuss here once reported a dream in which her face was swollen and painful. In the dream, she went to see a doctor, who treated her somewhat shabbily. "I had no choice," she said. "I was in pain and I needed help!"

The experience of pain as a condition of human contact continues into adulthood, and in analysis the patient will reexperience it in the transference. To overcome a masochistic way of relating requires a new experience as an adult analogous to that of the "terrible twos." When very young, these patients were deprived of the opportunity to be oppositional and provocative in the service of self-individuation. They now need a chance to have that experience in a containing or holding relationship to complete that phase of development. These patients are often highly sensitive and do well in life because they can accurately "read" others. They quickly learn the analyst's areas of vulnerability, which they skillfully test and unconsciously exploit. Surviving these provocations can be a growth-producing experience for both patient and analyst. I will now describe the first two years of an analysis in which such transferences were worked through and resolved.

CASE REPORT

Mary was a seriously depressed young woman with a masochistic character structure, and her therapy was characterized by continuous disruptions. As I struggled to focus on the center of her experiences, I repeatedly found myself saying things that either hurt or infantilized her. As I weathered each storm and helped repair each disruption without causing her to experience me as damaged by her or to feel forced to submit to my way of thinking, she gradually became stronger and more confident. As I was able to interpret her anxiety about maintaining her tie to me without having to submit to my desires and be used by me, she began to gain a sense of her own individuality.

Mary was a businesswoman in her mid-twenties who had been molested by her brother and her stepfather. She had left a therapist four years earlier when he tried to seduce her; she had been seeing that therapist for eighteen months for a long-standing depression. More recently, she had been seeing a biological psychiatrist who prescribed various medications. Two weeks before she contacted me, the end of an intense relationship had left her in despair and unable to work. She was losing hope and felt that time was running out. She said, with great discouragement, "I need to get my life in order—to feel some authenticity!" She was profoundly depressed and desperate.

Mary was the third of four children of an alcoholic father and a depressed mother. A brother, seven years older, had sexually molested her when she was 5 to 7 years old. He was subsequently jailed for robbery and attempted murder. Mary maintained contact with him, worried about him, and felt guilty for not helping him more. Another brother, two years older than Mary, had emotional problems. A third brother, four years younger, was alcoholic. Mary's father beat her mother and brothers, but not her. He punished her, on at least one occasion, by taking her to the country and driving off without her. It was his way of controlling her. Her parents divorced when she was 11 years old. Her mother remarried and gave birth to a girl when Mary was 12; subsequently, Mary's stepfather began to sexually molest her. She never felt that she could turn to her mother, who responded to her allegations by spanking her and calling her a baby. When Mary was sick or in pain, her mother withdrew from her. Even talking about her mother's behavior made Mary feel anxious and guilty for being critical. Mary assumed her mother's perspective at her own expense. She explained, for example, that her mother was afraid to love another child after the death of a 5-year-old son a year before Mary was born.

We began meeting face to face four times a week. Mary seemed fragile, and when she asked about the couch, I said it was optional; she was relieved to sit facing me. In the beginning phase of therapy, her depression gradually lifted as she felt understood by me in a new way. She kept expecting me to blame her for her "masochistic" behavior and to hold her responsible for the various incidents of molestation.

Mary then began to worry about her growing attachment and sexual attraction to me. She wanted to please me and she worried about being seduced by me. She expected that any sexual encounter would be her fault because she believed that men are unable to control themselves and that women are stronger and must take responsibility for what men do. Her sexual arousal intensified during sessions before weekends and holidays when she felt unsure about her ability to maintain her feeling of connectedness to me. I interpreted her past sexual experiences, although painful and humiliating, as her way of providing herself with a sense of human contact in the midst of feelings of emptiness and lifelessness, and as a way of stabilizing her crumbling sense of self (Stolorow 1975). Mary came to understand that, although she paid a high price in terms of pain, degradation, and humiliation, these sexual encounters ensured human contact and were preferable to feelings of coldness, isolation, and inner deadness. These were the only options she had known when she was growing up. Her new understanding gradually built up her inner strength and confidence. She began to sense an aliveness in her work and made rapid professional advances. Her personal relationships also improved, and she became able to accept warmth and tenderness from both men and women.

After about six months of therapy, the tone of our sessions began to change. Mary's eagerness to see me was replaced by a feeling of dread, and her comfort in being with me changed to restless agitation. "I hate coming here! I can't stand these sessions," she complained. "There's no point in continuing. I'm getting worse instead of better." Nothing I said seemed of any benefit to her. She was upset, and I felt helpless and guilty. I tried harder. She felt patronized and complained that I was just using her, that I was pressuring her to talk about painful and humiliating experiences. I became annoyed and irritated with her. I, too, began to dread the sessions and felt misunderstood and unappreciated. She complained either that I wanted her to change according to my expectations, or that I did not care if she changed and that I was aloof and indifferent to her. I felt stuck in a no-win position.

I considered various interventions. Should I point out that it was the increasing closeness in our relationship that frightened her and that she was resisting being involved with me? Although accurate, that interpretation would only make her feel more inadequate and defeated. Should I point out that her feelings of anger and hostility toward me were a displacement from the past? That would only make her feel hurt and criticized. Should I point out the distortions in her perception of me and set the record straight? That would certainly make her feel discounted, and would result in a reenactment with me of painful childhood experiences with her mother. This line of thought, although somewhat accurate, put the essence of the difficulty solely within Mary. The intersubjective approach to treatment, however, maintains that in some way I play a role in her difficulty, that she reacts to some perception of me that must be clarified and understood (Stolorow et al. 1987). Winnicott (1960, 1965a) once said that there is no such thing as an infant, explaining that there can only be an infant *and* a mother. Similarly, in an analysis there is not just a patient, but rather a patient–analyst dyad.

Mary anticipated that my response to her would be as traumatic as that of her early caregivers. Her resistance was an attempt to protect herself from being hurt by me. I knew that I would not use her or demean her, but I also knew that some signal from me must be triggering her fears. It was my task to survive the assaults and to decenter from my perspective of being misunderstood and provoked. To appreciate her efforts to protect her vulnerable sense of self, I needed to assume a perspective from the center of her self-experience.

Subsequently, each time that Mary was upset with me, I would comment on the increased tension and distance between us and ask her to help me. Could she remember, I asked, what I had said that was patronizing or critical or pressuring or discounting. I then listened carefully until I could say: "Yes, now that I hear my words coming back to me they do sound patronizing. No wonder you feel hurt and angry. I appreciate your bringing this to my attention." I did not apologize for what I said; I wanted to acknowledge her perception without indicating regret (Goldberg 1987). I wanted to observe the impact of my words. This response on my part always produced a powerful effect. She would immediately become calm and appear more settled and better integrated. She would then become sad, an indication of a sense of reintegration. She told me that she felt better and that she had overreacted; she could see and appreciate that I was trying to help her. My efforts to see things from her perspective helped bridge the gap between us, and she began to see things from my perspective without having to be compliant.

Mary then began to spontaneously recall additional incidents of being hurt, humiliated, patronized, and demeaned by her parents and her brothers. The genetic determinants of her conflicts became clearer. She revealed that when she was a child, complaining to anyone when she felt hurt was absolutely out of the question; in fact, it had never occurred to her that she had any right to complain. Complaints to her father resulted in violence, and complaints to her mother resulted in coldness and rejection that left her feeling guilty and destructive for "hurting" her mother. Mary had been deprived of the mirroring selfobject functions necessary to master these painful, intrusive experiences, and she had been deprived of the idealizing selfobject functions necessary to develop an inner appreciation of her strengths and abilities.

Mary had needed to challenge and provoke me as a response to the progress in our work. Initially, she had felt vulnerable in therapy and developed an idealizing selfobject transference in which she experienced me as a source of strength. She could feel strong and secure only as long as she remained allied with me. The price she paid for this new strength was to be a compliant, good little girl, a false-self type of personality like that described by Winnicott (1960, 1965b). Her task as she gained strength was to de-idealize me, to see me from a different perspective, and to realize her own strengths and resources. In early childhood, Mary had been deprived of the opportunity to experience the "terrible twos," a time in development when it is normal to be provocative and negative. She now needed to use me as a containing selfobject, as a structure against which she could push, in her process of self-differentiation.[2]

During this phase of therapy, Mary began to have financial problems, and money issues became central to the analytic conflict. I reduced her fee somewhat, but some unexpected expenses precipitated a crisis. After considerable discussion, we agreed to have two therapy sessions a week instead of four. The therapeutic momentum changed. Mary's outside life had settled down, and it was in our sessions that she complained bitterly about the increased tension with me and my lack of help in resolving it. The twice-a-week sessions began to resemble the early phase of therapy. She now looked forward to our meetings and found everything that I had to say quite

---

2. I am grateful to Dr. Bonnie Wolfe for suggesting this concept.

helpful. However, progress in her outside life had stopped, everything seemed to be on hold, and she was gradually becoming depressed.

We resumed meeting four times a week when I agreed to defer the payments if she could maintain at least a minimum payment. This arrangement worked until she changed jobs. Although she would eventually make more money in her new job, for now she made less. After considerable discussion, it became clear that she could not concentrate on what she wanted without worrying about its impact on me. She was trying to make her wishes conform to what she thought I expected. Although I do not usually practice self-disclosure, I decided to tell her that my practice was busy and that I did not need the money immediately. However, I was planning a prolonged vacation in about six months, after which I would have much less income; I would need to be paid then. I asked her whether she might be able to pay the balance at that time, an arrangement she thought realistic and fair.

The sessions resumed at four times a week, and the focus once more moved back into the transference with her complaints that I was making her miserable and not helping her. Her outside life once more blossomed, with great progress in both professional and personal relationships. She also became involved in a serious relationship with a young man, Bob, that was characterized by a genuine intimacy she had never before experienced.

Then Mary's success and her increased responsibilities led to time conflicts with her therapy appointments. She suggested canceling the Monday appointments so that she could have that time to organize her workweek better in order to relieve some of the tension she felt in trying to keep her co-workers happy. I interpreted her fear that reducing the number of sessions would displease me. She was relieved and admitted that she was afraid of being more on her own. "So much is going on that this is a time when I really need you!" We agreed to continue sessions three times a week on a trial basis.

There then developed a period of many canceled appointments; often Mary came only once a week. Sometimes she canceled in advance, and sometimes not until the last moment. She often waited until the end of a session to tell me she would not be back for a week, acknowledging her anxiety that I would be mad at her. She became depressed and discouraged. She complained that she had started clinging to Bob, was eating too much, and was gaining weight.

Although I charged Mary for the missed appointments, I found myself feeling frustrated and impatient with her. I used this feeling as the basis for an intervention, asking her if she expected me to become impatient with her. She responded: "I'm waiting for you to get mad at me for not showing up!" Our exploration of this expectation led to new memories of Mary's relationship with her mother, who had expected Mary to care for her without regard for her own needs.

Despite her new sense of freedom and self-sufficiency, Mary was struggling to extricate herself from feelings of enmeshment with me. Had I interpreted her cancellations as acting out or as an expression of anger toward me, she would have felt criticized and pressured to "take care" of me by complying with my expectations. She would either have to comply or become more resistant. Her understanding of these dynamics established her realization that she had some control over her therapy and her life. Her former appearance of fragility and vulnerability disappeared.

Nevertheless, the pattern of upsets and reconciliations continued until I went on vacation. When I returned—the time we had agreed that she would pay me—Mary gave me a check for much less than I expected. I was upset and felt betrayed. Not knowing what to say, I decided to say nothing. Following her cancellation of our next session, she came in quite distressed; she complained that she was getting worse and that she saw no point in continuing treatment. I said that I felt a disruption in our relationship had developed. I wondered if there was more distance between us since she had paid me and I had not told her that I was disappointed. Her agitation then stopped, and she calmly asked why I was disappointed. I said that there may have been a misunderstanding, but that I had expected a much larger check. She said in a hopeless tone of voice that there was a misunderstanding and that it would be best if she quit therapy. She also said that she wished she could see me in the evenings, when—she said seductively—she could make me happy. I interpreted her response as indicating that she experienced my disappointment as a pressure to take care of me, something she had to do if she was to preserve her tie to me. In the next session, Mary said that she felt better and had begun to think that she had not been properly caring for *our* relationship.

In the following weeks, Mary felt a new sense of strength, confidence, and progress. My ability to confront her with my disappointment without being damaged by her or retaliating and hurting her seemed to give Mary new confidence. For the first time, she was able to take control of her finances. I told her that I had no doubt that she would eventually pay me in full, and I interpreted her actions as revealing that it was difficult for her to make a decision without worrying about its impact on me and her need to comply with my expectations. She felt that reducing the frequency of the sessions to twice weekly would ease the financial pressure; nevertheless, she struggled with her conflicting feelings about taking care of me, yet doing what was best for her. After some struggle, she decided in favor of twice-weekly sessions, and subsequently both her job and her relationship with Bob improved. She also became able to start extricating herself from the enmeshment with her mother and her brother.

DISCUSSION

These sessions illustrate the establishment of selfobject ties, their disruptions, and the use of an intersubjective approach to reestablish them. This patient's ability to reestablish her connection with me without subordinating her own needs in the process was a new experience for her. When I gave her the message that I expected her to act or feel in a certain way, she attempted to comply, but then became more anxious. When I persisted in my point of view, an impasse developed. When she learned that she could do what was best for her, yet maintain the vital tie with me, she became less anxious and felt stronger.

My interpretation of this process led Mary to new memories of early traumatic experiences, and as she began to see her mother's and brother's perspectives without putting herself down, she was able to extricate herself from her enmeshment with them. She developed new longings to see her father after she recalled memories of warm experiences when he took her places and proudly showed her off to his friends. She continued to consolidate both professional and personal gains. The transference continued to be characterized by fluctuations, as her selfobject needs sometimes came to the foreground and at other times receded into the background.

In this case of developmental arrest, the patient was deprived as a child of essential selfobject responses from caregiving figures that were necessary for the development of a bold and vigorous sense of self. Her achievements and accomplishments independent of her mother were not validated, and she felt that she had no right to be proud of herself. Instead, she received a message that her accomplishments hurt her mother and put her in danger of losing her mother's support before she was ready to be on her own. Her intrapsychic conflict was that she had to subordinate her own needs, her own developing individuality, and her spontaneity in order to comply with her mother's needs, thus preserving the vital maternal tie (Stolorow and Brandchaft 1987).

Mary reexperienced this conflict with me in the transference neurosis. During the analysis of the transference, she developed insight into the genetic determinants of her conflicts and had a new experience with me. I interpreted to her that her actions revealed that it was safe to assert herself with me in a variety of provocative ways; she could see that I neither fell apart and withdrew from her nor retaliated and rejected her. She experienced me as being able to stick with her, as working with her to help bridge the disruptions in our relationship, and as being pleased with her development. When she understood this, she became able to experience her own self as a source of strength and understanding. She became able to provide more selfobject functions for herself when her selfobjects failed her. She could experience normal disappointment and frustration without feeling disrupted. Her self-development was once more underway.

This case illustrates how self psychology has influenced my view of transference. Previously, when feeling provoked, I would understand and interpret the patient's behavior as a displacement from the past, as a projection, and as a distortion. I saw myself as the authority who knew better. Now I look carefully for any element of reality in the patient's perception, no matter how small, before looking at the distortions.

Writers outside self psychology have expressed similar ideas about transference. For example, Gill (1984) defined the analytic process as the systematic exploration of the analyst's own contributions to the patient's transference responses. The nature of the transference is emphasized more than the frequency of visits or the use of the couch. Gill described a shift from viewing transference as a distortion to emphasizing the analyst's contribution to the transference: "The change in atmosphere is one from the patient being wrong and misguided to one in which his point of view is given initial consideration. . . . his rational capacity is respected rather than belittled. . . . after his point of view has been acknowledged . . . he is more likely to be willing to look for his own contribution to his experience" (p. 173).

Gill's ideas in this area are compatible with self psychology and imply modifications of technique and of analytic attitudes that can further expand our therapeutic horizons. Sensitive therapists have intuitively applied these techniques, but self psychology now provides a theoretical framework that facilitates teaching them to others.

I have found that treatment impasses indicate that I have lost sight of how my patient is experiencing me (Atwood and Stolorow 1984). I pride myself on being a calm and understanding analyst, so it is quite unpleasant when a patient experiences me as a sadist or as a molester. However, when I can recognize the dynamic involved in this situation, I can also realize that I have invariably been drawn into a reliving of my patient's early traumatic experience. My appreciation of my contribution to this experience leads not only to a resolution of the impasse, but also to a deepening of the therapeutic experience, with new insights and changes both for the patient and for myself.

18

A Countertransference Reaction to Budding Exhibitionism

Charles Coverdale

While most of the challenging countertransference situations are associated with the so-called borderline patient, other forms of relatedness may also provide the clinician with difficult moments. What follows covers only the first two dozen therapeutic hours, focusing on the twenty-fourth session of a continuing therapy.

The patient is a call girl in her early thirties, quite beautiful and very sexy by any standards. Movie and television stars abound in her life, some exclusively as dates and many exclusively as clients. In her first hour she wondered if I knew one of her clients, a well-known psychiatrist. Soon she tells of a desire to come to my house and dance for me, but takes my interpretation well. Provocatively, she licks her lips and runs her tongue across her teeth. At times she seems turned on, but my own reactions tell me she is excited by her own sexiness. She draws attention to aspects of her body beneath her form-fitting clothes, asking me to look. She is delighted by my noncomprehension of the jargon used by clients of call girls. She leaves cash on a small table next to the Kleenex and clock whispering, "I'll just sneak out now" on departing. She describes the perfection of her breasts and nipples caressing them through a thin blouse and announces during her twenty-third session that she is going to have breast implant surgery and will return to therapy after recovering.

Several weeks pass and she returns to therapy in her usual provocative garb, but with unusually large breasts. Sitting opposite me, she tells of her happiness with choosing the largest implants and excitedly describes them while caressing them through her spandex top. Then sliding her scoop neck down she exposes them while looking at them adoringly. She continues to comment on them for some time while caressing and holding them. She looks briefly at me and asks for agreement. I look at them warmly and say, "Well, I can see why you're so pleased, they are just beautiful." She lingers a moment more, then pulls her blouse back up.

Now that the reader is sufficiently outraged, I would ask you only to remain open-minded through the discussion. I did promise you that the selfobject transferences can create difficult and challenging countertransference reactions, but these very reactions provide the clues essential to understanding and interpretation.

Among the difficult aspects of this case is the fact that I have a bias against implants and plastic surgery in general. I view it all as elective mutilation, unnecessary, unnatural, and as buying into sexism and ageism. But this is not my therapy, nor is this useful countertransference (and moralizing has little place in analytic understanding). What is useful is that I did not feel very much sexually as she exhibited (and not because I don't enjoy looking at female nudity). Just moments after she covered her breasts I added, "You know, I have the sense that you are showing me your babies." My comment was right and based mainly on the fact that I was not much titillated. Rather, as I looked on, her self-caressing reminded me of a new mother holding and stroking twin babies' heads. Thank goodness she didn't ask me to hold them, as is common with new mothers in regard to their infants. But, even so, I was prepared to decline as I sometimes do with other women's babies.

I realize that the reader has likely formulated a belief that the therapist in this case is simply voyeuristically acting out and tacitly encouraging the patient to indulge his perversion. We'll return to this momentarily.

Voyeurism aside, there was a great deal that I did get from this incident. Suddenly it was clear to me why she was in her line of work, and what she gets out of her job. Each client allows her the possibility to exhibit anew and receive the joy of appreciative response. This awareness (which came from her exposing herself) and my communication of this awareness put her immediately in touch with a screen memory of a mother too busy to respond to her daughter's budding exhibitionism. Further, it became apparent that her family is fundamentally religious and somewhat uptight about appreciating the body and sexual matters in general. In the several sessions since then she has focused on unmet needs to be attended to by her mother. Thankfully, she trusted me to respond as she needed, having tested me (as I now can understand) to see if I was only self-interested.

With regard to the reader's belief in my voyeuristic acting out, I suppose that all those drawn to this profession tend toward the voyeuristic end of the continuum. Further, I admit to feeling a moment of enjoyment as she exposed herself; but, as she did, it was a remarkably unsexual occasion.

Now let's consider some alternatives. By way of contrast, one must wonder what if I had been uncomfortable with her physical display. Had I stopped her from showing herself, surely I would have frustrated her desires to be attended to, and would have retraumatized her in the same way her mother had while precluding access to the very information that explained why she so hungers for response. So hungry, in fact, is she that she is driven to risk subjecting herself to painfully humiliating situations. Fortunately, I did not interfere. I feel equally fortunate not to have misinterpreted. Had I seen it as a sexual ploy, it could have been interpreted as a power play or control issue. It would also have been possible to conceptualize it as an attempt for merger, a violation of boundaries, of a desire to corrupt or sabotage therapy. But all of these formulations would have been incorrect and accompanied by different behaviors on her part. Please note that she did not look at me, except briefly, while exhibiting; nor did she glance at the front of my trousers. I realize this as I review the hour.

So, if we stay close to the evidence, we can see that having received the desired mirroring, she was then left with a sense of completion and satisfaction. Then, following my comment about showing her babies, she responded with all the sweet intonation of a new mother giving a baby its due with the words, "My beautiful babies. I didn't realize it until you said it." With herself serving as her own narcissistic object, she wanted nothing more than to be joined in her self-adoration. At last, adoring mother and adored child were united.

Once again I was thankful for my own analysis, which helped me years ago to differentiate and understand complex and subtle feelings. I also recall having had, at one point in my own analysis, a fantasy of being seen naked by my female analyst, only to realize that it was not my grown body but that of my 3-year-old self that I had wanted seen. So, while not all exhibitionists are seeking mirroring, I do know of two who were. In twenty-four years of practice, I have been flashed only once, and I feel lucky to have depended on my countertransference reactions for guidance.

V

STRATEGIC EMOTIONAL INVOLVEMENT IN LISTENING TO NEUROTIC ISSUES

19

Emotional Involvement in Neurosis

THE PROBLEM OF NEUROSIS

At this point in the history of psychoanalysis it is difficult to speak definitively about any aspect of neurosis since it is no longer altogether clear how we can best make use of the concept. Freud's self-analysis seemed most clear when he was still oriented to the idea that the origin of neurosis lay in the problem of the father (Freud 1954). He believed that the theme of *Oedipus Rex*, which was reworked in *Hamlet*, had endured so long because it portrayed a set of deep and universal concerns. However, Kohut (1979) has pointed out that Freud's narcissistic relations to his preoedipal selfobjects were never analyzed. I have maintained that Freud's self-analysis ended when he reached the question of whether the origins of neurosis lay, instead, with the problem of mother; and further, that Freud's symbiotic issues, which emerged so clearly to end his self-analysis, were never analyzed—primarily because he had no analyst who could register in the countertransference and then speak in the analysis the themes of the replicated dyadic symbiotic exchange (Hedges 1992). Freud's subsequent theorizing was therefore limited to a certain set of relatively high-level developmental concerns that through time have become specified in terms of oedipal-level neurosis.

Following Kaplan (1978) and Loewald (1979), I have formulated a contemporary reading of Freud's (1924b) study of the Oedipus complex (Hedges 1983). By way of summary, it can be said that the 3- or 4-year-old child is caught between regressive longings for oneness with the (m)other and progressive strivings for independence. Psychic independence is achievable only when the child is able to identify with the third party and to see him/herself in relation to the second party. That is, independence implies a psychological capacity for contingent or triangular object relating. Who I am now depends on, is contingent upon, my knowing (cognitively and emotionally) who is who to whom in each triangular relationship. Love "object constancy" is defined as the capacity for lifelong reconciliations between the pull for dependent merger experiences and the pull for a sense of independent separateness. Intense parricidal and/or incestual conflicts produce advanced-level repressions that serve to evade the oedipal task of establishing constant and ambivalent object relations. The developmentally achieved capacity for symbolization can be used in the service of repression of oedipal conflicts or in the service of gradually relinquishing oedipal object cathexes and substituting them by means of identifications with parental and cultural authorities (i.e., the formation of the superego), and in interpersonal and cultural subliminatory activities. The waning of the Oedipus complex is seen as a lifelong process characterized by the intensity of oedipal cathexes and conflicts being progressively relinquished in the face of novel love relationships.

It is interesting to speculate on the possibility of Freud's analysis having continued through narcissistic, borderline, and psychotic (organizing) layers of his personality. Might then "neurosis" have come to be synonymous with "internalizations" in general rather than only oedipal internalizations? Many early studies in hysteria, as well as many later ones by Freud and his colleagues focusing on what they labeled "neurosis," would, by contemporary standards, likely be labeled "narcissistic" or "borderline." Some have speculated that neurotics were once seen in pure culture but no longer exist due to changing cultural conditions. Others suggest that our tools for observation and conceptualization have become more refined, so that much of what appeared neurotic in days gone by we now know how to see as developmentally less differentiated.

The bottom line on these debates seems to point toward the notion that the concept of neurosis can no longer be used as a complete description of any person's psychological makeup. Rather, neurosis describes a certain set of capacities—object constancy, triangular relatedness, ambivalence, symbolic representation, dynamic repression, and an internalized superego. These capacities are developed by people whose more foundational developmental experiences have been favorable. Analysts holding to the classical formulations regarding neurosis maintain that once these abovementioned capacities are achieved, the entire previous personality structure becomes retrospectively reorganized under the sway of new and powerful integrating principles. This latter doctrine is generally used to justify the continued use of classical technique (as opposed to an expanded or variable technique) since all preoedipal issues are taken to be under the sway of the symbolizing influence of a constant self and constant others and therefore accessible by means of Freud's original free association technique.

In contrast, the listening perspectives approach does not require taking a stand on the "truth" position of any theoretical proposition—including issues about what is to be counted as neurotic. The listening perspectives approach assumes that all well-developed people have experienced in one way or another previous levels of self and other personality organization. These earlier overlearned patterns of emotional responsiveness may be engaged in analysis through communication modes other than the verbal-symbolic mode that characterizes oedipal triangular communication. That is, all people with advanced-level neurotic capacities passed through a narcissistic selfother developmental phase, a borderline symbiotic phase, and a psychotic organizing phase. The self and other modes of relatedness that characterize each of these levels of development may, in any given person at a specified moment in time, dominate certain aspects of the personality or simply be retained as an aspect of the overall flexibility of personality functioning.

The critical question for psychoanalytic technique is: Under what conditions is one mode of emotional relatedness more strategic—in terms of promoting analysis—than another? I have devised two rules of thumb to help me when I am in doubt as to what mode of emotional relatedness is being presented for me to respond to. The first guideline regards the *content of the relatedness communication*. I try the (developmentally) lower possibility first. For example, I respond to some aspect of (preoedipal) deficiency experience rather than interpreting an (oedipal) conflict between wishes and inhibitions. If I am wrong, the effect is relatively harmless or regarded by the client as naive or Pollyanna-like and ignored. Whereas if I go for the apparently higher-level conflictual content and I am wrong, I have painfully missed the client's point so that the sequelae of a misunderstanding ensue, marking a breach in empathy.

The second guide to determining what mode of emotional relatedness is presently active regards the *form of the communication* (i.e., verbal or paraverbal). When in doubt, I begin at the highest level of abstraction—the verbal-symbolic. If I am wrong the result is usually harmless—my words will go unheeded or at worst branded as stupid or off the mark. If I begin my response trying to establish some sort of (preoedipal) self to selfobject resonance, merger sense, or organizing contact, I will likely miss the opportunity to capitalize on the critical symbolic possibilities of the moment.

To restate, *the content rule* implies that lower level relatedness concerns are more universal but also more idiosyncratic in nature and, therefore, it is more difficult to achieve a specificity, a tailoring, or a catering to individual needs. By going after the lower level, more personal, and idiosyncratic, I probably will not be all that wrong but will have missed the subtleties of the higher level content, which can certainly be repeated until I get it right. But if a more critical (lower developmentally) emotional relatedness issue is at stake and I begin babbling some abstract interpretation about internal conflict, then I am way off the mark and my attempt will be felt as insulting, unempathic, hurtful, or whatever. To restate, *the form rule* tells me whether the accent on my response needs to be a carefully worded response capturing exactly the verbal-symbolic nuance of our interaction, or whether what I say is not so important as the manner in which I say it or the way I receive or give my response, in order to dovetail with the emotional relatedness being offered at the moment.

The content and form rules are easy to remember if you recall that with older children it is very important exactly *what* you tell them, *how* you explain yourself. However, with an infant or toddler what is important in strategic emotional involvement is *the way you manage yourself and how you manage them*, not so much the words you use.

There is one postscript to these rules of thumb regarding the content and form of the strategic emotional response. In regard to working with "terrible twos" borderline experiences and "colicky" organizing experiences, nothing the listener attempts by way of emotional involvement will be satisfactory, for very different reasons. We simply have to begin with that realization. In terrible twos oppositionality there is considerable structure so that our interpretative work can regularly go toward such formulations as "No means yes, and yes means no," "There's going to be a witch here no matter what," or whatever interpretation best defines the moment (notice I didn't say "wins the day"!). With a colicky baby, transference reenactment, the contact effectiveness of each maneuver, to the extent it brings relief, lasts only a moment. The severe pain and fatigue of object relating and the inadequacy of all response is being expressed in turbulent, out-of-control ways. The temptation toward countertransference anger and retaliation for making me feel helpless or impotent is great. We can be sure this speaker is used to that kind of response from everyone else, so we have to find something to do that's better. The tendency toward exasperation and withdrawal when working on organizing experiences is likewise great and has to be forestalled in favor of sustained presence in the face of constant unpleasantness, which often amounts to chronic rage accompanied by threats of attack, self-injury, or abandonment. But the rules still hold—keep focused on the preverbal content of the emotional involvement (i.e., the ebb and flow of contact) rather than on the words, content, or "symptoms" (which are probably irrational, contradictory, or inflammatory at best). It is fine if the baby is cooing during diaper change, or on the pediatrician's table, but this is often not the case and you have to do your job anyway. Form-wise, babies generally love to listen to the sound of mother's voice and are much more likely to be responsive to other nonverbal kinds of emotional contact when the world is filled with lovely sounds, gestures, and smiles—so keep up the abstract while doing what you need to do. But don't expect your words to be understood or responded to in kind—at a time when baby's expressive needs require crying, screaming, threatening, provoking, and demanding.

This is all to say that we are sometimes in a quandary when working with a person who is clearly well developed. There is no question that our strategic emotional relatedness needs to be basically frame oriented—that is, private, protected, bounded, nonintrusive, time limited, neutral with respect to internal agency, nongratifying, and unperturbed by countertransference involvement. But the question today is: Under what conditions is it preferable, in terms of securing for analysis an emerging preoedipal issue, to move from a strictly classical frame technique to more variable responsiveness? On the one hand, it is easy to understand how a preoedipal concern or demand may emerge as resistance to analysis of some neurotic structure and therefore require verbal-symbolic interpretation. But on the other hand, blind adherence to a technical interpretive procedure that has been historically validated for analyzing neurosis—when what is being lived in the analysis is clearly not neurotic—is wrong and unnecessary.

I will forever be grateful to my analyst for the day he sharply instructed me to sit up facing him so we could discuss a pressing matter. One of my clients had left her psychotic husband. He had broken into the house, beaten her up, declared he had cancer and gangrene, and was chasing around town in his truck with his shotgun vowing to kill those whom he felt were responsible for his wife's disaffection. I was number one on the list. I was terrified when I arrived for my analytic hour. As soon as my analyst grasped the gravity of the situation, he knew that any neurotic panic element paled in the face of the truly dangerous situation I was in. I was in a state of panic and confusion. He promptly insisted that we go over my plan of action, my safety precautions, my relation to people in my office building, and my protection by the police. While this is a dramatically real example, I hope it serves to make the point that, neurosis or not, life sometimes simply has more pressing matters than analyzing oedipal castration anxiety. The same holds true for any preoedipal issue that remains salient for very long in an analysis. Unless it is given its due precedence, whatever later issues may be involved or superimposed will never have an opportunity to emerge for analysis.

Some readers may object: "But since the analysis of neurosis requires the analyst to be 'like an opaque mirror,' if the analyst has been more active (and therefore perhaps more disclosing) in interventions designed to secure preoedipal engagements for analysis, doesn't the patient know too much about the analyst's real emotional responsiveness to use her as an opaque mirror?" My answer: "Nonsense, analysis is not so delicate as some previous teachings would lead us to believe. If a person is needing to project an oedipal prohibition onto her analyst, I promise you she will find a way. This is not the problem. The problem that analysts (neurotically) fear is having to "wean" their clients from forms of relatedness (e.g., dependency) that feel good and that clients—at some level—do not want to give up." Searles (1979a) holds that at times analysts too are reluctant to give up these preoedipal relatedness modes because of their transitional object value to the analyst! But such difficulties are almost diagnostic in themselves. If such dilemmas arise, it can only be because there was a great preoedipal yearning that needed to be engaged in and responded to so that the person could find some way of relinquishing an addictive way of relating, which had not yet been represented in conscious (symbolic) thought. Perhaps the analyst's resistance to being the person bringing the bad news about the relatedness addiction, and the reasons to give it up, need to be looked at. I have written extensively on technique with preoedipal-level issues and how they can be brought into the analytic relationship for study (Hedges 1983, 1992, 1994c).

STRATEGIC EMOTIONAL INVOLVEMENT
IN INDEPENDENT RELATEDNESS[1]

Classical psychoanalysis, based upon Freud's original formulations regarding psychoneurosis, is clear on the problem of countertransference. According to this strict and narrow definition, countertransference is always unconscious in nature and springs from the infantile neurosis of the analyst. As such, its emergence into the analytic arena constitutes an impediment, an interference with the unfolding of the transference of the person in analy-

---

1. This section is reprinted with modifications from Hedges 1992.

sis. Since countertransference is by nature unconscious, there is no ready access to it except through consultation with a supervisor or through further analytic work by the analyst.

Freud (1910) wrote, "We have become aware of the 'countertransference,' which arises in [the analyst] as a result of the patient's influence on his unconscious feelings, and we are almost inclined to insist that he shall recognize this countertransference in himself and overcome it" (p. 144f). This moralistic attitude of Freud is echoed in his only other direct published reference to it (Freud 1915).

> Our control over ourselves is not so complete that we may not suddenly one day go further than we intended. In my opinion, therefore, we ought not to give up the neutrality towards the patient, which we have acquired through keeping the countertransference in check. [p. 164]

In a letter to Binswanger dated February 20, 1913, Freud expressed that the problem of countertransference is one of the most difficult technical problems in psychoanalysis. "What is given to the patient," Freud said, must be "consciously allotted, and then more or less of it as the need may arise. Occasionally a great deal." Later Freud set down the maxim: "To give someone too little because one loves him too much is being unjust to the patient and a technical error" (Binswanger 1956). Kohut (1971) used this notion of Freud's to authorize his own expanded analysis of countertransference responsiveness in the analysis of selfother transferences.

Reich (1951) bolstered the Freudian position by eliminating ordinary feelings from what is to be considered countertransference. She maintained that extremely intense positive or negative feelings for the patient are always countertransference and worthy of more psychoanalysis for the analyst or referral of the patient.

In the listening perspective for use with independent relatedness strivings, or for understanding triadic, contingent relationships, disruptive affects from the personality of the analyst may indeed be dilatory to the development of the analytic enterprise and are probably best handled in the way Freud and others have suggested, that is, through consultation or more personal analysis. The chief difficulty today concerning adherence to these precepts is being able to distinguish among countertransference responses arising in relation to independent relating, responses arising appropriately in relation to selfother transferences, and responses that may relate to symbiotic replications or organizing endeavors. At present the only gauge seems to be by estimation of the general issues characteristic of the person involved and what sort of material is currently being explored in the analysis. Lacking other criteria upon which to make a judgment, the analyst first ought to explore cautiously the earlier developmental possibilities in hopes that, if in error, the analyst will be experienced as merely irritating or misguided. If one initially assumes that it is one's own material, much may be missed and much damage done to the analysis (see Hedges 1992, Chapter 1).

Each of the four major forms of countertransference responsiveness constitutes strategic emotional involvement that arises naturally out of a listener responding empathically to different developmental issues through one of the four differential listening perspectives.

THE "OVERSTIMULATING" COUNTERTRANSFERENCE

So what might countertransference to neurotic issues look like? This is anyone's guess since any aspect of one's personality might become stimulated. *Overstimulating* is perhaps the key word to describe the kind of experience the analyst might be having. Since the main areas of impulse and inhibition are, in the broadest senses, sexual and aggressive in nature at the neurotic level, we might expect countertransference to be responsive to these drives, which are highly organized by the age of 5. As the repressed returns, it has the hallmark of infantile sexual and aggressive organization and will likely be felt as a sexual or destructive drive. The overstimulating countertransference will represent, in one form or another, the analyst's response to these drives. The response will arise from the analyst's personality. But beyond this we can say little of a general nature.

Though Freud (1915) taught that emotional involvement on the part of the analyst can be an impediment to the analytic process, we know that his forbearance certainly did not entail the schizoid withdrawal that has come to be a caricature of psychoanalysis (Roazen 1984). His notions of neutrality and evenly hovering attention clearly included an awareness that unconscious emotional responsiveness of the analyst was the central part of analytic practice (Heimann 1950).

The remainder of this chapter will pull from the literature a few interesting and even surprising ways in which analysts have noted that countertransference to neurotic issues may manifest itself. These case reports by prominent psychoanalysts point towards subtle and perhaps quite unexpected forms of countertransference involvement with neurotic issues. Following these vignettes will be a discussion of the problem of distinguishing oedipal from preoedipal transferences and countertransferences.

RESISTANCE EXPERIENCED AS HATRED

Resistance on the part of the analytic speaker to uncovering some unconscious material may reflect hatred of the original love object that is being transferred to the analytic listener. In reacting to transferential hatred with counterhatred the listener falls into a trap laid by his or her own neurosis. The listener is prepared to believe he or she is hateable because of infantile internal objects which were in turn hated. An example is discussed by Racker (1968), in which a listener's rejection of the female speaker's ways of resisting paralleled his internal rejection of deceptive parts of himself that she reminded him of. While the listener's annoyance with a speaker's resistance may be in part realistically or objectively justifiable, there are always elements of the listener's annoyance that are in part neurotic. Racker sees such reactions as unavoidable but expresses more optimism when the listener can be aware of these tendencies and attempt to keep their interference to a minimum.

THE ANALYST'S NEED FOR LOVE

Racker (1968) reports that when the analytic listener's need for love is thwarted in the analytic situation, his or her capacity for objective perception may be interfered with by such archaic images as the mother or breast that does not feed but robs, or the self image of the insatiable vampire.

LOCKED OUT OF MY ANALYST'S OFFICE

Blum (1987) provides an example of a masochistic-sadomasochistic transference-countertransference exchange in which the neurotic conflicts in both speaker and listener were not created *de novo* by the analytic situation. The countertransference was a reciprocal rather than a mirror version of the transference, which would have to be taken into account before a useful interpretation could be made.

> The . . . example concerns a sadomasochistic patient who was frequently late, demanding, and complaining in the analysis. She tended to frustrate, annoy, and provoke her student analyst. There was no sign that he liked working with the patient, and it rather seemed as though he girded himself for a struggle and was disappointed with the failure of his interpretations to have any effect upon the patient's complaints or her tendencies to mas-

ochistically act out. (Some analysts may unconsciously instigate, encourage, or enjoy the patient's acting out tendencies, unwittingly contributing to complications if not impasse in the analytic process.) On two occasions, the analyst locked the patient out of the office, forgetting to unlock the waiting-room door. One of these occasions was on the patient's birthday. In the next session, the patient spoke about an insolent waiter who kept the patient waiting unconscionably and who provided terrible service. The patient vowed never to return to the restaurant, but she did return to the analytic session. She did not refer directly to the lockout and was afraid of the intensity of her disappointment and rage which seemed to be outside of awareness. She could not discuss her thoughts of quitting or her fears of being thrown out by the analyst. The lockout was also a message that she interpreted as "get lost" and an act of neglect and rejection.

Another patient might have reacted with overt outrage, might have been openly critical of the analyst, or might even have been gleeful over the analyst's egregious error. In this situation, this masochistic patient elicited a sadomasochistic countertransference. Her final quitting of treatment was overdetermined by her transference conflicts and by the influence of the analyst's countertransference. But it is entirely possible that the patient's departure from treatment included a determinant of acting out of the countertransference fantasy of the analyst, like a child who tends to act out the unconscious fantasies of the parents. I previously described this (Blum 1982) as a malignant cycle of unresolved transference-countertransference, distinguishing between the countertransference as an analytic reality to which the patient was reacting and the spontaneous, irrational, unconscious fantasies of the patient about the analyst. This brings me to a point emphasized by Little (1951) and since then by many others. The countertransference always has an impact upon the analytic process when the analyst's reaction is more than an internal signal. The patient was actually persistently reacting to the analyst's chronic countertransference rather than only to the episodic lockouts. The candidate tended to be sleepy during the patient's sessions and was, in a sense, emotionally detached so that the patient felt tuned out rather than appropriate attunement. Her masochism was gratified in the passive/aggressive withdrawal of her analyst. A correct interpretation of the patient's masochistic transference fantasies would have to take into account the grain of truth of mistreatment and victimization within the fantasy and that the fantasy was anchored to a reality in the analytic situation. Some dimension of the mistreatment was not transference distortion but a correct perception of a rejecting analytic attitude of "lock out" to which the patient masochistically adapted. Here, interpretation and resolution of the countertransference would have been indispensable to a fuller understanding of the patient's tenacious masochistic transference onto the establishment of a progressive analytic process. The countertransference was a reciprocal rather than a mirror reflection of the patient's transference, and the neurotic conflicts of analyst and patient stem from both their individual pasts and were not created *de nouveau* in the analytic situation. It may be presumed that the patient's masochistic tendencies may not have been expressed, exploited, or gratified in the same form in other situations. The patient's fantasy memories of victimized rejection had a reality as well as a transference meaning. [pp. 99–101]

ORALITY IN THE COUNTERTRANSFERENCE

Racker (1968) reports an interesting instance in which an analytic trainee had been referred a case by an older colleague whom he experienced as a father figure. The patient was seen as having a great deal of anxiety and hunger so that the young analyst was inclined to feed her and, as a result, she improved considerably. But as she got better through this "masochistic submission" on the part of her therapist, he became more anxious and finally became ill himself. He understood his illness was somehow related to the case and that he was "giving himself to her, and abandoning himself, 'tearing himself to pieces,' 'ruining himself,' or 'killing himself' for her; all these expressions faithfully reflected the situation of the ego submitting to the archaic persecuting superego" (pp. 115–116). In the countertransference reaction the therapist hated her and blamed her for her "vampirism" which he later came to see as his own projected frustrated, voracious hunger that had been taken into his persecutory superego. Here, Racker formulates, the desire to please the father analyst acted as a superego demand causing him to submit to feeding her in order to feed himself—a token self-castration to avoid a fantasied real castration by the internalized father of the superego.

THE VICTIM TURNED PERSECUTOR

It is not unusual to hear listeners denigrate the behavior of their speakers when presenting their work to colleagues. In the following vignette the therapist is a candidate in analytic training presenting his work to advanced colleagues at his institute (Racker 1968). The defense illustrated is a familiar one in which the patient is seen as "no good" in an effort to reassure the listener himself that he is not incompetent. Analytic work on the therapist's defense is seen as necessary before the analysis can proceed.

The patient for the most part was silent and when she did speak was seldom sincere. The therapist was presenting the case in an ongoing case conference which was a part of his training. As he became more frustrated with her lack of progress and his failure he began blaming her, thereby projecting his sense of failure onto her and his sense of persecutory blame directly onto his colleagues in the case conference and indirectly onto her. She thus became the persecutor and he the persecuted.

TOO MUCH ATTENTION

One feature that characterizes the analytic situation is the tendency toward automatic activities on the part of the analyst. Jacobs (1987) relates an instance in which his *rapt attention* came to be revealed as an attitude from childhood that concealed negative and competitive feelings. He reports visual associations that recurred during hours with a particular man as an orator holding forth before an entranced audience. His failure to say much or to interpret to this man concealed pertinent countertransference feelings within one of our chief analytic instruments—the silence of empathic understanding.

> Some years ago, after I had begun analytic work with a man of considerable artistic talent and ingenuity, I discovered in myself an unusual phenomenon. I noticed that despite having listened to Mr. K. for better than four months I had not missed a word that he had spoken. This, I must confess, was for me a situation worth reflecting on for I was quite aware of a tendency, when tired, conflicted, or anxious, for my attention to drift in the direction of my own associations rather than those of the patient. This had not happened with Mr. K. and I was on the verge of considering myself cured when I gave some thought to the way that, in fact, I had been listening to him. Then I realized that in listening so alertly, so carefully, and with such rapt attention, I had done nothing more than trade one symptom for another. My listening had taken on a special quality that now I recognized as familiar. It contained within it something akin to awe and I realized that although I had missed nothing, neither had I offered much in the way of interpretation.
>
> I became aware, too, that there occurred in my visual associations to Mr. K. a frequently recurring theme; this involved the depiction of an orator or public speaker holding forth before an entranced audience. It did not take much more detective work for me to understand what had been happening. I had been listening to Mr. K., as, for years, I had listened to my father holding forth at the dinner table and, like the two-thousand-year-old man, expounding his personal view of world history. Long after dessert was served, I would sit transfixed listening to him spin tales of biblical times and of the *tsouris* experienced by Rabbi Joshua, later known by the name of Jesus. It was his show, and if I spoke at all it was simply to ask for more details—the equivalent of my interventions years later with my patient.

Mr. K.'s talent for storytelling and his transference wish for me to play the role of appreciative audience had transported me back four decades. I was listening as I had listened as a boy of ten, silently, intently, half-mesmerized. Only later did I realize that the particular way in which I listened was serving an old and familiar purpose: to keep from my awareness the negative and competitive feelings that I was experiencing toward the performer on stage.

Like the rather extended silences that, in this case, I found myself slipping into, silence in the analyst not uncommonly contains elements of countertransference. Familiar to all of us are the silences that reflect anger, boredom, depression, and fatigue. Familiar too are the silences of confusion, of retaliation, and of momentary identification. [pp. 170–171]

PARANOIC AND MASOCHISTIC DEFENSE IN THE COUNTERTRANSFERENCE NEUROSIS

Racker (1968) reports a vignette in which the analytic listener begins to hate his patient, which results in a considerable guilt reaction. He alternates between accusations against his patient and self-recriminations. When she falls into misfortune his hate becomes satisfied but his unconscious guilt holds him (magically) responsible. As she turns her transferential hatred and accusations on him, his unconscious self-persecution leads him into a series of reparation attempts in which he masochistically allows himself to be "eaten, bitten, and partially castrated for her" (p. 118). Racker discusses this instance and several others in terms of various manic defensive maneuvers, including exhibitionism, which a listener may employ as a part of his or her countertransference neurosis. The listener's reactions are seen as an impediment to analytic progress that requires further analytic work on the part of the listener.

SOME EFFECTS OF REPRESSED COUNTERTRANSFERENCE

Racker (1968) provides another example of a man who attacks his analytic listener. She reacts partly unconsciously with anger and depression, repressing the possibility of his sensing her reactions. The analytic speaker developed self-attacking physical symptoms, in response not only to his transference fantasy of having caused depression in his listener but also to actual repressed countertransference feelings. Racker cites another instance of a speaker expressing a lack of respect for his listener. The listener may feel narcissistically wounded and annoyed. But if he represses his annoyance because it is not consistent with the demands of his ego ideal or superego, he deprives himself of an important guide to understanding the speaker's transference. Likewise sexual excitement in the listener may point toward important seductive aspects of the transference. Racker concludes that repression of countertransference may well prevent access to appropriate technique.

"ANALYTIC CONSCIENCE" AS A PIECE OF COUNTERTRANSFERENCE

Using a countertransference example from Reich (1951), Racker (1968) shows the importance of having access to the total countertransference reaction in order to understand the total transference situation. Failure to consider all aspects of countertransference can be an impediment to analytic work. Early in the analysis Reich responded to a series of provocations with interpretations. Reich's technique had communicated that there was much room for freedom of expression and analytic tolerance.

> What the analysand aimed at doing was to test whether such tolerance really existed in the analyst. Reich himself later gave him this interpretation, and this interpretation had a far more positive effect than the first. Consideration of the total countertransference situation (the feeling of being provoked, *and* the "analytic conscience" which determined the fate of this feeling) might have been from the first a guide in apprehending the total transference situation, which consisted in aggressiveness, in the original mistrust, *and* in the ray of confidence, the new hope which the liberality of the fundamental rule had awakened in him. [Racker 1968, pp. 150–152]

ENACTING AN EARLY MEMORY THROUGH EMPATHY

Jacobs (1987) notes some unaccountable irritation following a particularly vivid session with a woman. He had seen what she saw, experienced what she had experienced, and felt what she had felt. After she left he began to associate to a childhood experience in which empathy with his mother contained resentment for her feeling victimized by his father. He demonstrates in this vignette that memories in the form of such enactments can distract the analytic listener's perception and understanding.

> Less well recognized as a potential conveyor of countertransference feelings is the kind of silence that, as analysts, we strive to achieve as part of our analytic instrument; the silence of empathic understanding. Precisely because this attitude is so important to us, so much emphasized, and in

reality so valuable in our work, countertransference elements that on occasion may be concealed within it are easily overlooked.

This fact was brought home to me in the course of analytic work with a middle-aged professional woman. During one session in particular I became aware in myself of unusually strong feelings of empathy. In that hour I was able to see what Mrs. A. saw, experience what she experienced, feel what she felt. It was with considerable surprise then, that after the patient had left the office I noted in myself some irritation with her and the thought that what she had told me was only one side of a complex story.

This reaction caused me to reflect on the material of our hour and, with the patient out of the room, once again to associate to it. It was then that I realized that the scene that Mrs. A. had depicted was entirely familiar to me and that in my adolescence I had played one of the central characters. Distraught over an argument with her husband, Mrs. A. had been unable to sleep. She waited up until her teenage son had come in from an evening out, and then talked to him at some length of her distress. He had listened and been understanding as I had been when, under similar circumstances, my mother had confided in me her hurt and anger over my father's behavior.

Now as I listened to Mrs. A. and imagined the scene she was depicting I had, unconsciously, become again the son at the kitchen table listening to and sharing his mother's upset. I had become the good listener, the empathic listener, but also the listener who had to conceal from himself some feelings of resentment at what he was hearing. It was only after Mrs. A. was gone that I, like the adolescent who, when alone, can experience certain emotions that do not surface in a parent's presence, became aware that my responses during the hour were only one side of a complex countertransference reaction. The other side, the resentment I felt over Mrs. A.'s presenting herself as the helpless victim and her husband as the brutish aggressor, had been defended against as similar emotions had been defended against years before: by the upsurge of the strongest feelings of empathy.

For many colleagues the experiences in childhood and adolescence of being an empathic listener to parents or other family members has played a role of importance in their choice of vocation. It is not a rare occurrence for the memories of these experiences to be evoked in the analytic situation. Then silently, outside of awareness, the analyst's usually valuable empathic responses may contain within them enactments of those memories. Enactments which, subtly, can alter and distort his perceptions and understanding. [pp. 171–172]

NEUTRALITY AS COUNTERTRANSFERENCE

Highlighting the complexity of analytic neutrality, Jacobs (1987) points out that our discussions of this basic analytic posture rarely include considerations of the relation of the forces of outer neutrality, which are an integral part of analytic technique, and forces of inner neutrality, which define one of the conditions required for that technique—conflict-free ego functioning. Tension between inner and outer aspects of an analytic listener's neutrality frequently underlie countertransference distortion. He illustrates this with a vignette in which he had worked so hard to remain neutral that he failed to notice the speaker's aggression or the counteraggression it stimulated in him as well as in others. It was a rapid heartbeat, dry mouth, and knotted guts that informed the listener of his anger. This inner force had been dimly perceived but not yet understood by him so that he unconsciously was overemphasizing the outer aspects of neutrality, thus introducing a distortion in his analysis of a young attorney.

> This was a man of outward charm and inner rage. So well concealed was his anger, however, that he appeared to all the world to be quite simply a man of utmost graciousness and wit. To his qualities of keen intelligence and sophistication was added a persuasive tongue, so that Mr. C. was known for his ability to attract clients. This talent he utilized in the analysis in playful, witty, and seemingly good-humored efforts to get me to render judgments on one or another of the fanciful—and invariably self-defeating—schemes and projects in which he was forever engaged.
>
> In the face of Mr. C.'s charm and persuasiveness I remained admirably neutral—or so I thought. Repeatedly, if not doggedly, I identified and interpreted his central inner conflicts; his obvious oedipal rivalry and his unconscious guilt as well as certain preoedipal attachments—all with no effect whatever on him. Not for many months was I able to confront Mr. C. directly either with the destructive impact of his behavior on his personal and professional life or with his aggression in the analytic situation.
>
> The reason for this was simple. Aggression in Mr. C., though deep and pervasive, was so well concealed, so covertly expressed, that for some time I was not consciously aware either of its presence or of the strong counteraggression that it was stimulating in me. In a vague and not easily definable way, I felt uncomfortable with him, and I began, therefore, in sessions to pay attention to my autonomic responses. With regularity I found, when working with Mr. C., that my heartbeat was rapid, my mouth dry, and my guts feeling tense and knotted. It became increasingly clear to me that these were bodily signs of concealed anger occurring in response to the covert anger directed at me.
>
> Because of this state of affairs, I was unable to attain a properly "neutral" (that is, relatively conflict-free) inner receptivity. Since I was not consciously aware of this situation, but in some intuitive way, perceived it, I unconsciously overemphasized the outer aspect of neutrality, its technical side. I became, as it were, not only a neutral analyst but a determinedly neutral one. Afraid in the face of Mr. C.'s persuasiveness—and the aggression that lay behind it—to lose my stance of neutrality, I lost what Sandler

has termed the analyst's free-floating responsiveness. In this case that meant the ability to confront Mr. C. more directly with his behavior both within and outside the analytic situation.

Reflection on my responses to Mr. C. led me to a memory that helped clarify some of the more specific countertransference reactions involved. As a youngster I had great admiration for an after-school sports group leader who, for a time, became for me a father surrogate. Bright, witty, and ingenious, he was also something of a provocateur with his charges. In ways that were both humorous and vexing, he would tease the boys about aspects of their dress or behavior. Increasingly I became angry at this leader, but because he was emotionally important to me I concealed my feelings both from him and myself.

It was not until, for quite other reasons, I left the group, that I realized how large a role aggression on both sides, mine as well as his, had played in our relationship. No doubt Mr. C.'s behavior in the analytic situation, which in many respects was similar to that of the group leader and other important figures of my childhood, aroused in me a familiar pattern of response. It was this response, with its emphasis on attempting to quiet an inner disturbance through greater emphasis on outer neutrality, that led to its inappropriate use. [pp. 173–174]

THE REPETITION AND RESISTANCE SCENARIO

Repetition is central to the working-through process so that an analyst becomes accustomed to providing the same or similar interpretation in a variety of circumstances. But a scenario can develop in which an interpretation is resisted by the client and given again and resisted until an unconscious battle ensues, which can well produce a stalemate not unlike experiences from the childhoods of both parties (Jacobs 1987).

Within the framework of what appears to be a necessary, if painstaking, process of repetition and the gradual working through of resistance, a formidable, if unconscious, battle has been joined. As a result of the arousal of infantile conflicts in both parties—analyst as well as patient—the process of repetition becomes a hammer blow against an iron door. The result, unless this transference-countertransference interaction can be identified and effectively interpreted, is the kind of stalemate that often characterizes such struggles in childhood. Even in situations in which the process of working through gradually takes place, the interaction between patient and analyst may bear the hallmarks of similar parent–child relationships. The analyst interprets and the patient accepts perhaps a fraction of his offering. Further interpretations may lead to the acceptance of additional fractions. No doubt this is what is meant by fractional discharge. Under favorable circumstances this situation may continue until the patient's mouth has opened wide enough for the analyst to slip in a few spoonfuls of his special nourishment. [pp. 174–175]

"LISTENING FOR TRANSFERENCE" SEEN AS COUNTERTRANSFERENCE

Since analytic culture is skewed in favor of the notion that mutative interpretations are always transference interpretations, most analytic listeners are continuously scrutinizing the analytic situation for signs of transference. But this biased way of listening may give rise to a defensive collusion with the stated purpose of exploiting the transference so that the emergence of other anxiety-laden material can be avoided.

> Such was the case with Mrs. G., a clever and sophisticated woman who oriented herself to others by picking up in them the slightest behavioral and verbal cues. During a difficult time in her life, when her husband had become acutely ill, she brought in material that contained within it detectable, though quite concealed, references to her analyst.
> Though it took a hawklike alertness to the barest hints of transference to dig out these nuggets, I was able to do so and was rather pleased at being able to interpret certain transference feelings that had not previously surfaced.
> Only after this period had passed and Mrs. G.'s husband had recovered did I become aware of how patient and analyst had utilized this transference material. Terrified that her husband would die and unable in the analysis to face this possibility, Mrs. G. had, unconsciously, made use of her knowledge that I invariably reacted with interest to transference material by feeding me bits and pieces of it as a decoy. For my part, Mr. G.'s life-threatening illness had reactivated some painful memories concerning personal losses which I, too, was eager to suppress. By joining with my patient in a particular kind of detective game called "locate the transference," I had colluded with her in doing just that. At this time in the analysis the central issue was not the subtleties of the transference—as important as these were—but Mrs. G.'s inability to face the reality of death; a reality that her analyst was also quite willing to avoid. [Jacobs 1987, pp. 178–179]

"CORRECT" INTERPRETATION AS COUNTERTRANSFERENCE

Analytic listeners are keenly interested in "correct" interpretations because it is said that such interpretations elicit material that confirms them. Jacobs (1987) questions what is meant by correct and why the client must react favorably. The vignette he uses illustrates a woman's lifelong attempt to create reparation for the sudden loss of her mother at age 4. She had terminated three marriages and frequently threatened to leave her analysis. Her listener interpreted her threats as a repetition of her treatment of her husbands and her stepmother. But she needed her stepmother so much she could never follow through on her ever-present plan to leave her. He pointed out that he wasn't the only analyst in town so in fact she was responding to him the way she had to her stepmother. The client became tearful and agitated and accused him of wanting to get rid of her. The profound depressive reaction that followed registered that she had received the true intent. She had heard his anger that echoed her stepmother and husband's—all of whom invited her to leave. The analyst had blocked out the angry reaction because it was unacceptable to him as a helping response. The correct interpretation had, however, made its way out.

> The overt, noisier, easily recognizable face of countertransference is well known to us in the form of slips, omissions, symptomatic acts, and more or less clear-cut pieces of acting out. Its other face is its muted one. Often well camouflaged within the framework of our traditional, time-tested techniques, this aspect of countertransference may attach itself to our way of listening and thinking about patients, to our efforts at interpretation, to the process of working through, or to the complex issue of termination.
>
> Less recognizable than its more boisterous counterpart and in some respects less tangible, this side of the problem of countertransference is no less important. For it is precisely those subtle, often scarcely visible countertransference reactions, so easily rationalized as parts of our standard operating procedures and so easily overlooked, that may in the end have the greatest impact on our analytic work. [pp. 181–182]

ANALYTIC TECHNIQUE AS A COUNTERTRANSFERENCE REPLICATION TO EARLY DEPRIVATIONS

Giovacchini (1986b) reports on a man who generally annoyed his analyst (Giovacchini) for no apparent reason except that the analyst never quite felt related to as a person. Historical information revealed that the patient's mother was chronically depressed and, though devoted to caring for her son's physical needs, was unable to relate to him as a person. No smiles or other animation were evident as the analytic relationship took on a quality of uninvolvement, thus replicating the early mother–child relationship. Giovacchini did not feel uncared for, or neglected, or merely related to as a selfobject, but all response to his personhood was simply lacking.

Giovacchini discusses the technical problems in treating people who have some advanced capacities for object constancy but whose relatedness is narrow and constricted. He formulates that, despite an apparently ordinary response to the analytic situation, such persons replicate the mother–child scenario in reversed manner, treating the analyst in the same manner that the parent treated him or her. *In these cases traditional technique serves only to replicate the formal but distant mother. Here the listener's neutrality does not aid in making transference relations stand out, but obscures them within the analyst's usual operational mode.* The speaker needs to repeat infantile deprivation but he or she also wants to be gratified to make up for the severe deprivation. The speaker needs to complain of the transferential deprivation that may leave the listener irritated and confused. If the listener fails to recognize the inevitability of the transference complaint, he or she may resist receiving these judgments about the analytic offering. No matter what is offered, it is off the mark or falls short. The listener may even attempt to offer more to compensate for the experienced deprivations; but this would simply be a misreading of the complaint that must be made and received.

Giovacchini is well aware of how needy many people are of responses that go beyond the traditional frame. In many of his other writings he describes how that offering might be made (Giovacchini 1975a,b, 1979, 1993). But in the following vignette his focus is on the person who has attained good development but needs to communicate early deprivation through the transference. He maintains that merely responding with a greater offering will not aid in the analysis. The transference must be understood for its special qualities, not necessarily responded to with more giving.

> I found myself reacting to a 35-year-old married man with annoyance, although there were no obvious reasons why I should have had such a feeling.
>
> The patient was a highly successful professional who was quite articulate and had an excellent command of the language. He had considerable wit and his descriptions of inner feelings and outer events were picturesque and entertaining. My feelings puzzled me.
>
> Perhaps I had anticipated what would happen. He continued in the same clever style, but he turned from description of the inner world of his psyche and of his environment to nagging and complaining about treatment. He had a rigid obsessive character configuration, and . . . unlike other superficially similar clinical situations, I did not believe the patient was withdrawing from me, shutting me out, or even diminishing my worth by projecting feelings of inadequacy into me. There were some such projections, but they did not dominate the transference, and even if they had, there was no reason why they should have interfered with the course of the analysis or have

upset me. In fact, none of the defensive adaptations I have mentioned should have been reason for concern. They are common enough defensive stances for patients suffering from structural problems and intrapsychic conflicts.

My description of my patient's mode of relating, which I found disturbing, requires amplification. I had the impression that he was not aware of me as a person. He made me feel as if I were unidimensional and lacked depth. I was only a vehicle for his needs, and the external world was simply revolving around him, having no other focus. This sounds to be the orientation of narcissistic patients, who deal with external objects as if they were selfobjects. Their analyses often cause the analyst to feel that he does not exist in his own right and apart from the patient. The therapist may even feel the type of anxiety that is characteristic of an existential crisis (Giovacchini 1972, 1979, 1993). This was not the situation with my patient. He did recognize me as separate and apart from himself but in a limited way.

At the beginning and end of sessions, he was always courteous and respectful, a contrast to his occasional outbursts of recrimination and sarcasm during the session. However, when feeling especially mellow, he might spend all of his time discussing topics he knew I found exciting and sharing intellectual interests with me. He seemed to be relating to me as a person; nevertheless, I did not feel as if he were. I still reacted as if I were being excluded although clearly this was not so.

I then realized that I was responding to his emotional tone rather than the content of what he said. Although his material was interesting, the way he presented it was tedious and dull. He never smiled and was totally devoid of humor as an affect although, as stated, he could be witty. He often looked depressed, confused, and perplexed but never animated, enthusiastic, or happy. At his best he would be calm and mellow. The combination of directing everything back to himself even when he began by focusing on something that interested me and his humorless mode of presentation made me uncomfortable. I was able to relax when I understood our relationship in terms of his infantile past.

As long as the patient could remember, his mother had been in treatment with a prominent analyst because of a chronic depression. When the patient was 6 months old, his mother had been hospitalized for several months. In spite of her severe emotional difficulties, he was told that she was a good and devoted mother. He remembered being well taken care of as a child but he could not recall ever chatting or playing games with her. Apparently, she was constantly depressed and never smiled.

She related to his immediate needs with a sense of immediacy but she could not go beyond the need-gratification level. I was able partially to reconstruct and speculate about the early maternal interaction from the way he related to me and from my countertransference responses. I also had the opportunity to gather information about the mother from her analyst, who emphasized that she had not been able to recognize her son as a person, but

> simply as a baby who had to be fed and changed. He confirmed that she
> never sang or cooed to him. In fact, since the analyst had been interested in
> her mothering behavior, he had asked her about the various developmen-
> tal milestones of her son's life. When questioned, she did not recognize that
> her child had a smiling response or felt stranger anxiety. Certainly, she had
> not tried to evoke a smile from him, and as far as her analyst could tell, she
> had not smiled in his presence. She did not seem to get any pleasure from
> her son. He was a chore that she conscientiously took care of but not a per-
> son whose presence would fill her with pride and a sense of accomplishment.
>   I felt exactly the same way. I also felt no pride or sense of accomplish-
> ment about the treatment relationship. We did not smile at each other and
> I took it to mean that he was not pleased to see me. To him, it meant noth-
> ing because, like his mother, smiling was a foreign habit.
>   I have emphasized that I was not being ignored in the same manner that
> some narcissistic patients totally exclude external objects and concentrate
> only on themselves. The mother's analyst was again helpful. He did not
> classify his patient's relationship with her son as being primarily narcissis-
> tic or engulfingly symbiotic. He believed that because of her depression she
> could only relate to external objects in a constricted fashion, which in re-
> gard to her son meant she could only relate to the immediacy of his needs.
> She could not deal with him as a person in his own right who was emerg-
> ing and developing as an autonomous human being. She had no intuition
> or empathy; she could not establish emotional resonance with him. She sim-
> ply looked after him in terms of physical needs, which permitted him to
> reach a developmental level that includes object constancy but a constricted
> view of external objects based upon his needs. He neither received nor gave
> emotional sustenance. [pp. 220–223]

Giovacchini continues with technical considerations for treating individuals whose object relations experience has been constricted, producing
defects, but who nevertheless had enough nurturance to have reached an
advanced level of (neurotic) object constancy.

> These patients relate to objects in a constricted manner, a reflection of the
> way their mothers related to them. They have attained a constricted form
> of object constancy.
>   Restricting the interaction with the patient to interpretations and the
> maintenance of a neutral stance is reminiscent of the constricted relation-
> ship with the mother, who could allow herself no emotional involvement
> with her child. The analyst is equated with the unavailable mother. The
> patient suffers the same infantile deprivation in the current treatment set-
> ting. This ordinarily happens in the transference relationship, but usually
> the analyst's neutrality creates a backdrop that causes infantile transference
> elements to stand out, whereas with these patients, infantile reactions blend

with the analyst's operational mode. Consequently, their transference implications are obscured, and the patient believes he is confronting a reality similar to the one he knew in infancy. [p. 226]

COUNTERTRANSFERENCE TO BEING USED FOR NEED FULFILLMENT

Giovacchini (1986b) provides another brief example of a well-structured woman who nevertheless elicited the countertransference feeling of being simply a tool of her needs.

> A 40-year-old married woman kept emphasizing how much she needed me to tell her things about the external world because she was too inept and helpless to be able to make critical judgments that would enable her to cope with the exigencies of her daily life. This meant that I was to evaluate everyday events and relationships so that she would know how to respond judiciously. If I did not grant her what she required she would alienate her husband and children and generally create chaos. She acknowledged that she was asking me to breathe for her. She dependently clung to other persons as well, who eventually distanced themselves from her because of her intense neediness. Her self-centeredness finally antagonized her family and friends, and I began to feel the same resentment. This patient did not recognize anyone except in terms of her needs, an example of the constricted object constancy I have been discussing.
>
> She quietly attacked me for not giving her what she needed. These were not vociferous attacks. On the contrary, she would revile herself for her weakness but, nevertheless, she was adept at quiet reproach. She indicated that I was being remiss in my role as therapist by never talking to her and she would ask me numerous questions which admittedly I usually did not answer. In many instances I did not know the answer, but I was also aware of a resistance within me that made me reluctant to respond.
>
> Still, I was far from entirely silent. I answered some of her questions and often made interpretations, sometimes spontaneously and not just as a response to a question. Whatever I said did not seem to count. She did not recognize my interpretations as interpretations or as answers. She viewed them as criticisms and either started arguing with me or attempted to justify herself, although I had been extremely careful to be nonjudgmental. I could feel her reaching out to me, and then when I responded she ignored the fact that I was trying to reciprocate. If she acknowledged my attempt to impart some understanding, she would follow what I said with another question demanding further clarification. If I fell into her trap she would continue questioning every one of my responses. She reminded me of a child who endlessly asks, "Why?" She was insatiable.

Her reactions made me feel that I was simply a tool of her needs without any human qualities. I felt frustrated and had to view my countertransference in terms of the immediacy of her needs and her constricted maternal relationship in which the patient felt constantly frustrated, a frustration she now provoked in her external world.

She related the following material, which clearly illustrates how irritating she could be. While having her hair done, she was chatting with her female hairdresser. She told the hairdresser about some of her problems with her children, especially with a son who was having difficulties during his freshman year in college. The hairdresser would respond to her request for advice by making some sensible suggestion. The patient would then object and reveal another aspect of the problem. Again the hairdresser would offer her a solution and again the patient would argue that it would not work. At the end of the appointment, the patient was astounded when the hairdresser had an outburst of anger and told her that she did not want to see her in her shop again. [pp. 226–230]

ALARM IN THE FACE OF RAGE

In another type of situation Volkan (1968) also distinguishes earlier and later developmental constellations. In the case reported, because of the advanced developmental issues involved, the listener feels no need to disclose the reaction; but rather he finds ways of interpreting—using an "anchoring point" in current reality to show the speaker the reaction that belongs to the man's historical past. Volkan sharply contrasts such interpretations of neurotic transference issues with countertransference reactions that arise in response to externalizations onto the analyst, which do not contain anchoring points that aid the analyst in pointing to the reactions as an emotional replication of symbiotic issues.

A neurotic patient of mine had a dominant mother who had customarily denigrated her husband. The father was accordingly perceived as ineffectual, and in spite of his considerable professional accomplishments, my patient considered *himself* to be ineffectual as well. His analysis revealed that this identification with the *degraded* image of his father also had been a defensive maneuver to deal with castration anxiety. As his analysis advanced, memories that showed other aspects of his father as a stronger man surfaced. This new development went hand in hand with his transference displacement onto me of his attitudes and feelings toward this stronger father. As might have been expected, they were accompanied by references to castration anxiety. In other words, to see his father as stronger was to expect castration at his hands—through transference neurosis, at the hands of the "stronger" analyst. His references to this were initially tentative, and his view of me as a castrator did not induce in me any particularly strong emotional response since my experience as an analyst had made me familiar in the course of my professional development and practice with being considered a castrator at some time or other by neurotic patients.

One day this patient, while lying on the couch at this stage of his analysis, calmly told me how amazed he was to recognize the pattern of the radiator grill in my office. He said that his father, who had been a mechanic, had made grills and had made a beautiful one exactly like mine for his own office. The patient thus acknowledged his father's manual skills and made him appear a strong man. After a deep silence the patient suddenly broke into a loud outburst of hostility toward me in which he cursed and raved. He made it clear that during the silence he had felt fear of me, thinking that I could hurt him and take advantage of him. His outburst was in the service of warding off my attack. Since he was usually obsessional and polite, his hostility took me by surprise, and I am sure I presented the appearance of someone under attack, having a quickened heartbeat and the sudden sweat of alarm. Regardless of this natural human response, my emotions did not lose their signaling functions; thus I was able to think that the patient's use of the radiator grill was a means of displacing behavior originally directed toward his father-castrator. His outburst was a protective maneuver against his projection of his own murderous impulses onto me. Moreover, it protected him from the possibility of homosexual surrender to his father. The reality of the grill in my office and its actual or fancied resemblance to the one in the office of his father gave an *anchoring point* for the interaction that took place between us. Within seconds I was in command of my counteremotions. I chose not to tell my patient about them since such knowledge on his part would burden him unnecessarily, but in due course the process was repeated and then was interpreted to him. This episode is but one example of many similar events that occur in our daily work.

I must emphasize that I do not equate this kind of counteremotion felt on one occasion with what we regard as a manifestation of a full-blown countertransference. I use it here simply as a microscopic example of a collection of such events, the macroscopic correlate of which is the full-blown countertransference reaction to the transference of a patient.

The analyst who is the subject of externalizations may lack the advantage of having an observable anchoring point in reality which precipitates or accompanies such processes; he is more at the mercy of what is attributed to him by his patient. He will, however, come to understand more of what is going on as the therapeutic process advances, and as he gains secondary process understanding of the affect-laden sensations he experiences as the recipient of his patient's split-off self and object representations. Even so, his countertransference responses are more likely to be generally unfamiliar to the analyst dealing with a patient who externalizes. It is likely that his training analysis, outside of relatively brief periods of extreme regression which seldom escaped the attention of his observing ego, has not provided him enough opportunity to identify with his analyst as he handles such externalization. [pp. 443–445]

COUNTERTRANSFERENCE ISSUES IN TERMINATION

As a final illustration of countertransference that may be in response to an oedipal or preoedipal set of issues, the end of therapy constitutes a loss for the listener as well as the speaker. Gorkin (1987) systematically considers many of the issues that might arise for the analytic listener. He also addresses the issue of disclosure. Under what circumstances and how much of the listener's reaction are suitable to disclose to the speaker?

> A few years ago I was in the uncomfortable position of having to dissolve my practice because I was moving out of the country. It was difficult to make the announcement of my impending departure to all my patients, but it was especially difficult with one particular patient. This patient, R., was a social work student who had been with me a relatively short time (two years). She was a person whose obvious talents were matched by an equally obvious narcissistic deficit. An only child, R. had been very close to her mother, also a social worker, who suffered from diabetes, a heart ailment, and a history of depression. The mother, out of her own narcissistic needs, had sought throughout R.'s life to protect her from the disappointments of daily life. So determined was she to accomplish this that she had managed to discourage R. from ever giving voice to her own experiences of disappointment and discouragement. Not until she entered treatment was R. able to look at this pattern, and then only after a good deal of trepidation. But she had finally begun to explore her relationship to her mother in great detail, and it was precisely as we were in the midst of this material that I had to announce my upcoming departure.
> As can readily be imagined, I was most reluctant to make this announcement to her. I felt sad and guilty. In my guilt I found myself quickly—much too quickly—wondering to whom I could send this "good" patient. For her part, R. initially took the announcement with measured calmness. She wanted to know where I was going and what had prompted me to leave, and (as I provided her with more than the usual number of details about my departure and plans) she ruminated about how hard it was for *me* to make such a move. Within a few sessions, however, her calm shifted to disappointment, anger, and sadness. She wept profusely, scolded me, and wept again. Having begun to mourn me, she could not stop. This went on for weeks, and I soon found myself becoming detached and tuning her out for

most of the session. Then, unwittingly, in reaction formation to my own underlying anger and guilt, I began hollowly "supporting" her, encouraging her to look at what we had accomplished and suggesting that she consider resuming treatment elsewhere.

It was at this point, with about a month to go before I left, that she brought me an article that she had just been assigned in class. The article was Miller's "The Drama of the Gifted Child and the Psychoanalyst's Narcissistic Disturbance" (1979). I was not then familiar with this article, but I soon realized that she had given me the right "assignment." As the article so clearly elaborated, like her mother I also had been unable to tolerate her depression and anger. In my own overwhelming guilt about leaving, I had attempted to stifle R.'s feelings and to encourage her to look at the "bright side" or, even more perniciously, to comfort me in my leaving. I had been unable to tolerate her mourning. Fortunately, in this instance, the patient was aware enough and brave enough to bring it directly to my attention, and I was able to do something about my countertransferential intrusion. And I will say, I hope without sounding too pollyannaish, that those final weeks of treatment turned out to be highly meaningful for R., and in no small measure, for me too.

This kind of situational pressure on the therapist probably occurs more often than we care to imagine. Any situation in the therapist's life that confronts him with loss can make it especially difficult for him to manage his patients' mourning reactions. Included here are such inescapable life circumstances as the death, illness, or long-term departure of loved ones, as well as serious illness or the trials of old age in oneself. In addition, new therapists and trainees frequently confront situational pressures of this sort as they find themselves having to terminate with many patients at one time. . . .

If we assume that the therapist's sense of loss is a part of the termination of long-term treatment, the question again arises of what might be usefully disclosed about this loss to the patient. It can be reasonably argued—and most "classical" analysts would probably so contend—that direct communication of this sort to the patient runs the risk of providing gratification to the patient; thus, by disclosing his sense of loss, the therapist may succeed in binding the patient to him even after they have parted.

This important argument should not be dismissed lightly. Above all, it would seem to apply in those cases in which less-than-satisfactory results have been achieved, or in which termination occurs after some years in serious deadlock. Here, statements of sadness or mourning on the therapist's part are likely to hinder the patient's ability to relinquish his tie to the therapist and may interfere with his eventually turning elsewhere for treatment.

In cases in which satisfactory results have been achieved, however, and the patient has been able substantially to work through his transference neurosis or psychosis and turn to other people in his environment for the richer satisfactions of day-to-day living, I would view it as a useful part of termination for the therapist to disclose some of his feelings of loss. At that point in the progression of the therapeutic relationship, the patient has generally become at least preconsciously aware of some of these feelings in his therapist, though in the regression that often occurs in the final phase, he may temporarily disregard this knowledge. It would seem to me that as part of the "mature" and far more equal relationship that obtains in the termination of satisfactory treatment, the therapist can feel free to let the patient openly know these things about himself. More to the point, the therapist's refusal to let the patient know of his sadness (as well as other feelings) may serve as a way of *not* acknowledging and validating the patient's independence and hard-won autonomy—not acknowledging, that is, the fact that the patient now can receive such gratification from the therapist without being unduly stimulated by it. Many therapists, including analysts, apparently do communicate their sense of loss in these circumstances, perhaps sensing that it is a "human" thing to do. My point is that it is also a "therapeutic" thing to do. [pp. 263–265]

In conclusion, there is ample clinical evidence to support Freud's original attitude that in the treatment of neurosis, countertransference is likely to be an impediment to the course of the analysis. The key question today revolves around how an analyst is able to distinguish countertransference responsiveness, which is specific to neurotic-level issues, from responsiveness to preoedipal aspects of personality. The simplifying notion that the personality retrospectively reorganizes preoedipal material into oedipal motifs is not only overly optimistic, but appears to reflect a rigid attitude on the part of analysts who wish to view all aspects of countertransference responsiveness according to one easy-to-remember, reductionistic formula. The case vignette in the next chapter illustrates how personalities typically mix oedipal and preoedipal issues.

20

The Sudden Violent Storm

Jacquelyn Gillespie

Editor's Comments

The general expectation at the level of object constancy is that countertransference reactions will be unhelpful or a detraction from the unfolding of the speaker's analytic associations. In the following example we see a well-developed woman suddenly decompensating in a life crisis, thus reviving a childhood trauma. Her regressive reactions create countertransference problems for the therapist that get in the way of the woman's therapeutic needs. Through the therapist's own analytic work and through consultation the equilibrium could be restored. The subsequent loss of the therapist (in the termination process) could then serve as a situation where the early loss could be worked through.

THE SUDDEN VIOLENT STORM

When she first came into my office, slowly and reluctantly, Karen collapsed into a chair. Her eyes were red and puffy from tears and lack of sleep. She withdrew from me as far as she could into the chair, occasionally stealing a wary glance in my direction without meeting my eyes. The diagnosis from her referring physician was acute depression with suicidal ideation. He recommended psychiatric hospitalization, but she was so resistant to the idea that she was sent to me to see if we couldn't find some way to manage the depression on an outpatient basis.

Karen's story: She had been on a boating holiday with her husband, 10-year-old daughter, and a couple of other young families, when a sudden violent storm arose. Although athletic and experienced with boats, Karen found herself unable to contribute to the activity necessary to manage the boat in high winds and waves. She ignored her husband's exasperated efforts to move her into action; instead, she huddled motionless, hugging her daughter. She said she felt sure that the storm was some punishment that would be visited on her and/or the ones she loved, for some unknown crime. An active Christian from a very early age, she now felt judged by God, who would surely drive her away and take away all safety and security from her life. It was not clear when or whence disaster would strike, only that it was a sure thing. She experienced an overwhelming terror, with hopelessness; it was impossible to envision a course of action open to her that would provide any relief.

The sense of dread did not dissipate after the ordeal was over. Karen retreated to the bedroom, alternately pacing the floor and lying on the bed in tears.

By the time she reached me, she had been through every possible variety of cajoling, encouragement, and threats from her well-meaning family, which had served, predictably, to enhance her already overwhelming sense of guilt and anxiety. Her husband was a military officer and kept a gun in a locked cabinet in the home. She sneaked the gun out of its cabinet and would sit on the side of the bed when nobody else was home, holding the gun, testing its weight, and wondering what it would feel like to have a bullet ripping through her, particularly if she botched the suicide. At the same time, a strong observing ego was horrified at these thoughts and terrified that she might indeed act upon them.

Although she understood that she would be safe from her own self-destructive impulses in a hospital, she nevertheless saw psychiatric hospitalization as another form of punishment that would underline her failure as a human being and would brand her forever as unstable and unfit for her profession. Well, I thought, at least that is strongly reality based; as a young attorney with a promising future, a stint in a mental health facility would do her no professional good.

As this woman continued to explain herself to me, I found myself uneasy. Although she found her circumstances unbelievably bizarre and completely exceptional, I was noting a typical onset of panic and depression associated with a current traumatic event that most probably suddenly broke down defenses against a traumatic event of early origin.

Although Karen's anxiety level was diminishing as we talked, mine was unaccountably rising, although I was barely aware of it at the time. We moved into examining Karen's earlier life. She was the oldest and favorite child of an older mother, who had died suddenly of a heart attack when Karen was 11 years old. Karen had been present, but her father had not yet returned from work. She had to take charge of the situation, call for medical help, and find supervision for her younger brother and sister. She received lavish praise at the time for "handling it all so well," which, in her family, meant that she showed little emotion. She had accepted that evaluation, and her presentation of the circumstances surrounding her mother's death was calm and intellectualized. I thought that this was an obvious place to start to explore the earlier material, but that I had better put some structure into this process.

Very professionally, I explained to her that we would do what we could to keep her out of the hospital, but that she would need to be seen daily until I was sure she was out of danger of suicide, and that she would need to see her physician to see about some mild medication to ease the anxiety while she was in crisis. I was getting ready to talk about releases of information to and from her doctor, and so forth, when it became apparent that she had finally understood that I would indeed work with her. That knowledge immediately precipitated a strong emotional reaction in which she flung herself to the floor and then tried to crawl into my lap. She needed to be held, she insisted, crying hysterically; she had to be close to me. I was taken by surprise and by the most intensely ambivalent feelings of wanting to hold her and rock her like a tiny infant, and also to shove her away. Although I was in no place to contemplate my countertransference issues right then, the material from that interaction stayed with me throughout our several years of therapeutic work together and remains vividly clear to me as I write this.

I thank God for my own intellectualizing defenses; they not only served me in good stead in remaining professional, but they also activated her own intellectualization. It seemed to be important to get some sort of defensive system back in operation to keep both of us out of a "Mommy-and-I-are-one" dance that would have seriously compromised our work. Speaking of compromise, however, I must acknowledge that I agreed to end our sessions with a hug for her. The promise of that brief physical contact served to keep her with me while our relationship developed. In our discussions of all this, very much later, we have both agreed that she came only for that hug for many of the more troubling of our early sessions.

At the intellectual level, however, I was able to explain to her that her need to have me be her mother was absolutely understandable, but that it was an impossibility. I was not her mother, and any attempt to make me into her mother would not work and simply set her up for another disappointment and loss. She was not convinced. The issue that made sense to her was my irritated comment, "Look, do you want to be one of those people who spend a lifetime in therapy, a sort of addictive thing?" She backed off in genuine horror. I pointed out the dangers of too much dependence on the therapist. While it turned out to have been a wise move with this particular patient, who had a strong internal ego structure, I have since shuddered at the kind of rejection this approach would have represented to a person with major weaknesses in characterological development.

I also told her that it would be much easier for me to hold her, to mother her as she wanted to be mothered, but again emphasized the distortion of the therapeutic relationship that would most probably ensue. I was aware of my own need to mother, and also of the need to push her away (which I did not see any reason to disclose) to an extent that I had never previously encountered.

Enter the countertransference; in this case, an immediate and intense issue. I was exhausted, emotionally and physically, and felt vaguely and diffusely guilty over the intensity and ambivalence of my feelings. This therapy took place several years ago, when Dr. Hedges was developing his concepts of the countertransference as an important therapeutic tool. I was already a convinced devotee of his listening perspectives approach, which allowed me to think of Karen as a well-developed personality with a major traumatic regression related to issues associated with her mother's death. While she was clearly struggling with symbiotic issues and a need to re-create the symbiosis within the therapy, there was no need to describe her as a borderline personality. I felt free to deal with the borderline aspects of her functioning at that time, without any need to consider her in a particular diagnostic category.

The countertransference issues were a different matter. Throughout the several years of our work together I grew to have immense respect and fondness for this bright young woman who worked so fiercely to face difficult repressed material associated with her psychosexual development, which had of course been affected by the loss of her mother just at the beginning of puberty. These issues were a relief to me, since I could focus there and avoid a good deal of the countertransference feelings that kept me floating back and forth, wondering if I was a "good-enough mother" and then wondering why I was becoming angry again with my long-dead mother and bringing those issues up obsessively in my own analysis.

I found myself jealous of the warm relationship that this young woman had enjoyed with her mother during her early years. Well, I reassured myself, the symbiosis had been wonderful but extended a bit long, leaving some maternal overprotection that was already leading to some incipient rebellion at the time of the mother's death. My own mother's emotional distance, I told myself, avoided the need to rebel, since she would never have noticed. Some advantages, there, surely? I knew better, of course. I wished I could have mourned for my mother in the same way she mourned for hers—with real longing for a relationship that had been profoundly satisfying. And I became a child again, angry that I did not have a mother like hers, and I remained always ready to establish a kind of familiar protective emotional distance. I used that intellectualized distancing to keep our therapy relationship comfortable for me, not for her, although I did not realize that at the time. No wonder she needed her hugs!

Her own transference issues were very much matters of attention in our sessions, and she was particularly sensitive to any vacations or absences on my part, over which I personally felt a great deal of guilt. She learned to cope with my time away quite well, with overt sadness but a firm insistence on being "realistic" and forcing herself to accept the circumstances. Her anxiety level increased once again at those times, however, and it was often necessary for her to resort to medication briefly to get through those difficult times. Holidays were particular sources of stress, as were birthdays and other special days marking transitions because they all seemed to represent the end of something without heralding new potential. Her daughter's completion of a school grade, a neighbor's moving away, remodeling her house, my change of office location—all seemed to evoke a similar style of anxiety, which resulted in a tighter grip on me.

Nevertheless, she was gradually gaining a more solid center, consolidating loss experiences into a more realistic framework, which began to show fruit when some real losses came to her. About two years into our work, when she was seeing me three times a week, she found that her mother-in-law had terminal cancer. Her initial panic was soon replaced with a wonderfully mature caring for the other woman. She found the inner strength to assume major responsibility for meeting the increasingly burdensome demands of an elderly woman in great pain, with only normal and reasonable fits of frustration and fatigue. At the end Karen was able to overcome the objections of the rest of the family in order to answer the woman's last wish for a visit from a priest, a very generous gesture from this very strongly Protestant young woman. During this time I found myself obscurely comforted by her caring, apparently identifying with this elderly woman who was being mothered so effectively by Karen.

As she became more and more secure, it became clear that we could continue to reduce our time together. As might have been expected, she had experienced difficulty when we moved from five to four to three days a week, and then to two, but the move to once a week was a particularly worrisome one. It was at this time, however, that we began to discuss the eventual termination of our work together. I don't know exactly who was more threatened by this—she or I.

By this time, however, I was able to handle the countertransference more overtly, and we talked about my own lack of trust in my own perceptions about our termination phase. "Termination phase!"—I should never have used the phrase. The terror associated with contemplating the sudden termination (death) of our relationship evoked regression on her part, anxiety on mine. We were not, of course, considering a sudden parting of the ways, but nevertheless I began to have no sense at all of how much contact was necessary for her and how much was necessary for me. I felt utterly insecure. I talked about my uncertainty with Karen, but feared that she might find my confusion an additional source of anxiety. To my surprise, she accepted my uncertainty with calm, even with some sense of relief. I am now sure that she had been experiencing my ambivalence; it was adding to her own anxiety.

With her permission, I sought supervision for the termination phase of our work together. Now I could turn, with unbelievable relief, to someone else to monitor the progress of the work. On the other hand, I experienced jealousy of the supervisor and real reluctance to turn over my "child" and myself to someone else; I was aware of my reluctance to let Karen belong, at least partially, to someone else. But, as the supervision progressed, I was able to achieve a comfort level with myself in the relationship with Karen that made it possible for me to feel comfortable with the gradual diminution of our contact—weekly, biweekly, monthly, bimonthly, then occasionally. And now the relationship still holds open the opportunity for contact, when the spirit moves. It turned out to be possible after all, as my countertransference issues became clearer and the resolution of them freed us both for a new phase in our relationship, to relinquish regularly scheduled contact and to move toward the kind of support an adult parent needs to be able to provide for an adult child.

VI

STRATEGIC EMOTIONAL INVOLVEMENT AND THE COUNTERTRANSFERENCE

21

Emotionality and Psychoanalysis[1]

Psychoanalytic theorizing is always ultimately concerned with the listening context of the consulting relationship. Ideas and concepts borrowed from the fields of biological and physiological evolution; infant and child development; philosophy, ethics, and religion; or the humanities, social science, and arts, may indeed be stimulating and interesting when considered in the light of psychoanalysis. But such wide-ranging speculative thoughts are relevant to psychoanalytic theory only insofar as they serve to elucidate human relatedness possibilities that come to be apprehended and responded to during the analytic hour. In no aspect of psychoanalytic thinking has it been more tempting to search abroad for solutions to perennially puzzling dilemmas than in the attempt to understand human emotions. Often spoken of as "affects," "feelings," or "feeling states," emotionality that characterizes the communicative exchange between the analytic couple continues to be an enigma. Part of the problem is that the study of individual human emotional activities blends imperceptibly on the one hand with constitutional and biological concerns and on the other hand with aspects of human life involving social relations and communication.

The purposes of this chapter are (1) to review the major ways in which human emotionality has been studied in the field of psychoanalysis; (2) to demonstrate how each of these ways of thinking about emotionality has served to lead away from, rather than toward, a greater understanding of the analytic emotional exchange; and (3) to survey some promising directions that have appeared in the psychoanalytic literature in the last decade. In the next chapter I will suggest some ways of considering human emo-

---

1. This chapter is reprinted with revisions from the *Southern California Bioenergetic Society Newsletter* [1990] 5(1):3–11.

tionality in the analytic relationship with specific technical considerations for the conduct of the analytic enterprise.

EMOTIONS IN THE CONSULTING ENCOUNTER

The literature dealing with the affects in the practice of clinical psychoanalysis begins with Karl Abraham's (1911) notes on "Manic-Depressive Insanity." Abraham traces the affective psychoses back to "an attitude of hate which was paralyzing the patient's capacity to love" (p. 143). Following Freud's formulations regarding the dynamics of paranoia in the Shreber case, Abraham puts forward the following dynamic formula for depression: "I cannot love people; I have to hate them." Through repression and projection the formula becomes altered to read: "People do not love me, they hate me . . . because of my inborn defects. Therefore I am unhappy and depressed" (p. 145).

Abraham believed morbid feelings of guilt resulted from "imperfectly repressed sadism," though "the idea of guilt contains the fulfillment of a wish . . . to be a criminal of the deepest dye, to have incurred more guilt than everyone else put together" (p. 146). "As a result of the repression of sadism, depression, anxiety and self-reproach arise," which bring a modicum of pleasure by reinforcing "masochistic tendencies." According to Abraham, both manic and depressive phases are thought to be "dominated by the same complexes," only the patient's attitude toward the complexes differs. In the depressive state, the person is weighed down and sees no other way out of misery but death. In mania, however, the person "treats the complex with indifference," returning "to a stage to which his impulses had not succumbed to repression, in which he foresaw nothing of the approaching conflict" (p. 147).

Freud's *Mourning and Melancholia* (1917) contrasts normal, conscious grieving in which "the world becomes poor and empty" (p. 155) with melancholia in which the ego itself becomes impoverished. He views melancholia as "related to an unconscious loss of a love-object" (p. 155). "The self-reproaches are reproaches against a love-object which have been shifted on to the patient's own ego" (p. 158). Freud maintains that melancholics "are far from evincing toward those around them the attitude of humility and submission that alone would befit such worthless persons; on the contrary they give a great deal of trouble, perpetually taking great offense and behaving as if they had been treated with great injustice" (p. 158f). Freud reasons, "the object-choice had been effected on a narcissistic basis, so that when obstacles arise in the way of the object-cathexis it can regress to narcissism. The narcissistic identification with the object then becomes a substitute for the erotic cathexis, the result of which is that in spite of the conflict with the loved person the love relation need not be given up" (p. 159f). He explains, "The self-torments of melancholics, which are without doubt pleasurable, signify . . . a gratification of sadistic tendencies and of hate, both of which relate to an object and in this way have both been turned round upon the self" (p. 162). Freud agrees with Abraham that both manic and melancholic disorders display the same content and "are wrestling with the same 'complex'" (p. 164). In melancholia the ego succumbs to the complex, but "in mania it has mastered the complex or thrust it aside" (p. 164).

These early views are elaborated in the subsequent work of Abraham (1924), who organizes the affects encountered in mania and obsessive-compulsive neurosis within a detailed framework of the now familiar early libidinal phases. Sandor Rado (1928) places emphasis on understanding the factor of infantile self-esteem in mania and depression. Otto Fenichel's (1945) therapeutic approach entails recognizing the depressed person's need for consolation and "narcissistic" or "oral" supplies. Edith Jacobson (1953) emphasizes the early dissappointments in parental omnipotence and subsequent devaluation of parental images in the child's ego formation.

Until Edward Bibring (1953) and David Rapaport (1953) offered ego psychological views on depression, the major writers continued to distinguish theoretically and clinically between two types of depression: (1) a simple, essential, endogenous or mild reaction typified by Freud's uncomplicated grief reaction or various forms of (ego) depletion or exhaustion, and (2) a severe melancholic syndrome characterized by narcissistic injury, lowered self-esteem, oral mechanisms of recovery and turning object directed aggression against the self.

Bibring (1953) redefines depression as an expression of an (affectively experienced) state of helplessness and powerlessness of the ego, irrespective of what may have caused the breakdown of the self-esteem establishing mechanisms. Bibring defines three groups of persisting aspirations that maintain self-esteem: (1) the wish to be loved, appreciated, and worthy; (2) the wish to be strong, superior, and secure; and (3) the wish to be good and loving, not hateful, aggressive, or destructive. According to Bibring, depression results from a tension between these narcissistic aspirations on the one hand and the ego's acute awareness of its real and imaginary helplessness and incapacity to live up to its aspirations on the other hand. Bibring does not view depression as a conflict between id, ego, superego, and environment, but rather as an intrasystemic ego conflict in which the ego collapses or becomes inhibited as a result of feeling unable to live up to its own aspirations. Depression represents an affective state of the ego characterized by helplessness and inhibition of functions. Bibring defines other affect states according to a similar ego psychological formula:

1. Depersonalization represents aggressive tensions that are barred from emotional and motor expression.
2. Boredom represents libidinal strivings that are prevented gratification, blocking goal- or need-directed behavior.
3. Anxiety represents a reaction to danger, indicating the ego's desire to survive.
4. Elation represents an ego response to an actual or imaginary fulfillment of the person's narcissistic aspirations.

Rapaport (1953) distinguishes three historical phases or approaches to consideration of the affects:

1. The *energy catharsis approach* equates affects with quantities of psychic energy. Affects prohibited from discharge are thought to remain fixed to the pathogenic fantasy and to find an outlet (to be discharged) in the innervation of conversion symptoms. The goal of therapy is to promote (through catharsis or hypnosis) the discharge of dammed-up affects (energies), thereby draining the pathogenic ideas of their force and influence.
2. The *id approach* views affects as motor and secretory processes controlled by *ideas* in the unconscious. Affects are released by and are indicators of unconscious wishes. *Affect-charges* and *ideas* are two forms of drive representations but they have very different vicissitudes. Ideas may remain conscious or become repressed as memory traces (actualities), while affects are always conscious and cannot be repressed but only remain as potentialities. That is, affects are always created *de novo* as a result of either environmental stimuli or recall of (preconscious or unconscious) ideas.
3. The *ego phase* utilizes Freud's (1923) tripartite structural theory to depict affects as ego functions or signals to be used by the ego. The ego theory of affects recognizes the innate character of affect-discharge channels and even the innate character of their thresholds and their relations to releasing stimuli. Freud (1926b) theorizes that these preformed affect-discharge channels are made use of by the ego for "safety valve" discharge by a whole series of conflicted or blocked drives that arise during the course of development. In the case of anxiety, Freud defines a series of conflicts related to specific danger situations in which anxiety typically becomes discharged. The

danger situations Freud speaks of are loss of the object, loss of the object's love, castration, and loss of the superego's love.

While Rapaport (1953) acknowledges the ill-advisability of premature attempts to make a definitive or comprehensive theory of affects, he sketches the following outline:

1. Affects use inborn channels and thresholds of discharge. At a developmental stage where the pleasure principle holds sway, drives strive for immediate discharge. When drive action is not possible, affects serve as safety valves, thus *appearing* to be discharge phenomena.
2. "Affect-charges" and "ideas" are both drive representations. Ideas are discharged onto the drive object while affect-charges discharge into the interior of the body through motor and secretory innervations.
3. The development of psychic structure begins with the operation of innate discharge regulating thresholds and is fostered by reality delays that establish a (defensive) ability to delay. Countercathectic energy distributions (defenses against pain or overstimulation) become organized (bound, neutralized) so as to constitute (ego) secondary processes.
4. Conditioned motivational and affect hierarchies thus constitute aspects of a developing psychic structure through which the ego (that originally only endured affects passively) gradually comes to tame the affects into anticipatory signals.
5. An ever-increasing hierarchy of psychic structure formation leads to the differentiation of id, ego, and superego, each with its economic, dynamic, and adaptive functions.

Rapaport's sketch of psychoanalytic affects theory can thus be seen to include three basic components: (1) inborn affect-discharge channels, (2) drive representations termed affect-charges, and (3) the taming of affect-charges into signals to be released by the ego when danger threatens.

Jacobson (1953) generally endorses Rapaport's formulations and additionally proposes the following classifications of affects:

1. Simple and compound affects arising from *intra*systemic tensions.
   a. Those arising from sexual or aggressive tensions in the id.
   b. Those developing in the ego (e.g., fear of reality, object love or hate, thing interests).
2. Simple and compound affects arising from *inter*systemic tensions.
   a. Tensions between id and ego.
   b. Tensions between ego and superego.

Jacobson maintains that classifying affects based upon "tensions" circumvents the problem of "conflicts," thereby providing a more comprehensive framework than might be employed in the study of the conflict neuroses. The type of affect, according to her schema, is implicitly defined from both the dynamic and structural points of view. Jacobson further maintains that affects can only be understood from the simultaneous study of perceptive experiences as well as conscious and unconscious ideational processes.

Elizabeth Zetzel (1965) and David Rubinfine (1968) examine and elaborate the Bibring and Rapaport ego psychology approaches, concluding that the "capacity to bear" depression and anxiety represents an important measure of ego strength and a developmental advance in the capacity for reality relations and reality testing. Jacobson (1971), however, criticizes Bibring's exclusive ego psychology approach as neglecting the role of object relations, the drives in general, and, specifically, conflicts around aggression, which for her are central in understanding depression. Citing Margaret Mahler's (1966) observations of toddlers, Jacobson attempts to show that basic depression is the outcome of an aggressive conflict caused by a lack of understanding and acceptance by the mother that reduces the child's self-esteem. She further criticizes Bibring, Rubinfine, and Zetzel for their failure to distinguish between neurotic states of depression and those that belong to the manic-depressive or schizophrenic groups of disorders. Jacobson considers a clear distinction between neurotic, borderline, and psychotic states as well as a distinction between different types of depressive states prerequisite for both psychoanalytic and neurophysiological research on depression in childhood and adult life.

Perhaps most appealing to contemporary clinicians are the theories of affect put forth by Otto Kernberg (1975, 1976, 1980a). Following a long-term and intensive study of borderline conditions, Kernberg offers massive revisions of classical and ego psychology theory and has combined them in an artful way with ideas taken from object relations theory. Kernberg's initial observation is that people with borderline development exhibit specific areas of "impulse disturbance." That is, variations in impulsiveness represent

> an alternating expression of complementary sides of a conflict, such as acting out of an impulse at some times and specific defensive character formations or counterphobic reactions against that impulse at other times. The patients were conscious of the severe contradiction in their behavior; yet they would alternate between opposite strivings with a bland denial of the implications of this contradiction and showed what appeared to be a striking lack

of concern over this "compartmentalization" of their mind. [Kernberg 1976, p. 20]

That is, "there exists what we might call a mutual denial of independent sectors of psychic life . . . or independent 'ego states,' repetitive, temporarily ego syntonic, compartmentalized psychic manifestations" (p. 20).

Kernberg's next observation is "that each of these mutually unacceptable 'split' ego states represented a specific transference paradigm, a highly developed regressive transference reaction in which a specific internalized object relationship was activated in the transference" (Kernberg 1976, p. 21). Kernberg suggests that the "chaotic transference manifestations" borderlines present might be understood as the oscillatory activation of those mutually unacceptable ego states representing what he calls "nonmetabolized internalized object relations."

He states:

Affects represent inborn dispositions to a subjective experience in the dimension of pleasure and unpleasure. Differentiation of affect occurs in context of the differentiation of internalized object relations; . . . affect and cognition at first evolved jointly, only to differentiate much later. . . . Pleasurable and painful affects are the major organizers of the series of "good" and "bad" internalized object relations. [p. 104]

Kernberg thus considers early positive and negative affect states the experiential basis for future development. Following Jacobson (1954, 1964) and Mahler (1968), he conceptualizes the infant's early task as first a differentiation of self-representations from object representations, followed rapidly by an integration of libidinally determined "good" and aggressively determined "bad" self and object representations (Kernberg 1980). Then it becomes possible to speak of "internalized experiences" or "ego states," which are thought to be the building blocks of personality and are assumed by Kernberg to be composed of (1) a representation of self, (2) a representation of an object, and (3) a positively or negatively weighted affective link.

Thus in Kernberg's view, these contradictory, oscillatory, internalizations or "ego states" are comprised variously of good, bad, self, and object experiences and, as such, are conceptualized as the normal developmental process he calls "splitting." By the third year, the infant is thought to begin integrating the good with the bad, giving rise to a wide "spectrum of affects." At the same time, through repression, it becomes possible for a constant integrated experience of self to become reliably differentiated from ambivalently held "constant objects."

It should be clear from the foregoing discussion that the clinical emphasis upon the affects has generally centered around the problem of depression and mania, good and bad, pleasurable and unpleasurable, or elated and depleted states. In contrast to the clinical discussions that revolve predominantly around depression and mania, theoretical discussions through the years have tended to revolve more around the affect of anxiety. Though Freud himself never developed a comprehensive theory of the affects, his various discussions of affect and anxiety have throughout the years represented a powerful theoretical paradigm.

FREUD'S THEORETICAL FORMULATIONS ON AFFECTS AND ANXIETY

Freud's earliest formulations of affect appear in relation to anxiety in the "actual neuroses." Anxiety is viewed as a transformation of dammed-up or (sexual) excitation in the nervous system finding its way out (1894, Draft E sent to William Fliess, published in 1950). However, in a subsequent paper on anxiety neurosis Freud (1894) writes:

> The psyche is overtaken by the affect of anxiety if it feels that it is incapable of dealing by an appropriate reaction with a task (a danger) approaching from the outside. In neurosis it is overtaken by anxiety if it notices that it is incapable of allaying a (sexual) excitation from within. Thus it behaves as though it were projecting this excitation to the outside. The affect (normal anxiety) and the corresponding neurosis stand in a firm relationship to each other. The former is a reaction to an exogenous excitation and the latter to an analogous endogenous one. [p. 189]

The distinction between affect as response to exogenous stimuli and anxiety as response to endogenous stimuli conflicts with Freud's earlier view in "actual neuroses," that anxiety is a transformation of accumulated tension due to some specific interference with the discharge of sexual tension.

Freud's yet later view of anxiety makes its first appearance in a 1909 footnote to *The Interpretation of Dreams*. Following a discussion about fantasies of life in the womb, Freud (1900) adds, "moreover, the act of birth is the first experience of anxiety and thus the source and prototype of the affect of anxiety" (p. 400). Freud's later view of the affects becomes crystallized by 1926 and is derived from his (1923) tripartite model of psychic structure. The problem of affects, according to this structural view, is completely subordinated to the problem of anxiety. Affects are considered more physiological, while anxiety is more purely psychological:

Anxiety is not newly created in repression; it is reproduced as an affective state in accordance with an already existing mnemic image. If we go further and inquire into the origin of affects in general, we shall be leaving the realm of pure psychology and entering the borderland of physiology. Affect states have become incorporated in the mind as precipitates of primeval traumatic experiences, and when a similar situation occurs, they are revived like mnemic symbols. [Freud 1926b, p. 19]

Thus in this later view, affects are physiological precipitates of early trauma (overstimulating experiences) that have become integrated into the mind. When similar circumstances arise later in life, affects become revived as symbols of early traumatic memories. Freud further draws a distinction between "automatic anxiety" in response to danger and anxiety used as a "signal" by the ego, thus eliminating the previous distinction of a generic difference between neurotic (sexual) and realistic anxiety (affect). The determinant of automatic anxiety is formulated by Freud as the traumatic situation. Trauma is conceptualized as helplessness of the ego in face of overstimulation (whether of external or internal origin). Anxiety as a signal is the ego's organized response to the threat of trauma. A threat is the potential presence of a "danger situation." The specifics of these internal dangers change throughout life, but their common form involves a loss or separation, which may lead to a situation of helplessness (i.e., accumulating tension resulting from unsatisfied desires). Thus the (internal) state of accumulated and discharged tension in Freud's earliest causal formulations is now reformulated as the traumatic or danger situation. Freud's four danger situations are loss of the love object, loss of the object's love, loss of the penis, and loss of the superego's love. Self psychologists have suggested adding to this list the loss of self cohesion, but perhaps this is implicit in various ways in Freud's four.

In summary, Freud's earliest view of affect is that it results from a damming up of sexual energy. Affects and affective anxiety are thus conceptualized as transformations of libidinal energy. Subsequently, he distinguishes between normal or realistic anxiety (affect), which arises in response to exogenous stimuli, and neurotic anxiety, which arises in response to endogenous (sexual) stimuli. By 1926 Freud formulates "automatic anxiety" as a response to danger situations and "signal anxiety," which serves to warn the ego of impending danger. These basic ideas have generally guided psychoanalytic theorizing about the affects until recently. Stimulated by limitations in traditional affect theory, or the clinical need for a broader framework in which to consider emotional experience, or perhaps even by advances in developmental and physiological psychology, several theoreticians have offered reformulations of affect theory.

RECENT INNOVATIONS IN AFFECT THEORY

Roy Schafer (1964) has correctly observed that the literature on the affects "is beset by three problems: heterogeneity of theoretical formulation; overemphasis on abstract metapsychological formulations, particularly economic formulations; and insufficient rigor in developing the connections between theory and observations made in the psychoanalytic situation" (p. 2). Schafer argues that because most analytic investigation revolves around emotional experience, it seems urgent to reexamine the means by which emotional experience is explored in the clinical situation. His 1964 work in this area specifies eight categories for organizing observations, which he proposes as down-to-earth, commonsense foundations upon which abstract formulations should be built. He seees no advantage in distinguishing between the terms *affect, emotion,* and *feeling,* since there is no general agreement in the field as to the merit of differentiating them in any particular way. It is easy to speak of affects in the abstract as if there were fixed and clear conceptual boundaries, but when sitting in the analytic chair an affect is always seen as part of complex phenomena that cannot be extricated from the ongoing stream of experience. Schafer is concerned about how we think about affects, though he is aware we usually must discuss them in their empirical contexts of wishes, defenses, ideas, ideals, and attitudes.

Here are the categories that Schafer suggests to guide our thinking about the emotional aspects of an event:

1. *Affect existence.* Is a specific affect present and being felt by the person? Is it being warded off or is it an unconscious potential at the moment? Or is the affect that is present artificial or superficial while true or deep feelings are absent?
2. *Affect formation.* Is a particular emotion forming in a specific situation and can it be identified? Is an emotion being represented or synthesized presently? Is a "preverbal" emotion becoming organized into verbal consciousness?
3. *Affect strength.* Can the relative intensity of existing and remembered feelings be clarified in relation to one another, as for example, in ambivalence? And are the feelings optimal in strength for reality orientation and for an inner sense of sincere involvement in one's life experience?
4. *Affect stimuli.* Unconsciously, if not consciously, people experience feelings as responses to specific stimuli. Is the person's designation of that stimulus accurate and complete? Are the stimuli internal or

external? Are they displaced from one object to another or from the current to the past or vice versa?
5. *Affect complexity and paradox.* Most emotions are blends or aggregates of various affect components. Are we observing condensations or fusions as distinct from ambivalence? In a single perhaps chronic affect are we analyzing the multiple tendencies that may be being experienced through expression of the same affect? And does one feeling paradoxically represent another perhaps opposite tendency as in a reaction formation?
6. *Affect location.* Can the affect presence be specified in a time context or in relation to other mental events? Are the affects properly experienced vis-à-vis a certain person or, in the case of loose boundaries or projection, is the affect more associated with certain self experiences? We speak of being touched, tickled, gripped, and of bodily processes being heavy, empty, hot, and tender. What body zones participate in the affect?
7. *Affect communication.* Through such communications as silence, minimization, exaggeration, obfuscation, displacement, rejection, uncertainty, confusion, intellectualization, somatization, or acting out, are the affects being communicated? If so, how accurately and completely?
8. *Affect history.* In examining an emotion in an analytic context, we are invariably wondering when, where, how, and with respect to whom or what has this emotion manifested itself before.

Schafer's eight categories can serve as reference points to foster analytic investigation into the occasions, meanings, functions, and changes of emotion. His work demonstrates that *affect analysis cannot be meaningfully separated* from the analysis of ideas, attitudes, fantasies, impulses, defenses, and all other categories of analytic experience.

Michael Basch (1975), in a detailed consideration of existing theories on the nature of depression, has provided a new series of hypotheses regarding human emotionality. Basch points out that theoreticians usually seek to establish some "unitary disease entity" but that "depressed behavior and mood may appear alone or in combination with other signs and symptoms, has a wide range of intensity with affects ranging from total incapacity to almost unnoticed discomfort, and is precipitated by a variety of factors presumed to be causal. To confuse an end result called depression with an underlying specific disease and search for its cause hinders both understanding and treatment" (pp. 485–486). Basch examines many of the explanatory principles of psychoanalysis and attempts to formulate depression as a "system disfunction."

Surveying a wide range of ideas in information theory, semiology, and studies of infant development, Basch concludes: "Far from being a passive creature to be shaped by his mother, the infant forms a system with her, using her capacities in the interest of his needs. Through his mimetic musculature he indicates whether he is optimally stimulated: if not, he sends signals that encourage the mother to search for and correct what is wrong" (p. 505). Basch further notes that "man is the only animal that becomes able to function symbolically in the course of normal development. . . . This indicates an evolutionary advance in kind, not just in degree, and its consequences for behavior are momentous" (p. 508). He adds that man "does not just live in the physical reality around him. The formation of a symbolic world, a world of concepts, creates a new environment in which a different relationship exists between the old and the new brain" (p. 510). Basch discusses extensively the infant's need for basic ordering of experience through the symbiosis and the subsequent formation of consistent self experiences. He demonstrates in a variety of ways that "depression refers to those consequences that follow from disturbances in the message processing function of the brain" (p. 531) due to disruptions in the ordering or process of information flow. He asserts that "depression should be considered a system disfunction rather than a particular illness or clinical picture. The behavioral system generated by the brain's operation is an open one which means that it sets its own goals on the basis of processing incoming stimuli and extracting their informational value. The systemic disturbance indicating that this process is no longer viable and that the system is converting from an open, transitional state into a closed reactive position is properly called depression" (p. 531).

Basch's views demonstrate a general modern trend toward considering human beings as open information processing systems in which complex affective signals serve to maintain interaction with other humans. As such, all affective colorations are assumed to have an important informational exchange value for the person in sustaining an active, alive sense of personhood. In the example of depression, Basch formulates that any one of a variety of causes can serve to provoke a limited or extensive closing off of exchange with the human environment resulting in the clinical picture known as depression.

In 1976 Schafer returned to studying the problem of emotion, this time in the context of forming a new language for psychoanalysis. In his book, Schafer critically examines the language of metapsychology, of internal and external world, and passivity that psychoanalysts have traditionally shown such a preference for. He begins with the assertion that emotions are not "things" and that we must forego speaking of them as substantive nouns.

Rather, Schafer advises that emotions are better conceived of and spoken of as actions or modes of action; that is, as verbs and adverbs. Emotions are best spoken of in the spirit of actions or activities that we engage in or as ways of engaging in life's many activities. In a thorough analysis of emotion language, Schafer shows that our common language uses "irrational, animistic fantasies about the anatomy, physiology, life cycle and social context of the body. We invoke the intestines ('guts'), the liver ('lily-livered'), the spine ('spineless') and the testicles ('no balls'), and we go on in this way about the stomach, spleen, buttocks, feces, urine, blood, senses, birth, death, contact and, time and again, the heart" (p. 275). Analyzing "heart" language as an extended example, Schafer shows how we unnecessarily concretize our emotions. Using happiness, love, anger, guilt, and fear, Schafer shows how each of these emotions in fact represents actions we engage in and that no loss is entailed by switching from noun usage to verb usage. For example, we have tended to speak of guilt as:

> a crushing load or a burden to be cast off; sometimes it is ghostly when we say it haunts or torments one. We often personify guilt as an inner tyrant, a judge, or policeman demanding that we be exposed and punished.... But by resorting to this language we no longer say (what is perfectly adequate to the occasion) that sometimes one judges one's own actions in an irrational, infantile, severly moralistic or punitive manner and especially that one does so unknown to oneself, that is unconsciously; we say instead that it is one's superego that (or who) judges one's ego (or self) in these ways. Thereby we set up superego as a personified entity of another sort; a so-called psychic structure that sets standards, prohibits, judges and punishes cruelly just as the parents of one's childhood once did or, with the help of exaggeration, seemed to do or seemed ready to do. [pp. 283–284]

In short, "it is inconsistent with action language either to speak substantively about the emotions and their activity or to render emotion-actions and emotion-modes through the use of bodily or other metaphors, the ideas feel and feeling and the limiting verb to be when it connects subjects with emotion-adjectives" (p. 293). Schafer points out that in Freudian language therapy consists of making unconscious things conscious or establishing ego where id or superego was. In action terms, the person is said to begin doing emotion-actions and doing actions in different emotion-modes. For example, a person is observed to begin welcoming friends rather than putting them off or acting less moodily. Schafer disallows the idea of storage and preservation of emotions or accumulating or displacing emotions.

An important logical extension of Schafer's action language arguments applied to human emotions is that "action, situation and emotion are all aspects of one description or explanation" (p. 339). "This interpenetration or co-determination of action, situation and emotion is not empirical; it is conceptual, logical, a priori. Consequently, the assumption of invariant lawful connections must be rejected in principle. The separations of emotional experience from action and situation is untenable" (p. 340). That is, we so often tend to assume that emotions are predictable and that one undergoes them passively. In taking such a view, we presuppose some lawful or predictable relations between action and situation on the one hand and emotion on the other. We may define both actions and situations in part by the emotional way in which a person is doing something, just as we may equally well define a person's emotion-actions and emotion-modes by stating his or her situation in certain ways.

In short, for Schafer emotion is not an entity, a quantity of psychic energy, the result of conflicting forces, an instinctual presentation, a physiological response, a sensation, a phenomenon governed by laws, a signal, or a passive experience with which one must cope. Emotion is an action or mode of action that people perform in the situations they define. People love and hate; they act joyfully, depressively, and guiltily. Emotions are enactments. Emotions are done, not had, and in most respects one may have access to them much as one may have access to any other action or mode of actions, whether it be one's own or another's.

Heinz Kohut (1971, 1977a, 1984) and the self psychologists as a group have written very little explicitly pertaining to the subject of human emotionality. Yet implicit in Kohut's concept of "empathy" as an observational tool (1959) is the requirement that the analyst must be attuned to the emotional life of the individual, especially as it pertains to issues of self cohesion and self fragmentation. Moreover, Kohut's central concept of "selfobject" resonance implies an ongoing fine-tuned emotional involvement and responsiveness. In contrast to the dearth of explicit theoretical focus on emotionality, the case studies of the self psychologists (Goldberg 1978, 1980) continue to demonstrate an exquisite awareness of and responsiveness to the vicissitudes of emotional life. Howard Bacal deals with emotional attunement in terms of "optimal responsiveness," a variation on Kohut's (1984) theme.

Daphne Socarides and Robert Stolorow (1984) have recently made good this deficit in the self psychology formulation of affect by contending that "selfobject functions pertain fundamentally to the integration of affect, and that the need for selfobjects pertains most centrally to the need for phase-appropriate responsiveness to affect states in all stages of the life cycle" (p. 105). They point out that the fundamental role of affectivity in organizing self-experience has been described in various ways by many analysts through time and has recently found confirmation in studies of infant–caregiver interaction.

> Affects can be seen as organizers of self-experience throughout development, if met with the requisite affirming, accepting, differentiating, synthesizing, and containing responses from caregivers. An absence of steady, attuned responsiveness to the child's affect states creates minute but significant derailments of optimal affect integration and leads to a propensity to dissociate or disavow affective reactions because they threaten the precarious structuralizations that have been achieved. [p. 106]

They maintain that the lack of required responsiveness interferes with the integration of affect states into the organization of self-experience, giving rise to defenses designed to preserve the "integrity of a brittle self-structure."

Basch (1983) is cited in this regard:

> Affect attunement leads to a shared world; without affect attunement one's activities are solitary, private and idiosyncratic. . . . [If] affect attunement is not present or is ineffective during these early years, the lack of shared experience may well create a sense of isolation and belief that one's affective needs generally are somehow unacceptable and shameful. [pp. 107–108]

Basch further proposes that defenses that appear in treatment are resistances against affects and stem from the lack of adequate affect attunement. Other aspects of development that depend upon selfobject attunement, according to Socarides and Stolorow are "(1) affect differentiation and its relationship to self-boundary formation, (2) the synthesis of affectively discrepant experiences, (3) the development of affect tolerance and capacity to use affects as self-signals, and (4) the desomatization and cognitive articulation of affect states" (1984, p. 108).

Socarides and Stolorow point to several important implications of their thesis for analytic treatment: (1) that defenses against affects "must be understood as being rooted in the patient's expectation or fear in the transference that his emerging feeling states will meet with the same faulty responsiveness that they received from the original caregivers" (p. 111), (2) that once the transference resistance against affects has been analyzed based upon the "dread to repeat" (Ornstein 1974) "the patient's arrested developmental need for the originally absent or faulty responsiveness to his emerging affect states will be revived with the analyst," and (3) that the importance in analyzing ruptures in the selfobject transference may not lie so much, as Kohut (1971) formulated, in "transmuting internalizations" resulting from "optimal frustration," but rather that the "central curative element may be found in the selfobject transference bond itself and its pivotal role in the articulation, integration and developmental transformations of the patient's affectivity" (p. 112).

In discussing depressed affect as an example of their theoretical formulations, Socarides and Stolorow maintain that what is crucial to the child's (or patient's) growing capacity to integrate his sadness and his painful disappointment in himself and others is the "reliable presence of a calming, continuing, empathic selfobject, irrespective of the 'amount' or intensity of the affects involved" (p. 113). The net result of their formulations represents a key contribution to the advancement of self psychology in their shifting of emphasis from "optimal frustration" to the "centrality of affect attunement." Socarides and Stolorow have convincingly put forward the claim that selfobject functions "pertain fundamentally to the integration of affect into the evolving organization of self-experience." Further, reliable affect attunement from selfobjects is thought to foster the differentiation, synthesis, modulation, and cognitive articulation of emerging emotion states, thereby contributing vitally to the structuralization of the individual's sense of self.

PSYCHOANALYTIC VIEWS ON MOODS

While there is no general agreement regarding how the terms *feeling, affect,* and *emotion* are to be used in psychoanalysis, more consensus prevails regarding the concept of mood. Weinshel (1970) speaks of the ambiguous, shadowy, or even "slippery" quality of moods but emphasizes their complex, highly refined, and relatively stable nature, pointing out that in this way moods are not unlike character traits. Jacobson (1957) points out that normal as well as pathological moods represent "a cross-section through the entire state of the ego, lending a particular, uniform coloring to all its manifestations for a longer or shorter period of time" (p. 68). She distinguishes moods sharply from the affect states in that particular qualities of the mood "brush off" on all other functions, whereas affect states relate to definite ideational representatives with feelings being vested in specific objects. Weinshel's (1970) definition is:

> [Moods] are psychological structures of varying complexity and stability, reflecting a certain degree of synthesis and organization, and depending on contributions from all three psychic systems.... In the moods, we can observe a mixture of affects as well as the products of varying defensive

activities directed against the affects. . . . The overall mood structure helps play a part in the binding of the affects; and the bound affects, in turn, contribute to the overall mood structure. At times the affective discharges associated with moods appear to be massive and relatively archaic; at other times, the affects involved reflect the development of highly differentiated affect discharge structures; and often both extremes coexist. [p. 315]

Christopher Bollas (1984) has contributed fundamentally to our understanding of moods, especially as they come to be established in the transference. He sees moods as being as necessary to the well-being of a person as dreams. "Whilst in a mood a part of the individual's total self withdraws into a generative autistic state in order that a complex internal task be allowed time and space to work itself through" (p. 203). For Bollas, a mood is a "space" licensed by a universal recognition of its necessity. "We need to experience moods" (p. 203). In "generative" moods a "special territory" is usually marked out which insures that mood experiencing is not mistaken by others for object directed communication. In contrast, a "malignant" mood is primarily aimed to effect some significant other, to coerce someone into some "capitulative activity." He quotes Greenson (1954): "Moods are not only derived from the internal representations of external objects, but are often the representations of one's own past state of mind; one's conception of oneself in the past" (pp. 73–74). Highlighting this mnemic quality of moods, Bollas defines moods as, "complex self states that may establish a mnemic environment, in which the individual re-experiences and re-creates former infant-child experiences and states of being. . . . As with a dream, so too with the mood: psychic reality is given a certain existential status in effecting our lived experience of external reality. . . . The psychic accomplishment of the mood may be as valuable as is the work of a dream" (p. 204). Because of the particular features of the analytic setting and process (Bollas 1979, Khan 1974, Winnicott 1975), "analysands create environments within the clinical setting and a living through of a mood is one of the idioms for the establishment of an environment" (Bollas 1984, p. 204).

Bollas maintains that a mood is "a special feature of a person's character, [which] actually conserves a former self state, although the way in which the usual person relates to the special self state will of course be both a representation of how the person interpreted and experienced the parental disposition to the self state represented in the mood, and, as such, both the self state and the usual self will constitute the person's character." Through case studies, Bollas illustrates that moods that are typical of a person's character preserve and contain being states experienced by the child in relation to the family, "experience-memory that is stored in the internal world as a conservative object."

Bollas believes that moods are often the existential registers of breakdowns that occurred in the parent–child relationship and that when a person goes into a mood he becomes that child self who was refused expression in relation to his parents. A self state that might have been integrated into the child's ongoing self development was rejected by the parents and conserved in the form of a mood. Such self states may become represented in the analytic transference as moods and, at times, may threaten a negative therapeutic reaction.

22

Emotionality and Human Relatedness[1]

LISTENING TO HUMAN EMOTIONALITY

From the beginning, psychoanalysis has constituted a process of *listening* to emotionality and to emotional involvements. Freud always recalled that he first understood the "power of the unconscious" the day his friend and colleague, Dr. Joseph Breuer, told him about his work with Bertha Pappenheim. Written up as the case of Anna O., Breuer describes his regular trips to Bertha's house to hear emotion-laden accounts of the thoughts and fantasies that daily occupied her. She reported great relief from her various "hysterical" symptoms with this procedure she called the "talking cure." The evening of the day Breuer pronounced her free of hysterical illness, Bertha had him summoned on an emergency basis, only to announce that she was pregnant and that the baby she was carrying was his. This event marks the clearest moment of entry of emotionality into the countertransference as Breuer fled her hysterical pregnancy to go on a second honeymoon with his wife.

Emotional catharsis (usually with the aid of hypnosis) was the earliest treatment tactic of Breuer and Freud (1893–1895) in which the patient was encouraged to remember the exciting events surrounding the occurrence of the symptom's first appearance—and to report them with full emotionality. Their theory was that the intense affects that produced hysteria had been deprived the normal "wearing away" process of forgetting and had become "strangulated" inside, thus producing the physical symptoms. Freud's subsequent free association technique evolved out of the same notion that persistent recall of significant memories with their associated

---

1. This chapter is reprinted with revisions from the *Southern California Bioenergetic Society Newletter* [1991] 6(1):2–6.

intense affective states produced the cure. Rather than merely following the doctor's suggestions, free association was designed to see whatever facet of the patient's unconscious presented itself spontaneously each hour. As the field of psychoanalysis evolved, the emphasis on the revival in present consciousness or unconscious (or id) imagery was regularly observed to be a highly charged emotional event. As the concept of interpretation became elaborated, thoughts and affects from the unconscious id were systematically interpreted, thereby becoming included in the realm of conscious ego functioning. James Strachey's (1934) classic paper on the "therapeutic action" of psychoanalysis conceptualized a mutative interpretation as a statement by the analyst mobilizing a quantity of id or instinctual energy (or intense emotionality) and directing it at the person of the analyst. An interpretation in the best sense has come to be considered a statement that was *simultaneously* true for a love relation of the past, contemporary love relations outside the analytic situation, and the current experience of the relationship with the analyst. Mutative interpretations are regularly thought to evoke a strong emotional response in the presence of and directed toward the analyst.

Through the years, intense emotionality encountered as a result of analytic interpretation has been considered and formulated in many different ways, as shown in Chapter 21. Seldom, however, has the emotional exchange occurring *between* the two participants per se been the focus of systematic study.

We live in a society in which emotional display is generally considered impulsive or irrational and looked upon with caution, if not openly devalued. In contrast, rational, cognitive thought processes involving restraint and control of emotionality are generally valued in our civilization. This factor alone (never mind possible defensive reactions on the part of analysts) may account for the general tendency in our field to shift the focus of investigation onto the rational, cognitive "ego" aspects of the analytic situation while generally neglecting or overlooking the centrality of emotional experience in the analytic interchange. Yet every practitioner knows differently. Daily in our consulting rooms we live through passionate outpourings, shattering emotional earthquakes, and emotional storms of the widest variety. Further, we know that at the end of a good day's work we are often emotionally drained or exhausted. The labyrinths of emotionality our work requires us to thread through regularly takes us on tours of the deepest and often some of the most uncertain and troubling aspects of our own emotional lives. The fact of our recognizing the importance of every analytic practitioner having undergone his or her own analytic experience, makes clear the primacy with which we consider our own emotional responsiveness in this kind of work. No other line of professional activity makes such a daily demand upon the affective life of the practitioner. One hour, we rejoice with new achievements of one person; the next, we are weighed down with pain and sadness only next to greet anger and accusations—and so on, in a quick sequence.

With the contemporary emphasis in psychoanalysis on listening to emotional concerns and issues stemming from life's earliest relationships, the importance of developing the countertransference response as a working tool has increased in importance. A wide variety of formulations have developed to help the practitioner tune in to his or her own emotional responsiveness and to *use* that responsiveness to feel and to understand what is being communicated—not so much in words, images, or ideas—directly into the most private regions of the analyst's own emotionality. Undoubtedly, the mesmerizing power of Heinz Kohut's emphasis on empathy owes much of its impact to the general awareness that the most important function during the analytic hour has to do with *emotional attunement* to the feeling states of the people who come for consultation.

Even the emphasis that Roy Schafer (1976) and Donald Spence (1982) have recently placed on the ongoing construction of personal narrations in analysis owes much of its force to daily experiences of emotional interchange in the analytic relationship and the mutual effort at rendering these emotional exchanges as creative life-history narrations. The studies of countertransference reported by Harold Searles (1979a) and Peter Giovacchini (1979b), and in a different vein Otto Kernberg (1975, 1976, 1980a) and others, have likewise served to expand general considerations of the analytic experience into the realm of mutual, reciprocal emotionality which is shared and understood by two. John Gedo's (1981, 1986) emphasis on the receipt of emotional experience and the necessity for the analyst in various circumstances to deliver his or her interpretation with affective force confirms the contemporary trend toward recognition of the importance of the affective exchange in psychoanalysis.

In my own work developing *Listening Perspectives* (1983), I have supported the Kohutian emphasis on emotionally attuned empathic responsiveness, but I have raised the two further questions: (1) Empathy with *what* and (2) in what *modes* can that empathy generally be achieved? I have proposed that the *listening* context of the consulting room be considered along lines first proposed by Jacobson (1954, 1964) in her work on the "self and object world." That is, my own work has revolved around an attempt to notice what aspects or experiences of self are emerging at a given moment. And what is the expressive relationship of those self experiences to the current experience of otherness—most immediately and specifically, the otherness that the analyst represents in the evolving relatedness context. Our interest in transference and countertransference in analysis has always been, and remains, experiencing and attempting to tease out and understand the emotionality of the analytic exchange and its constantly shifting focus from person to person in the analytic hour.

To my first question, "empathy with *what*?" I have proposed that we consider four broad forms of self and other relatedness as listening perspectives, metaphorically using a developmental schema (see chapter 15).

To my thinking, the gravest error of Freud and most other analytic thinkers has been the utilization of the commonsense assumption that people live their daily lives experiencing themselves as more or less separate entities from their significant others. Because our grammar utilizes personal pronouns (such as I, you, he/she, and them), and because people do speak as though they experience one another as separate actors or agents, classical analysis (and I might here add Kleinian analysis, ego analysis, and existential analysis as well), has tended to be formulated and experienced in terms of an object constancy mode, even though at the same time the fundamental concept of transference makes it clear that people do not generally tend to experience one another as separate and differentiated from their own emotionally charged ways of constructing and experiencing their world.

To my second question of how or in what ways can we most meaningfully consider the vastly different demands that empathic responsiveness to these four distinctly different forms of experience makes on analytic relatedness, I have concurred with the Freudian finding that emotional restraint and cognitively based verbal-symbolic interpretations serve well to *reflect* interpersonal—the so-called oedipal—modes of emotional exchange. Likewise, Kohut's emphasis on emotional attunement to the ebb and flow of experiences of self cohesiveness serves well to elucidate crucial aspects of "self to selfobject" *resonance*.

But to the Freudian "constancy" mode of empathy and the Kohutian "selfobject" mode of empathy, I have specified in my work (Hedges 1983) two additional forms of analytic empathy:

1. *Reverberation* through replication and eventual differentiation of symbiotic and separating emotional relatedness modes through the recreation of interpersonal "scenarios" in the analytic exchange.
2. *Contacting* emotionally charged perceptual and sensorimotor relatedness *extensions*, which represent attempts to organize environmental forms, in such as way as to foster the eventual establishment of a mutual cuing bond of human emotionality with the analyst.

VALUE SYSTEMS INVOLVED IN THE CONCEPT OF THE "CURE"

Kohut (1984) has rightly pointed out that the Freudian criterion of cure—the capacity for mature, heterosexual, genital object relationship—represents a limiting value system that serves to systematically bias the analytic relationship. He further maintains that the Kleinian criterion of cure—postambivalent object relations—likewise represents a series of biasing value judgments. He acknowledges that his own criterion of cure—"mature forms of self to selfobject resonance"—also represents the introduction of a value system into the analytic relationship.

I would add to Kohut's observations that the use of the separation-individuation developmental metaphor as a criterion of cure also runs the risk of introducing into the analytic relationship another value system with limiting effects—a value system that seeks to promote "growth, maturity, differentiation and individuation." I propose that we carefully restrict our use of such developmental metaphors to *defining a range of human relatedness possibilities* and that we refrain from placing values on how people relate to one another. The only possible value that might serve us in the ongoing analytic relationship is the value we attribute to evolutionary processes in general—that is, the progressive attainment of increments or increases in *flexibility* in the living out of various relatedness modes.

My own preference, however, is to attempt to restrict my value system in analysis to a *premium on listening and responding* as flexibly as possible to the various relatedness forms presented to me during each analytic hour. By continuing to expand my own range of listening possibilities, I not only seem to feel better about myself as a developing human being, but I believe the ways in which people are able to use me as a listening resource increase.

In *Soul Analysis* (1985), I maintain that the analytic experience derives its power from having one's personal, individual essence in its rich uniqueness reflected, resonated, reverberated with, and contacted by the person who assumes the analytic position. I have formulated the role of the analyst as one that ideally represents a repository of culturally derived wisdom about the nature of human relatedness. The function of the analyst is to listen to personal emotional communications (verbal and nonverbal) and to reverberate with personal forms of relatedness through the medium of culturally constructed forms.

J. Michael Russell, in his tour de force, "The Self in Contemporary Psychoanalysis" (1985), has "turned on its head" our usual way of considering the problem of the evolving sense of self, thus contributing further to questioning developmentally based value systems. Psychoanalysis has traditionally considered the earliest developing experiences as narcissistic and self-preoccupied, and human development as a gradual moving toward a consideration of others and their emotional separateness. Russell has shown that it is equally possible, and perhaps even more sensible and appealing, to consider human development as just the reverse. That is, Russell shows how, by virtue of cultural assumption, we are agents before we are born. Infants become immediately responsive to the cultural and linguistic community into which they are introduced at birth. Then, slowly, through a series of disappointments and frustrations with others in the human environment, a sense of self can be seen to evolve. That is, Russell has most interestingly been able to show that we become sensitive to and enmeshed with others from the beginning and that what we later come to call our "self" is the result of a series of retreats in the face of disappointment and frustration. Thus, Russell's formulations permit us to consider the range of human emotionality along quite different lines. Russell's work provides another basis for questioning contemporary attempts to place a positive value on independence and a negative value on various forms of social merger or enmeshment.

The work of Henri Wallon, a French psychiatrist, psychologist, and educator, similarly questions traditional developmental value systems (Voyat 1984). He has been a long-time critic of the ego psychologists and especially of the developmental research of Piaget. In *Soul Analysis* I have reviewed extensively the fascinating developmental theories of Wallon that parallel the Russell model just cited. I will mention briefly Wallon's views on human emotionality.

Based on a general consideration of the biological evolution of the psyche, Wallon considers the emotions as primary forms of interpersonal contact that are activated and available at birth and during the first few months of life. "The role of emotion in the behavior of the child and the influences they continue to exercise on that of the adult, openly or covertly, are thus not mere chance events or simple manifestations of disturbances of equilibrium. As *organizing phenomena*, emotions play a necessary role" (Hedges 1985, p. 150). In studying the display that constitutes emotionality, Wallon concludes that from earliest infancy human emotionality utilizes innate mimetic capabilities for the purpose of directing and controlling others in the environment to respond to one's needs. Emotionality is thus *for others*. This position has been echoed in recent philosophical studies such as those conducted by Robert Solomon (1984), in which the "rationality" of emotion has been studied as a set of social conventions whereby personal experiences are canalized in highly refined and ritualized forms of communication. Wallon, like Russell, points out that the self only becomes distinguished gradually from a matrix of total enmeshment with otherness in which the emotions serve as primary focus of expressive communication. Wallon points out that a child only expresses *for* others; if injured in solitary play there is no crying until the other appears. Wallon's penetrating analysis of emotion extends to the rhythm, movements, and attitudes of the social group, which achieve remarkable uniformity. Since emotionality derives its form from group behavior, the group itself then comes to represent a cohesive force derived from the participation of each individual, thus acquiring its capacity to exert an influence on human evolution. Wallon (Voyat 1984) states,

> The first systems of reaction that begin to develop in organized patterns—through the influence of the environment—are directed toward bringing about a fusion of feeling between the individual and those around him. Emotions may with good reason be regarded as the origin of consciousness since through their expression they delimit for the subject himself certain specific limits of feeling states. Emotions provide the initial spark to individual consciousness only through the group, with which they initially brought about his total fusion. [p. 43]

Much of Wallon's developmental theory is devoted to specifying stages and phases through which individual and cognitive consciousness slowly differentiates from its affective merger with group responsiveness.

Permit me now to conclude this survey with a series of tentative proposals for how we might best begin now to consider human emotionality in the listening context of the consulting situation.

1. All aspects of the analytic relationship are to be considered as actions and activities of two mutually engaged persons.
2. All emotionality is to be considered activity, and all activity is to be considered in its emotional aspects.
3. Emotionality is to be considered as constituting a way each person knows about, makes judgments about, and affects as well as is affected by the other.
4. Emotionality is to be considered neither in physiological nor sociological terms per se but rather as representing crucial psychological aspects of the interpersonal exchange.
5. Emotionality is to be understood as one person's primary mode of maintaining contact with another.
6. Human psychological development is taken as a continuously expanding appreciation of the limits of one's influence over another,

the fundamental awareness of those limitations coming as a result of interpersonal emotional exchange.
7. Emotionality is to be understood as playing a complex and significant role in the differentiation of representations of individual identity or "self" experience from representation of communal, group, or "other" experience—nowhere more clearly evident than in the differentiation typically achieved in the analytic situation.
8. Human traditions known to the analyst may provide categories and tools for expanding and differentiating psychological organization, but ultimately the personal discovery of the limitations of human categories and organizational principles remains an individual creative emotional activity that may take on an affective coloration of elation (success in individuation) or depletion (disappointment in loss of fusion) or both.
9. In analysis, one person looks to another for emotional resonance in order to create, integrate, or master new varieties of creative self experience, or in order to achieve novel self experiences apart from limiting patterns of (characterologically based) emotionality, or to achieve resonance with sustaining patterns of emotional withdrawal—as in generative moods.
10. An analytic experience is sought in order to dip into secured patterns of emotionality and, through reflection, resonance, reverberation, or contact with another, to discover (consciously, unconsciously, verbally, nonverbally) the limitations of one's characteristic patterns of emotional relatedness, thereby creating fresh emotional activities.
11. In analytic work, it is useful to consider human emotionality along a continuum of greater or lesser differentiation of self experiences from other experiences—that is, to employ the series of listening perspectives I have proposed.

Finally, I view emotionality as the central organizing feature of human life. Analysis seeks to study the interplay of emotional relatedness *forms* through various *modes* of empathic reflection, resonance, reverberation, and contact. The challenge for the future is to begin acknowledging and formulating in theory and in practice the various dimensions of the human emotional exchange that can and do enhance the listening context of psychoanalysis and psychotherapy.

23

Working the Countertransference

Central to the psychoanalytic enterprise is the complex interplay of emotions of the participants. The objectivist view of psychoanalysis has sought to suppress the subjective response of the listener in an effort to attain a clearer picture of the patterns of emotional responsiveness transferred onto the listener by the speaker. The emerging view of systematic subjectivity promoted by the listening perspectives approach is more in keeping with the epistemological tenets of our age of uncertainty.

I hope that this volume of countertransference studies based upon the emotional involvements of many speakers and listeners has demonstrated clearly the viability of utilizing these strategic involvements for the purpose of enhancing human relatedness potentials. Freely experienced emotional responsiveness evoked in an experiencing listener can be a powerful informer of the kinds of experiences the speaker is communicating through word, gesture, interaction, and overtone.

The historical caution about countertransference stirrings in analysts can be seen as justified in light of our present knowledge about how extremely complex transference-countertransference communications can be. That is, a listener may have an emotional response with certain subjective qualities. But deciphering its meaning and place in the overall relatedness picture is by no means a simple or straightforward endeavor. However, as this volume demonstrates, we now possess a century of experience in deciphering the kinds of emotional involvements that are likely to arise in the course of analytic relating and how to use them strategically for analytic gain.

But even more importantly, we have each other. We now live in a community of practicing listeners to whom we can turn for help in contextualizing enigmatic emotional responses that arise in the course of our work. In *Interpreting the Countertransference* (Hedges 1992) and *In Search of the Lost*

Mother of Infancy (Hedges 1994b) I have provided many actual transcripts of study groups that meet weekly to consider their work together and to submit to one another their most puzzling emotional involvements for group study. Many such study groups have begun forming throughout our community that will continue to sustain us in this difficult work.

At this juncture in our history it seems convenient, logical, and heuristic to allow ourselves to think in terms of four distinct varieties of emotional involvement. These four categories are derived metaphorically from studies of early childhood development as well as from a century of psychoanalytic experience. Rather than assuming we have arrived at definitive categories, or that we are ever likely to know with certainty the nature of the human psyche, our research needs to be interpreted as pointing toward ways of thinking about and listening to the multitude of possibilities in human emotional involvement that we can expect to arise in the course of relating.

I am deeply indebted to the many professional listeners who have contributed their thought and work toward making these studies possible. I am indebted also to the many people about whom they have written and who have given permission for aspects of their private lives to be made public in service of the expansion of human knowledge.

Freud opened up our field by courageously disclosing his dreams and slips of the tongue so that we might be encouraged to think about invisible aspects of ourselves. Freud's courage has been matched by those who have contributed their work here. May their example be matched by many others as we go forward together in the human endeavor of understanding the invisible complexities of strategic emotional involvement.

REFERENCES

Abraham, K. (1911). Notes in the psychoanalytical investigation and treatment of manic-depressive insanity and allied conditions. In *Selected Papers of Karl Abraham*, trans. D. Bryan and A. Strachey. New York: Brunner/Mazel.
——— (1924). A short study of the development of the libido. In *Selected Papers of Karl Abraham*, tr. D. Bryan and A. Strachey. New York: Brunner/Mazel.
Atwood, G. E., and Stolorow, R. D. (1984). *Structures of Subjectivity: Explorations in Psychoanalytic Phenomenology*. Hillsdale, NJ: Analytic Press.
Bacal, H. (1985). Optimal responsiveness and the therapeutic process. In *Progress in Self Psychology*, vol. 1, ed. A. Goldberg. New York: Guilford.
Balint, A. (1943). On identification. *International Journal of Psycho-Analysis* 24:97–107.
Basch, M. (1975). Toward a theory that encompasses depression. In *Depression and Human Existence*, ed. E. J. Anthony and T. Benedek. Boston: Little, Brown.
——— (1983). Interpretation: toward a developmental model. Cited in D. Socarides and R. Stolorow, *Journal of Psychoanalysis* 12.
Bibring, E. (1953). *The mechanism of depression*. Revised version of a paper presented at the Annual Meeting of the American Psychoanalytic Association, May 1951.
Binswanger, L. (1956). *Sigmund Freud: Reminiscences of a Friendship*, trans. N. Guterman. New York: Grune & Stratton.
Bion, W. R. (1955). Language and the schizophrenic. In *New Directions in Psycho-Analysis*, ed. M. Klein et al. London: Tavistock.
——— (1962). *Learning From Experience*. New York: Basic Books.
——— (1963). *Elements of Psycho-Analysis*. New York: Basic Books.
Blanck, G., and Blanck, R. (1979). *Ego Psychology II: Psychoanalytic Developmental Psychology*. New York: Columbia University Press.
Blum, H. (1987). Countertransference: concepts and controversies. In *Countertransference*, ed. E. Slakter. Northvale, NJ: Jason Aronson. (Originally published in *Psychoanalysis: The Science of Mental Conflict: Essays in Honor of Charles Brenner*, ed. A. D. Richards and M. S. Willick, pp. 229–245. New Jersey: Analytic Press, 1986.)
Bollas, C. (1979). The transformational object. *International Journal of Psycho-Analysis* 59:97–107.
——— (1983). Expressive uses of the countertransference. In *Shadow of the Object: Psychoanalysis of the Unthought Known*, ed. C. Bollas, pp. 200–236. London: Free Association Press, 1987.
——— (1984). Moods and the conservative process. *International Journal of Psycho-Analysis* 65:203–212.
——— (1987). *Shadow of the Object: Psychoanalysis of the Unthought Known*. New York: Columbia University Press.

Brandchaft, B. (1983). The negativism of the negative therapeutic reaction and the psychology of the self. In *The Future of Psychoanalysis: Essays in Honor of Heinz Kohut*, ed. A. Goldberg, pp. 327–359. New York: International Universities Press.

Brandchaft, B., and Stolorow, R. D. (1984). A current perspective on difficult patients. In *Kohut's Legacy: Contributions to Self Psychology*, ed. P. E. Stepansky and A. Goldberg, pp. 93–115. Hillsdale, NJ: Analytic Press.

Brenner, C. (1959). The masochistic character: genesis and treatment. *Journal of the American Psychoanalytic Association* 7:197–226.

Breuer, J., and Freud, S. (1893–1895). Studies on hysteria. *Standard Edition* 2.

Briggs, J., and Peat, F. D. (1984). *Looking Glass Universe: The Emerging Science of Wholeness*. New York: Simon & Schuster.

Casement, P. J. (1985). Analytic holding under pressure. In *Learning from the Patient*, pp. 129–139. New York: Guilford.

Coverdale, C. (1983). Two developmental lines in self psychology: selfobject empathy and interpretation. In Hedges, L., *Listening Perspectives in Psychotherapy*, pp. 93–99. Northvale, NJ: Jason Aronson.

Darwin, C. (1872). *The Expression of the Emotions in Man and Animals*. Chicago: University of Chicago Press, 1965.

De M'uzan, M. (1976). Countertransference and the paradoxical system. *Rev. Franc. Psychanal.* 40:575–590. (Trans. in Lebovici, S. and Widlocher, D., *Psychoanalysis in France*, pp. 437–451. New York: International Universities Press, 1980.)

Eissler, K. (1953). The effect of the structure of the ego on psychoanalytic technique. *Journal of the American Psychoanalytic Association* 1:104–143.

Ekstein, R. (1984). *Prolegomena to the study of the languages of psychoanalysis and psychotherapy*. Paper presented at the Newport Center for Psychoanalytic Studies, Newport Beach, CA, October.

Ekstein, R., and Motto, R. (1966). *Children of Time and Space of Action and Impulse*. New York: Appleton Century Crofts.

Epstein, L. (1993). Countertransference with borderline patients. In *Countertransference*, ed. L. Epstein and A. Feiner, pp. 375–405. Northvale, NJ: Jason Aronson, 1979.

Fenichel, O. (1945). Depression and mania. In *The Psychoanalytic Theory of Neurosis*, pp. 387–414. New York: Norton.

Firestein, S. K. (1978). *Termination of Psychoanalysis*. New York: International Universities Press.

Fliess, R. (1942). The metapsychology of the analyst. *Psychoanalytic Quarterly* 11:211–227.

Freud, A. (1937). *The Ego and the Mechanisms of Defense*. New York: International Universities Press.

Freud, S. (1894). Anxiety neurosis. *Standard Edition* 1:112.

―――― (1897). Extracts from the Fliess papers. Letter 71. *Standard Edition* 1:263–265.

―――― (1900). Interpretation of dreams. *Standard Edition* 4.

―――― (1905). A case of hysteria: three essays on sexuality and other works. *Standard Edition* 7:125–243.

―――― (1910). Future prospects of psycho-analysis. *Standard Edition* 11:141–151.

——— (1912). The dynamics of transference. *Standard Edition* 12:97–108.
——— (1915). Instincts and their vicissitudes. *Standard Edition* 14:111–140.
——— (1917). Mourning and melancholia. *Standard Edition* 14:237–260.
——— (1918). From the history of an infantile neurosis. *Standard Edition* 17:1–123.
——— (1923). The ego and the id. *Standard Edition* 19:3–68.
——— (1924a). The economic problem of masochism. *Standard Edition* 19:157–172.
——— (1924b). The dissolution of the Oedipus complex. *Standard Edition* 19:172–179.
——— (1926a). Negation. *Standard Edition* 19:235–242.
——— (1926b). Inhibitions, symptoms, and anxiety. *Standard Edition* 20:77–175.
——— (1932). New introductory lectures in psycho-analysis and other works. *Standard Edition* 22.
——— (1954). *The Origins of Psychoanalysis.* New York: Basic Books.
Gedo, J. (1979a). *Beyond Interpretation: Toward a Revised Theory for Psychoanalysis.* New York: International Universities Press.
——— (1979b). Theories of object relations: a metapsychological assessment. *American Psychoanalytic Association Journal* 27:361–373.
——— (1981). *Advances in Clinical Psychoanalysis.* New York: International Universities Press.
——— (1986). *Conceptual Issues in Psychoanalysis.* Hillsdale, NJ: Analytic Press.
Gill, M. M. (1984). Psychoanalysis and psychotherapy: a revision. *International Review of Psycho-Analysis* 11:161–179.
Giovacchini, P. L. (1972). *Tactics and Techniques in Psychoanalytic Therapy.* Vol. 1. New York: Jason Aronson.
——— (1975a). *Psychoanalysis of Character Disorders.* New York: Jason Aronson.
——— (1975b). *Tactics and Techniques in Psychoanalytic Therapy.* Vol. 2. New York: Jason Aronson.
——— (1979). *The Treatment of Primitive Mental States.* New York: Jason Aronson.
——— (1984). *Character Disorders and Adaptive Mechanisms.* New York: Jason Aronson.
——— (1986a). *Developmental Disorders: The Transitional Space in Mental Breakdowns and Creative Integration.* Northvale, NJ: Jason Aronson.
——— (1986b). Psychic integration and object constancy. In *Self and Object Constancy,* ed. R. Lax, S. Bach, and A. Burland, pp. 220–232. New York: Guilford.
——— (1988). *Countertransference—Triumphs and Catastrophes.* Northvale, NJ: Jason Aronson.
——— (1993). Countertransference with primitive mental states. In *Countertransference,* ed. L. Epstein and A. H. Feiner, pp. 267–304. Northvale, NJ: Jason Aronson, 1979.
Gleick, J. (1987). *Chaos: Making a New Science.* New York: Penguin.
Goldberg, A., ed. (1978). *The Psychology of the Self: A Casebook.* New York: International Universities Press.
———, ed. (1980). *Advances in Self Psychology.* New York: International Universities Press.
——— (1987). The place of apology in psychoanalysis and psychotherapy. *International Review of Psycho-Analysis* 14:409–417.
——— (1990). *The Prisonhouse of Psychoanalysis.* Hillsdale, NJ: Analytic Press.

Gorkin, M. (1987). *The Uses of Countertransference*. Northvale, NJ: Jason Aronson.
Green, A. (1986). The dead mother. In *On Private Madness*, The International Psycho-Analytical Library, No. 117, ed. C. Yorke, pp. 142–173. London: Hogarth Press and Institute of Psycho-Analysis.
Greenson, R. (1954). On moods and introjects. In *Explorations in Psychoanalysis*, pp. 61–74. New York: International Universities Press.
——— (1967). *The Technique and Practice of Psychoanalysis*. New York: International Universities Press.
——— (1978). *Explorations in Psychoanalysis*. New York: International Universities Press.
Grinberg, L. (1993). Projective counteridentification and countertransference. In *Countertransference*, ed. L. Epstein and A. Feiner, pp. 169–191. Northvale, NJ: Jason Aronson, 1979.
Hartmann, H. (1950). Comments on the psychoanalytic theory of the ego. In *Psychoanalytic Study of the Child* 5:74–96. New York: International Universities Press.
Hedges, L. E. (1983). *Listening Perspectives in Psychotherapy*. New York: Jason Aronson.
——— (1985). *Soul analysis*. Unpublished.
——— (1992). *Interpreting the Countertransference*. Northvale, NJ: Jason Aronson.
——— (1994a). *Remembering, Repeating, and Working Through Childhood Trauma*. Northvale, NJ: Jason Aronson.
——— (1994b). *In Search of the Lost Mother of Infancy*. Northvale, NJ: Jason Aronson.
——— (1994c). *Working the Organizing Experience*. Northvale, NJ: Jason Aronson.
——— (1994d). *Projective identification or reciprocal scripting in judicial processes*. Unpublished manuscript.
Hedges, L. E., Hilton, R., Hilton, V. W., and Caudill, O. B. (in press). *Therapists at Risk*. Northvale, NJ: Jason Aronson.
Hedges, L. E., and Hulgas, J. (1991). *Working the Organizing Experience*. Northvale, NJ: Jason Aronson.
Heimann, P. (1950). On counter-transference. *International Journal of Psycho-Analysis* 31:81–84.
Heisenberg, W. (1958). *Physics and Beyond*. New York: Harper Torchbooks.
Hilton, R. (1990). *Touching in psychotherapy*. Speech, Pacific Northwest Bioenergetic Conference, Edmonds, WA.
Hunter, V. (1994). *Psychoanalysts Talk*. New York: Guilford.
Hurn, H. T. (1971). Toward a paradigm of the terminal phase: the current status of the terminal phase. *Journal of the American Psychoanalytic Association* 19:332–348.
Jacobs, T. (1987). Countertransference enactments. In *Countertransference*, ed. E. Slakter, pp. 170–182. Northvale, NJ: Jason Aronson.
Jacobson, E. (1953). The affects and their pleasure–unpleasure qualities in relation to the psychic discharge process. In *Drives, Affects, Behavior*, vol. 1, ed. R. M. Lowenstein, pp. 38–66. New York: International Universities Press.
——— (1954). The self and object world: vicissitudes of their infantile cathexis and

their influence of ideational and affective development. *Psychoanalytic Study of the Child* 9:75–127. New York: International Universities Press.
——— (1957). Normal and pathological moods: their nature and function. *Psychoanalytic Study of the Child* 12:68–113. New York: International Universities Press.
——— (1964). *The Self and Object World.* New York: International Universities Press.
——— (1971). On depressive states: nosological and theoretical problems. In *Depression,* ed. L. Newman, pp. 167–184. New York: International Universities Press.
Kaplan, L. (1978). *Oneness and Separateness: From Infant to Individual.* New York: Simon & Schuster.
Kernberg, O. F. (1975). *Borderline Conditions and Pathological Narcissism.* New York: Jason Aronson.
——— (1976). *Object-Relations Theory and Clinical Psychoanalysis.* New York: Jason Aronson.
——— (1980a). *Internal World and External Reality.* New York: Jason Aronson.
——— (1980b). Lecture given at the conference on *The Narcissistic Personality,* Los Angeles, October, sponsored by the Los Angeles Psychoanalytic Society and Institute.
Khan, M. M. R. (1974). Role of phobic and counterphobic mechanisms and separation anxiety in schizoid character formation. In *The Privacy of the Self,* ed. J. D. Sutherland and J. B. Pantalis, pp. 69–81. New York: International Universities Press.
Kirsner, D. (1990). Mystics and professionals in the culture of American psychoanalysis. *Free Associations* 20.
Klein, M. (1946). Notes on some schizoid mechanisms. *International Journal of Psycho-Analysis* 24:97–107.
——— (1952). Some theoretical conclusions regarding the emotional life of the infant. In *Developments in Psycho-Analysis,* ed. J. Riviere, pp. 198–236. London: Hogarth.
——— (1957). *Envy and Gratitude.* New York: Basic Books.
Kohut, H. (1959). Introspection, empathy and psychoanalysis: an examination of the relationship between mode of observation and theory. *Journal of the American Psychoanalytic Association* 7:459–483.
——— (1971). *The Analysis of the Self.* New York: International Universities Press.
——— (1977a). *The Restoration of the Self.* New York: International Universities Press.
——— (1977b). *Psychodynamics of Drug Dependence.* National Institute on Drug Abuse Research, Monograph No. 12, May. Washington, DC: U.S. Department of Health, Education and Welfare.
——— (1979). Discussion at the UCLA Self Psychology Conference.
——— (1982). Introspection, empathy and the semi-circle of mental health. *International Journal of Psycho-Analysis* 63:395–407.
——— (1984). *How Does Analysis Cure?* Chicago: University of Chicago Press.

Kosinski, J. (1970). *Being There.* New York: Harcourt, Brace, Jovanovich.
Kuhn, T. (1962). *The Structure of Scientific Revolutions.* Chicago: University of Chicago Press.
Lacan, J. (1977). *Ecrits. A Selection.* New York: Norton.
Langs, R. (1982). *Psychotherapy: A Basic Text.* New York: Jason Aronson.
Little, M. (1951). Counter-transference and the patient's response to it. *International Journal of Psycho-Analysis* 32:32–40.
——— (1981). *Transference Neurosis: Transference Psychosis.* New York: Jason Aronson.
——— (1990). *Psychotic Anxieties and Containment. A Personal Record of an Analysis with Winnicott.* Northvale, NJ: Jason Aronson.
Loewald, H. (1979). On the therapeutic action of psycho-analysis. *International Journal of Psycho-Analysis* 41:16–33.
Lowen, A. (1975). *Bioenergetics.* London: Penguin.
Mahler, M. (1966). Notes on the development of basic mood: the depressive affect. In *The Selected Papers of Margaret Mahler, M.D., Vol. 2: Separation and Individuation,* pp. 59–76. New York: Jason Aronson.
——— (1968). *On Human Symbiosis and the Vicissitudes of Individuation, Vol 1: Infantile Psychosis.* New York: International Universities Press.
Miller, A. (1979). The drama of the gifted child and the psychoanalyst's narcissistic disturbance. *International Journal of Psycho-Analysis* 60:47–58.
Money-Kyrle, R. E. (1956). Normal countertransference and some of its deviations. *International Journal of Psycho-Analysis* 37(4–5):360–366.
Natterson, J. (1991). *Beyond Countertransference.* Northvale, NJ: Jason Aronson.
Norman, M. (1983). *'Night, Mother.* New York: Hill and Wang.
Ornstein, A. (1974). The dread to repeat and the new beginning: a contribution to the psychoanalysis of the narcissistic personality disorders. *Annual of Psychoanalysis* 2:231–248.
Piaget, J. (1937). *The Construction of Reality in the Child.* New York: Basic Books, 1954.
——— (1962). *Play, Dreams, and Imitation in Childhood.* New York: Norton.
Pontalis, J. B. (1977). *Frontiers in Psychoanalysis.* New York: International Universities Press.
Pope, K. S., Keith-Spiegel, P., and Tabachnick, B. G. (1986). Sexual attraction to clients: the human therapist and the (sometimes) inhuman training system. *American Psychologist,* Feb., pp. 147–157.
Pope, K. S., Sonne, J. L., and Holroyd, J. (1993). *Sexual Feelings in Psychotherapy.* Washington, DC: American Psychological Press.
Racker, H. (1968). The countertransference neurosis. In *Transference and Countertransference,* pp. 118–152. New York: International Universities Press.
Rado, S. (1928). The problem of melancholia. *International Journal of Psycho-Analysis* 9(4):420–438.
Rapaport, D. (1953). On the psycho-analytic theory of affects. *International Journal of Psycho-Analysis* 34(3):177–198.
Reich, A. (1951). On counter-transference. *International Journal of Psycho-Analysis* 32:25–31.

Reich, W. (1933). The technique of character analysis. In *Character Analysis,* trans. V. R. Carfagno, pp. 42–121. New York: Simon & Schuster, 1945.

Rickman, J. (1957). A survey: the development of the psychoanalytical theory of the psychosis. In *Selected Contributions to Psycho-Analysis.* New York: Basic Books.

Roazen, P. (1984). *Freud and His Followers.* New York: New York University Press.

Rosenfeld, H. (1987). *Impasse and Interpretation on the Treatment of Psychotic and Neurotic Patients.* London: Tavistock.

Rubinfine, D. (1968). Notes on a theory of depression. *Psychoanalytic Quarterly* 37:3.

Russell, M. J. (1985). *The self in contemporary psychoanalysis.* Presented to the symposium on "The Self in Contemporary Psychoanalysis." California State University Fullerton.

Savage, C. (1987). Countertransference in the therapy of schizophrenics. In *Countertransference,* ed. E. Slakter, pp. 115–130. Northvale, NJ: Jason Aronson.

Schafer, R. (1964). The clinical analysis of affects. *Journal of the American Psychoanalytic Association* 12:2.

——— (1976). *A New Language for Psychoanalysis.* New Haven: Yale University Press.

Searles, H. F. (1965). *Collected Papers on Schizophrenia and Related Subjects.* New York: International Universities Press.

——— (1975). Violence and schizophrenia. With J. M. Bisco, G. Coutu, and R. C. Scibetta. In *Countertransference and Related Subjects,* p. 288. New York: International Universities Press, 1979.

——— (1979a). *Countertransference and Related Subjects: Selected Papers.* New York: International Universities Press.

——— (1979b). The countertransference with the borderline patient. In *Advances in Psychotherapy of the Borderline Patient,* ed. J. Le Boit and A. Capponni, pp. 309–346. New York: Jason Aronson.

Sechehaye, M. A. (1951). *Symbiotic Realization.* New York: International Universities Press.

Segal, H. (1956). Depression in the schizophrenic. *International Journal of Psycho-Analysis* 37:339–343.

——— (1981). Notes on symbol formation. In *The Work of Hanna Segal: A Kleinian Approach to Clinical Practice,* pp. 49–65. New York: Jason Aronson.

Shapiro, S. (1989). The provocative masochistic patient: an intersubjective approach to treatment. In *Bulletin of the Menninger Clinic* 53:319–330.

Silver, A. S. (1989). *Psychoanalysis and Psychosis.* Madison, CT: International Universities Press.

Socarides, D., and Stolorow, R. (1984). Affects and selfobjects. *Annual of Psychoanalysis* 12/13:105–119.

Solomon, R. (1984). *What Is an Emotion?* New York: Oxford University Press.

Spence, D. (1982). *Narrative Truth and Historical Truth.* New York: Norton.

Stern, D. (1985). *The Interpersonal World of the Human Infant.* New York: Basic Books.

Stolorow, R. D. (1975). The narcissistic function of masochism (and sadism). *International Journal of Psycho-Analysis* 56:441–448.

Stolorow, R. D., and Atwood, G. E. (1979). *Faces in a Cloud: Subjectivity in Personality Theory*. New York: Jason Aronson.
—— (1981). Psychoanalytic phenomenology of the dream. Delivered as the William Menaker Memorial Lecture, New York University, New York, May 16. (Also in *The Annual of Psychoanalysis* 10:205–220, 1982.)
Stolorow, R. D., Atwood, G. E., and Brandchaft, B., eds. (1994). *The Intersubjective Perspective*. Northvale, NJ: Jason Aronson.
Stolorow, R. D., and Brandchaft, B. (1987). Developmental failure and psychic conflict. *Psychoanalytic Psychology* 4:241–253.
Stolorow, R. D., Brandchaft, B., and Atwood, G. E. (1987). *Psychoanalytic Treatment: An Intersubjective Approach*. Hillsdale, NJ: Analytic Press.
Stolorow, R. D., and Lachman, F. J. (1980). *Psychoanalysis of Developmental Arrests*. New York: International Universities Press.
Stone, L. (1962). *The Psychoanalytic Situation*. New York: International Universities Press.
Strachey, J. (1934). The nature of the therapeutic action in psychoanalysis. *International Journal of Psycho-Analysis* 50:275–292.
Tustin, F. (1972). *Autism and Childhood Psychosis*. London: Hogarth.
—— (1981). A modern pilgrim's progress: reminiscences of personal analysis with Dr. Bion. *Journal of Child Psychotherapy* 7(2): 175–179.
—— (1984). Autistic shapes. *International Review of Psycho-Analysis* 11:279–290.
Volkan, V. (1968). Transference and countertransference: an examination from the point of view of internalized object relations. In *Object and Self: A Developmental Approach*, ed. S. Tuttman, C. Kaye, and M. Zimmerman, pp. 429–449. New York: International Universities Press.
—— (1976). *Primitive Internalized Object Relations: A Clinical Study of Schizophrenic, Borderline, and Narcissistic Patients*. New York: International Universities Press.
Voyat, G., ed. (1984). *The World of Henri Wallon*. New York: Jason Aronson.
Weigert, E. (1952). Contribution to the problem of terminating psychoanalysis. *Psychoanalytic Quarterly* 21:465–480.
Weinshel, E. M. (1970). Some psychoanalytic considerations on moods. *International Journal of Psycho-Analysis* 51:313–320.
Winnicott, D. W. (1947). Hate in the countertransference. In *Through Paediatrics to Psycho-Analysis*, pp. 194–203. New York: Basic Books, 1975.
—— (1949). Birth memories, birth trauma, and anxiety. In *Through Paediatrics to Psycho-Analysis*, pp. 86–94. New York: Basic Books, 1975.
—— (1953). Transitional objects and transitional phenomena: a study of the first not-me possession. *International Journal of Psycho-Analysis* 34:89–97.
—— (1960). *The Maturational Process and the Facilitating Environment*. New York: International Universities Press.
—— (1964). The importance of the setting in meeting regression in psychoanalysis. In *Psycho-Analytic Explorations*, ed. C. Winnicott and D. Shepherd, pp. 96–102. Cambridge, MA: Harvard University Press, 1989.
—— (1969). Use of an object. In *Playing and Reality*. London: Tavistock, 1971.

——— (1970). *Dependence in childhood*. Speech given in Los Angeles.
——— (1975). Anxiety associated with insecurity. In *Through Paediatrics To Psycho-Analysis*. London: Hogarth.
Wolf, E. (1993). Countertransference in disorders of the self. In *Countertransference*, ed. L. Epstein and A. Feiner, pp. 445–464. Northvale, NJ: Jason Aronson, 1979.
Zetzel, E. R. (1965). The theory of therapy in relation to a developmental model of the psychic apparatus. *International Journal of Psycho-Analysis* 46:39–52.

CREDITS

The author gratefully acknowledges permission to reprint excerpts from the following:

"Countertransference: Concepts and Controversies," by H. Blum, in *Countertransference*, edited by E. Slakter. Copyright © 1987 by Jason Aronson Inc. Originally published in *Psychoanalysis: The Science of Mental Conflict: Essays in Honor of Charles Brenner*, edited by A. D. Richards and M. S. Willick, pp. 229–245, and used by permission of The Analytic Press, Inc.

"Countertransference Enactments," by T. Jacobs, in *Countertransference*, edited by E. Slakter. Copyright © 1987 by Jason Aronson Inc.

"Countertransference in Disorders of the Self," by E. Wolf, in *Countertransference*, edited by L. Epstein and A. Feiner. Copyright © 1993, 1979 by Jason Aronson Inc.

"Countertransference in the Therapy of Schizophrenics," by C. Savage, in *Countertransference*, edited by E. Slakter. Copyright © 1987 by Jason Aronson Inc.

"Hate in the Countertransference," in *Through Paediatrics to Psycho-Analysis*, by D. W. Winnicott. Copyright © 1958 by Basic Books, Inc. Reprinted by permission of BasicBooks, a division of HarperCollins Publishers, Inc.

Interpreting the Countertransference, by L. E. Hedges. Copyright © 1992 by Jason Aronson Inc.

'Night, Mother, by M. Norman. Copyright © 1983 by Marsha Norman. Reprinted by permission of Hill and Wang, a division of Farrar, Straus & Giroux, Inc.

"Normal Countertransference and Some of Its Deviations," by R. E. Money-Kyrle, in *International Journal of Psycho-Analysis*, vol. 37, nos. 4–5, pp. 360–366. Copyright © 1956 by the Institute of Psycho-Analysis.

"Projective Counteridentification and Countertransference," by L. Grinberg, in *Countertransference*, edited by L. Epstein and A. Feiner. Copyright © 1993, 1979 by Jason Aronson Inc.

"The Provocative Masochistic Patient: An Intersubjective Approach to Treatment," by S. Shapiro, in *Bulletin of the Menninger Clinic*, vol. 53, pp. 319–330. Copyright © 1989 by the Bulletin of the Menninger Clinic.

"Psychic Integration and Object Constancy," by P. L. Giovacchini, in *Self and Object Constancy*, edited by R. Lax, S. Bach, and A. Burland. Copyright © 1986 by The Guilford Press.

"Transference and Countertransference: An Examination from the Point of View of Internalized Object Relations," by V. Volkan, in *Object and Self: A Developmental Approach*, edited by S. Tuttman, C. Kaye, and M. Zimmerman. Copyright © 1968 by International Universities Press.

"Two Developmental Lines in Self Psychology: Selfobject Empathy and Interpretation," by C. Coverdale, in *Listening Perspectives in Psychotherapy*, by L. E. Hedges. Copyright © 1983 by Jason Aronson Inc.

The Uses of Countertransference, by M. Gorkin. Copyright © 1987 by Jason Aronson Inc.

INDEX

Abraham, K., 286, 287
Abuse. *See* Child abuse
Active replication, role of, 159
Affects, anxiety and, Freudian perspective, 292–294
Affect theory, recent, emotionality, 294–300
Alexander, F., 43
Analyst's need for love, neurosis, 257
Analytic conscience, as countertransference, neurosis, 262
Anxiety
 affects and, Freudian perspective, 292–294
 signal anxiety, disconnecting modes compared, 72
Attention, excessive, neurosis, 260–261
Atwood, G. E., 28, 43, 230, 241

Bacal, H., 42
Balint, A., 103, 107
Basch, M., 295, 296, 299
Bibring, E., 287
Binswanger, L., 255
Bion, W. R., 30, 59, 116, 119
Blanck, G., 103, 213
Blanck, R., 103, 213
Blum, H., 257
Body integrity, psychosis, 74–76

Bollas, C., 36, 60, 110, 117, 159, 184, 301
Borderline issues, 103–204
 boundary pressures, 197–204
 child abuse, 157–182
 countertransference, symbolic enactments in, 25–37
 incest, 183–196
 interrupted therapy, 127–139
 sadism and helplessness, 141–155
 symbiosis, 103–125
Boundary pressures, borderline issues, 197–204
Brandchaft, B., 210, 232, 233, 240
Brenner, C., 232
Breuer, J., 7, 42, 303
Briggs, J., 45

Child abuse, borderline issues, 157–182
Classical theory, uncertainty and, 41
Concreteness
 borderline issues, 27
 psychotic patients, 28
Confrontation, self and other transference, symbiosis, 105
Connection/disconnection dimension, free association compared, 79
Consciousness raising, psychoanalysis and, 5, 39

Constancy activity, empathy, 215–217
Content rule, relatedness communication, 251–252
Counteridentifications, projective, interpretation of, symbiosis, 118–119
Countertransference
  analytic conscience as, neurosis, 262
  analytic technique as replication, neurosis, 267–271
  boundary pressures, 197–204
  child abuse, 157–182
  correct interpretation as, neurosis, 266–267
  emotionality, 285–302. *See also* Emotionality
  empathic failure, 219–221
  empathy, 213
  erotic
    erotic transference and, symbiosis, 120–122
    gender-identification issues and, 124–125
    sadistic, 122–124
  exhibitionism, 243–245
  Freudian definition, 254–255
  language, 116–117
  listening for transference seen as, neurosis, 266
  listening perspective, therapist responsiveness, case illustration, 7–24
  masochistic-sadomasochistic transference–countertransference, neurosis, 257–259
  need fulfillment and, neurosis, 271–272
  neutrality as, neurosis, 263–265
  orality in, 259
  organizing-level, 59–64
    types of, 64–66
  overstimulating, neurosis, 256
  paradoxical thoughts as usable, symbiosis, 119–120
  paranoic and masochistic defense, in countertransference neurosis, 261
  projective identification, 114–116
  repressed, neurosis, 261–262
  sadism and helplessness, 141–155
  self and other transference, symbiosis, 110
  sexual, 79–90
  silence, 262–263
  split affect, symbiosis, 117–118
  symbolic enactments in, 25–37
  termination, neurosis, 274–276
  violence and, 73–74
  working of, 311–312
Coverdale, C., 223
Cure
  transference neurosis and, 127
  value systems and, 307–310

Darwin, C., 3
Death, of parents, borderline issues, 157–182
De M'uzan, M., 119
Denial, organizing-level countertransference, 64
Depression, ego psychology, 287–288
Developmental lines, empathy and interpretation, narcissistic issues, 223–230
Disconnecting modes, signal anxiety compared, 72
Dream analysis, psychosis, 91–100
Drive theory, structural approach and, 45

Early memory enactment, through empathy, neurosis, 262–263
Ego psychology, depression, 287–288
Eissler, K., 43
Ekstein, R., 5, 42, 59
Emergent self, listening perspectives, 51
Emotion, facial expression and, 3
Emotionality, 285–302
  affect theory, recent, 294–300
  consulting encounter, 286–292

INDEX 327

Freudian perspective, 292–294
moods, psychoanalytic perspective, 300–302
overview, 285–286
relatedness and, 303–310
Emotional response of therapist. *See* Therapist responsiveness
transference and, 4
Empathic engagement, countertransference, symbolic enactments in, 25–37
Empathic failure, narcissistic issues, 219–221
Empathy, 211–219
concept of, 211–212
developmental lines, narcissistic issues, 223–230
early memory enactment through, neurosis, 262–263
modes of, 212–216
organizing-level countertransference, 65–66
preoedipal issues, 216–219
Epstein, L., 114, 115
Erotic cathexis, narcissistic issues, 286–287
Erotic countertransference
case illustration, 79–90
erotic transference and, symbiosis, 120–122
gender-identification issues and, 124–125
sadistic, 122–124
Erotic transference, erotic countertransference and, symbiosis, 120–122
Exhibitionism, narcissistic issues, 243–245

Facial expression, emotion and, 3
False self, psychosis, 76–77
Fantasy, sadistic erotic countertransference, 122–124
Fear, psychosis, 66–68

Ferenczi, S., 43, 103
Fliess, W., 292
Form rule, relatedness communication, 251–252
Frame technique, variable responsiveness and, 42–45
Free association, connection/disconnection dimension compared, 79
Freud, A., 98, 106
Freud, S., 4, 7, 21, 22, 42, 43, 45, 46, 51, 52, 64, 72, 79, 106, 108, 111, 112, 127, 215, 232, 249, 254, 255, 256, 286, 287, 288, 289, 292–294, 303, 306, 312
Frustration, symbiosis, 114

Gedo, J., 43, 305
Gender-identification issues, erotic countertransference and, 124–125
Gill, M. M., 241
Giovacchini, P. L., 26, 29, 43, 57, 59, 70, 104, 267, 268, 269, 270, 271, 305
Gleick, J., 45
Goldberg, A., 21, 236
Good-enough mother, false self and, 76
Gorkin, M., 120, 122, 124, 274
Greenson, R., 301
Grinberg, L., 69, 113, 118, 119

Hartmann, H., 45
Hatred
psychosis, 66–68
as resistance, neurosis, 257
Healing, consciousness raising and, 5, 39
Hedges, L. E., 5, 47, 50, 59, 63, 88, 89, 103, 104, 105, 110, 117, 127, 153, 159, 184, 195, 249, 254, 256, 280, 306, 307, 308, 311, 312
Heimann, P., 7, 256
Heisenberg, W., 41
Helplessness, borderline issues, 141–155
Hilton, R., 20, 88

Hilton, V. W., 88
Historical truth, narrative truth and, 40–41
Holroyd, J., 80
Hunter, V., 26, 29, 37

Idealizing transference, narcissistic issues, 207–210
Identification, projective, self and other transference, symbiosis, 107
Identification with aggressor, symbiosis, 113–114
Incest, borderline issues, 183–196
Independent relatedness, neurosis, 254–256
Infancy
  self and other transference, symbiosis, 107
  symbiosis and separation, 49–50
Intellectual potency, loss of, symbiosis, 116
Interpretation
  correct, as countertransference, neurosis, 266–267
  developmental lines, narcissistic issues, 223–230
  of projective counteridentifications, symbiosis, 118–119
Interpretive control, terror of, psychosis, 69–70
Interrupted therapy, borderline issues, 127–139
Intersubjectivity
  masochism, narcissistic issues, 231–241
  narcissistic issues, 210–211

Jacobs, T., 260, 262, 263, 265, 266
Jacobson, E., 45, 46, 289, 290, 291, 300, 305
Jung, C. G., 43

Kafka, F., 63, 89, 96
Kaplan, L., 249
Keith-Spiegel, P., 80

Kernberg, O. F., 43, 50, 290, 291, 305
Khan, M. M. R., 301
Kirsner, D., 21
Klein, M., 107
Kohut, H., 20, 42, 43, 51, 64, 109, 207, 208, 209, 210, 211, 212, 214, 215, 217, 220, 222, 223, 224, 229, 230, 233, 249, 255, 298, 299, 305, 306, 307
Kosinski, J., 62

Lachman, F. J., 43
Langs, R., 43, 230
Language, symbiosis, 116–117
Life crisis, object constancy, neurosis, 277–282
Listening perspectives, 47–53
  metapsychology, 5–6
  myth and, 41–42
  personality in organization, 47–49
  psychosis, 66–77
  self
    emergent, 51
    other constancy, 52
  symbiosis and separation, 49–50
  therapist responsiveness, case illustration, 7–24
  variable responsiveness, 42–45
Little, M., 20, 57, 59, 104, 183
Loewald, H., 52, 249
Lowen, A., 186

Mahler, M., 49, 51, 183, 184, 291
Masochism
  incest, borderline issues, 186
  masochistic-sadomasochistic transference-countertransference, neurosis, 257–259
  narcissistic issues, 231–241
Masochistic defense, countertransference neurosis, 261
Memory enactment, early, through empathy, neurosis, 262–263
Miller, A., 275
Mimical self, psychosis, 76–77

INDEX

Mirror transference, narcissistic issues, 207–210
Money-Kyrle, R. E., 116
Moods, psychoanalytic perspective, 300–302
Motto, R., 59
Myth, listening perspective and, 41–42

Narcissistic issues
  developmental lines, empathy and interpretation, 223–230
  empathic failure, 219–221
  empathy, 211–219
    concept of, 211–212
    modes of, 212–216
    preoedipal issues, 216–219
  erotic cathexis, 286–287
  exhibitionism, 243–245
  intersubjectivity, 210–211
  masochism, 231–241
  transferences, 207–210
  unilaterally dependent relatedness, 222
Narrative truth, historical truth and, 40–41
Natterson, J., 40
Need fulfillment, countertransference and, neurosis, 271–272
Neurosis
  alarm and rage, 272–274
  analyst's need for love, 257
  attention, excessive, 260–261
  countertransference
    analytic conscience as, 262
    analytic technique as replication, 267–271
    correct interpretation as, 266–267
    listening for transference seen as, 266
    need fulfillment, 271–272
    neutrality as, 263–265
    orality in, 259
    overstimulating, 256
    repressed, 261–262
    termination, 274–276

    early memory enactment, through empathy, 262–263
    independent relatedness, 254–256
    life crisis, object constancy, 277–282
    masochistic-sadomasochistic transference–countertransference, 257–259
    paranoic and masochistic defense, in countertransference neurosis, 261
    problem of, 249–254
    repetition and resistance scenario, 265–266
    resistance, as hatred, 257
    structural approach, 22, 52
    victim turned persecutor, 259–260
Neutrality, as countertransference, neurosis, 263–265
Norman, M., 133

Object constancy, life crisis, neurosis, 277–282
Objectivity, subjectivity and, 40
Object relations, as paradigm, 45–46
Oedipal issues, neurosis, 22, 52, 249–250
Orality, in countertransference, neurosis, 259
Organizing activity, empathy, 213–214
Organizing-level countertransference, 59–64
  described, 59–64
  types of, 64–66
Ornstein, A., 299
Other constancy, self, listening perspectives, 52
Overstimulating countertransference, neurosis, 256

Paradoxical thoughts, as usable countertransference, symbiosis, 119–120
Paranoic defense, countertransference neurosis, 261
Passive replication, role of, 159
Peat, F. D., 45

Personality in organization, listening perspectives, 47–49
Piaget, J., 229
Pontalis, J. B., 116
Pope, K. S., 80, 88
Preoedipal issues, empathy, 216–219
Primitive energy, fear of, organizing-level countertransference, 64–65
Projective counteridentifications, interpretation of, symbiosis, 118–119
Projective identification
 countertransference, 114–116
 self and other transference, symbiosis, 107
 symbiosis, identification with aggressor, 113–114
Psychoanalysis
 consciousness and, 5
 moods, 300–302
 relatedness paradigm, 39–46
Psychosis, 57–100
 dream analysis, 91–100
 emotional involvement, 57–64
 hatred and fear, 66–68
 listening perspectives, 66–77
 organizing-level countertransference described, 59–64
  types of, 64–66
 sexual countertransference, 79–90

Racker, H., 257, 259, 261, 262
Rado, S., 287
Rage, alarm and, neurosis, 272–274
Rapaport, D., 287, 288, 289
Rapprochement, emergent self, 51
Recovered memory, incest, borderline issues, 195
Reich, A., 255
Reich, W., 43, 255, 262
Relatedness
 emotionality and, 303–310
 as paradigm, 45–46
 personality in organization, listening perspectives, 47–49

Relatedness communication, rules of, 251–252
Relatedness paradigm, 39–46
Relativity theory, uncertainty and, 41
Repetition, resistance scenario and, neurosis, 265–266
Replicating transference, self and other transference, symbiosis, 103–112
Repressed countertransference, neurosis, 261–262
Resistance
 as hatred, neurosis, 257
 repetition scenario and, neurosis, 265–266
Responsiveness, of therapist. *See* Therapist responsiveness
Rickman, J., 57
Roazen, P., 256
Rosenfeld, H., 57
Rubinfine, D., 290
Russell, J. M., 307, 309

Sadism, borderline issues, 141–155
Sadistic erotic countertransference, 122–124
Savage, C., 114
Schafer, R., 294, 295, 296, 297, 298, 305
Science, objectivity, 40
Searles, H. F., 26, 28, 43, 57, 59, 63, 73, 104, 121, 254, 305
Sechehaye, M. A., 76
Segal, H., 26, 28, 34
Self
 emergent, listening perspectives, 51
 object relations, 45–46
 other constancy, listening perspectives, 52
Self and other transference, symbiosis, 103–112
Self-conscious activity, empathy, 214–215
Self psychology, transference, 241
Separation, symbiosis and, listening perspectives, 49–50

INDEX 331

Setting, psychosis, 68–69
Sexual abuse, incest, borderline issues, 183–196
Sexuality, erotic countertransference, 79–90, 120–122
Shakespeare, W., 52
Signal anxiety, disconnecting modes compared, 72
Silence, countertransference, 262–263
Silver, A. S., 59
Socarides, D., 298, 299
Solomon, R., 308
Sonne, J. L., 80
Sophocles, 52
Spence, D., 305
Split affect countertransference, symbiosis, 117–118
Stern, D., 46
Stolorow, R. D., 28, 43, 230, 233, 235, 240, 241, 298, 299
Stone, L., 43
Strachey, J., 304
Structural approach
  drive theory and, 45
  neurosis, 22
Subjectivity, objectivity and, 40
Symbiosis
  concept of, 183–184
  empathy, 214
  erotic countertransference
    erotic transference and, 120–122
    gender-identification issues and, 124–125
    sadistic, 122–124
  frustration, 114
  identification with aggressor, 113–114
  intellectual potency, loss of, 116
  language, 116–117
  paradoxical thoughts, as usable countertransference, 119–120
  projective counteridentifications, interpretation of, 118–119
  projective identification, 114–116
  self and other transference, 103–112
  separation and, listening perspectives, 49–50
  split affect countertransference, 117–118
Symbolism
  in countertransference, 25–37
  dream analysis, 91–100

Tabachnick, B. G., 80
Termination
  borderline issues, 178–180
  countertransference, neurosis, 274–276
Terror, of interpretive control, psychosis, 69–70
Therapist responsiveness, 3–53
  listening perspective, case illustration, 7–24
  listening perspectives, 47–53
  overview of, 3–6
  relatedness paradigm, 39–46
Transference
  countertransference, listening for transference seen as, 266
  emotional response and, 4
  masochistic-sadomasochistic transference–countertransference, neurosis, 257–259
  narcissistic issues, 207–210
  self psychology, 241
Transference neurosis, cure and, 127
Truth, historical/narrative truth, 40–41
Tustin, F., 26, 91, 212
Twinship transference, narcissistic issues, 207–210

Uncertainty, classical and relativity theories and, 41
Unilaterally dependent relatedness, narcissistic issues, 222
Unknown thought, incest, borderline issues, 183–196

Values
    attack on, psychosis, 70–72
    cure concept and, 307–310
Variable responsiveness, frame technique and, 42–45
Violence
    borderline issues, 157–182
    countertransference and, 73–74
Volkan, V., 30, 117, 272
Voyat, G., 308, 309

Wallon, H., 308, 309
Weinshel, E. M., 300
Winnicott, D. W., 20, 21, 26, 28, 57, 61, 66, 67, 68, 69, 74, 75, 76, 103, 236, 237, 301
Wolf, E., 219
Working through, cure and, 127

Zetzel, E., 290

ABOUT THE AUTHOR

Lawrence E. Hedges, Ph.D., is the founding director of the Newport Psychoanalytic Institute, where he currently serves as Supervising and Training Psychoanalyst. Director of the Listening Perspectives Study Center, he is in private practice specializing in training psychoanalysts and psychotherapists in Orange, California. He is a training and supervising psychoanalyst in psychology and psychoanalysis at the California Graduate Institute and holds a faculty appointment at the University of California, Irvine, Medical School, Department of Psychiatry. Dr. Hedges is the author of numerous papers dealing with psychotherapeutic processes and the clinical texts *Listening Perspectives in Psychotherapy; Interpreting the Countertransference; Remembering, Repeating, and Working Through Childhood Trauma; In Search of the Lost Mother of Infancy, Working the Organizing Experience*, and the forthcoming *Therapists at Risk*.